SURVEY OF UNITED STATES INTERNATIONAL FINANCE 1952

BY

GARDNER PATTERSON

AND

JOHN M. GUNN, JR.

ASSISTED BY

JACK N. BEHRMAN

MARY B. FERNHOLZ

FRANCES C. HUTNER

INTERNATIONAL FINANCE SECTION

DEPARTMENT OF ECONOMICS AND SOCIAL INSTITUTIONS

PRINCETON UNIVERSITY

PRINCETON UNIVERSITY PRESS

London: Geoffrey Cumberlege, Oxford University Press
L.C. Card 50-12111

Printed in the United States of America
by Princeton University Press, Princeton, New Jersey

PREFACE

THIS is the fourth volume in a series that must still be regarded as an experiment. Its objective is the limited one of presenting an accurate and orderly record, and we have refrained from introducing any independent analysis of the many topics covered. We have, however, attempted to order the material so as to bring out such trends, conflicts, and inconsistencies as occurred, as well as progress toward achieving stated goals.

The present volume is concerned with the international economic and financial policies and activities of the United States during calendar 1952, and extensive references have therefore been made to the previous volumes, which provide background material for the year under review. Except for direct quotations, we have not cited the sources for every statement of fact but have limited the citations to what appeared to us the most helpful sources for persons desiring more detail than seemed suitable for inclusion in a survey.

Attention is again drawn to the fact that virtually all statistical data on international economic transactions are estimates and therefore are not only subject to wide margins of error but are frequently revised. An attempt has been made to include the latest estimates, and some of the data given in this volume for earlier years have been revised and so differ from those presented in the previous volumes.

We have again received much help from other members of the Department of Economics and Social Institutions in Princeton University, from Miss Dorothea Collins, Librarian of the Pliny Fisk Library of Economics and Finance, and from Mrs. Evelyn R. Barr, Librarian of the International Relations Collection, of the Princeton University Library.

A great debt is due many persons not connected with the University, including several holding official positions, who have checked various parts of this document for accuracy. Inasmuch as their help was asked for, and given, on an informal and unofficial basis and none of them had an opportunity to see the manuscript as it went to press, it would be improper to cite them by name. Full responsibility for the accuracy and form of the presentation is, of course, borne by those credited on the title page.

GARDNER PATTERSON, *Director*
INTERNATIONAL FINANCE SECTION

Princeton University
April 1953

CONTENTS

	Page
Preface	iii
Introduction	1
I. MILITARY ASSISTANCE	5
A. Legislative Issues	6
Broad Policy Issues	6
Military End-Item Assistance	16
a. Europe	16
b. Near East	23
c. Asia and the Pacific	24
d. Latin America	25
Defense Support	26
B. Implementation	31
Europe	31
a. Military end-item assistance	31
b. Offshore procurement	33
c. Defense support	36
d. Pace of European rearmament	42
e. European Defense Community	46
Near East and Africa	50
Asia and the Pacific	51
Latin America	53
II. ECONOMIC AND TECHNICAL ASSISTANCE GRANTS TO UNDERDEVELOPED AREAS	55
A. Bilateral Programs	57
Legislative Issues	57
a. Purposes of programs	57
b. Methods of financing	61
c. Form and amount of aid	62
Implementation	67
a. Technical Cooperation Administration programs	67
b. Mutual Security Agency programs	72
B. United Nations Expanded Program of Technical Assistance	72
C. Capital Assistance	77

III. OTHER GRANT ASSISTANCE ... 79
A. Israel and Palestine Refugee Programs ... 79
Legislative Issues ... 79
Implementation ... 84
B. Occupied Areas Program ... 87
C. Korean Reconstruction Program ... 90
D. International Children's Emergency Fund ... 93
E. Migration and Escapee Assistance ... 95
F. Miscellaneous Official Grants ... 99
G. Total United States Government Grants ... 100
H. Miscellaneous Government Unilateral Transfers ... 103
I. Private Remittances ... 103

IV. LOANS AND INVESTMENTS ... 104
A. United States Government Loans and Credits ... 105
Long-Term ... 106
a. Export-Import Bank: for own account ... 106
b. Export-Import Bank: for Mutual Security Agency ... 110
c. Export-Import Bank: for Defense Production Administration ... 111
d. Export-Import Bank: for Technical Cooperation Administration ... 112
e. Defense Materials Procurement Agency ... 112
f. Other ... 113
g. Total government long-term ... 114
Short-Term ... 114
B. Private Foreign Investment ... 114
Government Encouragement of Private Investment 114
a. Investment guaranties ... 117
b. Tax reforms and conventions ... 119
c. Investment treaties ... 121
d. Removal of obstacles to private foreign investment by foreign countries ... 121
Private Capital Movements ... 123
a. Long-term ... 123
b. Short-term ... 126
Note on German and Japanese Debt Settlements ... 128

V. INTERNATIONAL FINANCIAL RESOURCES: THE BANK, THE FUND, AND PROPOSED NEW INSTITUTIONS ... 130
A. International Monetary Fund ... 131
Lending Policy and Operations ... 133

Foreign Exchange Rate Policy ... 139
a. Exchange restrictions ... 139
b. Par values and exchange rates ... 143
Gold Policy ... 143
The Fund and the European Payments Union ... 146
B. The International Bank ... 148
Lending Policies and Operations ... 148
Marketing Operations and Financial Resources ... 155
C. Proposed New International Financial Institutions ... 158
An International Finance Corporation ... 159
An International Development Authority ... 162

VI. RECIPROCAL TRADE AGREEMENTS PROGRAM ... 167

A. Tariff Negotiations and Trade Agreements ... 171
B. Action under the Escape Clause ... 174
C. Customs Simplification ... 180
D. Seventh Session of the Contracting Parties ... 181
Complaints against the United States ... 182
Dollar Import Restrictions by Belgium ... 185
Consultations on Quantitative Restrictions ... 185
Waivers for the Schuman Plan ... 187
Accession of Japan ... 188
Administration of the GATT ... 189
Other Major Activities ... 190
E. Miscellaneous Encouragement of Imports ... 191
F. Conflicts between Trade and Agricultural Policies ... 192
Direct Import Controls ... 192
a. Fats and oils—the "Cheese Amendment" ... 192
b. Restrictions on meat and livestock imports ... 198
c. Sugar quotas ... 199
d. Tariff and other quotas ... 200
Export Subsidies ... 202

VII. STRATEGIC ASPECTS OF COMMERCIAL POLICY 204

A. Export Controls ... 204
B. Restrictions on Non United States East-West Trade ... 206
Note on United Nations Activities ... 213
C. Stockpiling ... 214
Program ... 215
Procurement and Supply Development ... 216
a. Procurement ... 217
b. Supply development ... 219
D. International Commodity Arrangements ... 221
International Materials Conference ... 222

Commodity Study Groups and Agreements 227
a. International Cotton Advisory Committee 227
b. Wool Study Group 228
c. Rubber Study Group 228
d. Tin Study Group 229
e. International Sugar Agreement 230
f. International Wheat Agreement 231
E. Temporary Suspension of Import Duties and Taxes 232

VIII. EUROPEAN ECONOMIC INTEGRATION 235

A. European Payments Union 238
Operations and Adjustments in Mechanism during 1952 240
Accomplishments and Problems 248
B. Trade Liberalization Measures 254
C. European Coal and Steel Community 257
D. Other Integration Proposals 263
E. European versus North Atlantic Integration 265

IX. UNITED STATES BALANCE OF INTERNATIONAL PAYMENTS, 1952 267

A. Current Account 270
Merchandise Trade 270
a. Exports 270
b. Imports 271
Invisibles 272
a. Income on investments 272
b. Transportation 274
c. Travel 274
d. Miscellaneous services 275
Export Surplus 276
B. Capital Account 278
Foreign Gold and Dollar Assets 278
Other Items 281
C. Errors and Omissions 281

Summary 282

Index 297

LIST OF TABLES

		Page
1.	Mutual Security Program Funds, Fiscal Year 1952-1953	15
2.	Military End-Item Grants Utilized, 1951-1952	34
3.	Defense-Support Aid Provided to Western Europe, 1951-1952	38
4.	ECA-MSA–Financed Shipments to Europe, by Major Commodity Groups, 1948-1952	39
5.	Administration Requests for Economic and Technical Assistance to Underdeveloped Areas, Fiscal Year 1952-1953	58
6.	United States Government Gross Foreign Grants, 1945-1952	101
7.	Net United States Capital Outflow, 1946-1952	105
8.	Export-Import Bank Operations, 1934-1952	107
9.	Mutual Security Agency–Export-Import Bank Loans Utilized, 1948-1952	111
10.	Long-Term Foreign Loans and Credits of the United States Government, by Program and by Area, 1952	115
11.	Net Outflow of Private Long-Term United States Capital, 1946-1952	124
12.	Factors Affecting Value of United States Private Direct Investments Abroad, 1950 and 1951	127
13.	International Monetary Fund Exchange Transactions, 1947-1952	136
14.	Net Foreign Gold Transactions by the United States, 1952	147
15.	International Bank: Loans Granted and Disbursed, 1947-1952	151
16.	International Bank: Currencies Disbursed and Currencies Repayable, 1947-1952	153
17.	Funded Debt of International Bank, December 31, 1952	157
18.	Position of Member Countries with the European Payments Union, 1950-1952	241
19.	Value of Intra-European Merchandise Trade as Percentage of Members' Total Trade, 1938, 1948-1952	250

20. International Transactions of the United States, 1950-1952 268

21. Direct Investment Income Receipts, by Area and Industry, 1951 273

22. United States Current Account Export Surplus, by Area, 1950-1952 277

23. Estimated Changes in Foreign Gold and Dollar Holdings, 1952 279

INTRODUCTION

NATIONAL security considerations became predominant in the determination of United States foreign economic policies following the outbreak of war in Korea, and, in effect, the nation abandoned the immediate pursuit of many of the previously established long-term economic objectives in favor of international economic and financial policies designed to strengthen quickly the military defenses of the non-Communist world.

In 1951 most of the official aid programs were subsumed under a single Mutual Security Program but throughout the year assistance was still being provided foreign nations via a series of more or less distinct programs having different, though sometimes overlapping, objectives. Western Europe continued to receive the lion's share of American financial aid, but greater emphasis than in the immediately preceding years was given to helping other areas—especially the so-called underdeveloped countries. Still, there were many who fervently believed that it was in the nation's interest to concentrate official aid more heavily in the Far East. The financing of shipments of military end-items to non-European areas was increased during 1951 but a larger proportion of the total aid than was the case with Europe was in the form of technical services and non-military goods, it having been concluded by the majority of American officials that facilitating the economic development of, and providing consumer goods to, many of the non-European nations were the most effective ways of keeping their peoples sympathetic to the cause of the West in the East-West struggle. Most of these efforts to increase production and standards of living in the so-called underdeveloped areas had barely gotten beyond the planning stages as 1951 ended, and serious differences had developed during the year between United States spokesmen and the representatives from many of the underdeveloped countries on almost every aspect of economic development, other than its desirability.

A major issue between Congress and the Administration in 1951 with respect to aid to Europe had been the extent to which the assistance should take forms other than military end-items and services. The Administration argued that large amounts of aid for "recovery" purposes per se were no longer needed (goods already in the pipeline were scheduled to continue their flow for many months) but that substantial help in the form of non-military goods and services would further the mutual defense effort by permitting the recipients to expand, by some multiple, their own production of military matériel and would also, by cushioning the rearmament-induced declines of consumption and investment in Europe, serve to strengthen the moral and psychological support of the European peoples for mobilization. Congress, however, was willing to provide only such "economic" aid as it thought would directly increase military production in Europe and insisted that the European Recovery Program should be terminated and no substitute created. Nonetheless, the question of whether, and if so to what extent and for what purposes, economic assistance should be provided Europe was destined to be debated at length during the year under review.

Shipments to Europe of military end-items nearly trebled in 1951 as compared with the previous year but were only a small fraction of those that were authorized by Congress and that were expected by the European countries. This small outflow of military equipment was due in part to the long term required to produce such matériel and to the competing demands for these goods by American forces at home and by United Nations forces in Korea. But it also reflected in part the failure of Europe to reach the level of mobilization that had been hoped for by the U.S. Government and involved sharp disagreements between Europe and the United States, and within Europe, as to the desirable and feasible pace of rearmament. American officials assumed a leading role in the extended discussions during the year attempting to reconcile the military "needs" of Europe with that area's political-economic "capabilities." At Lisbon early in 1952, a "plan of action" was agreed upon for the following year. This was, however, only a plan and, although it represented some cutback in earlier force goals and called for an accelerated flow of goods and services from the United States, a host of the economic problems of creating "balanced collective forces" in the North Atlantic area were still unsolved. The role of Germany in the North Atlantic defense effort constituted another major unsolved problem and some of the basic issues involved in creating a European Army were still to be settled.

United States officials repeatedly emphasized during the year that the necessity for rearming made it even more imperative that the economies of Europe be "integrated." The treaty constituting the European Coal and Steel Community was signed but it was still only on paper as the year ended. The European Payments Union was facing serious operating problems as 1952 began and had made virtually no progress toward its goal of facilitating the return by its members to the practice of world-wide currency convertibility and nondiscriminatory trade. The related trade liberalization measures suffered severe setbacks late in 1951 and in early 1952 when the United Kingdom and France reimposed many of the trade barriers previously removed.

The increasing concern over possible aggression by Soviet-bloc countries also resulted in a widespread adaptation and reorientation of the nation's international commercial policies. The U.S. Government tightened still further the controls on its exports to potential enemies and, at Congressional insistence, exerted increasing pressure on other friendly nations to restrict further their exports to Communist areas. This curtailment of non United States East-West trade was giving rise to several new problems as the year ended. In the light of the "mad scramble" that had developed after Korea among the Western nations for many strategic and critical materials, arrangements were made at United States initiative in early 1951 for a voluntary system of international allocations (via the International Materials Conference) and by the end of the year few complaints were being heard from abroad that the United States was "hogging" available supplies. Nonetheless, there was growing concern in the United States as to the adequacy of the production of many raw materials, not only for immediate rearmament needs and for the requirements in the event of a general war, but also for the anticipated expansion of the United States economy. Acquisitions for the official stockpile were therefore continued but commodities in inventory as the year ended were valued at only slightly more than one-third the objectives. Increasing assistance was given under the Technical Assistance

Program and by the Export-Import Bank and the International Bank to expanding the production abroad of such goods but several of the countries receiving contracts, technical assistance, and loans repeatedly emphasized that the production pattern thus being encouraged by the United States was not in conformity with their own plans for economic development.

In spite of the concern in the United States over the adequacy of the production of many raw materials, the huge foreign grants being provided by the U.S. Government, and the strong internal inflationary pressures, Congress during 1951 had pursued a protectionist policy on imports. This action was bitterly criticized by many in the United States (and abroad) who—emphasizing the growing "need" of the United States for imports, the importance to American producers of export markets, and the increasing doubts as to the wisdom and feasibility of continuing large-scale official aid to foreign countries—argued that the time was overdue for a drastic reduction in United States import barriers.

In sum, 1951, as every other year, left behind a host of unsolved problems, and the following chapters survey the actions taken during 1952 to meet them and the new ones that emerged.

I · MILITARY ASSISTANCE

In an effort to "contain" Communism, the U.S. Government began in 1947 a large-scale program of assistance to Greece and Turkey in the form of military end-items. Two years later, Congress approved the Mutual Defense Assistance Act, designed primarily to discharge some of the obligations to aid European rearmament that had been assumed under the North Atlantic Treaty, and the U.S. Government began to regard foreign military assistance as a long-term undertaking. While military matériel was given in increasing amounts during the following two years to many countries in the Far East, the Middle East, and Latin America, by far the most was sent to Europe. And for the world as a whole the amounts of "economic" assistance still greatly exceeded "military" aid.

The year 1951 marked a pronounced shift in the purposes for which aid was provided to Europe; assistance under the European Recovery Program was terminated (except for items in the pipeline) and the objectives of American assistance were determined primarily by considerations of military defense rather than of economic recovery of that area. In other areas, however, assistance in the form of military matériel or for "defense support" was relatively less important, in part because it was believed the danger of aggression was less acute, in part because of the inability of many of the countries to utilize military equipment, and in part because it was thought that many of those nations were not yet wedded to the ideals and purposes of the West and still had to be "won over." To encourage these other countries to identify themselves with the cause of the West, the U.S. Government provided economic and technical assistance for the purposes of raising living standards and accelerating economic development.

Most of these various aid activities were placed under the single Mutual Security Program in 1951, and as such were reviewed in a single chapter of our *Survey—1951*.[1] During 1952, however, the justifications offered by the Administration for providing military assistance were not closely related to those for extending so-called economic and technical assistance to areas where relatively little effort was being made by the United States to expand foreign defense forces. To bring out this distinction and to facilitate the presentation of policy formulation and activities under each broad type of program, the various grant programs are divided in the present volume into three chapters: "Military Assistance," "Economic and Technical Assistance Grants to Underdeveloped Areas" (including much of what in earlier *Surveys* had been contained in the chapter entitled "Point Four Program"), and "Other Grant Assistance."

A. *LEGISLATIVE ISSUES*

In formulating the 1952 policies with reference to the military security aspects of the Mutual Security Program, it was almost unanimously accepted in both the Executive and Legislative Branches that the issue was not whether the Program should be continued but rather how much aid should be provided and what forms it should take. Many of the questions regarding the military assistance program centered around the amount and kind of aid proposed for particular areas, but there were a few broad policy issues relating to the economic and technical as well as military assistance portions of the Mutual Security Program as a whole. The most important of these issues were those surrounding the purpose of the Program, the nature of the Communist threat, and the ability of the United States to continue to extend large amounts of foreign aid on a grant basis.

Broad Policy Issues

In discussing the central purpose of the Mutual Security Program, Administration officials presenting the proposed legislation to Congress repeatedly stressed that the security of the United States was the first obligation of the U.S. Government, that this

[1] See Chapter I of our *Survey—1951* for an account of United States policy on foreign military assistance during that year, together with references to earlier volumes of the *Survey* for a record of the policies and activities during 1949 and 1950.

goal depended in part on the security of the free world, and that "the Mutual Security Program is the keystone of the whole collective security effort of the free world. Without it, the time when we will reach a position of relative security is too far distant, and the risk is too great."[2]

Administration witnesses reiterated their belief that "the whole Communist policy is one which will take advantage of weakness,"[3] and that such a policy would possibly lead to armed attack. Contrarily, they testified, the policy of the free world was merely to gain security—defined as follows: "By security we mean, in the first place, actions which will result, so far as any action on our side can result, in the prevention of war. It is the prevention of war, the maintenance of peace, which is the primary goal."[4] As on previous occasions, the Administration asserted that the rearmament of the West was to be carried only to the point where an attack could be withstood long enough to mobilize fully the free world's forces; no attempt would be made to create an attacking force—only a "resisting" one. But the creation of armed forces was

[2] "Mutual Security Act of 1952," *Hearings on a Bill to Amend the Mutual Security Act of 1951, and for Other Purposes*, U.S. Senate, Committee on Foreign Relations, 82d Cong., 2d Sess., March-April 1952, p. 26. Other sources used extensively in the preparation of this section were the following: "Continuance of the Mutual Security Program," Message from the President, *H. Doc. No. 382*, 82d Cong., 2d Sess., March 6, 1952; "The Mutual Security Program for Fiscal Year 1953," *Committee Print*, House Committee on Foreign Affairs and Senate Committee on Foreign Relations, 82d Cong., 2d Sess., 1952; "Mutual Security Act Extension," *Hearings on H.R. 7005*, House of Rep., Committee on Foreign Affairs, 82d Cong., 2d Sess., March-April 1952; *H. Rpt. No. 1922*, May 12, 1952; *S. Rpt. No. 1490*, April 30, 1952; *H. Rpt. No. 2031*, June 4, 1952; "Mutual Security Appropriations for 1953," *Hearings*, House of Rep., Subcommittee of the Committee on Appropriations, 82d Cong., 2d Sess., June 1952; *H. Rpt. No. 2316*, June 26, 1952; "Supplemental Appropriation Bill, 1953," *Hearings on H.R. 8370*, U.S. Senate, Committee on Appropriations, 82d Cong., 2d Sess., June 30, 1952; and *S. Rpt. No. 2076*, July 2, 1952.

In presenting the 1951 program, the Administration had been castigated for a poor organization of materials and halting testimony. It did a much better job in 1952, receiving the plaudits of the Congressional Committees for clear and detailed presentations. These were made possible partly by the prior work of the Temporary Council Committee of NATO. The public, however, cannot know all the details of the case presented, for much of the testimony was in "executive session" and many statements in public sessions were made "off the record," particularly when the questioning pertained to military programs and policies in the United States and foreign countries.

[3] *Hearings on H.R. 7005*, *op.cit.*, p. 143.

[4] *ibid.*, p. 142. See also Cowen, Myron M., "Component Parts of the Mutual Security Program: Military Aid, Defense Support, Technical Assistance," Department of State *Bulletin*, May 5, 1952, pp. 702ff.

that the projected expenditures for trying to "save" others would "bankrupt" (undefined) the United States but also that the continuation of deficit spending by the Government—Congress was in no mood to raise taxes—was causing inflationary pressures that were making the dollar "unsound." Some also maintained that, in any case, United States production was not yet geared to the volume of military output presumed under the proposed domestic and foreign rearmament programs.

At the very outset of the hearings, the members of the House and Senate committees considering the proposal questioned Administration witnesses as to the "advisability" of cuts in the amount requested. The unanimous response was that the request was not padded in any respect; that the large sums "reflect the size of the peril and the dimensions of the need"; that the program was less costly "than any other means" of attaining security; that "the consequences of a budgetary deficit are . . . insignificant compared with the dangers to our very existence which would follow an undue reduction either of the national security program as a whole or of the vital mutual security segment"; and that no cut, however small, was "acceptable" if an "equilibrium" of forces in Europe was to be attained at the "earliest possible moment."[4] General Gruenther asserted that "half-way" measures would not permit the completion of the program agreed upon at Lisbon in February 1952 and that acceptance by the Supreme Headquarters Allied Powers in Europe of half a program of aid because it was so voted by Congress would not mean that even half the mission could be accomplished; a military operation could not succeed half-way—it was either won or lost.[5]

It was clear as the hearings progressed that Congress was determined not to authorize the full amount requested, and in reporting the bill to the floors of their respective houses both Congressional committees stated that they had weighed the threat of Communism with that of bankruptcy of the United States

legislation but received a warm welcome in some quarters of Congress. (See *Hearings on H.R. 7005*, *op.cit.*, pp. 890-895, 897-899, and *Congressional Record*, May 21, 1952, pp. 5775-5776, and May 23, 1952, pp. 6002-6003.)

[4] See "Mutual Security Act of 1952," Senate, *Hearings . . .* , *op.cit.*, pp. 9, 44-46; *Hearings on H.R. 7005*, *op.cit.*, pp. 136, 293-295; and "Mutual Security Appropriations for 1953," House, *Hearings*, *op.cit.*, p. 180.

[5] See *Hearings on H.R. 7005*, *op.cit.*, p. 304.

economy and had decided to recommend a cut of $1 billion from the Administration's request but had concluded that any further cuts would increase the eventual cost to the United States of its security program.[6]

Administration officials were in almost unanimous agreement that any cuts imposed by Congress should be over-all and in the aggregate and not in specific items, stating that Administration experts would be more capable of determining the items and areas that could best withstand any reduction of aid. Although the members of the Congressional committees did not, in the public record at least, raise many questions about the allocations proposed by the Administration, Congress did nonetheless allocate the $1 billion reduction among the various titles. However, transfer authority between titles was left at 10 percent, as in the 1951 Act, and though the Administration had requested only a 5 percent transfer authority between "military" and "economic" parts of each title, the 1952 Act again allowed a 10 percent transfer.

The committees, and Congress, accepted the Administration's recommendation that all the authorized aid be in the form of grants. Previous programs had specified that some of the "economic" aid was to be extended on a credit basis, but the Administration, in particular the National Advisory Council on International Monetary and Financial Problems, again advised that Europe was already burdened with all the debts she could service in the near future and that other areas needing aid on a credit basis could borrow from the Export-Import Bank and the International Bank. Administration officials stated they were opposed to "fuzzy lending" and argued that established lending agencies could adequately meet the foreseeable needs. They argued also that a requirement that some of the authorized aid be in the form of loans might "jeopardize the security of loans we have already made." Congress was convinced by these arguments, and the final legislation repealed the provision written into the 1951 legislation requiring that at least 10 percent of the funds made available for economic assistance be provided on a credit basis.[7]

[6] See *Congressional Record*, May 21, 1953, pp. 5739-5740, 5755-5757. *The Economist* wrote that this amount was the minimum cut expected and that, in fact, the bill had easier passage than the Administration had anticipated. (See *The Economist*, April 5, 1952, p. 22, and May 17, 1952, p. 440.)

[7] See *Survey—1951*, pp. 33-34.

Both committee chairmen (Senator Connally and Congressman Richards) reported to their respective houses that committee members would not take the risk of cutting below the aggregate of $6.9 billion reported out, stating that, in the view of General Eisenhower, further cuts would probably necessitate "drastic revision of the whole program" of Western rearmament.[8] Chairman Richards also asserted that further "deep" cuts would "leave a gap in our security defense line," and would "increase the cost of our own defense manyfold because if Western Europe were lost, we would need a huge increase in our own Army, Navy and Air Force to have any chance of meeting Russia on equal terms if trouble should start. . . ." He added that without the program United States forces stationed abroad would have to be increased and the risk taken that fighting would take place on American soil "instead of many thousands of miles away."[9]

Despite these statements, several amendments were introduced in both houses to cut the authorization by amounts ranging up to another $1 billion (and one amendment was offered to transfer all the funds to the United States Air Force for its build-up). Arguments used in support of the cuts were generally not directed at the details of programs in any area or to any particular title. Rather, they were founded on the desirability of reducing Government expenditures in order to curtail inflation and to maintain fiscal "soundness"; on dissatisfaction with many aspects of the Administration's foreign policy; on what some regarded as inadequate reliance on United States air power to safeguard the nation; on reports of waste and overlapping in procurement under the Program; on delays in obligating funds previously provided and in obtaining delivery of matériel; on political uncertainties abroad; and on what many regarded as the insufficient efforts of aid recipients.[1]

[8] *Congressional Record*, May 26, 1952, p. 6027. For the text of the answer by General Eisenhower, then Supreme Commander of Allied Forces in Europe, to Connally's cabled query on the effect of a cut in the program, see Department of State *Bulletin*, May 26, 1952, pp. 840-841.

[9] *Congressional Record*, May 21, 1952, p. 5736.

[1] Some Congressmen thought that the use of MSA funds to publicize its operations was improper since it persuaded American voters that the program should be expanded or sustained. An amendment in the 1952 Act prohibited MSA from using its funds to "propagandize" but allowed publication of "information." On the

In reply, opponents of additional reductions added to the reasons cited above that to do so would undercut European defense efforts and would be regarded by many in the rest of the world as indicating lack of Congressional interest in the aims of the North Atlantic Treaty Organization (NATO). Speaker Rayburn felt it necessary to step down from the dais to make a strong plea against the United States being there with "too little and yet too late again," maintaining that every dollar was being "spent for peace," that the chances of another war were large, and that the costs of it would overshadow this program plus the costs of the domestic Military Establishment; he concluded with a plea for "soul-searching and cool calculation" before voting to tear down a program that had not yet been built up.[2]

Those favoring a reduction of the amounts recommended by the committees were in the majority, however, and the President's request was cut $1.7 billion by the House and $1.2 billion by the Senate in their authorizing bills. The conference report stated that in reconciling the difference every item was examined carefully, but apparently in order to reach agreement the time-honored technique of "splitting the difference" was used, for an aggregate of $6.4 billion was authorized—$1.5 billion less than the Administration's request.[3]

In presenting the Administration's case for a full appropriation of the authorized funds, Director for Mutual Security Averell Harriman urged that there be no further cuts on the ground that such cuts would endanger lives of American soldiers through a reduction of European forces (he stated, for example, that three

---

origin of the amendment, see *Congressional Record*, May 27, 1952, pp. 6104-6105, and May 28, 1952, pp. 6262-6271.

For one of the more carefully prepared statements urging further reductions in the total appropriations, see the statement by Senator Paul Douglas in *Congressional Record*, May 27, 1952, pp. 6113-6127.

[2] *Congressional Record*, May 23, 1952, pp. 5978-5981.

[3] In addition, the authorization raised from $1.0 billion to $1.2 billion the ceiling on the amount (procurement cost) of "excess" United States military equipment that could be sent abroad under the Program. For such goods, only the costs of rehabilitation, packaging, and shipping are charged against foreign-aid funds.

The House bill allowed a transfer of $1 billion of equipment from the Military Establishment if the National Security Council determined it was advisable, but this provision was later amended to require payment by MSA to the Defense Department, so that there was no net addition to MSA funds. (See *Congressional Record*, May 21, 1952, p. 5742; May 22, 1952, pp. 5849-5853; and May 23, 1952, p. 6003.)

ground divisions in Europe would be lost by a 15 percent cut in direct military aid) and through a delay in rearmament abroad. The question, he stated, was not "Can we afford such a program?" but "Can we afford to survive?"[4] He emphasized that time was still an important element in the program and that cuts would extend the final date of preparedness. He concluded that "To reduce a program that is soundly conceived and that we can clearly afford amounts to a deliberate enlargement of the risk. It is a gamble for which I should not like to be responsible."[5] Secretary of Defense Lovett testified that the full authorization was needed to maintain the scheduled rearmament build-up agreed upon at Lisbon, which itself was "not completely adequate from a military standpoint." He also testified that any cut would increase the already existing military risk: ". . . an appropriation in any appreciably lesser amount than that authorized by the enabling act will require such drastic downward revision of the defense build-up as most seriously to endanger our national security." He also stated that further cuts would discourage Europe in its efforts to such a degree "as to undo much of the good work already accomplished" and would jeopardize the creation of a European Defense Community.[6]

The Administration presented to the Appropriations Committees extensive and detailed justifications for each title and each type of aid under them,[7] but the final Congressional action was to provide appropriations of $6.0 billion—nearly $450 million less than had been authorized. The President's request, the authorization, and the actual appropriation, by title and type of aid, are given in Table 1, below. On July 15, the President denounced these cuts as leaving an appropriation that was "inadequate and was arrived at in an effort to present the American people in an election year with the illusion of economy rather than with the reality of an adequate collective defense." Every dollar cut out, he emphasized, meant "a loss of much more than a dollar's worth of strength for the free world." He also chose for special mention the 55 percent cut in technical assistance to Asia and in the contributions to the UN program of technical assistance, and asserted

[4] "Mutual Security Appropriations for 1953," House, *Hearings, op.cit.*, pp. 174-179.

[5] *ibid.*, pp. 180-181. [6] *ibid.*, pp. 205-206. [7] See *ibid.*, pp. 289-765.

that the "American people should carefully note the strange fact that prominent among the proponents of this cut were some of the very individuals who have shouted loudest that we are not

TABLE 1

Mutual Security Program Funds, Fiscal Year 1952-1953[a]
(millions of dollars)

Title and Program	*Presidential Request*	*Congressional Authorization*	*Congressional Appropriation*
I. Europe			
Military end-items	4145	3416[b]	3128
Defense support	1819	1282	1282
Spain[c]	0	(25)	(25)
II. Near East and Africa			
Military end-items	606	560[b]	499
Economic and technical	55	51	51
Palestine refugees	65	60	60
Israel	76	70	70
III. Asia and the Pacific			
Military end-items	611	565[b]	541
Economic	258	202	203
Technical	150	119	68
IV. Latin America			
Military end-items	62	58[b]	52
Economic and technical	22	20	20
V. Other			
Multilateral technical assistance	17	15	9
Migration	10	9	9
Children's welfare (ICEF)	0	16	7
Ocean freight subsidies	3	3	3
Grand Total	7900	6448	6002

Details may not add to totals because of rounding.
a) The Administration request that any funds unobligated as of June 30, 1952 be carried over was also granted.
b) In addition, a total of $200 million of excess equipment was authorized to be provided to any countries under the Program, raising the amount of matériel in this category that could be transferred to $1.2 billion.
c) A minimum of $25 million out of the funds for military end-items and/or defense support was set aside for extension of aid to Spain.
Sources: "Mutual Security Act of 1952," *H. Rpt. No. 2031*, 82d Cong., 2d Sess., June 4, 1952, p. 15, and Supplemental Appropriation Act (P.L. 547, 82d Cong.), July 16, 1952.

doing enough in Asia." He concluded that the cuts were "the falsest kind of economy" because they would "in the long run cost us much more."[8]

[8] Department of State *Bulletin*, August 4, 1952, p. 200.

Military End-Item Assistance

The military assistance extended to foreign areas by the U.S. Government in recent years has fallen into two broad categories: military end-items and commodities intended to facilitate the production *within* the recipient countries of military end-items. The debates during 1952 on continuing to supply aid of the latter category (which the Administration had called "economic" aid in 1951 but chose to designate as "defense-support" aid in 1952) are discussed later. The present section attempts to record the issues that were raised in Congress concerning the provision of military end-items, for which the Administration requested new appropriations of $5.4 billion.[9]

As in the previous year, the Administration presented its requests broken down according to four major areas: Europe, the Near East and Africa, Asia and the Pacific, and Latin America.

a. EUROPE

The largest portion of military assistance during 1950 and 1951 went to Europe, principally on the grounds that Europe was prepared and able to make effective use of the aid and that the loss of Europe to Russia would so strengthen the military potential of the latter that the United States would have to go on a "full mobilization" basis. The Administration used the same arguments to justify its program for the fiscal year beginning in mid-1952. It stated that equipment was being sent to Europe not because it believed that war was imminent, but rather because it believed that strengthening the NATO countries would prevent aggression by Russia. A few critics of the Administration questioned the advisability of concentrating so much of the aid in Western Europe, arguing that Russia probably wanted the United States to centralize its efforts there so that Russia could more safely choose

[9] In addition to authorizing grant aid, the original Mutual Defense Assistance Act, of 1949, permitted nations that had joined the United States in collective defense arrangements to buy military goods in the United States for cash through the U.S. Military Establishment. In the 1952 Mutual Security Act the provisions relating to reimbursable aid were amended to allow such sales to Latin American countries and to "any international military organization or headquarters when, in the opinion of the President, such assistance will further the purposes of this Act," and it allowed, with the consent of the President, delayed payments up to sixty days after delivery; it also increased the limit on outstanding contracts from $500 million to $700 million.

another battle area. There was, however, no significant pressure in Congress to provide more aid than the Administration planned to other areas, and the majority of the members of the Legislative Branch agreed that the bulk of whatever aid was provided should go to Western Europe.

In presenting its program to Congress, the Administration requested new appropriations of $4.14 billion (plus authority to use any unobligated portions of previous appropriations) for military end-item assistance to Europe.[1] This amount, officials reported, was the result of adjusting "what is desirable to what is possible" for both Europe and the United States,[2] and was based on the program agreed upon at Lisbon in February 1952.[3] In anticipation of questions as to how long the United States would find it desirable to extend some $4 to 5 billion of aid per year, the Director for Mutual Security pointed out that the military "requirements" of the free world were subject to frequent changes and that NATO made a continuous review of the needs[4] so that "It is impossible to predict with precision the size of the United States contribution beyond the coming year or how long it should be continued."[5] The Administration spokesmen stated that, to insure that American aid was used most effectively to build up European forces

[1] For a detailed statement of the legislative request of the Mutual Security Agency, see *Hearings on H.R. 7005, op.cit.*, pp. 1118-1132.

[2] This sum did not include anticipated American contributions to "infrastructure" (operational and logistic facilities for the joint use of all the NATO forces), since it was planned that these costs would be met from funds appropriated to the U.S. Military Establishment for military construction, rather than, as they had been in 1951, from Mutual Security Program funds. At Lisbon in February 1952, the United States had agreed to contribute 43 percent of the estimated expenditures of $426 million during 1952 for such construction.

The "infrastructure" military construction program abroad was delayed in 1951 and early 1952 due to lack of agreement as to payment of taxes by the United States on infrastructure and other mutual defense structures in Europe. Congressional committees were adamantly opposed to the United States' paying any foreign taxes on any of the projects or items under the aid programs. The Administration testified that sufficient amounts were being withheld from aid payments to insure that no taxes would be paid and that agreement with the foreign countries on nonpayment was expected during the year. (See *Hearings on H.R. 7005, op.cit.*, pp. 143-144; "Mutual Security Act of 1952," Senate, *Hearings . . . , op.cit.*, pp. 87-88; and *H. Rpt. No. 1922*, 82d Cong., May 12, 1952, pp. 24-26.) Tax-relief agreements had been signed with most, if not all, aid recipients by the end of 1952.

[3] See *Survey—1951*, pp. 38-42 for a summary of the Lisbon agreements.

[4] For details as to the procedures used in determining the amount of aid scheduled for the European countries, see "Mutual Security Act of 1952," Senate, *Hearings . . . , op.cit.*, pp. 278-284, 322-326.

[5] *ibid.*, p. 6.

quickly, the rearmament program agreed upon at Lisbon had set out a system of priorities. General Bradley reported that the priorities as then established for United States military assistance applied only to equipment for firmly planned NATO forces plus some equipment for non-NATO forces in Europe provided such forces were in existence or mobilizable, and only the highest priorities under each of these two categories were to be met. He added that equipment of a "questionable" operational value would not be furnished, nor would equipment producible by the recipient.[6] It was planned that the determination of which country met what priority was to be largely the responsibility of the NATO supreme commanders, who would recommend action to the U.S. Department of Defense, which in turn was to have the final determination as to the disposition of aid. Aid programs by country were to be modified and altered in accordance with the actual performance of each country in meeting the Lisbon goals: "Performance will be the test, as reflected in the NATO commander's priority recommendation."[7]

In addition to showing concern as to the ability of the United States to "bear the burden," the major questions raised by Congress in considering the Administration request for military end-item assistance for Europe centered around issues of whether "effective" use had been made of previously appropriated funds. Some Congressmen thought that the U.S. Government, by publicly stating that the security of Europe was "vital" to that of the United States, had encouraged the Europeans to be lax in their own rearmament efforts. They also asserted that it was evident that the United States would not surrender to the Russians if Europe were lost but would defend itself on European as well as on American soil and therefore that a policy statement that European defense was "important" but not "vital" to American defense would cause Europe to look more to its own security rather than depending so much on American forces and aid.[8]

Administration witnesses responded to these doubts as to the state of the morale and efforts of the Europeans by testifying that

[6] *ibid.*, pp. 26-27. Secretary Lovett stated that aid would consist of the "more complicated matériel which Europe is not geared to produce in the quantity required. . . ." (*ibid.*, p. 21.)

[7] *ibid.*, p. 19; see also pp. 27-28, 194, 339.

[8] See, for example, *Congressional Record*, May 21, 1952, p. 5743.

both the willingness to defend themselves and their tangible contributions to their own mobilization had picked up greatly during the past year and that the responsible Ministers in those countries were anxious to build up European defenses.[9] Some Congressmen thought that, while the Ministers might be "anxious," the "common man" was not at all eager to rearm if the burden was to be on him. These Congressional critics were greatly disappointed in the rate of rearmament in Europe, which, they said, had as its goal by the end of 1952 only 50 divisions against the more than 200 at the command of Stalin. In reply, Administration officials reminded Congress that France (which had been singled out for censure) was making a major military contribution to the whole free world's defense in Indochina[1] and that the cost of the campaign was greater than the value of American military aid to France. They asserted that France would be able to meet all her NATO commitments unaided if her forces were withdrawn from Indochina.[2]

Administration witnesses also testified that the need not only for continuing but for expanding military aid was a reflection of the same factors that necessitated the expansion of expenditures on domestic military forces in the United States from some $12 billion in fiscal year 1951 to $52 billion in fiscal year 1953. Further, Harriman stated, 1953 was to be a year of "large-scale capital build-up. Thereafter . . . requirements for the further capital build-up should taper off. When the capital build-up is completed, an expanded European economy, and an expanded European munitions production, should make it possible for the European countries themselves substantially to maintain their own defense forces at an adequate level."[3] Secretary of Defense Lovett testified that it was planned that the 1953 funds, plus unexpended previous aid authority, "will complete the unit equipment of

[9] Extensive testimony, both on and off the record, was given by the United States Special Representative in Europe, Ambassador Draper, and by General Gruenther on the military and economic conditions in Europe. See *Hearings on H.R. 7005, op.cit.*, pp. 215-305.

[1] Under Secretary of State Bruce testified that the French were "collectively crazy" if they were fighting in Indochina only to protect their investments there—as some Congressmen had suggested—since, he said, the cost for a single year of the military operations in that area exceeded the value of all French investments there.

[2] *Hearings on H.R. 7005, op.cit.*, pp. 173, 332.

[3] "Mutual Security Act of 1952," Senate, *Hearings . . . , op.cit.*, p. 6.

ning on July 1, 1953, 75 percent of the United States military aid be supplied solely through the European Defense Community and not to individual countries. All such mandatory amendments were successfully opposed, largely on the grounds that "persuasion" and "advice" would be more effective, that administration of the aid would be exceedingly difficult if it were tied to any specific schedule of integration, and that such measures would force Britain into the European Defense Community against its will.[9] The final Act merely *permitted* the Administration to extend aid directly to NATO, the European Coal and Steel Community, and "the organization which may evolve from current international discussions concerning a European defense community."

Funds for military assistance to Europe were also allowed to be used in non-NATO European countries that were willing to resist Russian aggression even though there were no formal commitments that they would fight in defense of the West if other European countries were attacked. It was anticipated that Yugoslavia and Spain would be the major beneficiaries. No funds were requested separately for any such country but the Administration did ask that the amounts that Congress had set aside in the 1951 Act for Spain and that were as yet unallocated pending agreements with Spain be carried over. The majority of Congress showed no misgivings lest the Administration fail to provide adequate amounts to Yugoslavia but were less certain as to the intentions of the Executive Branch vis-à-vis Spain; therefore, Congress decided to set aside for Spain another $25 million to be used for "military, economic and technical assistance" in addition to the 1951 reservation of $100 million. The 1952 Act also allowed the use of up to $100 million ($20 million for any one country) without regard to the eligibility conditions of the Act;[1] this authority allowed extension of aid to such countries as Iran, which had balked at signing the stipulated bilateral agreement, and to others

[9] For the discussion, see "Mutual Security Act of 1952," Senate, *Hearings . . .*, *op.cit.*, pp. 99, 191-192; and *Congressional Record*, May 21, pp. 5744-5745, and May 22, pp. 5872-5876.

[1] There were no important substantive changes in the eligibility requirements for recipients of aid under the program, but a new subsection was added to the 1951 Act (Section 511c) clarifying the intent of Congress. See *Survey—1951*, pp. 31-32 for the eligibility conditions in the 1951 Act.

such as Poland and Czechoslovakia if they became "disaffected and could be pried loose from Russia."[2]

Out of the military funds requested for Europe, the Administration stated that it planned to use some $1 billion for offshore procurement (in Europe) of end-items. While the Administration had made small amounts of such purchases in the past, this decision to "untie" a substantial portion of American aid was regarded as a major change in policy and was one that European officials had been urging during 1951 and one that Congress found readily acceptable. Besides lightening the burden on certain sectors of the United States economy already under strain, the purposes were to make use of certain "idle" productive capacity in Europe and to expand the productive capacity in areas closer to the place of use, which in turn, it was anticipated, would result in an earlier independence of Europe from military end-item aid. Further, such dollar payments were seen as constituting an important source of dollar earnings needed to help fill the gap left in some of the European balances of payments by the abandonment of the European Recovery Program aid and the diversion, in some countries, of current output from exports to rearmament.

At the same time, the expanded production of end-items in Europe was expected to increase the demand for many imports, especially raw materials, and to result in a larger demand on the United States for "defense-support" aid—discussed below.

b. NEAR EAST

Almost all of the military end-item assistance scheduled for the Near East was to go to Greece, Turkey, and Iran. The last-named country had not signed the standard agreement required in the law of those receiving such assistance and therefore no aid was being provided in early 1952 although a United States military mission was in Iran. It was largely because of this situation that the Administration requested that the "escape clause" from the eligibility requirements, noted above, be inserted.

Most of the testimony on the military aid program for this area, including that for the proposed Middle East Command, was "off the record," but all agreed that the programs for Greece and Turkey had been "eminently successful." Administration officials re-

[2] "Mutual Security Act of 1952," Senate, *Hearings . . . , op.cit.*, p. 165.

ported that these programs were now tapering off, having arrived at a "funding" status, where most of the major capital items needed only to be maintained and provisioned; however, some funds were scheduled to be used to expand the air power of these nations. Congress was impressed with the low cost of the rearmament programs in these two countries and asked why the same economy could not be imposed on Europe. The major reason, according to the Administration, was that the cost of maintenance and supply of a Greek or Turkish soldier was much less than that of a European, inasmuch as the former received something like the equivalent of twenty-one cents per month as pay, received one uniform for his entire two years' service and only one pair of shoes each six months, and often slept in unheated barracks. Many Congressmen expressed the hope that it would prove feasible to end aid to these two countries in the near future but there were no indications that the majority of Congress believed this would be the case. The Administration held out little hope of Greece's being able to maintain an effective military force in the foreseeable future by itself, but it did give as its opinion that Turkey could be self-sustaining if the military burden were lessened somewhat.

There was apparently no serious inclination in Congress to trim this particular program, either because of the way it had been administered or because of any doubt as to the wisdom of aiding these countries, but the area nonetheless shared in the over-all cut imposed in the final authorization and appropriation acts, as was shown in Table 1, above.

C. ASIA AND THE PACIFIC

Military end-item aid to South Korea and to the United Nations forces fighting there was being supplied out of funds appropriated for the U.S. Military Establishment and was not considered a part of the Mutual Security Program under discussion here. Much of the deliberation on the Mutual Security Program for the Far East again was "off the record" but Administration officials stated that most of the military end-item assistance requested ($611 million) was scheduled for Indochina, Formosa, the Philippines, and Thailand, with the first two to receive the largest amounts.

The programs for the Philippines and Thailand were, they reported, already on a "maintenance level."

Witnesses asserted that the Administration considered Indochina to be the most important area in Asia from a strategic viewpoint, excluding Korea, and aid was being shipped there under "a very high priority." Compared with 1951, a substantial increase in assistance (to be sent directly to the Army of the Associated States and not through France) was planned because "If the situation in Indochina can be cleared up, not only will Southeast Asia be stabilized but the French position in Europe—and thereby the entire NATO defenses—will be measurably improved."[3] The *immediate* aim of the program was to equip the Vietnamese forces in order to make it possible successfully to defend the area and, thereby, to instill in them the willingness and eagerness to do so.

The aim of the program in Formosa, officials said, was to be that of insuring the "integrity of that island" and of laying a foundation for the complete reorganization of the Chinese forces there along United States lines. Training was the most important part of the program and was being carried out under the supervision of the second largest United States military mission then serving abroad. Some funds were also scheduled to be used for the improvement and expansion of equipment, especially air and naval craft. The Administration considered that the current program was highly successful and that it promised to reduce the future need for American assistance. There was little discussion of the feasibility of establishing a "Far Eastern OEEC" or "NATO" as had been urged in previous years.

As with the Administration's programs for the Near East, Congress did not seriously question the desirability of continuing the military-aid program to the Far East; though the Administration proposals for this area felt the effects of the economy drive in Congress, the pruning was less (percentagewise) in the case of this area than for any other, as was shown in Table 1, above.

d. LATIN AMERICA[4]

The program for Latin America was, as with all the others, an extension of the 1951 aid program. It was aimed at providing

[3] "Mutual Security Act of 1952," Senate, *Hearings . . . , op.cit.*, p. 24.

[4] The 1952 law included in this title also the "non-self-governing territories of the Western Hemisphere."

equipment and training necessary to help national forces there defend the area, with the objectives of securing the sources of, and access to, strategic materials and of lessening the probability in time of crisis of having to station large numbers of United States troops in that area. The Administration planned that most of the equipment needed by these countries would be purchased by them either directly or under the reimbursable provisions of the Act and only $62 million was requested by the Administration for grants. The Administration reported that the program of military end-item assistance for Latin America was to be solely on a "maintenance" level after fiscal year 1953. As in 1951, some members of Congress questioned whether most of the Latin American countries were doing all that was feasible for their own security, but there was no disposition to abandon the aid program and the final appropriation was only $10 million less than that requested by the Administration.

Defense Support

An integral part of the Administration's military assistance program for Europe (but not for other areas) was the provision of some $1.8 billion of what the Administration chose in 1952 to call "defense-support" aid, that is, consumption and production goods designed to facilitate the expansion of output in Europe required by that area's "dangerously extended" programs of rearmament. Most of such assistance was to be in the form of raw materials, machinery, and equipment to be used in the production of armaments in Europe, but a part was scheduled as civilian-type consumption goods (including foodstuffs) to facilitate the European nations' redirecting more of their resources from the production of goods for internal civilian consumption and/or for export into armament production.[5] This "defense-support" aid, coupled with the Mutual Security Agency's productivity drive in Europe, was aimed at so increasing European production as to make possible the greater defense effort called for by the NATO plans agreed upon at Lisbon.

Of the total defense-support funds requested for Europe, some

[5] For some statements by the Administration on the need for "defense support," see "Mutual Security Act of 1952," Senate, *Hearings . . . , op.cit.*, pp. 94-95, 270-271, 341-351, and *Hearings on H.R. 7005, op.cit.*, pp. 139-141.

$400 million was for non-NATO members in Europe and for Greece and Turkey, with nearly half of this scheduled for ERP-type assistance to Austria and Greece. Of the $1.4 billion requested for the Western European NATO members, by far the largest share (about $600 million) was scheduled for Britain—which was maintaining large defense forces, was then producing about 60 percent of Europe's total armaments, was seen as the "workshop of Western Europe," but was scheduled to receive no more military end-item assistance than was Belgium-Luxembourg or Holland. France, the other large recipient, was to receive $400 million, with the balance distributed among the remaining members.

Aid of this sort had been provided during 1951 but in that year Congress had been especially severe in pruning the Administration's requests for what was then referred to as "economic aid." These cuts were made largely because the requests by the Administration were not convincingly presented and Congress considered that it was nothing more than a continuation of the European Recovery Program, which it was determined to end.[6] In 1952 the Administration prepared its case more carefully. Anticipating that many in Congress would again identify this aid with that extended under the Marshall Plan, which was legislatively ended as of June 30, 1952 and which had expired administratively at the end of 1951, the Administration spokesmen stated at the outset of the hearings that defense-support aid was "not the same thing we were doing under the Marshall plan. The Marshall plan was designed to help Europe rebuild its civilian economy from the disastrous consequences of war. Defense support is also a form of economic assistance, but it is for an entirely different purpose. It is to make it possible for our friends in Europe to expand their defense efforts for our common security."[7] ". . . this is almost the heart and soul of the NATO program,"[8] and it is not only "the most important single item as it relates to the development of security in Europe"[9] but will actually save the United States money in obtaining a given state of security.

Administration witnesses testified that the mobilization effort of

[6] For a summary of the debate in 1951, see *Survey—1951*, pp. 19-24.
[7] "Mutual Security Act of 1952," Senate, *Hearings . . .* , *op.cit.*, p. 5.
[8] *ibid.*, p. 95.
[9] *Hearings on H.R. 7005*, *op.cit.*, p. 57.

the Western European members of NATO, including the proposed defense-support aid from the United States, was scheduled to reach an aggregate expenditure during the year 1952-1953 of the equivalent of $14 billion, said to be equal to about 10 percent of these countries' gross national products. Moreover, Administration officials argued, taking account of the low real per capita incomes in Europe, the portion of this 10 percent that they paid themselves was more of a burden on the people of Europe than was the some 18 percent of their gross national product that the people of the United States were spending on rearmament. In addition, they stated, the $14 billion estimate was too low for comparison with United States expenditures since the money payments and standards of living enjoyed by the European soldier were much less than those of his American counterpart. The Administration stressed that of major importance in the above $14 billion was the $1.4 billion of defense support included in it,[1] which would enable the European recipients to add some $3 billion to their own defense expenditures.[2] That is, without the projected defense-support aid, they argued, Europe could spend only about $10 billion on defense and such a low rate would place "in jeopardy that most important move [the European Defense Community] toward European unity"; the whole integrated defense set-up might well collapse; and the only substitute might be more American troops, which, the spokesmen for the Administration estimated, might cost the United States some five and one-half times the cost of any reduction in defense-support funds.[3]

It appeared early in the hearings that many in Congress agreed with Senator Connally that "as a general proposition . . . the United States can't go on forever appropriating these large sums of money to the United Kingdom and to France and to all of these powers. If they are not willing to do something for them-

[1] The remaining $0.4 billion of the requested $1.8 billion of defense-support aid was scheduled to go to non-NATO nations and to Greece and Turkey.

[2] Of this $3 billion, about one half would be an increase in "hardware" production in Europe and the rest would be in the form of clothing, barracks, airfields, etc. (See *Hearings on H.R. 7005*, *op.cit.*, pp. 571, 573 for statistics on projected defense-support items.) Examples of the "multiplying effect" of defense support on European armaments production may be found in "Mutual Security Act of 1952," Senate, *Hearings* . . . , pp. 565-566, and S. *Rpt. No. 1490*, 82d Cong., April 30, 1952, p. 35.

[3] *Hearings on H.R. 7005*, *op.cit.*, pp. 258-267, 327, 329, 528-529, 1061-1062.

selves in defending themselves, it is not our obligation to take over that responsibility."[4] In defense of the Administration's request, senior officials stated that the planned efforts of the European countries "approach the limits of their capacities. To go beyond these limits would produce a strain in their political, economic, and social structures which would endanger both their security and ours, and might well wreck everything we are trying to accomplish."[5] They testified further that the limitations on Europe's effort were real and significant: (1) a per capita income equal to only about one-third that of the average United States citizen, of which the percentage taken by taxes was equal to that of the United States even though Europeans still had not replaced many of their personal durable goods lost during the war; (2) serious inflationary trends accelerated by the Korean war; and (3) heavy military commitments elsewhere (for example, France was reported as having spent more in Indochina over the past five years than it had received under the Marshall Plan).

In an effort to prevent cuts in their request for defense-support funds, Administration officials asserted that this aid was "inseparable" from military end-item aid, and that the two types could not be distinguished "with any accuracy." (For example, a tank might be produced in Europe with some of the materials financed by defense-support funds, or, the tank might be sent there complete by the United States as end-item aid—and in each case similar matériel would be placed in defense of Europe.) They also affirmed that in the light of differences in the production potential of the various countries, each type of aid was necessary if the resources of the West were to be used most effectively and that it was difficult to determine the relative importance of each. Some Congressmen, remembering the savings of dollars promised when defense support was substituted for military end-item aid, questioned whether more of the former might not be extended at the expense of the latter. Administration officials replied that the programmed defense-support aid was about the limit of that which could be economically and effectively employed inasmuch as it would tax the European economy nearly to capacity to make use of the supplies scheduled.

[4] "Mutual Security Act of 1952," Senate, *Hearings . . . , op.cit.*, pp. 40, 41.
[5] *ibid.*, p. 12.

Some Congressmen, understanding that defense support was designed to utilize more completely the existing productive capacity in Europe, asked whether or not offshore procurement—the purchase with dollars in Europe of military end-items for Europe—could be substituted for defense support, thus relieving the drain on goods from the United States. The reply given by the Administration was that these two techniques were not substitutable: some countries did not have excess plant and manpower but did need defense-support funds to provide raw materials; while others had excess capacity, could obtain raw materials, and would produce if orders were received. It was anticipated, they added, that some countries would need both types of aid because an increase in offshore procurement *could* carry with it a greater demand for imported materials. But, it was thought, the dollars supplied under the offshore procurement procedure would usually provide sufficient funds for purchases of any additional imported raw materials required. The witnesses finally admitted that it would be *possible* to expand offshore procurement to cover most of both needs but stated that it would not result in any savings for the United States and would confuse the purposes of the aid.

The Administration's case for defense-support funds was more convincing to the Congressional committees than it had been in 1951, and there was no serious threat of eliminating this type of assistance. Indeed, in reporting to the House on the Mutual Security Act, the Foreign Affairs Committee stated that it had cut only 10 percent off this portion, and that "to cut this part of the bill further would be a tragic mistake."[6] The Senate committee was a little less generous, recommending a reduction of some 17 percent. On the floor, however, the sentiment was strong for more substantial reductions (in part because of the general economy drive and in part because many Congressmen were not convinced that some of the proposed aid would not be used for "recovery" purposes)[7] and the final authorizing act reduced the

[6] *Congressional Record*, May 21, 1952, p. 5738.

[7] During the debate the President had written the Congressional committees that all but six or seven of the ECA responsibilities should be transferred to the Mutual Security Agency (see Department of State *Bulletin*, April 7, 1952, pp. 555-559). This suggestion disturbed many members of Congress and an amendment was accepted from the floor of the House that eliminated all reference to

requested $1.8 billion to $1.3 billion; this amount was left intact in the subsequent appropriation bill, as was shown in Table 1.

In order to channel as much of the defense-support aid as possible into military assistance, the provisions in the 1951 Mutual Security Act regarding the use of counterpart funds (local currency deposited by aid recipients in amounts equivalent to the dollar cost of United States goods and services received by them on a grant basis) were amended to provide that all future accumulations of such local currencies should, with minor exceptions,[8] be used only for the purposes—production of military end-items and defense-support activities—for which dollar aid was being extended. This restriction excluded the use of counterpart funds for retirement of government debt, which the Administration had for years under the European Recovery Program regarded as a major anti-inflationary device, and which had been one of the major uses of such funds by many countries during the European Recovery Program period.

B. *IMPLEMENTATION*[9]

Europe

a. MILITARY END-ITEM ASSISTANCE

As was brought out in the hearings discussed above, deliveries of military matériel to Europe—as well as to other areas—had been

the Economic Cooperation Act of 1948, as amended, and substituted the provisions of Section 503 of the 1951 Mutual Security Act. This section delineates the responsibility of the Director for Mutual Security without mention of economic assistance that is not directly related to mutual defense efforts.

[8] The Mutual Security Act of 1952 required that $100 million of counterpart funds be used as a revolving loan fund for extension of credit to private business enterprises in Europe *and* as a source of financial support for activities under the Benton amendment, which was designed to encourage free private enterprise in Europe (see *Survey—1951*, pp. 32-33).

[9] The important official sources of information on activities under the Mutual Security Program in 1952, and the principal sources of material included in this section are the following publications of the Mutual Security Agency: *Second Report to Congress on the Mutual Security Program*, Wash., D.C., June 30, 1952; *Supplement to the Second Report . . .*, Wash., D.C., 1952; *Third Report to Congress on the Mutual Security Program*, Wash., D.C., December 31, 1952; and Draper, W. H., Jr., *Report to the President*, Paris, August 22, 1952 (also printed in full in the Department of State *Bulletin*, September 8, 1952, pp. 353-360). For more detailed statistical data on the Mutual Security Program, see U.S. Department of Commerce, *Foreign Aid by the United States Government* (quarterly), and the following publications of the Mutual Security Agency: *Report to the*

smaller during 1951 than had been planned.[1] In addition to the reasons cited in Congress for the lag there was some evidence that a contributory factor had been the high priority that the Defense Department had given to building up military stockpiles within the United States as compared with supplying matériel to foreign countries. The President in January 1952 directed that after the requirements of Korea and other active battle areas had been met, the Defense Department should allocate military equipment in such a manner as to insure that those forces that would first be engaged in case of war—United States forces in Europe, other North Atlantic Treaty Organization forces, as well as the forces of certain other allies—would be adequately equipped. This decision, together with the steadily increasing output of most items by United States manufacturers and an accelerating program of rearmament in Western Europe itself, resulted in a large increase in shipments of United States-financed goods, with the value of such aid "utilized"[2] being nearly 75 percent greater during the

---

Public Advisory Board (monthly); *Procurement Authorizations and Allotments* (monthly); and *Paid Shipments* (monthly). See also Shepler, C. E., "Foreign Aid in Fiscal Year 1952," *Survey of Current Business*, October 1952, pp. 6-11, and Kerber, E. S., "United States Foreign Aid in 1952," *Survey of Current Business*, March 1953, pp. 13-19.

For reports on the military assistance programs of the United States in years prior to 1952, see earlier issues of this *Survey* and U.S. Department of Commerce, *Foreign Aid by the United States Government, 1940-1951*, Wash., D.C., 1952.

[1] Data on the amount of military assistance given by the United States to various United Nations forces in Korea have not been made public and are *not* included in any of the statements for foreign assistance given in this document. Such aid is financed out of the regular Defense Department appropriations and not from foreign aid appropriations.

[2] For the definition of "utilized" see footnote (a) to Table 2. Unless otherwise specified, the value figures for military end-item assistance used in this document are Department of Commerce data and include ocean freight, administrative expenses where allocable, United States contributions to the infrastructure program, and the expenses incurred by the United States in its various programs for training European military forces. They thus differ from some of the data released by other branches of the Government, which are not always so inclusive.

In addition to military assistance provided on a grant basis, the Mutual Security Act authorized the President to transfer, and to enter into contracts for the procurement or transfer of, military equipment, materials, and services to foreign countries on a reimbursable basis. Through October 1952 forty-one countries had placed orders under this authority totalling $601 million (apparently about $150 million was placed prior to 1952), of which $356 million was paid in full in advance. Actual deliveries through October totalled $156 million, including some $65 million prior to January 1, 1952. Such orders are merged with the procurement program of the United States defense forces, thereby permitting more orderly use of American productive facilities.

first half of 1952 than during the last half of 1951. Still, at some $750 million, this was at a rate of only about one-third that authorized by Congress.[3] The Mutual Security Agency reported at midyear that, while deliveries were well behind the forecasts made at the beginning of the year, the lag had not had "a serious impact on the rate of activation of forces in Europe. . . ."[4] The value of aid furnished fell off slightly during the third quarter but during the last three months of the year shipments spurted upward and certain items—tanks and jet aircraft were specifically mentioned—were said by American officials to be flowing on an "impressive scale." Still, for the year as a whole the value of such military aid to Europe, as shown in Table 2, was less than $2 billion, raising the total since the beginning of the Mutual Defense Assistance Program in 1949 to just over $3.2 billion.

The continuance of large requirements for matériel in Korea, certain delays in munitions production in the United States, and the lack of facilities in Europe to receive the goods were again cited by the Administration as the causes for falling short of the programmed deliveries. In the letter transmitting his final report to Congress on the Mutual Security Program, President Truman took occasion to tell the new Administration that "we need to find methods to expedite delivery of end-item military equipment" and that "we must hold to the principle that those who may be called upon to fight first should be adequately equipped first."[5]

b. OFFSHORE PROCUREMENT

The Administration's policy of greatly expanding "offshore procurement," that is, purchasing with United States aid funds military end-items produced abroad for transfer to foreign govern-

[3] President Truman exercised the power given him in the Mutual Security Act to transfer up to 10 percent of the funds appropriated under Title I (Europe) between expenditures for direct military assistance and for defense support and to transfer up to 10 percent of the funds appropriated under any title to the same kind of assistance under any other title. In February he transferred $478 million of the funds appropriated for military end-item assistance in Europe to "defense-support" purposes in five European countries. In order, among other things, to provide more military equipment to French and Indochinese forces fighting the Communists in Indochina, the President in May also transferred $153 million from the appropriation for military end-item assistance under Title I (Europe) to military assistance under Title III (Asia and the Pacific).

[4] *Second Report to Congress on the Mutual Security Program*, *op.cit.*, p. 10.

[5] *Third Report to Congress on the Mutual Security Program*, *op.cit.*, p. XII.

TABLE 2

Military End-Item Grants Utilized, 1951-1952[a]
(millions of dollars)

	1952					
	1st Quarter	*2nd Quarter*	*3rd Quarter*	*4th Quarter*	*Total*	*1951*
Europe[b]	283	476	452	741	1952	915
Near East and Africa[c]	79	75	46	100	300	184
Asia and the Pacific[d]	49	72	139	131	391	296
Latin America	32	18	6	3	59	61
Unallocable Administrative Expenses[e]	13	10	8	6	37	37
Total	456	651	651	981	2739	1493

a) Represents military end-items provided by the Defense Department under the Mutual Security Program, as well as small amounts during 1951 and 1952 of aid under the Greek-Turkish Assistance Act of 1948, as amended, and small amounts of military aid financed under the China Aid Act of 1950.
Grants "utilized" represent shipments when goods are procured by U.S. Government agencies and cash payments by the Government when other methods of procurement—including offshore procurement—are used. Excess equipment provided on a grant basis is included at original acquisition value. When such equipment is sold under the reimbursable provisions of the Mutual Security Act, the excess of original cost over the amount received from the sale is included as a grant. This item has been of great importance in the case of Latin America.

b) Includes $72.3 million of contributions by the U.S. Government to the multilateral construction program (infrastructure) during 1952.

c) The bulk of this aid went to Greece and Turkey, members of the North Atlantic Treaty Organization. Included are small amounts of military aid financed from funds provided in the Greek-Turkish Assistance Act of 1948, as amended.

d) Excludes the value of military items supplied the United Nations forces in Korea. Includes in 1951 a small amount of military aid financed under the China Aid Act of 1950.

e) Includes both counterpart funds and dollars used by various agencies of the U.S. Government in administering the military aid programs.

Sources: Compiled from data in Department of Commerce, *Foreign Transactions of the U.S. Government, Foreign Aid,* Wash., D.C., April 1952, Appendix Table 6, and Department of Commerce, *Foreign Aid by the United States Government,* Wash., D.C., March 1953, Appendix Table 3.

ments, was welcomed by European officials as well as by the majority of Congress, but activity here was also below the expectations of many.[6] Among the reasons cited for the delays were the time required to adapt United States contracting procedures

[6] While it is true that, in general, the policy of the United States has been to tie its aid funds to purchases in the United States, 31 percent of the value of all the commodities financed by the Economic Cooperation Administration had been purchased outside the United States. (See earlier issues of this *Survey* for details.)

to those in Europe, to negotiate special tax agreements under which taxes were waived on military production financed by the United States, to determine sources of production and delivery schedules, and to receive competitive bids.

Contracts for offshore procurement under the military aid program began to be negotiated toward the end of 1951 and by mid-1952 contracts for a total of some $620 million had been signed, but only an additional $130 million worth were let during the last half of the year.[7] These contracts covered, among other items, naval vessels, electronics equipment, ammunition, tanks, planes, and spare parts; France received nearly half, in value terms, of the contracts let,[8] followed by Italy with about one quarter of the total and the United Kingdom with one fifth.

Many of the end-items ordered under the offshore procurement program required several months to produce and since, in general, the Defense Department pays at the time of delivery, actual dollar expenditures during the year totalled only some $80 million. In June, faced with an acute need for dollars, the French Government negotiated a two-year $200 million loan from the Export-Import Bank to be repaid as deliveries of matériel under offshore procurement contracts were accepted by the Defense Department; just over three quarters of this loan had been used by the end of the year and the balance of the credit was cancelled. Of the above $80 million in payments by the Defense Department, over half was used by France to repay a part of the Export-Import Bank loan. The U.S. Government anticipated that during the first half of 1953 the rate of placing contracts would increase greatly—over $800 million worth of new contracts were anticipated—but

[7] These figures do not include orders financed from regular Defense Department appropriations for military equipment to be used by United States forces. Details are not available but scattered data indicate that such orders were larger than in previous years, but still small, and that probably a large portion of them were placed in Canada.

[8] $200 million worth of the contracts placed in France were in fulfillment of pledges made at the North Atlantic Council's meeting at Lisbon in February. Additional orders were subsequently placed in France, at French request, for production already programmed as part of the French defense effort but which the French authorities stated the nation's budget could not finance. Even with this assistance, it was reported that the French internal budget could not provide funds for all the production planned at the North Atlantic Council meeting in February.

it was thought that the rate of dollar payments would rise only moderately.[9]

While this program was of modest dimensions, most observers agreed that it was serving the intended purpose of increasing the production bases abroad and so contributing to the ability of European nations to assume a greater responsibility for their own defense, and that, from the point of view of the balance of payments problems of European countries,[1] this method of financing military assistance from the United States was, in the short run and within limits, preferable to providing equipment produced in the United States.[2]

C. DEFENSE SUPPORT

Nearly $1.8 billion of so-called "defense-support" or "economic and technical" aid was provided by the Mutual Security Agency to the Western European countries during 1952, as compared with over $2.5 billion of such aid to these countries during the preceding year.[3] The rate of extension of aid for these purposes was

[9] Military aid extended via the offshore procurement procedure is included in, and is not in addition to, the total amount of aid discussed in the preceding section.

[1] The offshore procurement device was used to facilitate a settlement of Belgium's creditor position in the European Payments Union. (See Chapter VIII, Section A. For some unofficial reports favoring an extension of the offshore procurement procedure, see *Fortune*, October 1952, pp. 112ff.; and *The Economist*, December 13, 1952, pp. 759-760, and December 20, 1952, p. 827. Its extension was also recommended by the so-called Sawyer Mission. (See *Foreign Commerce Weekly*, December 22, 1952, p. 16.)

[2] There was no public evidence that officials had given serious thought to the question of whether the reallocation of resources in Europe and the United States involved in this program, as compared with the United States' providing the finished goods directly, was likely to make more difficult Europe's problem of balancing her international accounts when the rearmament crisis was over.

[3] These totals include the assistance given to Spain and Yugoslavia, as well as to those countries that had participated in the European Recovery Program and/or were members of the North Atlantic Treaty Organization. All of the aid to Spain during the year was under the $62.5 million loan authorized by Congress in 1950. None of the $125 million of grant aid that Congress had appropriated in 1951 and 1952 had been spent by the end of the year under review. United States military and economic survey teams had visited Spain and the Departments of State and Defense had spent several months during the year attempting to negotiate agreements with Spanish authorities providing (a) for the construction of air and naval bases in Spain to be available for use by the United States in time of war and (b) for the provision of military and economic assistance to that country. The press reported that the failure to reach an agreement by the end of 1952 was due primarily to the efforts of the Spanish authorities to obtain more aid than was contemplated by the Executive Branch, to get permission to use more of the aid for non-defense purposes, and to obtain official statements from the United States

tapering off during the year and the annual rate during the last quarter of 1952 was less than $1 billion. As Table 3 shows, the largest recipients were the United Kingdom, France, and Italy, which countries accounted, respectively, for 27 percent, 19 percent, and 12 percent of the total.[4]

This economic assistance was designed to pay for goods and services, obtainable for the most part only with dollars, that it was judged would further the rearmament of the European countries and that it was believed those countries could not pay for out of their own dollar earnings or reserves. Of the paid shipments during the year two thirds, by value, came from the United States and one sixth from Canada, with a large part of the remainder going for petroleum from countries in which American

---

that Spain was a full partner in the West's anti-Communist activities. (For a discussion of the question of American aid to Spain, see *Survey—1951*, pp. 14-15, 21, 104-105, and the references cited therein. See also *Congressional Digest*, Wash., D.C., March 1953, pp. 71-96.)

The Yugoslav emergency relief program had been completed in 1951 and was followed by an agreement between Yugoslavia on the one hand and the United States, the United Kingdom, and France on the other whereby the latter countries agreed "in principle" to underwrite up to the equivalent of $120 million (the United States share was $80 million) Yugoslavia's deficits for the period ending in mid-1952. (See *Survey—1951*, pp. 65-66.) A second tripartite conference was held in Washington in early 1952 and the Governments of the United States, the United Kingdom, and France agreed to provide the equivalent of $99 million (the United States share was $78 million out of Mutual Security funds) for the year ending in mid-1953. This aid was intended to strengthen Yugoslavia's defense potential and to help preserve her independence from Russia. In addition to this economic aid, the United States provided large, but unspecified, amounts of military matériel to the Yugoslav forces. (Department of State *Bulletin*, November 24, 1952, pp. 825-826, gives an official account of the reasons for aiding Yugoslavia.) Yugoslavia became indirectly linked to the NATO nations early in 1953 upon the signing of a treaty of friendship and collaboration with NATO members Greece and Turkey.

[4] In February 1952, the President transferred $478 million of the fiscal year 1951-1952 military appropriations for Europe to defense-support activities. $300 million of this was allocated to the United Kingdom, previously scheduled to receive no economic aid during the year ending in mid-1952. In view of the serious drain on Britain's international reserves that had taken place during preceding months, the Director for Mutual Security concluded in early 1952 that unless $300 million of United States aid were provided Britain for materials related directly to the defense effort her defense production would have to be cut by more than twice that amount. France was allotted $100 million of the transferred funds to prevent impending cuts in defense production, and the balance was allotted to Greece, Turkey, and Yugoslavia to permit greater defense production in those countries than would otherwise have been possible. (For details of these transfers and justifications for them, see Department of State *Bulletin*, February 11, 1952, pp. 236-237, and February 25, 1952, pp. 317-318.)

TABLE 3

Defense-Support Aid Provided to Western Europe, 1951-1952[a]
(millions of dollars)

	1952		*1951*	
	Grants	*Credits*	*Grants*	*Credits*
Austria	95.0	—	160.8	—
Belgium-Luxembourg	8.0	12.8	52.6	2.7
Denmark	8.0	2.3	62.0	—
France	284.9	53.0	460.2	16.0
Germany	75.7	20.3	381.9	3.6
Greece	136.9	2.5	204.1	1.3
Iceland	4.6	1.0	7.4	1.8
Ireland	0.2	—	15.1	9.5
Italy	187.5	23.0	298.9	0.8
Netherlands	71.8	16.0	150.1	—
Norway	19.3	12.3	49.3	—
Portugal	1.8	6.3	1.4	18.9
Spain	—	12.3	—	17.1
Sweden	cr. 3.5[b]	—	27.0	—
Trieste	cr. 0.2[b]	—	7.8	—
Turkey	55.7	11.4	39.1	19.5
United Kingdom	424.5	67.9	224.5	11.3
Yugoslavia	80.2	—	54.8	—
European Payments Union[c]	—	—	195.4	—
Unallocable[d]	72.4	—	63.2	—
Total	1522.7	241.1	2455.6	102.5

a) Includes European Recovery and Mutual Security Program aid. Credits include only that portion of the Mutual Security (European Recovery) Program aid extended on a credit basis, including loans (through September 1952) in dollars and counterpart funds made by the Defense Materials Procurement Agency for its own account and for the account of the Mutual Security Agency to expand production of strategic and critical materials in the European countries and their dependent overseas territories. Both grants and credits are on the basis of utilizations rather than allocations or authorizations. Aid "utilized" represents the value of shipments when goods are procured by the U.S. Government and cash payment when other methods of procurement are used.

b) Accounting adjustments.

c) Includes only the payments by the U.S. Government to the central fund of the European Payments Union. Various payments made by the United States to the Union members to cover their deficits in the Union are included in the figures for the individual countries.

d) Includes both dollars and counterpart funds used for certain administrative expenses in carrying out the defense-support program, certain technical assistance supplied by MSA-ECA, as well as postal and freight payments on relief parcels. Also included are grants for the Provisional Intergovernmental Committee for Movement of Migrants from Europe.

Sources: Compiled from data in Department of Commerce, *Foreign Transactions of the U.S. Government, Foreign Aid,* Wash., D.C. April 1952, Appendix Tables 4, 5, 9, and Department of Commerce, *Foreign Aid by the United States Government,* Wash., D.C., March 1953, Appendix Tables 3, 5.

investment was important.[5] Table 4 shows that, on the basis of the value of paid shipments, there was a pronounced shift, as compared with aid provided during the period of the European Recovery Program, in the types of goods provided. While many of

TABLE 4

ECA-MSA–Financed Shipments to Europe, by Major Commodity Groups, 1948-1952

(in percentages)

Commodity Groups	*1952*	*1948-1951*
Food, feed, and fertilizer	17.0	36.4
Fuel	20.9	15.5
Raw materials and semifinished products	41.7	32.8
Machinery and vehicles	19.2	14.3
Miscellaneous	1.2	1.0
Total	100.0	100.0

Source: Mutual Security Agency, *Monthly Report to the Public Advisory Board*, Wash., D.C., December 31, 1951, pp. 42-43, and December 31, 1952, p. 53. These documents provide a detailed commodity breakdown.

the goods financed by the U.S. Government were such direct military-support items as metals for use in military equipment, chemicals for the production of ammunition, and machinery and equipment for matériel-producing industries and for the construction of military facilities, perhaps as much as half of the expenditures were for such commodities as cotton, food, coal, and petroleum products, which did not enter directly into the rearmament programs.[6]

[5] The Mutual Security Act requires that, if available, at least 50 percent of the MSA-financed shipments from the United States (and homebound cargoes of strategic materials financed with dollars or counterpart funds) by cargo ship, liner, and tanker, be in United States bottoms. Through mid-1952, the latest date for which figures are available, these requirements were surpassed with respect to cargo ships and liners, but the Mutual Security Agency found that American-flag tankers were not available on what it considered reasonable terms and conditions and it invoked the "non-availability" clause of the law exempting tankers from the 50 percent American-flag requirement.

The Public Advisory Board for Mutual Security recommended that the 50 percent requirement not be applied to countries that permit American shipping to compete on a "fair" basis.

[6] The Mutual Security Agency estimated (*Press Release No. 78*, December 30, 1952) that the total industrial output in Western Europe in 1952 was some 2 percent greater than in 1951 and nearly 50 percent greater than in 1947-1948. It was also estimated that European agricultural production increased by 3 percent over the preceding year and by more than 30 percent over 1948. For a detailed

An important aspect of the European Recovery Program in Europe had been the partial financing of the establishment and/or modernization of specific industrial projects that it was believed would increase the viability of Europe.[7] By 1951 this program was being sharply curtailed as more emphasis was placed on the so-called "productivity drives" rather than additional investment in plant, and during 1952 only one new project was approved—grain handling and storage facilities in Turkey, calling for $2.5 million of MSA funds. However, the Agency did approve the expenditure of an additional $22.7 million in supplemental dollar financing of previously approved projects, mostly for plants producing iron and steel products.[8] The Mutual Security Agency also continued the Economic Cooperation Administration's technical assistance program in Western Europe, expending some $14 million during the year. Details as to the purposes of such payments were not published.

Each country receiving economic and technical—as distinct from military end-item—assistance on a grant basis from the Mutual Security Agency must deposit in special accounts local currency (called counterpart funds) in amounts equivalent to the dollar cost of the aid received.[9] Between 90 and 95 percent of these deposits are reserved for use in the countries making the deposits and the remainder are reserved for the use of the U.S. Government. Although these moneys did not constitute any increase in the real resources of the country and the effect of their expenditure or immobilization could be offset by the monetary and fiscal policies of the recipients, the U.S. Government believed that they played an important role in influencing internal monetary and investment policies.[1] The Mutual Security Act of 1951

analysis of Europe's economic position and problems at the end of 1952, see Organization for European Economic Cooperation, *Europe—the Way Ahead*, Paris, December 1952. See also Williams, J. H., "End of the Marshall Plan," *Foreign Affairs*, July 1952, pp. 593-611.

[7] See *Survey—1951*, p. 54, and the references cited therein.

[8] Paid shipments under this program during the year totalled approximately $95 million, most of them being in fulfillment of previous commitments.

[9] For details on the accumulation and use of counterpart funds, including details by country and by purpose of use, see Mutual Security Agency, *Local Currency Counterpart Funds*, Wash., D.C. (monthly).

[1] See *Survey—1951*, pp. 55-56, and the references cited therein for a brief account of the activities and policies regarding the use of these funds in earlier years.

had specified that the equivalent of $500 million of counterpart funds should be used in the year ending in mid-1952 for defense purposes and, as noted earlier, the 1952 Act specified that, except as otherwise provided in the law, these funds were to be used only for purposes for which the dollars provided in the Act would be available.

Deposits in counterpart fund accounts during 1952 for the use of the depositing countries totalled the equivalent of nearly $1.5 billion and the Mutual Security Agency approved withdrawals of a slightly larger amount. Of the approved withdrawals only $0.3 billion was used to retire government debt held by central banks. This was in sharp contrast with earlier years when amounts ranging from one fourth to four fifths of the deposits were used for anti-inflationary purposes, that is, permitted to accumulate or used to retire public debt held by central banks. Of the withdrawals approved during the year, just over two fifths were for such clear-cut military purposes as construction of military installations, and procurement and production of military matériel for the armed services. The remainder were channeled into land reclamation projects, the construction of public buildings and housing facilities, and a wide variety of projects designed to promote production.

The so-called "Moody Amendment" to the Mutual Security Act of 1952 provided that not less than the equivalent of $100 million of counterpart funds should be used for the purpose of implementing the 1951 "Benton Amendment,"[2] which was intended to encourage competition in Europe and to develop and strengthen the free labor movements there. The Mutual Security Agency reported at the end of 1952 that negotiations for setting up programs under this amendment had reached an advanced stage in eleven European countries. These programs were designed to raise productivity, to eliminate restrictive marketing and labor practices, and to lower the sales prices for finished products. Details are not available but it was stated that the funds were to be made available, apparently on a loan basis, to individual plants to finance new techniques and new designs, and to provide technical assistance, research, education, and demonstration. Actual expenditures under this program had not begun at the end of

[2] See *Survey—1951*, pp. 32-33.

the year. The so-called Sawyer Mission concluded in December that the Benton-Moody Amendments should be repealed, arguing that, though they were well intentioned, the provisions were unwise—in that they undertook to assume a direction of certain policies and practices in various countries in Europe that "we have neither the wisdom, the experience, nor the resources to carry out" —and had proven "unworkable."[3]

In earlier years, at least 5 percent of the deposits in the counterpart fund accounts were reserved for use by the U.S. Government, but, as noted earlier, the 1952 Mutual Security Act specified that from June 20, 1952 this was to be raised to not less than 10 percent. Because of a change in reporting techniques, it is not possible to determine from the public data actual expenditures of these funds by the United States during the year, but, apart from the equivalent of a few million dollars that was used by the Defense Materials Procurement Agency to purchase strategic materials for the United States stockpile and to finance projects for the development of their production,[4] the expenditures were primarily to cover a portion of the administrative and the operating expenses of official United States agencies in Europe and to meet a portion of the costs of the information services of the Mutual Security Agency.[5]

d. PACE OF EUROPEAN REARMAMENT

Following the review of the military requirements for adequate defense, on the one hand, and the evaluations of the economic and political capabilities of the various European members of the North Atlantic Treaty Organization to rearm, on the other, that were made by the Temporary Council Committee (the "Three Wise Men") in late 1951 and early 1952, the North Atlantic Council of Ministers met at Lisbon in February and set specific goals to be met at the end of the year. These included making available to the NATO Command 25 divisions in a state of combat readiness, 25 divisions in the form of a quickly mobilizable reserve, 4,000 operational aircraft, and 1,600 naval vessels. The armed forces of the United States in Western Europe (6 divi-

[3] *Foreign Commerce Weekly*, December 22, 1952, pp. 18-19.

[4] See Chapter VII, below.

[5] Some members of Congress criticized the Administration for using counterpart funds to build "luxurious" housing for official American personnel in Germany.

sions) were included in these goals but not included were contributions by Greece, Turkey, and Western Germany. At the same meeting the principle of establishing a European Defense Community in which Germany would make a major contribution was heartily endorsed; Greece and Turkey were welcomed into the NATO; the administrative structure of NATO was reorganized; and it was decided that an annual review should be made by the Organization of the defense requirements and capabilities of the members.[6]

For security, and possibly other, reasons details as to the progress made during the year toward these goals were not made public and the official statements were all carefully qualified. But the record is clear that, while European defense production, recruitment, and training had all increased, the goals were not wholly met.[7] In April General Eisenhower, then Supreme Allied Commander, Europe, reported that there were some thirty divisions in being and readily mobilizable, and in midyear the Mutual Security Agency reported that there would be some delay in reaching the targets by the end of the year—especially with respect to the twenty-five reserve divisions—but that it would not be of "major significance" and would not involve any basic changes in the plans for the military build-up.[8] During the summer there was much speculation in the press as to the extent of the failure to meet the Lisbon goals and General Ridgway, who

[6] See *Survey—1951*, pp. 38-49, and the references cited therein for a summary of the Temporary Council Committee's report, the issues that preceded it, and the decisions taken at Lisbon.

For comprehensive studies of the problems of Western rearmament, see Royal Institute of International Affairs, *Atlantic Alliance: NATO's Role in the Free World*, London, 1952; Bolles, B. and Wilcox, F. O., *The Armed Road to Peace: An Analysis of NATO*, New York, 1952; Middleton, D., *The Defense of Western Europe*, New York, 1952; and "The Impact of Rearmament on Western Countries," *Public Finance* (The Hague), no. 1-2, 1952.

[7] The Mutual Security Agency reported that in value terms expenditures on rearmament by the European NATO nations (the United Kingdom and France accounted for over three fourths of the total) during the last few months of 1952 were at a rate more than 25 percent higher than in the first few months of the year and that further increases were expected in 1953.

For a detailed unofficial account of the problems and progress of European rearmament as of the end of 1952, see the five articles by Hanson W. Baldwin in the *New York Times*, issues for January 12-16 inclusive, 1953, pp. 1, 8, 13, 7, 4, respectively. See also Wilmot, C., "If NATO Had to Fight," *Foreign Affairs*, January 1953, pp. 200-214, and Murphy, C. J. V., "A New Strategy for NATO," *Fortune*, January 1953, pp. 80ff.

[8] *Second Report to Congress on the Mutual Security Program, op.cit.*, p. 8.

had replaced General Eisenhower, stated in October that his Command had not been given the "minimum military requirements" for the defense of Europe, despite the fact that Soviet military strength was growing.[9] In its report for the period ending in December 1952 the Mutual Security Agency stated that the 1952 force goals, "established purposely on optimistic assumptions," were "largely realized," with the naval objectives "considered met," 25 active divisions "largely up to the required standards," and the goal of 4,000 aircraft "nearly met." The bulk of the deficiencies, it declared, were to be found in the strength, both in men and in equipment, of the reserve divisions.[1]

Among the most frequently cited reasons for the failure (whatever its extent) to meet the Lisbon commitments were that the goals were extravagant and unreal in the first place and that the economies of Europe were unable to support the program without what were regarded as unacceptable sacrifices in the standards of living of the people. Many Europeans still felt it impossible to prevent Russia's overrunning most of Europe and therefore saw no point in rearming; others believed that the threat of war had receded; still others believed that American atomic power was a sufficient deterrent to Russian aggression.[2] Some officials, particularly in France and, to a lesser extent, in the United Kingdom, stressed the drain on their exchange reserves and their extra-European military commitments as reasons for their failure to meet the goals. Some officials also claimed that the pace of their nation's rearmament had been restricted by the failure of the U.S. Government to provide as much assistance as planned and others maintained that making realistic plans for their own rearmament efforts was virtually impossible since the United States made commitments as to its contributions only for one fiscal year at a time.[3]

[9] For some of the press comment, see *U.S. News and World Report*, September 12, 1952, pp. 41-42; *The Nation*, August 23, 1952, pp. 149-150; and *The Economist*, August 23, 1952, pp. 432-433.

[1] *Third Report to Congress on the Mutual Security Program*, *op.cit.*, p. 1. In his final appearance before the Senate Foreign Relations Committee, Secretary Acheson in mid-January 1953 stated that the Atlantic Community nations were then so strong in Western Europe that the Communists could not overrun the area without first giving their intentions away by a military build-up.

[2] For an account of the official British reasons for "stretching out" their defense program, see *The Economist*, February 28, 1953, pp. 547-549.

[3] President Truman took cognizance of this consideration when he told the incoming Congress in early 1953 that in his opinion it would be desirable to

There were also some complaints that the "paralysis" in United States foreign policy occasioned by the Presidential election and the change in administration had forced the European countries to delay making the decisions needed if they were to meet the objectives set at Lisbon.

The North Atlantic Treaty Organization's institutions in Paris carried out their assignment of preparing an annual review of the progress achieved during the year toward creating "balanced collective forces" and of recommending military goals for 1953, after taking into account the experiences during 1952 and reconciling the cost of the forces deemed desirable by the military authorities with an assessment of the political and economic capabilities of members.[4] In mid-December cabinet members from all the NATO countries met in Paris and reviewed these various progress reports and recommendations. But the United States officials present were members of an outgoing administration and did not feel competent to take decisions on most questions, including the making of estimates as to the amount and form of future United States aid, and it was therefore agreed that another meeting should be held in the spring of 1953 at which time the results of the 1952 "review" would be further considered and firm force goals for 1953 established.

The Ministers did agree in December on an additional infrastructure program estimated to cost the equivalent of some $230 million.[5] They also reiterated their earlier statements that the de-

---

develop a longer-range approach than the one-year renewal of the military aid program, which had been the practice up to that time.

[4] For an authoritative account of the failure through 1952 of NATO to deal effectively with the economic problems of its members, see Spofford, C. M., "NATO's Growing Pains," *Foreign Affairs*, October 1952, pp. 95-105.

There was but little evidence during the year that a concerted effort was being made to create a "coordinated arms program," in the sense that, as a matter of policy, each member should specialize in producing certain items for the whole community with the result that no one country would be in a position of producing all of its own requirements (see *Survey–1951*, p. 43). In December the Council of Ministers did take occasion to note that progress was being made in the "coordination of production" of defense equipment and to direct formally that more study should be given to this problem and to further standardization of equipment. (See the communiqué of the North Atlantic Council reprinted in the Department of State *Bulletin*, January 5, 1953, p. 3.)

[5] Infrastructure refers to certain fixed military facilities—particularly airfields and related installations—that are used jointly by the NATO forces. This program was begun in 1950 by five of the continental nations, and in September 1951 the United States and Canada joined in the financing of additional construction esti-

fense of Europe called for the early establishment of the European Defense Community; formally agreed that the war being fought by the French forces in Indochina deserved the continuing support of the NATO Governments; approved proposals for establishing a Mediterranean Command; and decided that, if a choice must be made, more emphasis should be placed on increasing the effectiveness of existing forces than on expanding their numbers.[6]

e. EUROPEAN DEFENSE COMMUNITY

The problem of organizing the defense of Western Europe has since 1949 been intensified by the difficulties of reaching agreement as to the role of Germany. After Korea, the U.S. Government concluded that large-scale German participation was a necessary condition to the building of adequate defenses. In late 1950 the then French Premier, Pleven, whose Government had an acute fear of a resurgent Germany, proposed that a European Army be created, composed of the forces of several nations, including Germany, and be placed under a supranational authority. After several months of skepticism, American officials became convinced that this device promised to be the most effective feasible means for obtaining early and substantial participation by Germany in the defense program and throughout 1951 the U.S. Gov-

mated to cost the equivalent of $221 million. At Lisbon in February 1952 a further expansion was agreed upon that was estimated would cost $426 million. The "fourth slice" of the program was estimated to cost the equivalent of $473 million, of which the December 1952 approval for $230 million was the first installment. The United States portions of the costs for the last three "slices" were some 48 percent, 43 percent, and 40 percent respectively, with a portion of the dollars coming from Mutual Defense Program appropriations and the remainder from the appropriations to the Defense Department. Actual expenditures under the Mutual Security Program began in 1952 and totalled $73 million by the end of the year.

[6] The full texts of the official communiqué and related statements on the meeting are reprinted in Department of State *Bulletin*, January 5, 1953, pp. 3-8. The Ministers gave only a brief nod to the concept of developing, in any formal sense, the North Atlantic Community that had been discussed at some length in 1951 (see *Survey—1951*, pp. 44-45). Specifically, they adopted a resolution stating that the Governments "should seek by individual and collective measures to strengthen their political and economic capacities. . . ." There was an unconfirmed report in the fall that France had submitted a proposal to the Organization for creating some form of common defense budget among the members. Precise details of any such arrangement were not published and there was no indication that the U.S. Government, which would be expected to be a chief contributor, was willing seriously to consider such a proposal. For a succession of unofficial articles arguing for the creation of a "common budget," see the various issues of *The Statist*, August 1952 through January 1953, but especially the November 1952 issues.

ernment actively encouraged the creation of a European Defense Community.[7] As noted earlier, during the hearings in the spring of 1952 on the Mutual Security Program, Congress expressed keen interest in, and virtually unanimous approval of, the concept of a European Army and in the law authorized the Mutual Security Agency to provide funds directly to such an organization when and if it was created.

Following many months of negotiations, representatives of Germany, Belgium, France, Italy, Luxembourg, and the Netherlands on May 27 signed a treaty establishing the European Defense Community.[8] The agreement was long, complex, and contained many special provisions and exceptions, and only the central features need be listed here. There was to be created a European Air Force and a European Ground Force, the latter to be composed of *groupements* (slightly smaller than United States divisions) from each of the signatories. These groups were to be integrated at the army corps level, with each corps containing three or four divisions of different nationalities. Member states would be permitted to maintain armed forces outside the Community only for specified purposes: internal security, use in non-European territories with respect to which the nations had assumed defense responsibilities, and international missions assumed by them in Berlin and Austria or by virtue of a decision by the United Nations. The forces of the Community were to be assigned to the Supreme Commander of the North Atlantic Treaty Organization.

The administration of the Community was to be by a series of institutions similar to those of the European Coal and Steel Community: a Commissariat, a Council of Ministers, an Assembly (the Schuman Plan Assembly with nine additional members), and a Court of Justice (identical with the Schuman Plan Court). The Commissariat was to be supranational in character and was to be the principal executive agency of the Community with responsibility for, among other things, coordinating the training and re-

[7] See *Survey—1951*, pp. 40-49 for a brief account of the various forms this encouragement took.

[8] The text of the treaty may be found in *Senate Document, Executives Q and R*, 82d Cong., 2d Sess., June 2, 1952, pp. 167-251. For an unofficial background account of the steps leading to the signing of the European Defense Community Treaty, see Walton, C. C., "Background for the European Defense Community," *Political Science Quarterly*, March 1953, pp. 142-169.

cruitment of the defense forces, preparing a common military budget (after consultation with the governments of the member states), and granting licenses for the production, export, and import of war matériel. The authority of the Commissariat was, however, extensively circumscribed. The Council of Ministers, composed of one member of the government of each member state, was to "harmonize the actions of the Commissariat with the policies of the Governments of the Member States" and by a unanimous vote could issue directives to the Commissariat. Among other things, the Council had to agree unanimously to the total amount of the Community's budget and the amount of each member's contribution thereto; a two-thirds majority was required before the proposed distribution of expenditures could be implemented. A two-thirds majority of the Council was also required before the regulations, prepared by the Commissariat, governing the granting of licenses for the production, export, and import of military equipment and supplies could become effective and the Council had to be consulted on the selection of the superior military officers. The Assembly, whose members were selected by the parliaments of the member states or by direct voting, was given general supervisory powers over the Community and by a two-thirds vote could force the resignation of the Commissariat. Among its many other powers, the Assembly could, within specified limits, propose changes in the common budget of the Community and, by a two-thirds majority, could reject the budget as prepared by the Commissariat and approved by the Council.

French spokesmen, as well as those of the other signatories to the treaty, had repeatedly expressed fear that the proposed European Army would be looked upon by the United States and Britain as permitting them to withdraw their forces from Europe and that, the European Army notwithstanding, once Germany had rebuilt her forces she would again embark on military ventures against them. To allay these fears, the United States and Britain formally declared at the time the European Defense Community Treaty was signed that they would regard any action that threatened the "integrity or unity" of the Community as a threat to their own security and that they were resolved to station such forces on the continent of Europe as they deemed "necessary and appropriate to contribute to the joint defense of the North Atlantic Treaty area. . . ."[9]

The day before the treaty setting up the Community was signed, the United States, the United Kingdom,, and France finally signed a "contractual agreement" with the Federal Republic of Western Germany that had the effect of giving the latter virtually complete control over her domestic and foreign affairs, with the following major exceptions: Western Germany could not make a separate peace treaty with Russia; the other three powers retained the right to maintain forces in Western Germany and to intervene if the stability of the German Government should be threatened by an internal uprising; and certain restrictions were kept on the production of heavy military equipment in Germany, subject to exceptions that might be permitted by the European Defense Community.[1]

The European Defense Community was seen by the U.S. Government as an essential factor in the new relationship between Germany and the Allied powers established by the agreements ending the occupation. It was therefore expressly provided that the conventions, the protocols to the North Atlantic Treaty, and the European Defense Community should come into force at the same time. The U.S. Senate gave its approval to the conventions and the protocols and they were signed by President Truman on

[9] The text of this declaration may be found on pages 253-254 of *Senate Document, Executives Q and R, op.cit.*

While Germany was not a member of the North Atlantic Treaty Organization, she was given a guarantee of assistance should she be attacked. This took the form of a protocol to the North Atlantic Treaty, signed on May 27 by all of its members, stating that an armed attack on any of the members of the European Defense Community would be considered an attack against all the parties to the North Atlantic Treaty. A similar guarantee was extended by Germany to all parties of the North Atlantic Treaty in a protocol to the European Defense Community Treaty. For more discussion of the issues involved in these agreements, see Department of State *Bulletin*, June 16, 1952, pp. 931-933, 947-951, and June 23, 1952, pp. 971-979.

[1] The text of the conventions, together with statements by President Truman and Secretary of State Acheson, are reprinted in *Senate Document, Executives Q and R, op.cit.*, pp. 1-165. In addition to the main convention, several related ones were also signed. One was concerned with bringing to a conclusion existing Allied programs in Germany; another made provision for logistic requirements of the Allied forces in Germany and for the personal status of the members of such forces. A finance convention established the general principles governing the amount of the German financial contribution to the common defense, including the Federal Republic's share of the costs of the European Defense Community and the cost of maintaining United States, British, and French troops in Germany.

August 2, 1952. They had not, however, entered into force by the end of the year since none of the parliaments of the signatory nations had ratified the Defense Community treaty. Opposition to ratification was apparently widespread. Only brief summaries of the major reasons need be presented here. In Germany, there were many who did not want their nation to rearm, on the ground that such action would goad the Russians into aggression against them, or that their security was not threatened by the Russians, or that their economy could not "bear the burden," or that it would serve to postpone reunification of East and West Germany. There were also influential groups in Germany that believed that their nation would not be given a prominent enough role in the Community and some questioned the constitutionality of the treaty. In the other nations, most of the opposition, apart from that of the Communists, grew out of the fear that, despite the safeguards, Germany would dominate the Community and, in time, once again threaten their national security, especially since the United Kingdom did not plan to become a member of the Community. There were also objections stemming from the belief that the treaty involved an unacceptable limitation on the members' sovereignty and freedom of action.[2] On the other hand, sentiment in favor of the European Army within the United States Government was as strong as ever as the year ended.

Near East and Africa

Of the fourteen countries eligible for military aid under Title II (Near East and Africa) of the Mutual Security Act of 1952,[3] only three—Greece, Turkey, and Iran—actually received such assistance during the year, and in each case the shipments were in continuation of programs in effect for several years. Greece and Turkey, members of the North Atlantic Treaty Organization, obtained most of the $300 million of aid utilized in this area. The military assistance provided to Iran was on a modest, though undisclosed, scale, having been suspended from January 8 to April 24,

[2] See *The Economist*, November 22, 1952, p. 522; December 13, 1952, pp. 760-761; December 20, 1952, pp. 799-800; and January 24, 1953, p. 194.

[3] Greece, Turkey, Iran, the seven Arab States (Egypt, Iraq, Jordan, Lebanon, Saudi Arabia, Syria, and Yemen), the independent countries of North Africa (Ethiopia, Liberia, and Libya), and Israel.

pending Iran's agreeing to comply with the conditions of aid as specified in the law.[4]

While negotiations were carried on during the year, no progress was recorded toward creating the Middle East Command, a regional defense arrangement that had been proposed in 1951 by the United States in conjunction with France, Turkey, and the United Kingdom.[5] The major obstacles to the creation of such an organization were the general apathy felt by the Arab States toward the West, the "what's in it for us?" feeling among the officials of many of the Arab nations, and the continued tensions between the Arab States and Israel.

Except for the "defense-support" aid to Greece and Turkey, discussed in the preceding section, the assistance provided in forms other than military end-items and services by the U.S. Government to the countries in this area was intended primarily to encourage their economic development rather than directly to support their defense forces and is therefore discussed in Chapter II.

Asia and the Pacific

Military aid was extended during 1952 to four countries in the Far East and Pacific area: the Republic of China on Formosa, the Associated States of Indochina, the Philippines, and Thailand.[6] The value of military aid provided rose steadily during the year and totalled $391 million, with the annual rate during the last six months rising to some $540 million, as shown in Table 2, above. In general, military assistance to these countries had the limited objective of developing forces capable of discouraging attacks from abroad and of maintaining internal security. In all these countries the aid was supervised by United States Military Advisory Groups, which were also active in local training programs.

Although details were not made public, it was officially stated that "a substantial percentage" of the aid provided to this area went to train and reequip the Chinese forces on Formosa. High priority was also given to the delivery of military equipment to

[4] For a list of these conditions, see *Survey—1951*, pp. 30-32.

[5] See *Survey—1951*, pp. 50-51.

[6] Although no new aid was programmed during the year to Indonesia, there were small deliveries of military supplies that had previously been approved under the Mutual Defense Assistance Program. This assistance was mostly in the form of vehicles and light arms for the national police of Indonesia.

the armed forces of the French Union and the Associated States of Indochina and this was regarded by American officials as having played a major role in the war against the Communists in Indochina.[7] As noted above, the commitment of French forces in Indochina continued to limit France's participation in the mutual defense efforts in Western Europe and the United States therefore gave increasing support to building up the armies of the Associated States, under French tutelage, with the hope that this would permit the French to transfer some of their forces back to Europe. United States military aid to the Philippines and Thailand was small during the year.

The three "security treaties" that the United States had signed in 1951 with Japan, the Philippines, and Australia and New Zealand were ratified by the signatories and entered into effect in 1952.[8] Under the last two treaties each of the parties declared that "an armed attack in the Pacific Area on any of the Parties would be dangerous to its own peace and safety,"[9] and all were bound "separately and jointly by means of continuous and effective self-help and mutual aid" to "maintain and develop their individual and collective capacity to resist armed attack." The short treaty with Japan provided that the United States could maintain land, air, and sea forces in and about Japan and that such forces and Japanese "facilities" were to be combined for the maintenance of peace in the Far East; no provision was included in this treaty for "continuous and effective self-help and mutual aid." A formal meeting was held during the year of the Council of the so-called ANZUS group—Australia, New Zealand, and the United States—but no such meetings were held in connection with the other two treaties. The meeting of the ANZUS Council was largely exploratory and organizational in character.

While these treaties referred to the desirability of "development of a more comprehensive system of regional security in the Pacific Area" and were viewed in some foreign quarters as skeleton organizations from which regional security organizations like

[7] *Second Report to Congress on the Mutual Security Program*, *op.cit.*, p. 24.

[8] For the texts of these treaties, see Department of State, *Treaties and Other International Acts Series*, Wash., D.C., Nos. 2491, 2493, 2529.

[9] It is to be noted that this is similar to the language of the Monroe Doctrine and is less of a commitment than the North Atlantic Treaty undertaking that "an armed attack against one . . . shall be considered an armed attack against them all."

the North Atlantic Treaty Organization might evolve,[1] there were no indications from any official United States sources that further extensions of the Pacific defense pacts in the near future were being contemplated, although the Administration, and Congress, did hope the time might come when an over-all Pacific pact would be feasible.[2] At the first session of the Council of ANZUS, held in August, the delegates concluded that "it would be premature . . . to attempt to establish relationships with other states or regional organizations."[3]

The economic and technical aid provided to Formosa and Indochina was considered to be in close support of the military aid programs there, but it also was intended, as in the other countries in that area, to help them increase and diversify their production of non-military goods; the economic aid provided the Far East and Pacific area during 1952 is therefore discussed in the following chapter.

Latin America

In 1951 the Mutual Security Act had provided that military assistance on a grant basis could be extended to Latin American countries after a finding by the President that plans prepared by the Inter-American Defense Board for the defense of the Western Hemisphere would require the participation of certain of the other American Republics. The President made such a finding with respect to several of these countries in December 1951 and negotiation of the necessary bilateral military assistance agreements began. By the end of 1952 agreements had been signed with seven of these nations.[4] The press reported that some of the Latin American countries were reluctant to sign, or to ratify, these agreements on the grounds that they carried an implied commitment to send troops abroad, that the aid was designed

[1] See, for example, *The Economist*, August 9, 1952, pp. 321-322, and *The New Statesman and Nation*, August 9, 1952, p. 150.

[2] See "Japanese Peace Treaty and Other Treaties Relating to Security in the Pacific," *Hearings*, U.S. Senate, Committee on Foreign Relations, 82d Cong., 2d Sess., and Department of State *Bulletin*, September 29, 1952, pp. 471-475 for a general survey of America's policy in the Pacific area in 1952.

[3] Department of State *Bulletin*, August 18, 1952, p. 245.

[4] Brazil, Chile, Colombia, Cuba, Ecuador, Peru, and Uruguay. The agreements with Brazil and Uruguay had not been ratified by those countries at the end of the year. Negotiations had also taken place with Mexico and the Dominican Republic but no agreements had been signed at year's end.

primarily to meet United States objectives rather than to meet what these nations regarded as their own needs, and that military agreements invite aggression.[5] The actual provision of military aid on a straight grant basis began in July and went to Chile, Colombia, Cuba, Ecuador, and Peru. The amounts shipped were small, however, and most of the $59 million of military end-item grants recorded as utilized by Latin America during the year (see Table 2, above) represented the excess of the acquisition cost over the sale price of "excess" United States military equipment purchased by the various Latin American nations. This aid was intended by the United States to help the recipients perform certain tasks—especially the protection of sea lanes and the defense of strategic areas (including sources of critical raw materials) against sea and air attack—that it was believed the United States might otherwise have to perform.

As in the other non-European areas, grants supplied by the U.S. Government to Latin America in forms other than matériel and related services were primarily designed to facilitate its economic development and therefore are discussed in the following chapter.

[5] See, for example, *New York Times*, February 21, 1952, p. 6; October 27, 1952, p. 9; and December 17, 1952, p. 15. The State Department denied these charges. (See Department of State *Publication 4917*, Wash., D.C., March 1953.)

II · ECONOMIC AND TECHNICAL ASSISTANCE GRANTS TO UNDERDEVELOPED AREAS

UNDER its Technical Cooperation Program (Point Four), the Mutual Security Program, and through various United Nations programs, the U.S. Government in 1951 had extended small but growing amounts of economic and technical assistance grants[1] to a large number of so-called underdeveloped areas of the world —usually defined, for working purposes, to mean those with low per capita incomes: Latin America, Africa, the Middle East, Southeast Asia, and the Far East, excluding Japan and Communist areas.[2] These activities took several forms, and there was considerable disagreement, perhaps even more than over most of the international economic activities of the U.S. Government, within the Executive Branch as to the form and purpose of the aid and as to its relation to other international economic policies of the Government.[3]

An important justification back of the Point Four Program and the United States grants to the United Nations technical assistance program was a humanitarian concern over the crushing poverty suffered by many of the peoples in the underdeveloped areas, but the Government also expected them to serve the political and economic interests of the United States in various ways, the more important being that they would (a) expand the sources of urgently needed raw materials, (b) help prevent people from embracing or succumbing to Communism, (c) contribute toward world peace by aiding the establishment of responsible and representative governments, and, in the words of President Truman,

[1] Loans by the U.S. Government are discussed in Chapters IV and V.

[2] Some European countries received technical assistance under the European Recovery Program and, later, the Mutual Security Program, but this aid was industrial in character and was therefore largely of a different sort from that extended to other areas.

[3] See the chapters entitled "Point Four Program" in the previous three volumes of this *Survey* for an account of the evolution of that program.

by striking "at the conditions of misery that envelop half the people of the earth,"[4] and (d) increase United States foreign trade.

By the end of 1951 several broad operating principles had been established by the Technical Cooperation Administration. Important among these were that: (a) the programs were to be primarily ones of teaching and showing, supported by adequate supplies and demonstration equipment, with emphasis to be on simple tools and equipment; (b) the problems of hunger, disease, and illiteracy were to be taken up first; (c) projects undertaken were to be cooperative, with some of the funds and administrative services being provided by the recipients; (d) the work was to be performed with the people rather than with their governments; (e) wherever practical, the assistance was to be provided through the United Nations and the Organization of American States; and (f) private agencies and institutions were to be used extensively. Further, it was a considered policy to supplement technical assistance by encouraging the flow of capital from private local and United States sources into productive enterprises in the areas.

The aid programs in the various Southeast Asian countries under the administration of the Economic Cooperation Administration-Mutual Security Agency had objectives similar to those of the Point Four Program, plus that of alleviating the impact on this region of military activities, but, in contrast to the Point Four activities, most of the funds were used to supply commodities rather than technical services and the basic operating principles were patterned after those of the European Recovery Program.

During 1951, several of the recipient countries had attempted, primarily in the United Nations, to get commitments from the United States to increase its grants-in-aid, particularly in the form of funds for economic development via a new International Development Authority to be established under the United Nations. The United States Executive Branch had successfully opposed, or at least postponed, assuming any such responsibilities, and Congress in that year had shown a willingness to finance *technical services* to be provided on a "grass-roots" basis but had made it clear that it was opposed to any new program for giving

[4] Department of State *Bulletin*, April 21, 1952, p. 607.

away large amounts of *commodities* and had evidenced much more sympathy for the Point Four programs than for those of the Mutual Security Agency.

A. *BILATERAL PROGRAMS*

Legislative Issues[5]

In presenting its requests for the 1952 Mutual Security Program, the Administration divided the proposed aid into three main categories: military assistance, defense support, and economic and technical assistance. The first two have been discussed in Chapter I, above. The last encompassed aid of three types: bilateral technical assistance administered by the Technical Cooperation Administration; bilateral economic aid (with emphasis on commodities rather than technical assistance) administered by the Mutual Security Agency; and multilateral aid, largely technical assistance, extended through the United Nations and the Organization of American States. For these purposes the Administration requested Congress to appropriate one-half billion dollars in new funds, and to authorize the carryover of any unobligated funds from previous appropriations, to be distributed among areas as shown in Table 5.

a. PURPOSES OF PROGRAMS

Administration officials and their supporters in Congress in 1952 defended the extension and expansion of economic and technical aid to the underdeveloped areas primarily on the grounds that such assistance was an effective weapon against Communism in these areas and would facilitate the increased production of many raw materials urgently needed by the United States and Western Europe. It was therefore, they argued, a "security program in a very real sense."[6] In the words of the Director for Mu-

[5] Readers desiring more detailed information than is given here are referred to the following sources: "Mutual Security Act of 1952," *Hearings*, U.S. Senate, Committee on Foreign Relations, 82d Cong., 2d Sess., March-April 1952; "Mutual Security Act Extension," *Hearings on H.R. 7005*, House of Rep., Committee on Foreign Affairs, 82d Cong., 2d Sess., March-April 1952; *H. Rpt. No. 1922*, 82d Cong., May 12, 1952; *H. Rpt. No. 2031*, 82d Cong., June 4, 1952; and International Development Advisory Board, *Guidelines for Point 4*, Wash., D.C., June 5, 1952.

[6] At the outset of the hearings, the Director for Mutual Security, Mr. Harriman,

TABLE 5

Administration Requests for Economic and Technical Assistance to Underdeveloped Areas, Fiscal Year 1952-1953

(millions of dollars)

Near East and Africa[a]—economic and technical	55
Asia and the Pacific—economic[b]	258
technical[c]	150
Latin America—economic and technical	22
Multilateral[d]—economic and technical	17

a) Excludes the Israel and Palestine refugee programs, but includes Technical Cooperation Administration aid to Egypt, Ethiopia, Iran, Iraq, Israel, Jordan, Lebanon, Liberia, Libya, Saudi Arabia, Syria, and Yemen.

b) Mutual Security Agency programs in Indochina, Thailand, Burma, Indonesia, the Philippines, and the Republic of China on Formosa. The Korean Rehabilitation Program was considered separately.

c) Technical Cooperation Administration programs for the following South Asian countries: Afghanistan, Ceylon, India, Nepal, and Pakistan.

d) Includes contributions to both the United Nations and the Organization of American States.

Source: "Mutual Security Act of 1952," *H. Rpt. No. 2031*, 82d Cong., 2d Sess., June 4, 1952, p. 15.

tual Security: "Development in these areas will provide raw materials for the continued growth of our own economy and those of other free nations. It will give hope to these people for a better life in a free society and should, in time, strengthen the nations of these areas so that they can in the future, without special help from us, be self-reliant members of the free world."[7]

testified that discontent with their lot was more intense than ever in underdeveloped areas, that the United States sympathized with this feeling, and that nationalism was growing apace. He concluded that unless "we provide technical and economic assistance, and do it promptly, to help these people begin to improve their conditions, there is serious danger that they will fall into the trap of the shrewd and ruthless Communist machine which is cynically promising quick cures for age-old ills. This would be just as grave a blow to our security as if they fell to Communism through armed attack." ("Mutual Security Act of 1952," Senate, *Hearings, op.cit.*, p. 7.)

The International Development Advisory Board (a group of private citizens that the law required the President to appoint to advise, and consult with, the Secretary of State on major policy problems pertaining to the Point Four Program) asserted in their midyear report that Point Four aid should be distinguished from military programs and that the philosophies underlying them should be kept separate, adding that the former was "fully justifiable without reference to military or military-support objectives." (See their *Guidelines for Point 4, op.cit.*, p. 4.)

[7] "Mutual Security Act of 1952," Senate, *Hearings, op.cit.*, pp. 8-9. See also the statements by President Truman and Secretary of State Acheson in Department of State *Bulletin*, April 21, 1952, pp. 607-612, and by Eric Johnston in Department of State *Bulletin*, May 12, 1952, pp. 747-751.

In 1952, for the first time, there was in the public hearings some direct questioning of the basic assumption that economic development would serve to weaken the appeal of Communism to the peoples of the underdeveloped countries. Some Congressmen expressed concern lest the process of economic development, accelerated by foreign aid, result in such a disruption of existing institutions that it create an "anarchy and confusion" conducive to the growth of Communism.[8] In reply, Secretary of State Acheson recognized that it was not certain that the results hoped for would be obtained by this means. He went on to testify that a requisite for the program's success in gaining allies was that the people to be aided must have a strong desire to "maintain their independence and work out their own national futures in their own way,"[9] but that if such a determination existed then it was in the United States interest to help them eliminate "the conditions in which disaffection can breed."

Related to this concern were the convictions of many Congressmen that the U.S. Government should not attempt to force "reforms" on the aid recipients,[1] should not attempt to impose United States standards—particularly labor standards—on them, and should undertake an aid program only when it was asked for and wanted. In their view, one crucial test of whether aid was really wanted was the willingness of foreign governments to use substantial amounts of their own resources for ends consistent with the Program's aims.

The Administration assured Congress that it was only "helping governments to bring about reforms that their people believe are due" and that the United States participated in specific projects only when satisfied that the aided people and their governments could, and would, in due course, "take over."[2] With respect to whether the aid was wanted, as measured by the will-

[8] Mr. Harriman had previously stated that the Mutual Security Agency actively supported land reforms and the establishment of free trade unions in the aided countries. ("Mutual Security Act of 1952," Senate, *Hearings*, *op.cit.*, pp. 7-8.)

[9] "Mutual Security Act Extension," *Hearings on H.R. 7005*, *op.cit.*, p. 152.

[1] In some midyear recommendations, the International Development Advisory Board stated that Point Four is "an instrument of orderly change, an attack upon the status quo" and that "any departure from this concept would tend to diminish the acceptance and effectiveness of the program." (*Guidelines for Point 4*, *op.cit.*, p. 3.)

[2] *Hearings on H.R. 7005*, *op.cit.*, pp. 928-929, 1001-1002.

ingness of the recipient nations to contribute some of their own resources, the Administration reported that local contributions in Latin America were never less than in a one-to-one ratio with United States contributions and in some cases were as high as thirteen to one, with the average being three to one. It added that most of these were older programs initiated by the Institute for Inter-American Affairs and that the United States contribution tended to decline as a given program continued. Thus, the newer programs, especially in the Far East, required much greater United States support, and in some cases "nothing" had been considered a "fair share" to be borne by the foreign country in the initial stages of a project.[3] The Act for International Development of 1950 required that recipients "pay a fair share" and while many in Congress were critical of the interpretation that nothing could be a fair share and were also dissatisfied with some of the Administration practices in this regard, the existing law was not amended on this point.[4]

The majority of Congress agreed that assistance of this type was wanted by the recipients and was a proper technique for the United States to gain allies abroad. There was also wide agreement that technical and economic aid of some amount was the "offensive" part of an over-all mutual security program that was largely "defensive" in character.

The national security objectives of the program, as manifested by its anti-Communist aim, were tied in closely with dependence of the United States on imported strategic materials.[5] The Administration and its Congressional supporters gave extensive testimony on the dependence of the United States on imports of various strategic minerals and metals, and argued that the proposed technical and economic aid to underdeveloped areas would both increase production of strategic commodities abroad and

[3] "Mutual Security Act for 1952," Senate, *Hearings*, *op.cit.*, pp. 634, 715, and *S. Rpt. No. 1490*, *op.cit.*, pp. 38-39.

[4] In its *Guidelines for Point 4* (*op.cit.*, pp. 6-7), the International Development Advisory Board stated that aid should be used "only to provide materials, equipment, or supplies which cannot be furnished by the cooperative government itself." They added that the minimum fair share of the recipient over any reasonable period should be in the ratio of at least one to one and should gradually rise to 100 percent.

[5] For an outline of the fiscal year 1953 program for the procurement of basic materials, see "Supplemental Appropriation Bill, 1953," *Hearings on H.R. 8320*, U.S. Senate, Committee on Appropriations, 82d Cong., 2d Sess., June 1952.

gain friends willing to export them to the United States. These objectives were quickly accepted by Congress and there was little discussion of them or disposition to prune those portions of the Administration's request that it could be shown would serve these purposes.

b. METHODS OF FINANCING

Some members of the Legislative Branch, as in earlier years, expressed the opinion that the areas to be aided could and should finance a large part of the needed *commodity* imports by borrowing abroad. Administration spokesmen agreed that economic development programs should be financed by loans "to the greatest extent possible, and through the established lending institutions,"[6] and emphasized that it was their policy that the bulk of the foreign exchange needed for the "ultimate development" of these areas must come from private sources,[7] supplemented by loans from the Export-Import Bank and the International Bank. They hastened to add, however, that until the local economies had reached a condition such that they could attract capital from these sources, the United States "must be prepared in some instances to make special grants for development."[8] They therefore urged Congress not to require that any of the funds made available under the Mutual Security Program be provided on a loan basis. Congress finally respected the Administration's request and the 1952 Act repealed the provision (Section 522) of the 1951 Act requiring that at least 10 percent of "economic" aid be extended as loans. The Act had never required that any of the "military" or "technical assistance" aid be provided on a credit basis.

As in the previous year, there were several in Congress who believed that at least some of the countries scheduled to receive aid, especially those that were benefiting from the increased world demand and prices for raw materials, were not in serious balance of payments difficulties and could and should pay for technical assistance (as well as for any imported commodities needed) from their own foreign exchange holdings. After some discussion, these

[6] *Hearings on H.R. 7005, op.cit.*, pp. 587-596; see also pp. 951-952.

[7] See Chapter IV for a discussion of activities by the U.S. Government designed to encourage private American investment abroad.

[8] On these questions, see also "Mutual Security Act of 1952," Senate, *Hearings*, *op.cit.*, pp. 8, 117, 592, 593, and *Guidelines for Point 4, op.cit.*, p. 5.

legislators accepted the Administration's statements that the described conditions did not exist in many of the countries scheduled to receive aid under the program and that, in any case, the ministries in the underdeveloped countries that were responsible for health, agriculture, public works, etc.—that is, those activities on which Point Four was concentrating—were frequently not very influential in their governments and therefore needed the prestige that experts financed by the U.S. Government gave to recommendations for development if such projects were to receive the wholehearted support of the foreign government.[9]

C. FORM AND AMOUNT OF AID

In presenting its requests for economic and technical assistance, the Administration preferred to emphasize the interdependence of the two but Congress insisted on drawing a more or less sharp distinction between the policy of providing underdeveloped areas with goods on the one hand and with services on the other. As in 1951,[1] the majority of Congress were much more sympathetic to supplying aid of the latter category than of the former, in part because of the lower costs and in part because of the emotional appeal of a program of teaching individuals how to help themselves to improve their economic status.

This issue of economic versus technical aid also involved the question of which U.S. Government agency would administer the programs, with Congress expressing a strong preference for the Technical Cooperation Administration rather than the Mutual Security Agency, which, for this purpose, it regarded as carrying the mantle of the Economic Cooperation Administration. In their original presentation, Administration spokesmen stated that the programs in the Near East and Africa and in Latin America would be administered by the Technical Cooperation Administration but that it was planned that, except in India, Pakistan, Nepal, Ceylon, and Afghanistan, all the programs in the Far East and Pacific area would be administered by the Mutual Security Agency. They stated that this decision was taken on the grounds that (a) these programs had been begun by ECA and were cur-

[9] See "Mutual Security Act of 1952," Senate, *Hearings*, *op.cit.*, pp. 645-650; see also p. 590.

[1] See *Survey—1951*, pp. 79-80.

rently being administered by the Mutual Security Agency and (b) that it would facilitate coordinating this type of aid with the military assistance being provided, or that might at some future time be judged necessary, to this area. Under this arrangement, over half of the total amount requested for economic and technical assistance funds was to be administered by the Mutual Security Agency. But Congress was reluctant to approve such a distribution of responsibility. It insisted that, as a general rule, all economic and technical assistance should be administered by the Technical Cooperation Administration except where it obviously was of the direct military-support type—as in Formosa, Indochina, the Philippines, and Thailand—and specified that the programs for Burma and Indonesia be shifted at once to the jurisdiction of the Technical Cooperation Administration. Congress also gave as its view that at an appropriate later time all the economic and technical assistance to Southeast Asia should be placed under the Technical Cooperation Administration's direction.

There was little discussion on the proposed Point Four programs for the Near East and Africa and for Latin America—the Israel and Palestine refugee programs were treated as distinct operations and are discussed in the following chapter. In the first place, the amounts involved were small—$55 million for the former, of which about one half was for the Arab States, and only $22 million for the latter—and the Administration testified that the bulk of these funds was to be used to provide technical assistance at the village or individual level, with only such commodities being provided as were absolutely necessary to make the technical assistance effective. In the final authorization and appropriation laws, these requests were pruned less than 10 percent.

Except for the case of Burma and Indonesia noted above, Congress did not seriously question the proposed Mutual Security Agency economic aid programs in Asia—Formosa, the Philippines, Indochina, and Thailand—since these were regarded as directly supporting the military efforts of these countries. But the proposed Point Four programs in the Asia and Pacific area were debated at length because in two cases—India and Pakistan—the

Administration proposed to provide relatively large amounts of materials as well as technical services.

Administration officials insisted that these programs involving provision of large amounts of commodities were bona fide Point Four projects but were not to be regarded as typical. They were justified as part of an accelerated program rather than as a change in the Point Four concept. The officials argued that there was less time than had been thought earlier to improve the economic well-being of these nations if they were to survive as independent governments and, by implication, to remain friendly to the United States. They emphasized that those nations that were scheduled to receive large quantities of commodities were newly independent and therefore did not yet have strong, stable, and efficient governments. Further, there were among these peoples "a rising tide of demand for speed on the economic side," and "a revolution of rising expectations" that carried with it a feeling that the success of the nationalist movement depended on rapid economic development and rising standards of living. Were it not for the expansionist pressure being exerted by the Kremlin, and the danger of internal subversion, the Administration said, the United States might safely spread its help in the process of development over twenty to fifty years, but, given the "Kremlin drive," "we cannot afford the risk of doing it the slow way," and "in order to enable these Asian governments . . . to survive as independent governments—it is necessary to enable them to make much more rapid progress in the meeting of rising expectations than would be possible without assistance from us."[2]

The types of assistance to meet this problem, said Administration officials, were not only technical services and the materials and equipment needed if the technical services were "going to make any sense," but, in some instances, shipments of consumption goods to tide these countries over the critical periods until the basic economic development projects began to bear fruit.

[2] *Hearings on H.R. 7005*, *op.cit.*, p. 923, and "Mutual Security Act of 1952," Senate, *Hearings*, *op.cit.*, pp. 8, 117, 592-593. The International Development Advisory Board stated in mid-1952 that "Point 4 cannot and should not encompass operations calculated to produce quick results through large and dramatic projects." The report did recognize that it might be "necessary or advisable, in certain circumstances, to accelerate or expand operations in one country or another" but that this could be done in such a way as not to violate the "fundamental character" of Point Four. (See *Guidelines for Point 4*, *op.cit.*, p. 3.)

Administration witnesses testified that, in some of the Far Eastern areas, especially India, the economic plight was centered on the failure of food production to keep pace with the growth in population and that the proposed aid should therefore include shipments of food as well as technical and economic assistance to expand local production.[3]

These statements, and those outlining the Administration's plans for using a part of the aid to improve health and sanitation facilities, led some Congressmen to urge that the program should place more attention on measures for limiting population growth, lest the result be increased demands in the future for greater shipments of American food to provide for an increased population for which the United States would be at least partly responsible. They argued that the Administration's program would cut the death rate but not the birth rate, that "our hearts [have] run away with our heads," and that not enough "fundamental thinking" had been done on these matters.[4] This was the first time since the inception of the Point Four Program that Congress had publicly considered its demographic aspects. In 1951, Administration spokesmen in the United Nations had strongly urged that specific and extensive study be given by the Economic and Social Council to the problems of population growth and its effect on economic development,[5] but in the public discussion before the Congressional committees in 1952, Administration officials did not direct themselves to these problems or give any evidence that they had given them careful study.

Of more immediate concern to Congress, however, was its feeling that the Administration's 1952 proposals represented not just a "speed-up" in the earlier programs, or those programs "writ large," as the Administration argued, but rather a fundamental change in their character and a shift in emphasis from "grass-roots" technical assistance to large-scale economic aid and fi-

[3] For details on India's difficulties as seen by the Administration, see "Mutual Security Act of 1952," Senate, *Hearings*, *op.cit.*, pp. 15, 397-401. See also Bowles, C. B., "The Partnership Which Must Not Fail," Department of State *Bulletin*, February 4, 1952, pp. 161-166, and Thorp, W. L., "India's Participation in Economic Development Programs," Department of State *Bulletin*, February 25, 1952, pp. 291-296.

[4] For the discussion of the population problem, see *Hearings on H.R. 7005*, *op.cit.*, pp. 996-997.

[5] See *Survey—1951*, p. 96, fn. 4.

nancial support. Some of these critics stated that programs of the latter sort in underdeveloped areas might be justifiable but, if so, they should be defended on their own merits and not disguised as Point Four. These Congressmen therefore urged that there be a separation by the Administration of its proposals for "technical assistance" from those for "economic aid" so that the integrity of the former would be preserved and so that Congress could vote its preference, if any, between the two.[6] Administration officials refused to make any such separation. They argued that all the proposed aid was for technical assistance "in the current definition of that term."[7]

But the majority of the Congressional committees considering the proposal agreed with the member who said that "this thing has plumb run away from the original conception."[8] During the debate on the floors of Congress, critics of the program pointed out that in some areas the Technical Cooperation Administration planned to spend fifteen to twenty times as much for commodities as for technical services and that the average ratio for all the programs was approximately four to one. They charged that the Point Four Program was "fantastically swollen beyond any possibility of doing the kind of job" Congress had originally intended it should do.[9] The House therefore approved an amendment that would have restricted the amount spent for commodities in any country by the Technical Cooperation Administration to no more than three times that spent for technical advice and services. This provision was not included in the final law, primarily on the ground that it deprived those administering the program

[6] See "Mutual Security Act for 1952," Senate, *Hearings*, *op.cit.*, p. 580, and *Hearings on H.R. 7005*, *op.cit.*, pp. 948-949. Members of Congress also questioned whether the Administration had adequately considered the "absorptive capacity" of the recipient countries for aid, asserting that aid was apparently requested on the basis of "wants or needs" and not on their ability to use it efficiently. (See *H. Rpt. No. 1922*, *op.cit.*, p. 52.) The Administration's position was that while many recipient countries ask for large amounts and inappropriate forms of aid (Secretary Acheson stated that a typical request was "We want a steel mill"), the programs recommended to Congress did not approach the absorptive capacity of the scheduled recipients.

[7] *Hearings on H.R. 7005*, *op.cit.*, p. 931.

[8] *Hearings on H.R. 7005*, *op.cit.*, pp. 936-937. See also the debate on these points in the *Congressional Record*, June 28, 1952, pp. 8549-8554, and July 3, 1952, pp. 9251-9286.

[9] See *Congressional Record*, May 21, 1952, p. 5744.

of needed discretion, but Congress pointed out that its view on the appropriate relation between goods and services was recorded.

On the floors of both houses, the supporters of the Administration's program repeated the arguments given by Administration spokesmen before the committees for speeding up the Point Four activities in certain Asian countries and urged their colleagues to show "compassion" for the poverty-stricken areas of the world. But the majority of Congress concluded that a change in concept was at issue, that the United States could not, and should not, attempt to raise the standard of living of the entire world, that the only responsibility that the Government should assume in this regard was that of sharing the nation's "know-how," and that the previously approved program of aiding underdeveloped areas should not be permitted to become a great new "give-away" program.

In the enabling legislation Congress therefore reduced the authorizations for aid to Asia and the Pacific area from the $408 million requested by the Administration to $321 million and the subsequent appropriation totalled only $271 million: $203 million for economic aid (including direct "military-support" activities) to be administered by the Mutual Security Agency, and $68 million for the Point Four program of technical assistance. This more than halving of the funds requested for Point Four activities in Asia was specifically designed to restrict this program to what Congress regarded as its original purpose.

Implementation[1]

a. TECHNICAL COOPERATION ADMINISTRATION PROGRAMS

The greatest emphasis in the Point Four Program during 1952, as in the previous year, was on efforts to increase agricultural pro-

[1] Official reports on the accomplishments and problems of the Point Four Program during 1952 were sketchy. The more important official sources, and the sources of most of the material in this section, were: Mutual Security Agency, *Second Report to Congress on the Mutual Security Program*, Wash., D.C., June 30, 1952, and *Third Report to Congress on the Mutual Security Program*, Wash., D.C., December 1952; Department of Commerce, *Foreign Aid by the United States Government, 1940-1951*, Wash., D.C., 1952, and *Foreign Aid by the United States Government*, Wash., D.C., March, 1953; Department of State, *Land Reform —A World Challenge*, Economic Cooperation Series 29, Wash., D.C., February 1952; Bennett, W. T., Jr., "Economic Structure of Pan Americanism," Department of State *Bulletin*, August 11, 1952, pp. 207-211; Seager, C. H., "Point Four's

duction, especially of food, to improve health, and to promote education in the aided areas. About half of the funds and the personnel in the programs during the year were directed toward expanding the production of food and fibers and another 20 percent of the resources were allotted to various health and education programs.[2] Other major fields in which assistance was rendered were transportation and communications, public administration, industrial development, and land-use reform.

Total expenditures under the regular Point Four Program during calendar 1952—excluding the aid to Israel refugees discussed in the following chapter—were some $62 million, as compared with approximately $35 million in 1951.[3] Of the 1952 expenditures, $25 million went to eleven Near Eastern and African countries, $16 million to nineteen Latin American countries, $13 million to eight Far Eastern nations,[4] and $8 million was for un-

Impact in the Middle East," and related articles, Department of State *Bulletin*, September 22, 1952, pp. 449-454; Department of State *Bulletin*, October 6, 1952, pp. 535-537; Howard, H. N., "The Development of United States Policy in the Near East, South Asia, and Africa," Department of State *Bulletin*, December 15, 1952, pp. 936-946; Bingham, J. R., "Understanding Point Four," Department of State *Bulletin*, December 29, 1952, pp. 1016-1018; and Department of State, *Aspects of Point Four Progress*, Economic Cooperation Series 34, Wash., D.C., 1952.

For a discussion of some of the economic, social, and political problems of developing underdeveloped countries, see Hoselitz, B. F. (editor), *The Progress of Underdeveloped Areas*, Chicago, 1952, and Frankel, S. H., "United Nations Primer For Development," *Quarterly Journal of Economics*, August 1952, pp. 301-326. For a critical appraisal of the administration and implementation of the program, see Hanson, S. G., "The Press Looks at Point IV," *Inter-American Economic Affairs*, Autumn 1952, pp. 51-69.

[2] Some of the specific projects undertaken in the various efforts to expand agricultural production were: demonstration of new cultivation methods; distribution and instruction in the use of improved seed and breeding stock; education in the use of fertilizers, import of fertilizers for demonstration purposes, and assistance in establishing fertilizer factories; improved water conservation and use; reforestation; assistance in setting up commodity grading standards and improvements in other marketing practices; insect and pest control; and assistance in developing storage facilities. In the public health programs, the principal emphasis was on training local nationals, with most of the actual work being preventive or demonstrational in nature.

[3] These data include small amounts of counterpart funds reserved for the use of the United States and disbursed for purposes regarded as benefiting the aided country.

[4] Through the "Colombo Plan," the British Commonwealth of Nations was undertaking a program of aid for its Asian members, with aims and methods similar to those of the Point Four Program. Although the U.S. Government expressed interest in its work and maintained contact with the Plan's permanent council through the American Ambassador at Colombo, it took no action at a high level

allocable administrative expenses. The number of experts and technicians serving abroad under the Point Four Program more than doubled in 1952, and totalled nearly 1,400 as the year ended. The programs in each nation were small, as Congress had demanded, and during the year only two countries—Iran and India—received assistance valued at more than $2.5 million.[5] No details were published as to the ratio of contributions by foreign governments to those of the U.S. Government for the programs as a whole, but the percentage in Latin America rose slightly during 1952 and, on the average, these countries spent the equivalent of four dollars for each one dollar granted by the United States. In the Middle East, however, local contributions averaged less than two thirds of the American grants for the period from the beginning of the program through June 1952.

In keeping with its general policy of making extensive use of private agencies, the Technical Cooperation Administration by the end of 1952 had signed over 100 contracts with 88 private institutions and agencies, over half of such contracts being with educational institutions. Such contracts usually called for training foreign technicians in the United States but some also involved sending American technicians abroad. While expenditures under such procedures accounted for less than 10 percent of the total disbursements, the Government regarded this mode of operation as holding great promise for the future because it made possible the hiring of highly skilled persons and specialized facilities for short-term jobs. The Ford Foundation, using its own funds, was increasingly active in Point Four-like activities during 1952; its biggest program (scheduled to cost some $2 million) was in India, where it was cooperating with the Indian Government and the Technical Cooperation Administration in a large community de-

to integrate planning of the Point Four Program with the Colombo Plan. For a discussion of the latter plan, see Malenbaum, W., "The Colombo Plan: New Promise for Asia," Department of State *Bulletin*, September 22, 1952, pp. 441-448. For excerpts from the first annual report of the Consultative Committee of the Colombo Plan, see *Current History*, August 1952, pp. 106-112.

[5] The special coordinator for economic and technical assistance in the Near East stated in late 1952 that a more ambitious and spectacular program was needed in that area and that the assistance should be concentrated on a few major enterprises rather than scattered over a large number of small undertakings. (*New York Times*, December 6, 1952, p. 2.)

velopment program primarily designed to increase agricultural production, improve health, and encourage small village industries. During the latter part of the year the Ford Foundation was studying the possibility of helping to finance several small technical assistance projects in various Near Eastern countries. As it had for many years, the Near East Foundation was also carrying out small-scale technical assistance projects in the Near East and the Rockefeller Foundation was helping to improve wheat and corn seeds in Mexico.

Recruiting suitable personnel continued to be one of the major problems in implementing the Point Four Program. In addition to the difficulties created by the inability of the Government in many cases to match the remuneration and security competent technicians received in private employment, it was found that many of those sent out proved unable or unwilling to make what was regarded as the necessary cultural adjustment to the area to which they were assigned, were too impatient for results, and were inclined to "do" rather than to "show others how to do." It was also found that the technicians sometimes were inclined to attempt to solve economic development problems by spending large sums of money and by encouraging the foreign countries to install the best and most modern techniques, paying little if any attention to the question of whether they were economically appropriate, given the particular resources of the foreign country. One senior Point Four official reported that the number of technicians that could be sent abroad was also limited by the fact that many countries simply did not want too many Americans "wandering around."

In most countries actual operations under the programs were just getting under way as the year ended and while there was concrete evidence in many individual cases of increased production and improvements in health attributable to the programs, there was as yet no convincing evidence that it had lessened the appeal of Communism to the aided peoples. The Deputy Administrator took occasion, moreover, to emphasize that the programs were not regarded as "a carrot for which we try to exact a political *quid pro quo*," and, with particular reference to Iran, to warn that economic and technical assistance would not "necessarily" keep a country friendly to the United States.[6] Similarly, the programs had not yet been in operation long enough to determine whether they would serve to augment appreciably the supply of strategic and critical materials available to the free world, the second major objective of the program stressed before Congress during the year. It is worth noting, however, that less than 10 percent of the experts in the field were concerned with developing natural resources and only a few of these were working on mining projects.[7] It was also noteworthy that the Administrator of the Program reported in early 1953 that the Technical Cooperation Administration had so far been able to do virtually nothing directly to encourage private foreign investment in the underdeveloped areas—one of the responsibilities placed on it by the Act for International Development.[8]

Throughout the year various Administration spokesmen tended in their statements to the public to play down the anti-Communist aims of the Program and its contribution to expanding the production of strategic materials. President Truman summarized these statements when he took the occasion of his final message to Congress in early 1953 on the Mutual Security Program to say that, while the Point Four Program was destroying "the conditions under which totalitarianism can grow," "These programs of technical assistance would be vitally important quite apart from the communist conspiracy. Our basic desire is to help other people to help themselves build decent conditions of life in which they can find political and social security."[9]

[6] Bingham, J. R., "Understanding Point Four," Department of State *Bulletin*, December 29, 1952, pp. 1016-1018.

As in previous years, Russia continued to charge that the United States was using the Point Four Program to "dominate" the so-called underdeveloped areas. For a United States reply denying these charges, see Department of State *Bulletin*, December 1, 1952, pp. 871-876.

[7] The President's Materials Policy Commission in its *Resources for Freedom*, published in June 1952, recommended that greater emphasis than in the past be given by the Technical Cooperation Administration to geological surveys, preliminary explorations for minerals, and advice on mining technology.

The so-called Sawyer Mission recommended that special attention be given in the Point Four Program to increasing the production of those foodstuffs and raw materials that Western Europe had historically received from the countries of the Eastern bloc. (*Foreign Commerce Weekly*, December 22, 1952, p. 19.)

[8] Andrews, S., "The United States and the Underdeveloped Areas," Department of State *Bulletin*, Wash., D.C., February 23, 1953, pp. 306-310.

[9] Mutual Security Agency, *Third Report to Congress on the Mutual Security Program*, *op.cit.*, p. X.

b. MUTUAL SECURITY AGENCY PROGRAMS

The Mutual Security Agency disbursed over $137 million[1] in its economic and technical assistance programs during 1952, of which $77 million went to help Formosa, nearly $23 million to help Indochina, and $17 million to help the Philippines. Approximately $5 million each was received by Thailand, Burma, Indonesia, and Korea.[2] Some of the funds for Formosa and Indochina were spent for technical assistance, principally directed to increasing agricultural production and improving health services, but most of the aid to those countries was designed to complement the programs of military aid and took the form of commodities, especially fertilizer, raw cotton, bread grains, machinery, and chemicals. These goods served to increase current production and consumption in those countries and to reduce the threat of inflation caused by their military defense efforts. The programs for the other countries were similar to the Point Four activities, with most of the funds being used to provide technical help for expanding food production, improving the health of the population, and training government administrators. Responsibility for administering the program in Burma and Indonesia was, as noted above, transferred to the Technical Cooperation Administration in midyear.

B. *UNITED NATIONS EXPANDED PROGRAM OF TECHNICAL ASSISTANCE*[3]

Shortly after President Truman announced, in the January 1949 inaugural speech, his "bold, new program for making the bene-

[1] Included is the equivalent of $3.4 million in counterpart funds reserved for the use of the United States which were spent for purposes regarded as benefiting the foreign country.

[2] In its semiannual reports to Congress the Mutual Security Agency did not mention any activities in Korea but the Department of Commerce reported that that nation had received $5.2 million of aid during that year for "economic and technical assistance" from the Mutual Security Agency.

[3] For more complete information on the United Nations Expanded Program of Technical Assistance than is given here, see, in addition to the other sources cited in this section, *Fourth Report of the Technical Assistance Board to the Technical Assistance Committee*, UN Doc. E/2213, Vols. I, II, May 8, 1952; *United Nations Bulletin*, December 1, 1952, pp. 545-556, 575-576; *Audit Reports Relating to Expenditure by Specialized Agencies and Technical Assistance Funds*, UN Doc. A/C.5/518, November 25, 1952; UN Doc. E/2209, April 21, 1952; UN Doc. ST/DPI/Ser. A/74, January 12, 1953; and UN Food and Agriculture Organiza-

fits of our scientific advances and industrial progress available for the improvement and growth of underdeveloped areas," the Administration stated that it planned, wherever practicable, to cooperate with the United Nations in implementing such a program. Shortly thereafter, American delegates to the United Nations took the initiative in encouraging that body, and its various specialized agencies, to expand their efforts in this field.[4] Many months were required to agree upon the initial program and general policies to be followed. Subsequently, many member governments were slow in making their contributions, with the result that the Expanded Program was not actually begun until late 1950. Activities were accelerated, but were still modest, during 1951 and by the end of that year the equivalent of some $17.5 million had been paid into the United Nations by the member states (including $10 million by the U.S. Government) but actual expenditures had reached the equivalent of only some $6.3 million, with an additional sum having been obligated, and $3 million having been placed in a special reserve.[5]

Spokesmen for some of the underdeveloped countries recorded during 1951 their dissatisfaction with the scope and size of the United Nations program, especially the small amounts of capital goods supplied. United States delegates in the United Nations, on the other hand, said that they were favorably impressed with the record to date but recommended that more attention should be given to training and demonstration projects and to setting up carefully selected pilot plants. They also suggested that it might be desirable for the United Nations to provide somewhat larger amounts of supplies and equipment than had been provided in the past but insisted that the major emphasis should continue to be on technical services. These recommendations were formally accepted by the Economic and Social Council early in 1952 and

tion, *Activities of FAO under the Expanded Technical Assistance Program, 1950-1952*, Rome, May 1952. Detailed information on the late months of 1952 was not available as this *Survey* went to press; complete reports for this period were to be provided to the Sixteenth Session of the Economic and Social Council, which was scheduled to open on June 30, 1953.

[4] The United Nations and its specialized agencies were already in 1950 extending small amounts of technical assistance to member nations. These activities, financed from their regular budgets, were continued after the Expanded Program was initiated and are not included in this summary.

[5] For a brief description of the organizational structure of the United Nations Expanded Program, see *Survey—1949*, pp. 72-73.

member governments were requested to contribute at least the equivalent of $20 million for the 1952 activities.[6]

In his original request to Congress for funds to carry on the Mutual Security Program for the year ending in mid-1953, the President asked for an appropriation of $17 million for the United States contribution to the Expanded Program of Technical Assistance of the United Nations, including $1 million to be transferred to the program being undertaken by the Organization of American States.[7] Administration witnesses assured Congress that the bulk of these funds would be for services of United Nations experts, with only small amounts being spent for such commodities as were vital to the success of the teaching, demonstration, and pilot-plant projects. As in previous years, the Administration justified channeling some of its aid for technical assistance through the United Nations on the grounds that extending aid through that organization would help allay fears abroad of "intervention," that it would serve to diminish the force of Communist assertions that the program was just another instance of American imperialism, and that there were many excellent technicians in foreign countries available to these organizations. Congress accepted these justifications, but, as in previous years, many were reluctant to contribute funds to a program over which the United States did not have a controlling voice. This consideration, together with the general sentiment in Congress that the United States should not contribute more than one third to the expenses of the United Nations, resulted in a final appropriation of $9.2 million for these multilateral activities for the year ending in mid-1953.

[6] See *Survey—1951*, pp. 81-83, and the references cited therein for a more complete account of the United Nations program during the years 1949 through 1951.

[7] The activities of the Organization of American States (OAS) have been similar to those of the Point Four Program, but have placed greater emphasis on training local personnel, especially in the fields of agriculture, public health, public administration, education, and public housing. In 1951 the United States had pledged $0.9 million to the technical assistance program of the Organization of American States, and it pledged $1 million in 1952, but it specified in both years that its actual contribution would be limited to not more than 70 percent of the total contributions to the program. The actual contributions by the United States in 1952 were $1.2 million, raising the total for the two years to $1.5 million. (For more information on the technical assistance activities of the OAS, see Pan American Union, *Annals of the Organization of American States*, Wash., D.C. An official account of the background of the Organization of American States may be found in Department of State *Bulletin*, January 7, 1952, pp. 9-11.)

Sixty-five of the eighty-odd nations belonging to the United Nations or to one or more of the participating specialized agencies pledged contributions to the expanded program during calendar 1952. During the year the equivalent of some $18.5 million was actually paid in, including $12 million by the United States. Expenditures under the program, including some from funds provided earlier, amounted to $16.9 million and 527 separate projects were in operation in October or had been completed by that time, some seventy countries having received assistance in one form or another.[8]

Activities under the United Nations program during 1952 were comparable with those of the United States Point Four Program, with most of the emphasis being on increasing food production and improving public health and education facilities.[9] While the program continued to be primarily one of furnishing technical assistance, pilot plants and demonstration projects were given more emphasis than in the preceding year. This shift in emphasis had the full approval of the United States representatives in the United Nations and the recipient countries welcomed it.

As with the Point Four Program, the most difficult immediate problem in administering the United Nations technical assistance program was in recruiting qualified and "sympathetic" experts.[1]

[8] From the beginning of the program through 1952 over 1,600 experts, representing more than sixty nationalities, had been employed to render assistance in various countries. In addition, some 2,700 fellowships had been granted to citizens of fifty of the so-called underdeveloped countries for training and study abroad. In the period ending December 31, 1951, of the 797 technical experts employed, 217 had been United States nationals and, of the 845 fellowships granted during the same period, 228 involved periods of study in the United States.

[9] See "Aids to Libya's Progress," *United Nations Bulletin*, March 1, 1953, pp. 171-172. The United Nations also urged land reform in many of the underdeveloped countries during the year. (See UN Department of Economic Affairs, *Land Reform: Defects in Agrarian Structure as Obstacles to Economic Development*, UN Publication Sales No.: 1951.II.B.3; *Land Reform: Progress Report of the Secretary-General*, UN Doc. A/2194, September 29, 1952; and UN General Assembly, *Official Records*, Seventh Session, Second Committee, 224th-230th Meetings, December 1-5, 1952.)

[1] For studies of the problems of administration, see Sharp, W. R., *International Technical Assistance: Programs and Organization*, Chicago, 1952, and *Fifth Report of the Technical Assistance Committee to the Economic and Social Council*, UN Doc. E/2304, July 18, 1952. See also *Tenth Report of the Administrative Committee on Co-ordination*, UN Doc. E/2161, December 13, 1951; *Report of the Technical Assistance Committee on the Administration of the Expanded Program*, UN Doc. E/2238, May 29, 1952; and Keenleyside, H. L., "Administrative Problems of the Technical Assistance Administration," *Canadian Journal of Economics and Political Science*, August 1952, pp. 345-357.

In addition to the problems, noted above, encountered by the United States Technical Cooperation Administration, the administrators of the UN program complained that countries were too insistent on obtaining the services of individuals who were well known rather than those who were less famous but nevertheless technically qualified. In reply, spokesmen for the underdeveloped countries stated that it was often necessary for an expert "to have a reputation" if his advice was to be followed, especially if he was advising upon administrative matters. The UN Technical Assistance Board also reported that while there had been some improvement as compared with the previous year, governments requesting assistance frequently were not administratively prepared to make use of such aid.

A more serious problem, United Nations officials reported, was that to be effective the technical assistance demanded required capital investment of a size that could not be supplied by the United Nations and often was regarded as beyond the capacity of the country concerned to supply. Related to this was the policy problem that arose from the assertions by representatives of some of the underdeveloped countries that they should not be required to pay the local costs of foreign experts; some delegates asserted that certain countries had not requested as much technical assistance as they believed they needed because of the size of these local costs. The United States took the position in this discussion that local costs should be borne by the United Nations only if the recipient country were exceptionally poor and it were clearly demonstrated that it was unable to pay them. Some modifications in the rules concerning local costs were made, but the changes tended to be consistent with the position of the United States.

The United Nations Technical Assistance Board also reported that in many countries several independently administered technical assistance programs (those of the various United Nations agencies, those under the Point Four Program, and those under the regional schemes of the Colombo Plan and the Organization of American States) were under way and that this was creating problems of avoiding duplication of effort and competition for experts and facilities. The official reports issued during the year emphasized, however, that strenuous efforts were being made to coordinate the various activities and that these efforts were meeting with success. Another policy problem during the year arose from the fact that some contributions to the United Nations program were made in inconvertible currencies. Some of the contributors of such funds complained that their contributions were being used too slowly and expressed the fear that their parliaments might be reluctant to make future funds available if the earlier ones were not used. As the year ended, special efforts were therefore being directed to investigating ways of increasing the use of such inconvertible currencies.

The United States delegate stated that the U.S. Government was "generally satisfied" with the United Nations technical assistance program and supported the resolution to establish $25 million as the goal for contributions in 1953. He successfully opposed any formal action on a proposal that the program should aim at an eventual level of operations of $100 million a year and that the goal for 1954 should be set at $40 million. In its mid-year report, the Technical Assistance Board had stated that a "major" problem in its operations arose from its inability to know far in advance how much money it would have at its disposal. While recognizing the problem, the United States delegate argued that plans for future years should depend upon accomplishments in immediately preceding periods and that in view of the problems noted above a sudden large rise in the rate of contributions would not bring corresponding benefits. He added that, in any case, the United States Congress, under established procedures, did not make appropriations for years in advance.

C. *CAPITAL ASSISTANCE*

United States officials in 1952, as in earlier years, stated that if the bilateral and multilateral technical assistance programs were to be successful they must be complemented by capital investment. The United States position, however, was that most of such capital must come from within the underdeveloped countries, while the spokesmen for such countries insisted that their nations were so poor that only small and inadequate amounts of capital could be obtained internally. In the United Nations, United States delegates accepted "in principle" the desirability of an expansion in the flow of capital from the richer to the poorer nations but argued that most of such foreign capital should come from private sources and existing public institutions. The spokesmen for the potential capital-importing countries, on the other hand, insisted that until their economies reached a higher level of production and productivity they could not attract adequate funds from private foreign sources or from established lending agencies.[2]

The various activities of the Government during 1952 to encourage private United States foreign investment are discussed in Chapter IV, as are the so-called economic development loans made by the Export-Import Bank. The International Bank also gave emphasis to such loans during the year and several countries arranged loans from the International Bank that were related to technical assistance they were receiving. There were extensive discussions in the United Nations on the question of establishing a new International Finance Corporation and an International Development Authority to supply capital goods to the underdeveloped countries. These are taken up in Chapter V.

[2] Some of the delegates from the so-called underdeveloped countries asserted that their potential foreign exchange earnings were an unreliable source of funds for their economic development in view of the historic instability in the prices and volume of primary products in international trade and because of an alleged long-term tendency for their terms of trade to deteriorate. These questions were discussed at length during the year and, over United States opposition, the General Assembly passed a resolution calling for three studies, all designed to make recommendations for measures to achieve an "adequate, just, and equitable relation" between the prices of primary products and the prices of manufactured goods. (General Assembly Resolution 623 [VII], December 21, 1952.) See *United Nations Bulletin*, January 1, 1953, pp. 3-6, 36-40. See also UN Department of Economic Affairs, *Instability in Export Markets of Underdeveloped Countries*, UN Publication Sales No.: 1952.II.A.1, and UN General Assembly, *Official Records*, Seventh Session, Second Committee, 214th-223rd Meetings, November 19-December 1, 1952.

III · OTHER GRANT ASSISTANCE

Both within and outside the authority granted by the Mutual Security Act, the U.S. Government during 1952 extended grant assistance of types other than the "military" and the "economic and technical" discussed in the preceding two chapters. The more important of these were the Israel and Palestine refugee programs, assistance to occupied areas, and contributions to various internationally sponsored programs of aid to particular groups or areas. None of these was a new activity and some of them had been going on for several years.[1]

A. *ISRAEL AND PALESTINE REFUGEE PROGRAMS*

Legislative Issues

The broad justifications given by the Administration for an aid program to Israel for the relief and resettlement of refugees coming into that country, on the one hand, and, on the other, to the Arab States that had received the refugees from the 1948 war in Palestine were similar to those presented in justifying similar programs in 1951: to help prevent economic conditions in those nations that might increase internal political instability; to encourage a political settlement between Israel and the Arab States and to help integrate Israel into the Near East area; and to stimulate the economic development of the area and thus create conditions favorable to the viability and defense of the region.

The Administration requested $76 million of "emergency" assistance to Israel for the year beginning in mid-1952, to be administered by the Technical Cooperation Administration.[2] Among

[1] For an account of these programs in earlier years, see *Survey—1951*, pp. 34-36, 63-72, and the references cited therein.

[2] This was in addition to $3 million requested under the Technical Cooperation Administration's regular technical assistance program. This $79 million may be compared with a total of $65 million of Mutual Security Act funds that had been allocated for aiding Israel during the previous fiscal year. The 1951 Act authorized up to $50 million for refugee and resettlement projects and the Mutual Security

the reasons given by the Administration for aiding Israel, other than those mentioned above, were the heavy costs placed on Israel by its immigration program, which, it was stated, had relieved the burden of displaced persons on European powers and so, indirectly, on the United States; humanitarian and political considerations stemming from the past persecution of many of the Israelis and from the desire of the American people to relieve suffering and to strengthen the economic and political independence of the new state; and the responsibility for helping discharge what the Administration regarded as a commitment by the U.S. Government to "maintain Israel." The Administration also pointed out that a case could be made for generously aiding Israel because that nation could at fairly short notice produce up to 200,000 soldiers, many of them having been trained by the British during World War II.[3]

The proposed program was seen as a "balance of payments" program of the Marshall Plan type and was designed, in general terms, to help "maintain [Israel's] population [at austerity levels] while developing a self-sustaining economy."[4] It was proposed that approximately three fifths of the funds requested be used for meeting current consumption needs, including a certain amount of housing and farm machinery, and the remaining two fifths be devoted to economic development purposes, especially transport, power, irrigation, industry, and fishing. The problem of helping Israel was considered an urgent one because her foreign exchange reserves were "exhausted" and she was living from "hand to mouth" on current receipts and short-term borrowing from abroad; prices were "soaring"; and industry was "crippled" because of the lack of foreign exchange to purchase raw materials. Administra-

Agency allotted another $15 million for general economic and technical assistance under Section 203 of the Mutual Security Act of 1951.

[3] For details on the Israel and Palestine refugee programs, see "Mutual Security Act of 1952," *Hearings on a Bill to Amend the Mutual Security Act of 1951, and for other Purposes*, U.S. Senate, Committee on Foreign Relations, 82d Cong., 2d Sess., pp. 668-681, 700-714; "Mutual Security Act Extension," *Hearings on H.R. 7005*, House of Rep., Committee on Foreign Affairs, 82d Cong., 2d Sess., pp. 762-799; "Mutual Security Appropriations for 1953," *Hearings*, House of Rep., Subcommittee of the Committee on Appropriations, 82d Cong., 2d Sess., pp. 593-626; S. *Rpt. No. 1490*, April 30, 1952, pp. 45-49; and *H. Rpt. No. 1922*, May 12, 1952, pp. 57-58. These documents are the sources of most of the information included in this section.

[4] "Mutual Security Act of 1952," Senate, *Hearings . . .* , *op.cit.*, p. 701.

tion spokesmen stated that they anticipated that aid to Israel for similar purposes would be necessary for at least two or three years beyond fiscal year 1952-1953 but they refused to make a specific estimate as to when aid should be terminated, stating that it was "an indefinite situation." They stressed that in their judgment Israel would be "an element of strength" in the East-West struggle if she were aided but if not she might be one of "weakness."

Officials of the Executive Branch agreed with many members of Congress that the program of aiding Israel could not be dissociated from the problems of the surrounding areas and countries, especially those created by the presence in the Arab States of nearly 900,000 refugees (150,000 families) from Palestine. Since 1950 these refugees had been receiving help through the United Nations Relief and Works Agency for Palestine Refugees in the Near East, with United States contributions accounting for some 60 percent of the total expenditures.[5] Through 1951 nearly all of the funds had been spent for relief rather than resettlement purposes.[6]

The Administration believed that this aid to the Palestine refugees had served United States purposes by preventing the "catastrophe" that it was believed would otherwise have been brought about by famine, disease, and unrest, but it also recognized that almost no progress had been made in making these people self-supporting and that increasing attention must be given to "reintegration" as distinct from "relief" activities. These general sentiments were shared by many other members of the United Nations, who recognized the deteriorating effects on the refugees of camp life and ration lines and who were ever conscious of the danger

[5] Over 1,000,000 names had been on the relief rolls in 1949 and the decrease to 900,000 by 1952 was due in large part to the elimination of double rations, to the removal of some non-refugees from the lists, and to the fact that a few of the refugees had resettled themselves. Only to a minor extent was the decline the result of the resettlement activities of the United Nations agency.

For a detailed tabulation of pledges and contributions of the various governments to the United Nations Palestine Refugee Program through 1951, see "Mutual Security Appropriations for 1953," *Hearings, op.cit.*, p. 597.

[6] A State Department spokesman testified before Congress in the spring of 1952 that the widely publicized 1949 recommendation of the Clapp Mission (see *Survey—1949*, pp. 56-59) for a broad Near East program of public works and economic development "was later abandoned on the grounds that it was more expensive than relief and it was leading to no conclusion to the [refugee] problem." (*Hearings on H.R. 7005, op.cit.*, p. 777.)

that funds for relief would not continue indefinitely. In January 1952, therefore, the United Nations General Assembly approved a resolution calling on members to contribute the equivalent of $250 million by mid-1954, of which only one fifth would be used for relief purposes and the balance for capital investment and other activities designed to make the refugees self-supporting members of the various Near Eastern economies, but without prejudice to their interests in repatriation and compensation.[7] The U.S. Administration frankly regarded this investment program as ambitious in light of the "stagnant" and "deteriorating" economies of the Arab States and the fact that most of the Arab officials were prone to regard the problem chiefly as a political one. Nonetheless, for political, social, and humanitarian reasons it strongly supported the United Nations resolution.

Therefore, in addition to $23 million for technical assistance to this area under the regular Point Four Program (discussed in the preceding chapter), the Administration requested Congress to provide $65 million for United States contributions to the United Nations Palestine Refugee Program for the fiscal year ending in mid-1953. In supporting this request the Administration spokesmen testified that the relief and resettlement of the Arab refugees from Palestine was of growing importance to the security of the United States, in view of the then current Anglo-Egyptian dispute over the Suez Canal and the Sudan, the continuing Communist propaganda exploiting the plight of the Palestine refugees, and the fact that the presence of the refugees served as a constant reminder to the Arab world of what many considered the anti-Arab intervention by the West in the Palestine case. Also present in the considerations of both the Executive and the Legislative Branches of the Government were the facts that "this little part of the world . . . is where the oil comes from . . . ,"[8] and that relieving the human suffering of these peoples was ". . . important in the hearts and minds of the people of the United States."[9]

Administration spokesmen stated that it was possible that the

[7] Department of State *Bulletin*, February 11, 1952, pp. 224-227.

[8] "Mutual Security Act of 1952," Senate, *Hearings* . . . , *op.cit.*, p. 679. Almost no oil was produced in the particular countries having refugees but important pipelines crossed them and there were close political, religious, cultural, and economic ties between these nations and those Arab States that did produce oil.

[9] "Mutual Security Act Extension," *Hearings on H.R. 7005*, *op.cit.*, p. 14.

proportion of the total cost borne by the United States in the United Nations program might be greater than in the past but that the Administration proposed to limit its contribution to not more than 70 percent of the total; that it would contribute only a proportionate share of the relief funds; and that payments would be made for the "reintegration" program only if such a program were "firm," were accepted by the countries concerned, and led to corresponding reductions in the relief rolls. While many members of Congress expressed disappointment that up to that time the United Nations program had been primarily a relief operation, the majority agreed with the Senate Committee on Foreign Relations that "humanitarian, economic, and political considerations dictate that, in the national interests of the United States, these refugees cannot be allowed to starve while their future is being settled."[1]

Many Congressmen insisted that the programs for Israel and the Palestine refugees were designed to meet similar problems—those raised by displacement of persons—and could see little justification for the differences in amount of United States funds to be provided for the two groups. Several considered that the Israeli-Arab tensions were so strong and so fraught with threats to peace that the U.S. Government should show impartiality by providing the same amount of funds for each program. Administration witnesses testified that the Arab States would in fact receive a total dollar aid, including Point Four activities, of $88 million compared to a total of $79 million for Israel. They also pointed out that the Arab States would obtain additional aid from other United Nations sources and that some of them at least had access to international lending agencies, whereas Israel's credit was already exhausted.

But several Congressmen were not satisfied with a policy of providing approximately equal *aggregate* amounts for the two areas. These legislators asked why Israel should receive almost 100 times more per capita than the Arab States. Administration spokesmen offered several justifications, in addition to pointing out that such per capita comparisons were of limited significance inasmuch as some of the Arab States were relatively wealthy in foreign exchange. A State Department official testified that the

[1] S. *Rpt. No. 1490, op.cit.*, p. 47.

Israeli Government was attempting to establish European rather than Near Eastern standards of living for its citizens and that the U.S. Government had a responsibility for aiding this effort because of the United States "acquiescence" in the policies that led to the emigration from European displaced person camps to Israel of persons who went with the hope and expectation of being able "to maintain the standards to which they were accustomed . . .";[2] he went on to argue that the United States did not have a similar responsibility for the migration of the Arabs out of Palestine. Furthermore, Administration spokesmen stated, the Israelis could not survive on the living standards of the great bulk of the Arab population and it was necessary to maintain relatively high living standards in Israel in order to keep that nation politically and economically stable. The tenor of the Congressional questioning showed that many members of the Legislative Branch were critical of Israel's policy vis-à-vis the Arabs and were less enthusiastic over the United States' extending aid to Israel than they had been in 1951, when, it will be remembered, $50 million of emergency aid to Israel was provided on the initiative of Congress rather than the Administration.

Nevertheless, the Administration's program suffered only minor cuts at the hands of Congress. The final law authorized the expenditure of $70.2 million during the fiscal year ending June 30, 1953 for emergency aid to Israel (plus $2.8 million of technical assistance) and $60 million for American contribution to the United Nations Palestine Refugee Program (plus $21.7 million of technical assistance to the Arab States). The subsequent appropriation law provided these amounts.

Implementation

Only the most summary official statements were released during the year on implementation of the Israel Aid Program, but a large (though unspecified) portion of the funds was used during the first three quarters of the year to liquidate maturing short-term debts that Israel had previously accumulated. Taking into ac-

[2] "Mutual Security Act of 1952," Senate, *Hearings . . . , op.cit.*, p. 670. The fact that less than 4 percent of the post-1948 immigrants came from Western Europe, America, and Oceania and that all the rest came from the Arab States, Asia, the Balkans and Central Europe, and Africa was not brought out in the hearings.

count both these expenditures and new purchases out of the aid funds, well over half the $82 million actually spent by the United States during 1952 for aiding Israel[3] went for the purchase of food and fuel; and "substantial" additional amounts were used to buy such other current consumption items as fodder, seed, fertilizer, textile raw materials, and leather. Considerably less than the proposed 40 percent of the aid was used for so-called economic development purposes, with such expenditures as were made being concentrated on housing, irrigation, electric power and transportation equipment, and spare parts for agricultural and industrial machinery.

That the outgoing Administration foresaw the need for continued aid and was less than fully satisfied with what had been accomplished with past assistance was indicated in the final report to Congress of the Truman Administration on the Mutual Security Program, transmitted in early January 1953, which stated that "it is hoped that increased emphasis can be placed on developmental projects, rather than relief needs, as the program progresses." It went on to say that "Intensive studies of Israel's financial problems were undertaken in connection with the economic aid program and the Israeli Government is now taking steps to adjust its economic activities to a level commensurate with its financial capabilities."[4]

Only $22 million was actually transferred by the U.S. Government to the Palestine Refugee Program during calendar year 1952 and most of this was used to provide food, shelter, and medical attention. The U.S. Administration believed that, as before, this relief aid helped prevent these refugees from threatening the internal order and security in the countries where they were located, but it was recognized that again very little had been accomplished in settling them in self-supporting occupations.

The United Nations Relief and Works Agency, in keeping with the January 1952 General Assembly resolution, negotiated with the various Arab Governments for specific resettlement projects designed to take the refugees off relief while not prejudicing their interests in repatriation or compensation for property left in

[3] This total figure includes small amounts disbursed under the Point Four technical assistance program in Israel.

[4] Mutual Security Agency, *Third Report to Congress on the Mutual Security Program*, *op.cit.*, p. 10.

Palestine.[5] Although there was some evidence of increased willingness on the part of the host nations to cooperate with the Agency in this attempt to find more permanent solutions to the refugee problem, these negotiations consumed more time than had been hoped, and the Agency reported in the autumn that relief costs for the fiscal year 1952-1953 were exceeding by nearly 40 percent those anticipated in the program set out in the General Assembly resolution. Subsequently, the Agency, with United States support, publicly urged the governments in the area to cooperate more generously with the Agency in its work and obtained from the General Assembly authority to spend more than had been planned on relief during the year ending in mid-1953.

In the United Nations discussion of the Palestine refugee problem during late 1952 the United States delegate stated that his Government agreed with the Agency that more attention must be put on development projects and "that large projects . . . should be sought. Individual projects, the principal goal of which was to enable the refugees to live by their own efforts, could be successful only if co-ordinated with each other and with the economic development of an area of which they would become a useful part."[6] He went on to say that the Executive Branch was ready to ask Congress for further contributions to the program on condition that other nations bear a "fair share" of the cost.

Such plans, however, were not welcomed by the governments of the Arab States. Their representatives urged that a greater proportion of the available funds be used for direct relief purposes and they stressed "the undesirability of linking aid to the refugees with any plans for the economic development of the Near East. Such development must depend solely on the efforts of the countries concerned and not be made the object of political pressure

[5] For official details on the Palestine Refugee Program, see United Nations, *Annual Report of the Director of the United Nations Relief and Works Agency for Palestine Refugees in the Near East, Covering the Period 1 July 1951 to 30 June 1952*, General Assembly, *Official Records*, Seventh Session, Supplement No. 13 (A/2171), New York, 1952, and *Special Report of the Director and Advisory Commission of the United Nations Relief and Works Agency for Palestine Refugees in the Near East*, UN Doc. A/2171/Add.1, 1953. For a summary of the General Assembly discussion in October 1952, see *United Nations Bulletin*, November 15, 1952, pp. 438-443.

[6] UN General Assembly, *Official Records*, Seventh Session, Ad Hoc Political Committee, 4th Meeting, 27 October 1952, p. 11.

from outside."[7] The delegates to the United Nations from the Arab States continued to insist that the only "acceptable" answer to the Arab refugee problem was repatriation, a solution that Israel refused to accept.

B. *OCCUPIED AREAS PROGRAM*

The programs for Government and Relief in Occupied Areas (GARIOA) had been a major part of the United States foreign grant programs in the years immediately following the war.[8] By early 1951, however, these activities had been reduced to relatively small operations, almost entirely restricted to the Ryukyu Islands, former Japanese possessions that the United States continued to control as an occupying power. For operations under this program for the fiscal year beginning in mid-1952, the President requested Congress to provide $11.8 million, as compared with an appropriation of $22.5 million for the previous fiscal year. The decrease was attributed to the fact that local production and exports were increasing because much of the extensive damage inflicted on these islands during World War II had been repaired and to the fact that the United States military were making substantial dollar expenditures there.[9] Still, it was argued, United States military activities in the islands enhanced the need for imports by taking large amounts of the arable land for military installations and by demanding higher local standards of public health, police protection, and other services for the benefit of American forces.

Most of the funds requested of Congress in 1952 were to be used for supplying grain, food, fuel, and other immediately consumable products; small amounts were included for education, reorientation, and exchange of persons.[1] There was nothing in the

[7] *ibid.*, p. 15. For some unofficial views on the Palestine refugee program, see Schechtman, J. B., *The Arab Refugee Problem*, New York, 1952, and Stevens, G. G., "Arab Refugees: 1948-1952," *Middle East Journal*, Summer 1952, pp. 281-298.

[8] See *Survey—1951*, pp. 66-67, and the references cited therein for a discussion of these programs during 1949-1951.

[9] It was stated in the hearings that in mid-1952 the Department of Defense currently had United States military construction projects under way in the islands that would cost more than $200 million. Only a part, unspecified, would be disbursed in the Ryukyus.

[1] $1.8 million of the 1952 request was for administrative expenses, including a small amount for the United States administrative expenses in Trieste.

request for capital goods, but the Administration asked Congress to extend for another year the availability of some $1.7 million of previously appropriated funds earmarked for various construction projects. It was stated in the hearings that these amounts would complete the construction projects that it was appropriate for the United States to finance.[2]

American interest in the Ryukyus was justified by Administration spokesmen primarily on the grounds that the islands, especially Okinawa, were bastions of great strategic importance to the United States. Huge supply depots for American forces in the Far East were located on them and at that time all the heavy bombers engaged in the Korean War were based there. Under the program, it was stated, the United States was teaching the people to govern themselves, subject to United States approval of any of the local governments' actions; was attempting to establish a standard of living comparable to that enjoyed before World War II; and was trying to place the islands on a self-supporting basis.[3] Members of Congress showed little inclination to question the desirability of the United States' "digging in" and making a permanent military base of the more important of these islands and there was no disposition to cut substantially the amount of money requested by the Administration for government and relief operations. The amount appropriated to the Department of Defense for this program for the year beginning in mid-1952 was $11 million, plus the $1.7 million carryover mentioned above. Actual expenditures during the year were $22 million but the annual rate during the last six months was only $9.5 million.

Immediately after the war, provision of most of the economic aid by the United States to Western Germany and Austria had been under the Defense Department's Government and Relief in Occupied Areas Program, but these aid activities were soon transferred to the European Recovery Program—and its predeces-

[2] For detailed official statements on the U.S. Government's programs and past activities in the Ryukyus, see "Mutual Security Appropriations for 1953," House, *Hearings, op.cit.*, pp. 1-46.

[3] Administration officials pointed out, however, that the United States should anticipate assuming some financial responsibility for the economic well-being of this area for a long time in the future. The islands had been a deficit area in the Japanese Empire and the United States had purposely removed the Japanese from the islands and as a result stripped the latter of trained personnel in both government administration and senior business management, with resultant deleterious effects on production.

sors in the case of Austria[4]—and were continued through 1952 under the Mutual Security Program, as discussed in Chapter I. In mid-1949 the military government in Western Germany was replaced by the Allied High Commission, in which the United States was a member, and a similar High Commission, with less authority and with Russia as a member, had been operating in Austria since the end of the war. These Commissions exercised some control authorities and carried out certain security, health, propaganda, education, and exchange of persons programs. Congress had provided $26.9 million[5] for such Government in Occupied Areas programs in these two countries for the fiscal year ending in mid-1952 and the Administration requested $20.5 million for similar purposes ($16.7 million for Germany and $3.8 million for Austria) during the year beginning in mid-1952.[6] These were not, strictly speaking, grant programs, and these expenditures are not included in the various statistical calculations of United States grants in this document. Nevertheless, the funds were provided in the mutual security appropriations and in view of the special nature of these operations they may appropriately be described briefly here.

It was anticipated at the time of the hearings that the four-power occupation of Austria was likely to continue for some time since the three Western occupying powers had been unable to agree with Russia on the terms of a peace treaty for Austria. With respect to Western Germany, however, it was considered that the signing of the contractual agreement between West Germany, France, the United Kingdom, and the United States that had taken place in late May 1952 marked the end of the occupation period and it was planned that, once the contractual agreement was rati-

[4] For some statistics on the amount and form of aid prior to 1949, see *Survey—1949*, p. 40.

[5] $26.25 million in the regular appropriation, plus $0.63 million in the special increased pay legislation.

[6] These requests do not include some $2.6 million requested in State Department appropriations for consular and similar activities in these two countries. Also excluded are local currency expenditures—estimated at the equivalent of $31 million in deutsche marks in 1952-1953 for Western Germany plus the equivalent of $80.4 million of deutsche marks for economic aid to Berlin, and $6.2 million in Austrian schillings. The local currency needed in previous years had come primarily from occupation costs (in Germany) and counterpart funds, but in 1952 the Administration asked—and was given—authority also to draw marks and schillings against United States surplus property credits (dollar debts) in Germany and Austria.

fied, the Office of United States High Commissioner in Germany would be replaced by an Embassy.[7] But it was also expected that the Embassy would have to carry out many tasks in connection with these conventions that were not usually the function of an Embassy,[8] together with certain unusual "public affairs" activities. The latter were largely such operations as maintaining information centers and newspapers, preparing and financing radio broadcasts and films, and sending Germans to the United States for short periods, all of which were directed at maintaining American influence in German local affairs and, in particular, at strengthening those democratic movements and attitudes in Germany that would insure German "integration" with the West and German participation in the defense of the West.[9]

Congress raised no serious objections to these programs and provided an appropriation of $19 million for the Government in Occupied Areas Program in Western Germany and in Austria during the year ending in mid-1953. An American Embassy was not established in Germany during 1952 as anticipated, however, and the Office of the United States High Commissioner continued to function since neither France nor Germany had ratified the contractual agreement.[1]

C. *KOREAN RECONSTRUCTION PROGRAM*

At the end of World War II the southern part of Korea was occupied by United States forces, who provided relief supplies to the local people under the Government and Relief in Occupied Areas Program. The Republic of Korea was established in 1948 in South Korea, and on the first of January 1949 the United States extended formal recognition to the new nation and at the same

[7] The text of the contractual agreement, together with several other related documents, including the treaties constituting the European Defense Community and the European Coal and Steel Community, were published as *Senate Document, Executives Q and R*, 82d Cong., 2d Sess., June 2, 1952.

[8] For example, United States courts, some military security controls, displaced persons programs, coal and steel control, and special responsibilities in Berlin.

[9] For a statement of United States policy vis-à-vis Germany in mid-1952, see "Mutual Security Appropriations for 1952," *op.cit.*, pp. 48-173. See also "Supplemental Appropriation Bill, 1953," *Hearings on H.R. 8370*, Committee on Appropriations, U.S. Senate, 82d Cong., 2d Sess., pp. 1-85.

[1] The implementation of the contractual agreement was conditional on the ratification of the European Defense Community and it was with respect to the latter that serious difficulties arose during the year. See Chapter I, above.

time transferred to the Economic Cooperation Administration the responsibility for administering United States economic aid. Shortly thereafter, President Truman asked Congress to approve a Korean Aid bill envisaging a three-year economic recovery program, with $150 million being requested for the first year. This proposal became a part of the bitter conflict between the Administration and important sectors of Congress over American policy in China and an amended bill was finally approved in early 1950; subsequently a total of $110 million was appropriated for the first year of the program and another $90 million for the year beginning in mid-1950.[2]

Following the outbreak of fighting in Korea in June 1950, American economic aid was immediately geared into the strategy and logistics of the United Nations military forces, and activities by the Economic Cooperation Administration were sharply curtailed. With strong United States support, the United Nations late in that year assumed responsibility for post-hostilities relief and reconstruction and to this end created a United Nations Korean Reconstruction Agency. The initial program approved by the United Nations called for an expenditure by the new Agency of the equivalent of $250 million during the first year of full-scale operations after the end of the war. Of this amount, the U.S. Administration pledged $162.5 million, subject to Congressional approval.[3] Pending the end of hostilities, emergency relief assistance to the South Koreans was being handled by the Unified Command in Korea and the United States contributions were filled out of Army stocks and charged against Department of Defense appropriations. Such grants were valued at $132 million in 1952, raising to $253 million the value of civilian relief goods and services supplied by the Army from the outbreak of hostilities. The American contributions accounted for over 95 percent of the

[2] See *Survey–1949*, pp. 47-49, and *Survey–1950*, pp. 57-59 for more details on the development of policy during those years. For additional information on the 1952 program, see "Mutual Security Act of 1952," *op.cit.*, pp. 774-782; *S. Rpt. No. 1490*, *op.cit.*, p. 49; and *H. Rpt. No. 1922*, *op.cit.*, pp. 61-62. For an official account of the economic problems of Korea and details on the work of the United Nations economic organizations there, see United Nations, *Report of the Agent General of the United Nations Korean Reconstruction Agency*, General Assembly, *Official Records*, Seventh Session, Supplement No. 19 (A/2222), 1952, and UN Doc. A/2222/Add.1, 1953.

[3] As of early 1952, other nations had pledged or contributed the equivalent of some $44 million against the total fund.

value of such supplies received from all United Nations member states.

In 1951 the Administration asked Congress to appropriate $112.5 million of new funds for the American contribution to the UN Korean Rehabilitation Agency and to reappropriate and make available for transfer to the UN Agency some $50 million of unobligated funds previously appropriated for Economic Cooperation Administration activities in Korea. Spokesmen for the Executive Branch stated that the Agency did not plan to begin operations until the fighting stopped but that funds should be provided at once in order that the Agency could proceed to determine future policies and specific programs. Congress was sympathetic to the United Nations program but saw little need to provide at that time the amounts asked and limited its action to reappropriating the unspent $50 million originally provided to the ECA for Korea and to authorizing, but not appropriating, an additional $45 million, with any transfers of commodities by the Army to the Agency at the cessation of fighting to be deducted from this authorization.

The Administration asked Congress again in 1952 to honor the $162.5 million pledge. This time the request was as follows: (a) the undisbursed balances (about $40 million) of the previously appropriated $50 million should be carried over; (b) the $45 million authorized in the previous year should be continued; and (c) not more than $67.5 million of civilian relief supplies in the United States Army pipeline to Korea at such time as the Korean Rehabilitation Agency took over should be made available to that Agency, the value of such transferred goods being counted as a United States contribution to the United Nations organization but one that would not be deductible from (a) or (b).

Congress did not seriously question the Administration's assertion that it was "established policy" of the United States to help Korea recoup some of the losses suffered in the Communist aggression by providing economic assistance via the United Nations when hostilities ceased. The majority of the Legislative Branch also agreed that funds should be provided in advance so that the Agency could begin to commit large amounts immediately at the end of the fighting. With little debate or discussion Congress therefore honored the Administration's request.

However, only $10 million was transferred by the Administration to the Agency during 1952, and this took place during the first three months of the year, under the authority of the 1951 legislation.

During the first part of 1952 the Agency continued to make specific plans for its future operations and entered into certain agreements with the Unified Command regarding tasks to be performed at the end of the fighting. Some Agency personnel were seconded to the United Nations Civil Assistance Command and a few small projects were being carried out by the Agency itself, including the provision of some technical assistance, seeds, mobile medical clinics, etc. But late in the year—in view of the failure to reach an armistice agreement, the creation of a reasonably stable military front, and the deepening despair of the Korean people over the delays in rehabilitating those parts of the country south of the fighting front, which despair carried with it what many regarded as serious threats to the United Nations political and economic objectives in Korea—an agreement was reached between the Agency, the Unified Command, and the UN Commander-in-Chief in Korea whereby the Rehabilitation Agency, in close cooperation with the civil assistance program of the Unified Command, was to begin at once its task of rehabilitation. Specifically, the program called for the expenditure of some $70 million in the first six months of 1953, of which $14 million was to go for the importation of such essential commodities as food, timber, and fertilizers, and the balance for rehabilitating Korean agriculture, industry, transportation, power, and health and education facilities.

D. *INTERNATIONAL CHILDREN'S EMERGENCY FUND*

With United States support, the United Nations General Assembly in late 1946 established the United Nations International Children's Emergency Fund. During its first three years, the Fund, for which Congress had authorized American contributions of some $75 million, continued supplementary feeding programs, largely in the war-devastated countries of Europe, that had been originated in the immediate post-hostilities period by the United Nations Relief and Rehabilitation Administration. By 1950 there was strong sentiment in the U.S. Government to terminate the Fund on the grounds that it was "ineffective," that the "emergency" needs had been met, and that the permanent and fundamental problems of child welfare could be better handled by some new long-term arrangements. Despite this stand, the General Assembly in late 1950 voted to continue the Fund for another three years and emphasis was thereafter shifted from mass feeding in Europe to a more comprehensive maternal and child health program in Asia, Africa, and Latin America, especially in rural areas. Early the following year the Administration asked Congress to appropriate $12.5 million for the period ending in mid-1951, but the latter, after expressing strong opposition to the past practice whereby the United States contributed nearly three quarters of the Fund's budget,[4] appropriated only $5.75 million.

In August 1951, President Truman asked Congress to authorize an appropriation of $12 million for the year ending in mid-1952. The Senate approved the request at that session of Congress but the House took no action and early in the 1952 session the Administration, stressing the humanitarian interest of the United States in the program, urged the House to give its approval. In addition, Congress was asked to authorize another $12 million in United States contributions for the remainder of the life of the Fund.[5] In the final authorizing act Congress cut the two requests by some 30 percent, that is, to $16.5 million for the period through calendar 1953, and specified, over Administration objections, that the United States contribution during this time should not exceed one third of the Fund's total budget. The Fund had set up a target budget for the two and a half years beginning in mid-1951 equivalent to some $50 million and the authorization was equivalent to one third of this. In the debate over the actual appropriation, however, the Legislative Branch, while willing to have the United

[4] It should be noted that each nation receiving food matched the Fund's contribution with local foodstuffs of an equivalent caloric value.

[5] See *Survey—1951*, pp. 68-69, and references cited therein for more details on United States policy vis-à-vis the Children's Fund. For an official United States statement on the Fund in June 1952, see "Mutual Security Appropriation for 1953," *op.cit.*, pp. 761-765. See also *S. Rpt. No. 1490*, *op.cit.*, p. 58, and *H. Rpt. No. 1922*, *op.cit.*, pp. 74-75. See also, Lenroot, K. F., "Development in Long-Range International Programs for Children," Department of State *Bulletin*, June 16, 1952, pp. 962-965. For a detailed official statement of the work of the Children's Fund as of late 1952, see *United Nations International Children's Emergency Fund, Report of the Executive Board*, Economic and Social Council, *Official Records*, Fifteenth Session, Supplement No. 2, October 1952.

States contribute one third of the total budget, anticipated that contributions by the other members would be far below the amounts assumed in the Fund's target budget and therefore appropriated only $6.7 million for the year ending on June 30, 1953.

Transfers by the U.S. Government to the Fund during calendar 1952 totalled $6.7 million; this raised total United States contributions to $87 million, over 70 percent of total contributions by all governments to the central account of the Fund. In the United Nations during the year United States representatives commended the Fund on its work, welcomed the extension of its programs in the less-developed areas, urged greater emphasis on permanent child welfare and health services, and expressed the hope that other member governments would continue their contributions so that the work of the Fund could go forward without interruption in 1953.[6]

E. *MIGRATION AND ESCAPEE ASSISTANCE*

During the period from the end of World War II to the beginning of 1952, the U.S. Government contributed some $237 million to the International Refugee Organization for the care and resettlement of refugees.[7] Large, but unknown, contributions were also made by private voluntary agencies. At Congressional insistence, official grants to the International Refugee Organization ceased in early 1951 and that institution was terminated in January 1952 after having aided in the resettlement of over a million displaced persons.[8] In anticipation of the end of the International Refugee Organization, a United Nations High Commissioner's Office for Refugees, whose operating funds were to come from the United Nations general budget, had been created early in 1951 and was given the general task of protecting refugees, especially the some 400,000 "hard core" cases left by the International Refugee Organization, primarily by intervening with governments to acquire

[6] Department of State *Bulletin*, September 8, 1952, pp. 376-377.

[7] The U.S. Government also made large grants for the care and resettlement of refugees through the United Nations Relief and Rehabilitation Administration, the Israel Aid Program, the United Nations Relief and Works Agency for Palestine Refugees in the Near East, and the Aid to Korea programs.

[8] See *Survey–1951*, pp. 34-35, 69-70, and the several references cited therein for details on United States policies and activities vis-à-vis refugees during the years 1949-1951.

citizenship for these persons.[9] Many in the United States, and elsewhere, believed there still remained a large unsolved and politically dangerous problem of refugees in Europe, but the U.S. Government was unwilling to make further large financial contributions for European refugees as such.

On the other hand, in implementing the European Recovery Program various agencies of the U.S. Government had become concerned with the problem of "surplus manpower," arising from normal population growth as well as migration from Eastern Europe, in certain of the European countries—especially Germany, Italy, Greece, and Austria—and in 1950 Congress, without specifically setting aside any funds, had empowered the Economic Cooperation Administration to encourage the migration of such labor out of Europe to areas where manpower was in greater demand. Little was accomplished that year and in 1951 Congress specifically set aside $10 million of the Mutual Security Program funds for encouraging migration out of Europe. Subsequently, in November and December, the United States sponsored a Conference on Migration at Brussels at which a "Provisional Intergovernmental Committee for the Movement of Migrants from Europe" (PICMME) was formed, the United States delegation agreeing to contribute for the first year the $10 million that Congress had provided for migration purposes.[1]

In 1951, Congress, on its own initiative, had also authorized the use of up to $100 million of the funds for military assistance to Europe to assist escapees from Iron Curtain countries to enter the military service of the NATO forces or for "other purposes." In March 1952, President Truman allocated $4.3 million for this use but stated that for reasons of security only a small number of such escapees could be taken into the armed forces of the NATO

[9] The Ford Foundation made a $2.9 million grant to this organization in 1952, specifying that the money was to be used for projects in a program seeking a permanent solution of the refugee problem, with particular emphasis on young people and on vocational training. For a summary of discussions in the United Nations during late 1951 on the work of the High Commissioner's Office and on migration in general, see *United Nations Bulletin*, February 1, 1952, pp. 133-139.

[1] For reports on the activities of this migration committee, see articles by G. L. Warren in Department of State *Bulletin*, January 14, 1952, pp. 50-52; February 4, 1952, pp. 169-173; April 21, 1952, pp. 638-640; July 21, 1952, pp. 107-109; and January 12, 1953, pp. 64-66. For a summary of the discussions on migration during the seventh session of the U.N. General Assembly in the latter part of 1952, see *United Nations Bulletin*, December 15, 1952, pp. 590-591.

countries and that the balance must either emigrate to other areas or be trained and equipped to carry out "productive work" in the North Atlantic area.[2]

In its request for extension of the Mutual Security Program for the year beginning in mid-1952, the Administration asked Congress to continue the authority to aid escapees and to provide another $10 million for contributions to the work of the Committee for the Movement of Migrants. President Truman also asked Congress to liberalize the immigration laws and to approve a three-year emergency program authorizing the admission of 300,000 persons over and above the current quotas.[3]

The Administration stated that the migration program for 1952 was an experimental one and that, if it worked as planned, it was hoped that within five years, and with virtually the same amount of dollars per year from the United States, "a substantial part of the surplus population of Europe" could be moved. It also asserted that "large numbers" would have to be transferred if "we are going to make any real dent on surplus population in Europe."[4] In view of the unwillingness of Congress either to liberalize the existing immigration laws or to approve the President's request for an emergency immigration program, the Administration anticipated that after 1952 the bulk of the migrants from Europe would go to Canada, Australia, and Latin America, with but very few coming to the United States.

Congress raised few objections to continuing the 1951 authority to aid escapees (indeed, many legislators expressed disappointment that so little of the 1951 funds had been spent) or to making another contribution to the newly established Migration Committee. It extended the former authority for another year and ap-

[2] The United States ignored the charge by Russia in the United Nations that these escapees were to be used "for armed intervention and for the overthrow of governments. . . ." (UN Economic and Social Council, *Official Records*, Fourteenth Session, 633rd Meeting, July 8, 1952, p. 495.)

[3] See "Mutual Security Appropriations for 1953," *op.cit.*, pp. 751-757 for details on United States policy and the proposed activities for the Migration Committee. For a comprehensive policy statement by President Truman on the overpopulation problem in Europe and what the United States might do to help solve it, see Department of State *Bulletin*, April 7, 1952, pp. 551-555. For a paper on the problem as seen by an Italian, see del Giarlino, J. G., "International Emigration Problems," *Review of Economic Conditions in Italy* (Rome), May 1952, pp. 179-195.

[4] "Mutual Security Appropriations for 1953," House, *Hearings*, *op.cit.*, p. 756.

propriated approximately $9 million for the migration program for fiscal year 1953.

The Provisional Intergovernmental Committee for the Movement of Migrants from Europe formally began to function in February 1952, taking over the fleet of ships operated by the International Refugee Organization, and by year's end twenty-one nations had joined.[5] The Committee planned early in the year to move some 137,000 migrants during 1952, the vast majority to come from Austria, Germany, Greece, Italy-Trieste, and the Netherlands, and to go to Canada, Australia, Latin America, New Zealand, Israel, and the United States. A budget of the equivalent of $41.4 million was finally adopted for the year 1952, with the United States contribution coming from the funds earmarked for such purposes in the Mutual Security Program appropriation plus $3.2 million provided by Congress to help move ethnic Germans to the United States under the Displaced Persons Act.

Data on operations through the end of the year are not available, but nearly 63,000 migrants were moved in the first nine months, of which over 36,000 came to the United States.[6] At its October meeting, the Committee reported that probably no more than 100,000 would be moved during the year and that total income available to it would be the equivalent of about $30.3 million, of which the United States would contribute $9 million. At this meeting representatives from some of the immigration countries (Australia, Brazil, Chile, and Venezuela) argued that the Committee could make the hoped-for impact on the problems of surplus manpower and refugees in Europe only if it were established on a permanent basis and its functions expanded to include the "encouragement" of colonization projects in the receiving countries. The United States representatives stated they were not

[5] Australia, Austria, Belgium, Bolivia, Brazil, Canada, Chile, Denmark, France, Germany, Greece, Israel, Italy, Luxembourg, the Netherlands, Norway, Paraguay, Sweden, Switzerland, the United States, and Venezuela.

[6] The United States was scheduled to receive 38,000 during 1952, largely ethnic Germans who had fled from areas east of the Iron Curtain. These persons were authorized to enter the United States under special provisions of the Displaced Persons Act of 1948, as amended, and were in addition to the 330,000 who had entered under the other provisions of this Act since 1948. It was anticipated that the immigration authorized under this Act would be virtually completed by the end of 1952 since the authority to issue such visas expired on June 30, 1952. See the *New York Times*, August 20, 1952, p. 6 for a summary of the final report of the Displaced Persons Commission.

prepared at that time to consider prolonging the Committee beyond the end of 1953 or to authorize the Committee to engage in the management, operation, or financing of colonization projects. The decision finally taken was to extend the Committee for one more year, to change its name to "Intergovernmental Committee for European Migration," to make its staff available to interested governments to help in developing a formula for the financing of colonization projects that might facilitate the presentation of such projects by the governments to the International Bank, and to plan on moving 120,000 people during calendar 1953 on a budget equivalent to $36.8 million.

Little information was published during the year on activities under the escapee program and no data were given as to the numbers of escapees who had entered military service in the NATO forces. Some 2,600 such persons had been resettled overseas, or were awaiting departure at year's end, with the Migration Committee providing the transportation. Contracts had also been entered into between the U.S. Government and several voluntary agencies to provide food, clothing, and medical care to the escapees. The President had made no allocations of dollars for this program beyond the original one of $4.3 million but apparently nearly $2 million in European counterpart funds had been made available.[7]

F. *MISCELLANEOUS OFFICIAL GRANTS*

Congress in 1947 authorized the Department of Agriculture to cooperate with the Government of Mexico in a program for eradicating foot and mouth disease in Mexico. During 1952 some $2.9 million was spent by the Agriculture Department for this purpose, raising the total expenditures from the beginning of the program to $88.1 million. In addition, the U.S. Government has from time to time purchased canned beef in Mexico under a program to provide an alternative market for cattle that normally would come into the United States. Some of this meat may have been sold for a loss, but details are not available and neither the purchases nor the losses, if any, are included in Table 6. The Department of Agriculture was given authority, commencing in

[7] See Mutual Security Agency, *Third Report to Congress on the Mutual Security Program, op.cit.*, pp. 7-8.

1949, to donate to private and international welfare organizations operating abroad certain surplus food products that had been acquired under various agricultural price-support operations. Through 1951 commodities that cost the Government $81.3 million had been given away but there were no such donations during 1952.

When the Communists gained control of mainland China in 1949, Congress authorized the State Department to use certain of the unexpended funds from previous grant programs for that area to aid Chinese students who were stranded in the United States. This law was subsequently extended and amended to include certain Korean students and $1.4 million was spent during 1952, raising the total to $6.6 million. During 1952 the State Department also spent $3.8 million in completing work on certain public service reconstruction projects that had been authorized under the Philippine Rehabilitation Act in 1946.[8]

G. *TOTAL UNITED STATES GOVERNMENT GRANTS*

The total amount of U.S. Government grants extended during 1952 and from the end of the war through 1952 are shown in Table 6, broken down into major programs and areas of destination. Aid extended on a credit basis is *not* included in this table but is given separately in Table 10. The table on total grant aid does include aid extended under indeterminate terms, some of which for earlier years, as noted below, was later classified as loans or credits.

The data in this table are gross and include the ascertainable dollar costs of administering the various grant aid programs as well as those expenditures of United States-owned foreign currency counterpart funds that were made in administering the aid program and for other purposes regarded as of benefit to the foreign country. Excluded from the table are grants from abroad to the U.S. Government and the returns on grants. These totalled $151 million during 1952, of which $91 million was counterpart fund deposits reserved for the use of the United States and $60 million represented the return of certain lend-lease naval vessels by France, the United Kingdom, Greece, and Yugoslavia. These

[8] For a summary of these programs, see *Survey–1951*, pp. 62-63, and the references cited therein.

III. OTHER GRANT ASSISTANCE

TABLE 6

United States Government Gross Foreign Grants, 1945-1952[a]

(millions of dollars)

	1952	*1951*	*July 1, 1945— Dec. 31, 1952*
By Major Program			
Mutual Security			
Military aid[b]	2739	1493	4819
Economic and technical assistance[c]	1849	2709	12801
Civilian Supplies to Occupied Areas[d]	154	366	5340
United Nations Relief and Rehabilitation	—	—	2589
Post-UNRRA and Interim Aid	—	—	854
Philippine Rehabilitation	4	12	634
Greek-Turkish Aid[e]	—	—	650
International Refugee Organization	—	8	241
International Children's Emergency Fund	7	6	87
Lend-Lease	—	—	1932
Other[f]	3	51	300
Total	4756	4645	30246
By Major Area			
Western Europe and Dependencies[g]	3775	3592	21626
Other Europe[h]	—	—	1036
Near East and Africa[i]	105	20	129
Asia and the Pacific[j]	712	826	6140
Latin America	79	75	292
Unallocable[k]	85	132	1023
Total	4756	4645	30246

a) In most instances these data represent shipments where goods are procured by U.S. Government agencies and cash payments by the Government where other methods of procurement are used. They include the ECA-owned counterpart funds spent for administration and other services deemed of benefit to the countries concerned. Dollar costs for administering all aid programs are also included. Aid extended on a credit basis is *not* included here but in Table 10.

b) Includes military grant aid extended under the China Aid Act as well as military assistance provided under the Mutual Defense Assistance Act and the Mutual Security Act. Not included is the value of military supplies provided to Greece and Turkey under the Greek-Turkish Assistance Act prior to 1951 or the value of military matériel supplied to several nations under the lend-lease program. Available data do not permit a breakdown of the aid provided under these programs as between military and economic.

c) Includes grants provided under the Economic Cooperation Act, the Mutual Security Act, the Act for International Development (Point Four), and the Smith-Mundt Act, and by the Institute for Inter-American Affairs. Also included is the value of supplies given Yugoslavia under the special Yugoslav Aid Program.

d) Includes civilian supplies furnished to Korea by the Defense Department, as well as civilian supplies provided under the Government and Relief in Occupied Areas Program.

(Notes continued at bottom of next page)

returns totalled $140 million in 1951. Thus, *net* grants extended during 1952 were just over $4.6 billion.

Reverse grants during the period from the end of World War II through 1952 totalled $1.2 billion, of which half represented counterpart fund deposits for the use of the United States, 10 percent represented cash payments on war account settlements, and the balance were reverse lend-lease and the return of lend-lease goods. In addition, $1.3 billion of the recorded grants (principally lend-lease) were subsequently changed into long-term credits. Thus, net grants from the U.S. Government to the rest of the world in the seven and one-half years following the end of the war totalled approximately $27.8 billion.

---

e) The small amounts provided under this program in 1951 and 1952 have been included in "Mutual Security, Military Aid."

f) The total for the postwar period includes grants by the Department of Agriculture of surplus foods valued at $81 million ($46 million worth of these in 1951); contributions of $88 million to the eradication of foot and mouth disease in Mexico ($3 million of these in 1952 and $5 million in 1951); $11 million of contributions by the U.S. Government to the American Red Cross for foreign war relief; and $120 million out of the $500 million 1942 Treasury Stabilization Loan to China.

g) Includes grants to OEEC countries and their dependencies plus Finland and Yugoslavia. Also includes contributions to the European Payments Union and the Provisional Intergovernmental Committee for Movement of Migrants from Europe. Military aid to Greece and Turkey under the Mutual Security Agency is included in "Near East and Africa."

h) Includes grants to Czechoslovakia, Poland, Russia, Albania, Hungary, and Spain.

i) Includes *all* grants to Egypt, Ethiopia, Israel, Saudi Arabia, the Union of South Africa, Iraq, Jordan, Lebanon, Liberia, Libya, and Syria, but only *military aid* to Greece and Turkey under the Mutual Security Program.

j) Includes grants to Australia, China, Indonesia, Japan and the Ryukyu Islands, Korea, New Zealand, Philippines, Pakistan, Nepal, Afghanistan, Ceylon, India, Burma, Indochina, Thailand, and the Caroline, Mariana, and Marshall Islands.

k) Includes contributions to the International Refugee Organization, United Nations, United Nations Relief and Rehabilitation Administration, International Children's Emergency Fund, and American Red Cross; Department of Agriculture donations; and certain administrative expenses.

Sources: Compiled from data given in Department of Commerce, *Foreign Transactions of the U.S. Government, Foreign Aid*, Wash., D.C., April 1952, Appendix Tables 2 and 6; Department of Commerce, *Foreign Aid by the United States Government*, Wash., D.C., March 1953, Appendix Tables 1 and 3; and Department of Commerce, *Survey of Current Business*, Wash., D.C., March 1953, p. 15.

H. *MISCELLANEOUS GOVERNMENT UNILATERAL TRANSFERS*

In addition to grants, the U.S. Government also made certain other unilateral transfers during the year, primarily divestments by the Alien Property Custodian, pensions, and payments on miscellaneous claims. These totalled, *net*, $130 million during 1952, raising the total Governmental net grants and unilateral transfers to over $4.7 billion.

I. *PRIVATE REMITTANCES*

The downward trend in private remittances that had occurred since the end of World War II stopped during 1952 and, at a *net* of $415 million, the volume of such payments—by individuals and institutions and in cash and in kind—was virtually the same as in the previous year.

IV · LOANS AND INVESTMENTS

Except during the immediate post-World War II period, the bulk of United States official aid extended foreign countries in recent years has been on a grant rather than credit basis, it having been concluded that most countries would in the foreseeable future find it exceedingly difficult to finance their "essential" imports—including goods needed for rearmament—and should not be burdened with additional interest payments, and that any substantial increase in official loans would discourage the outflow of private capital. Still, Congress did from time to time require that a portion of United States aid extended under the various Government assistance programs be on a credit basis and the Export-Import Bank continued to make modest amounts of loans, concentrating after 1948 on so-called economic development projects, with growing emphasis, after Korea, on helping to finance the exploitation and development abroad of strategic and critical materials urgently needed in the United States. The activities of the Bank, especially in the latter sphere, were greatly expanded during 1952 with the result, as Table 7 shows, that net foreign loans by the Government were nearly three times as large as during the previous year.

In contrast to the general policy of limiting official loans, the Government for several years has, through a variety of devices, been attempting to encourage an expanded outflow of private foreign investment. Many nations, however, evidenced little interest in, and in some cases even hostility toward, the efforts of the U.S. Government to improve the climate abroad for private investment; and United States private investors, in the face of many attractive domestic alternatives and what they regarded as appreciably greater risks abroad, showed little enthusiasm for making foreign investments other than in petroleum and, to a lesser but growing extent, mining and smelting. Although total private investments declined again in 1952, as shown in Table 7,

TABLE 7

Net United States Capital Outflow, 1946-1952[a]

(millions of dollars)

Year	Total as a Percentage of Exports of Goods and Services[b]	Total	GOVERNMENT Long-term	GOVERNMENT Short-term	PRIVATE Long-term[c]	PRIVATE Short-term
1946	21	3381[d]	3262[d]	—250	59	310
1947	24	7956[d]	6849[d]	108	810	189
1948	10	1750	973	—87	748	116
1949	7	1256	474	173	796	—187
1950	10	1481	127	37	1168	149
1951	6	1229	140	23	963	103
1952[p]	6	1350	409[e]	45	831	65

p) Preliminary.

a) Excludes Government grants, unilateral transfers, and private remittances.

b) In calculating these percentages, subscriptions by the U.S. Government to the International Bank and Fund have been excluded.

c) Includes net purchases of debentures sold or guaranteed by the International Bank.

d) Includes subscriptions to the International Bank and Fund of $323 million in 1946, and $3062 million in 1947.

e) The small discrepancy between this figure and that calculable from Table 10 is due to the inclusion in the latter (but not in the above table) of loans made by agent commercial banks under the guarantee of the Export-Import Bank and the inclusion in this table (but not in Table 10) of certain minor Government investments abroad, such as those by the Reconstruction Finance Corporation in the abaca plantations in Central America.

Sources: Department of Commerce, *Balance of Payments of the United States, 1949-1951*, Wash., D.C., November 1952, pp. 156, 160, and Department of Commerce, *Survey of Current Business*, Wash., D.C., March 1953, pp. 8-9.

there was a moderate increase in private direct investments and they were somewhat more diversified than in the previous years.

A. *UNITED STATES GOVERNMENT LOANS AND CREDITS*[1]

Although Congress did not insist for the year beginning in mid-1952, as for previous years, that a portion of the economic assist-

[1] Most of the material in this section was taken from the following official publications: National Advisory Council on International Monetary and Financial Problems, *Semiannual Report to the President and to the Congress for the Period October 1, 1951–March 31, 1952*, Wash., D.C., 1952; National Advisory Council on International Monetary and Financial Problems, *Semiannual Report to the President and to the Congress for the Period April 1–September 30, 1952*, Wash., D.C., 1953; Export-Import Bank of Washington, *Fourteenth Semiannual Report to Congress*, Wash., D.C., June 30, 1952; Export-Import Bank of Washington, *Fifteenth Semiannual Report to Congress*, Wash., D.C., December 31, 1952; and

ance extended under the Mutual Security Program be provided on a credit basis, the official aid extended by the U.S. Government to foreign countries on a loan basis during 1952 was nearly two and one-half times that of each of the previous two years and accounted for nearly 9 percent of the net foreign aid provided. The increase was attributable primarily to the expanded activities of the Export-Import Bank and to the fact that virtually all of the "economic aid" under the fiscal year 1951-1952 Mutual Security Program that Congress had specified should be on a credit basis was utilized during the first half of calendar 1952.

Long-Term

a. EXPORT-IMPORT BANK: FOR OWN ACCOUNT

Congress had increased the lending authority of the Export-Import Bank (EIB) in 1951 by $1 billion, raising to $4.5 billion the amount of loans it could have outstanding at any one time, and during 1952 the Bank authorized a total of some $538 million in new loans,[2] over twice the amount recorded in the previous year. Actual disbursements (including those by agent banks at Export-Import Bank risk) totalled $478 million and, with $271 million of principal repaid and $72 million collected for interest and commissions, the Bank made a larger net contribution to financing the United States export surplus than in any year since 1947.

The scope of the Bank's operations was widened somewhat in 1952 as compared with the previous year, both in number of countries receiving the loans and in the purposes of the credits. In keeping with the policy set out in the previous year when requesting Congress to expand its lending authority,[3] increased emphasis was given during 1952 to loans designed to expand the production of strategic materials abroad. Some $115 million of the new authorizations was for such purposes, nearly half of this going to South Africa and Australia to help construct various facilities for the production of uranium. These credits were ex-

---

Department of Commerce, *Foreign Aid by the United States Government*, Wash., D.C., March 1953.

[2] This excludes $58 million of loans authorized by participants without recourse to the Bank.

[3] See *Survey—1951*, pp. 102-103.

TABLE 8

Export-Import Bank Operations, 1934-1952

(millions of dollars)

	New Credits Authorized[a]	*Authoriza-tions Ex-pired or Cancelled*	*Loans Disbursed by EIB & Its Agent Banks*	*Principal Collected by EIB & Its Agent Banks*	*Interest and Com-missions Collected*	*Credits Out-stand-ing Dec. 31*
By Area—1952						
Western Europe[b]	284.5	86.7	240.2	217.3	47.7	1654.6
Eastern Europe	—	—	—	2.1[c]	1.3[c]	41.2
Latin America	153.1	59.6	100.4	44.2	17.4	508.4
Middle East	—	—	31.3	4.5	3.6	126.3
Africa	64.9	—	27.2	1.7	1.0	38.0
Asia and the Pacific	30.8	0.1	76.6	1.2	1.0	121.9
Canada	5.0	—	2.4	—	0.2	5.7
1952 Total	538.3	146.4	478.1	271.0	72.2	2496.1
By Period						
1951	244.2	29.6	204.1	134.5	68.2	2289.0
1950	554.8	37.0	199.9	160.0	64.4	2219.5
1949	241.0	19.4	184.8	143.7	60.9	2179.6
1948	117.2	325.9	428.9	261.2	57.3	2138.5
1947	540.6	23.5	824.5	95.5	}	1970.7
1946	1184.3	122.6	1029.8	40.3	}85.8	1241.7
1934-1945	2308.5	438.5	562.4	310.3	}	252.1
Cumulative Total, 1934 through 1952	5728.9	1142.9	3912.6	1416.5	408.9	

Details may not add to totals because of rounding.

a) Excludes credits authorized by participants without recourse to the Bank. Such participations are frequently included in the global figures published by the Bank and have been included in similar tables presented in previous numbers of this *Survey*.

b) The OEEC countries, including Greece and Turkey, plus Finland, Yugoslavia, and Spain.

c) From Poland.

Sources: Compiled from Export-Import Bank of Washington, *Eleventh, Thirteenth,* and *Fifteenth Semiannual Report to Congress*, Wash., D.C., 1950, 1951, and 1952, respectively; Department of Commerce, *Foreign Transactions of the U.S. Government, Foreign Aid,* Wash., D.C., April 1952, Appendix Tables 8-11; and Department of Commerce, *Foreign Aid by the United States Government*, Wash., D.C., March 1953, Appendix Table 5.

tended at the request of the Atomic Energy Commission, which had contracts to buy uranium from these countries, and additional aid was provided the South African enterprises by the British Ministry of Supply. Most of the rest of the credit authorizations for these purposes went to Brazil to assist in financing the production of manganese; relatively small loans were authorized to assist in the financing of the expansion of nickel and cobalt production in Canada, tungsten production in Bolivia, and sulphur production in Mexico. Most of these borrowers from the Bank had contracted to sell a part of their output to the U.S. Government.

Approximately one quarter ($137 million) of the new loan authorizations were intended to facilitate the economic development of the aided countries and tied in with the general objectives of the Point Four Program; in some cases, the Export-Import Bank loans were directly related to specific Point Four-sponsored projects.[4] Nearly half of the authorizations in this category were to be used to purchase supplies needed to expand electric power production in Brazil,[5] the Philippines, and Colombia. Loans were also authorized to improve and extend railroads in Brazil and Portuguese Africa and to help finance the importation of agricultural equipment and supplies by the former country. Small credits were authorized to modernize steel production in Mexico and the production of cast iron pipe in Brazil. An unusual type of loan for the Export-Import Bank, but one used by the International Bank on occasion, was authorized late in the year when arrangements were completed for a $5 million line of credit in favor of several Philippine banks for relending to private business firms in the Islands.

The Bank continued during the year to use some of its resources to assist foreign buyers to purchase raw cotton in the United States, one of the major activities envisaged when Congress established the Bank in 1934, and loans totalling $73 million were authorized for this purpose to borrowers in France, Germany,

[4] There was nothing in the official reports of the Export-Import Bank or the International Bank, nor would one have expected there would be, to indicate that there had been competition between them as to the making of loans for financing basic facilities abroad, but Mr. Maffry referred to the existence of such "confusing and frustrating competition" and stated that it was "one of the most embarrassing anomalies in the international financial relations of the United States." (Maffry, A., *Program for Increasing Private Investment in Foreign Countries*, Report prepared for Technical Cooperation Administration, Department of Commerce, and Mutual Security Agency, December 18, 1952 [mimeographed], p. 19.)

[5] The Bank pointed out that the $41 million loaned to seven subsidiaries in Brazil of the American and Foreign Power Company would not only facilitate the economic development of that company but would also "protect" a large investment by United States stockholders.

Austria, and Spain.[6] In June, the Bank authorized a $50 million credit to Belgium, to finance various imports, on the condition that participation in the loan by United States private banks be permitted. Subsequently, $45 million of the credit was taken over by thirty-two commercial banks.[7]

The largest single loan authorization during the year was in direct support of the European defense effort. A $200 million credit was opened in favor of the French Government in June for the purpose of permitting that country to receive immediately the dollar proceeds of contracts placed in France under the offshore procurement program by the U.S. Defense Department for the production of military end-items to be delivered and paid for at later dates.[8] The loan agreement provided that disbursements were to be limited to the dollar amounts of such contracts placed during the fiscal year ending in mid-1952 and that the Bank would be repaid as deliveries were accepted by the Defense Department. Only $154 million of such contracts were placed and the balance of the credit was cancelled during the latter part of the year; $49 million had been repaid at the end of 1952.

The Bank, which had previously been criticized—but never in the halls of Congress—for "tying" its loans to purchases in the United States, reported during the year that because of shortages in the United States it had to face "with increasing frequency" the question of whether to permit its dollars to be used to make purchases in other countries. No details of the specific decisions taken were published, but, as in earlier periods, the great bulk of the Bank's disbursements were used to buy United States-produced goods and services.[9]

[6] During the year $38 million of unused cotton credits authorized in 1945 were cancelled. It may also be noted that not all of the controversial $125 million line of credit extended to Argentina in 1950 was utilized (see *Survey—1950*, p. 128) and $28.5 million was cancelled in 1952.

[7] The Bank also authorized a credit to Italy of $4.7 million to purchase civilian-type aircraft in the United States and the American supplier extended additional credit of $1.2 million.

[8] See Chapter I, Section B(b).

[9] The Bank reported a net profit of $50.7 million during the year, after paying $21.6 million of interest on funds borrowed from the U.S. Treasury Department. On June 30, the Bank also paid and declared a $20 million dividend to the U.S. Treasury on the $1 billion of the Bank's capital stock held by the Treasury. This was the second such dividend payment, the first having been made in 1951.

b. EXPORT-IMPORT BANK: FOR MUTUAL SECURITY AGENCY

In 1948, 1949, and 1951 Congress, over the objections of the Administration, provided that a certain part of the "economic," as distinguished from "military," aid authorized for the European Recovery Program–Mutual Security Program should be provided on a credit basis.[1] The countries to receive aid on this basis and the terms—lenient—of these "fuzzy" loans were determined by the Director for Mutual Security in consultation with the National Advisory Council on International Monetary and Financial Problems, but the loans were administered by the Export-Import Bank. In extending the Mutual Security Act for another year, Congress, in 1952, respected the Administration's wishes that it not be required that a part of the aid funds be extended on a credit basis, but during the calendar year $184.4 million of credits under the 1951 and earlier legislation were utilized by the various European governments, raising the total since 1948 to $1.3 billion. Except for a token payment by Belgium, there had been no payment on principal; repayments under most of these loans were scheduled to start in 1956. Interest on these loans did become payable in 1952, however, and just over $13 million was received during the year under review.

In 1950 Congress authorized a special $62.5 million loan to Spain in the Act appropriating funds for the Economic Cooperation Administration.[2] The Export-Import Bank acted as agent for the Administrator of the European Recovery Program–Mutual Security Program for this loan and $12.2 million was disbursed during 1952, raising the total to $29.4 million, most of which had been used to purchase cotton, fertilizer, wheat, coal, railroad equipment, and tractors and spare parts. As with most of the loans under the Mutual Security Program, repayments were scheduled to commence in 1956.

In the face of an urgent need for wheat in India as a consequence of a drought and the locust plagues, Congress approved an India Emergency Assistance Act in 1951 that provided that up to $190 million worth of food grains could be supplied India on a

[1] See *Survey—1951*, pp. 33-34, and the references cited therein.

[2] See *Survey—1950*, pp. 13-17, for a brief account of the background of this action. See also Chapter I, Section B, above.

TABLE 9

Mutual Security Agency—Export-Import Bank Loans Utilized, 1948-1952[a]

(millions of dollars)

	1952	*1948-1952*
Belgium-Luxembourg	12.8	65.2
Denmark	2.3	33.3
France	43.2	225.6
Germany	16.9	16.9
Iceland	1.0	5.3
Ireland	—	128.2
Italy	22.6	95.6
Netherlands-Indonesia	16.0	166.7
Norway	4.2	39.2
Portugal	6.1	33.6
Sweden	—	20.4
Turkey	11.4	85.0
United Kingdom	47.9	384.8
Total	184.4[b]	1299.8[b]

a) Data given by the Export-Import Bank on disbursements of loans under this program differ in some cases from the above data because the Mutual Security Agency frequently extended assistance on an indeterminate basis and subsequently classified it as a "credit." In such cases, the Export-Import Bank made its disbursements at the time of classification rather than when the aid was actually transferred, the basis for the Department of Commerce data given in this table.

As of the end of 1952, credits of $2.9 million to Belgium, $3.1 million to Portugal, and $0.2 million to Turkey had been authorized by the Mutual Security Agency and the Export-Import Bank but had not been utilized by those countries.

b) The loans to Spain and India noted in the text are not included here but are included in Table 10.

Sources: Department of Commerce, *Foreign Aid by the United States Government*, Wash., D.C., March 1953, Appendix Table 5, and Department of Commerce, *Foreign Transactions of the U.S. Government, Foreign Aid*, Wash., D.C., April 1952, Appendix Table 8.

loan basis.[3] The general administration of the loan was by the Mutual Security Agency, with the Export-Import Bank serving as agent. Nearly $84 million worth of grain was shipped during 1952, raising the total utilization of the loan to $189.7 million. Repayments on this loan were scheduled to commence in 1957, but over $2 million of interest was received during 1952.

C. EXPORT-IMPORT BANK: FOR DEFENSE PRODUCTION ADMINISTRATION

Congress concluded in 1951 that some of the loans that might be judged desirable for expanding the production of strategic and critical materials abroad would be so risky as to fall outside the

[3] For details, see *Survey—1951*, pp. 105-108.

provisions of the Export-Import Bank Act. The Defense Production Act (Section 302) was therefore amended to authorize the President to make special provisions for loans for such purposes to private business enterprises. The President subsequently[4] authorized the Export-Import Bank to make these loans, upon receipt of individual "certificates of essentiality" from the appropriate defense agencies, from funds provided in the borrowing authorizations of the Defense Production Act. This program got under way in 1952 and five loans had been authorized by the end of the year, in an amount of $44 million, but only $0.2 million had actually been disbursed. One of the loans was for the same manganese project in Brazil for which the Bank authorized a credit from its own funds, noted above; two were for the production of copper and cobalt in British East Africa and Northern Rhodesia; one was for a zinc-processing plant in Mexico; and the other was in connection with two sisal-processing plants in Haiti. In each case, some agency of the U.S. Government had a contract to purchase at least a part of the products being produced and the proceeds of such sales were assigned to the Bank until the loans were repaid.[5]

d. EXPORT-IMPORT BANK: FOR TECHNICAL COOPERATION ADMINISTRATION

During the summer, the Government of Pakistan asked the U.S. Government for emergency aid to help alleviate the effects of a serious failure in the wheat harvest. In September, the Administration authorized a $15 million loan for the purchase of cereals out of Mutual Security Program funds, to be administered by the Technical Cooperation Administration through the facilities of the Export-Import Bank.[6] Through 1952, some $6.6 million of the loan had been utilized but contracts had been signed obligating all of the funds.

e. DEFENSE MATERIALS PROCUREMENT AGENCY

Beginning in 1949, the Economic Cooperation Administration–Mutual Security Agency loaned relatively small amounts of dollars

[4] Executive Order 10281, August 28, 1951, Section 311.

[5] For further details on these loans, see Export-Import Bank of Washington, *Fifteenth Semiannual Report to Congress*, Wash., D.C., December 1952.

[6] The terms were similar to those of the 1951 emergency wheat loan to India: thirty-five-year maturity, principal repayments to begin in 1958, and an interest rate of 2½ percent with the first payment due in September 1956.

and somewhat larger amounts of the counterpart funds reserved for United States use to facilitate the exploration for and production of strategic materials and resources in various European countries and their dependent overseas territories. In general, the dollars were used to purchase United States equipment and services and the counterpart funds to pay local expenses. These funds were to be repaid, including interest, in the commodities whose production they facilitated. In late 1951, the outstanding loans and responsibility for making new loans were transferred to the newly established Defense Materials Procurement Agency. This program gained momentum in 1952[7] and was expanded to include Canada and Latin America. During the first nine months (data for the last quarter of the year were not available as this document went to press) nearly $8 million in dollars and the equivalent of over $40 million in counterpart funds were disbursed, raising the total since 1948 to $23 million in dollars and the equivalent of just over $63 million in various European currencies. Most of the dollar loans during the year under review went to help finance projects in Canada and Jamaica and the bulk of the loans in counterpart funds went to undertakings in Southern Rhodesia, French Morocco, and Norway. Data on repayments of these loans were not published.

f. OTHER

The balance—$7.4 million—of the $65 million interest-free loan from the U.S. Government to the United Nations for helping to finance the construction of the permanent headquarters in New York was disbursed during the year and $1 million of principal repayment was received. Liberia was recorded as having received $1.6 million of lend-lease credits during 1952, but apparently this represented delayed billings and expenditures by the U.S. Navy for the construction of a port in that country.

The U.S. Government received during 1952 some $78 million in principal repayments and $35 million in interest on the various lend-lease and postwar surplus property credits. The United Kingdom made the scheduled $119.3 million of principal and interest payments on the 1946 U.S. Treasury loan. Repayments of

[7] The Defense Materials Procurement Agency had available dollars and counterpart funds transferred to it by the Mutual Security Agency as well as dollars obtained under the Defense Production Act.

$27 million of principal and $7 million of interest were received on other active outstanding loans—the Philippine refunding operation, Maritime Administration ship sales, and various Reconstruction Finance Corporation loans.

g. TOTAL GOVERNMENT LONG-TERM

Summary data on the total long-term U.S. Government loans and credits utilized during the year, together with the principal repayments and interest collections, are given in Table 10. Excluded from the outstanding obligations as of the end of the year are World War I debts, which were considered no longer active.

Short-Term

The U.S. Government short-term assets abroad increased by a *net* of $45 million during 1952. Almost nothing was published about the sources of these flows beyond the fact that they represented changes in the short-term holdings of various Government agencies that conducted overseas operations. It is probable that accumulations of counterpart funds reserved for United States use under the various aid programs accounted for most of this outflow.

B. *PRIVATE FOREIGN INVESTMENT*

Government Encouragement of Private Investment

During 1952 both Congress and the Executive Branch, supported by most vocal sections of the business community[8] and by the findings and conclusions of several groups charged by the Government with looking into various aspects of the nation's international economic policies,[9] continued to emphasize the

[8] For a summary of recommendations made by various private business organizations and individuals, as well as Government-appointed groups, for steps to encourage private investment abroad, see "Staff Memorandum on Increasing the Flow of Private Capital into Underdeveloped Areas," *Committee Print*, House of Rep., Committee on Foreign Affairs, 82d Cong., 2d Sess., March 27, 1952, pp. 24-27. This report also gives much detail on the actions that had been taken by the Government to encourage private investment as of early 1952.

[9] The more important of these reports were: Maffry, A., *Program for Increasing Private Investment in Foreign Countries, op.cit.*; The President's Materials Policy Commission, *Resources for Freedom* (the so-called Paley Report), Wash., D.C., June 1952, Vol. I, pp. 63-72, and Vol. V, pp. 107-128; International Development Advisory Board, *Guidelines to Point Four*, Wash., D.C., June 5, 1952, pp. 5, 9-10;

TABLE 10

Long-Term Foreign Loans and Credits of the United States Government, by Program and by Area, 1952

(millions of dollars)

	Utilized[a]	Principal Collected[b]	Interest & Commissions Collected[c]	Outstanding Indebtedness Dec. 31, 1952[d]
By Program				
Export-Import Bank:				
On own account[e]	478	271	72	2503[e]
For Mutual Security Agency	281	*	16	1519
For Defense Production Administration	*	*	*	*
For Technical Cooperation Administration	7	*	—	7
Defense Materials Procurement Agency[f]	48	1[g]	*[g]	86
State Department:				
United Nations Building loan	7	1	—	63
Treasury Department:				
British loan	—	45	74	3660
Lend-lease credits[h]	2	24	22	1528
Surplus property	—	52	12	905
Philippine funding	—	3	1	28
Defense Department:				
Surplus property	—	—	—	157
General Services Administration:				
Surplus property	—	2	1	12
Maritime Administration	—	18	5	137
Reconstruction Finance Corporation	—	6	1	59
Total	823	423	204	10663
By Area				
Western Europe and Dependencies[i]	481	339	167	8665
Eastern Europe[j]	—	4	6	316
Near East and Africa[k]	60	7	5	228
Asia and the Pacific[l]	167	20	8	829
Latin America	101	52	18	548
Canada	6	1	*	14
United Nations	7	1	—	63
Total	823	423	204	10663

Details may not add to totals because of rounding.

* Less than $500,000.

a) "Utilized" means cash disbursements for loans and value of goods delivered under the various property credits, or principal amount of mortgages received for sales contracts or billings.

b) "Principal collected" represents the payments received and applied to the reduction of outstanding indebtedness, including payments received through agent banks of the Export-Import Bank.

(Notes continued at bottom of next page)

desirability of an expanded outflow of private foreign investment. Private investment, it was believed, would furnish necessary capital to complement the technical assistance being provided by the Point Four Program and would accelerate the economic development of underdeveloped countries, help enlarge the productive capacity abroad of goods needed for an expanding United States economy, offset some of the undesirable consequences at home and abroad of reducing official grant aid, and promote the spread of private enterprise abroad.

The Administration, as in earlier years,[1] sought to encourage private investment primarily by making available investment guaranties, by continuing to negotiate conventions on tax reform, and by attempting to arrange for additional investment treaties. Many members of Congress were dissatisfied with the efforts of the Administration in the past[2] and several amendments in general

---

c) "Interest and commissions collected" represents payments actually received.
d) "Outstanding indebtedness" represents utilizations from the beginning of the program through 1952 less principal repayments.
e) Includes loans utilized and principal collected by agent banks at Export-Import Bank risk. The total outstanding includes a participation of $7 million by another (unspecified) agency.
f) These data are through September 30, 1952 only.
g) Incomplete.
h) Includes lend-lease current credits, lend-lease credit offsets to grants, and lend-lease silver credits.
i) OEEC countries, including Greece and Turkey, plus Finland, Spain, and Yugoslavia.
j) Czechoslovakia, Hungary, Poland, and the U.S.S.R.
k) Egypt, Ethiopia, Iran, Israel, Lebanon, Liberia, Saudi Arabia, and the Union of South Africa.
l) Afghanistan, Australia, Burma, China, India, Indonesia, Japan, Korea, New Zealand, Pakistan, the Philippines, and Thailand.

Source: Compiled from Department of Commerce, *Foreign Aid by the United States Government*, Wash., D.C., September 30, 1952, Appendix Tables 6-8, and December 31, 1952, Appendix Tables 5-6.

---

and Department of State, *Pacific Coast Conference on Private Investment in International Development*, Economic Cooperation Series 36, Wash., D.C., December 1952.

[1] See *Survey—1951*, pp. 83-90, and the references cited therein for an account of policies and activities during that and earlier years.

[2] Congress was especially displeased with what it regarded as a virtual failure of the Administration to implement the so-called Benton Amendment to the Mutual Security Act of 1951, which was intended, among other things, to improve the climate abroad for private enterprise. In 1952 Congress therefore enacted the so-called Moody Amendment, directing the use of $100 million in counterpart funds to advance the purposes of the Benton Amendment. (See Chapter I, Section B, above.) For a statement by the Director for Mutual Security on what had been

terms were added to the Mutual Security Act in 1952 designed to eliminate barriers to, and provide incentives for, larger private investments abroad. Specifically, various agencies of the Government were ordered to "encourage a greater participation by private capital in the guaranty program," to "conduct a thorough study of the legal and other impediments . . . to private investment abroad" and ". . . the means whereby these impediments can be removed or decreased," to "accelerate a program of negotiating treaties of commerce and trade," and to " find and draw the attention of private enterprise to opportunities for investment and development in underdeveloped areas."[3]

a. INVESTMENT GUARANTIES

The investment guaranty program (commitments by Government agencies, in return for a fee, to *convert* into dollars certain returns on approved private direct foreign investments that could not be converted through normal channels and to *compensate* in dollars for losses arising from expropriation or confiscation of approved investments), initiated as a part of the European Recovery Program in 1948, was continued in 1952 under the Mutual Security Program.[4] This device had not accomplished, and was

done to implement the Benton Amendment, see "Mutual Security Act Extension," *Hearings on H.R. 7005*, House of Rep., Committee on Foreign Affairs, 82d Cong., 2d Sess., pp. 113-121, 1032-1038.

[3] Mutual Security Act of 1951, as amended, Section 516 b, c, d, e. For details on the background of these amendments, see *H. Rpt. No. 1922*, 82d Cong., 2d Sess., pp. 62-64, 104.

Spokesmen for the U.S. Government and several other governments, as well as some American businessmen, expressed the belief during the year that some of the deterrents to private international investment could be overcome if foreign capital were to invest "in partnership" with local capital, sharing both equity and management of the enterprises established. For a proposal designed to encourage private investment to assume a larger role in economic development abroad by the creation of special investment companies, see Javits, J. K., "Foreign Aid through Investment Companies," *Commercial and Financial Chronicle*, April 17, 1952, pp. 18-19.

Eric Johnston, Chairman of the International Development Advisory Board, suggested selecting a "laboratory country" in which the United States and the local government would make an intensive cooperative effort to discover means of overcoming the barriers to foreign investment. (See Department of State *Bulletin*, May 12, 1952, pp. 747-751.)

Two private agencies, the National Planning Association and the Carnegie Foundation, announced during the year a joint project to make case studies of successful United States investments abroad and to publish the results as a guide to future investors and policy makers.

[4] Summary information on the policies and activities of the investment guaranty

not accomplishing, what its supporters had anticipated, and the Sawyer Mission expressed a view often advanced by the business community when it stated in late 1952 that investment guaranties had served to reduce pressure on foreign governments desiring foreign investments to create the conditions necessary to attract it.[5]

Some Congressmen in early 1952 found it "disheartening" that only $45 million[6] of an authorized $200 million had been committed in investment guaranties, and there was some feeling that the Administration, which had been enthusiastic as to the potentialities of this device in 1949 and 1950, had not wholeheartedly supported the program. Nonetheless, Congress continued to believe that this technique could be effective in inducing larger private investments and, while no substantive changes were made in the law, the Director for Mutual Security was directed to encourage private investors to make more use of the guaranties and was asked to liberalize the criteria for investments eligible for guaranties.[7]

Private investors, however, showed even less interest than in the previous year and only eight new guaranties, totalling $5.9 million, were issued during 1952.[8] Two of the new guaranties

---

program prior to 1952 may be found in *Survey—1951*, pp. 84-86, and the other references cited there.

For a discussion and assessment in mid-1952 of the program, see The President's Materials Policy Commission, *Resources for Freedom, op.cit.*, Vol. V, pp. 110-115.

[5] *Foreign Commerce Weekly*, December 22, 1952, p. 17.

[6] This included nearly $12 million that had been used to insure the convertibility into dollars of the local currency proceeds of exports of informational media. During the first nine months of 1952 some $2.3 million of informational media guaranties were issued. From the beginning of this program in 1948 through September 30, 1952, such guaranties had been issued in the amount of $14 million, of which approximately $3 million had been cancelled and $7.1 million had been liquidated by the conversion by the U.S. Government of foreign currency receipts into dollars. These conversions may be compared with fees collected by the Government of only $212,000. Apparently the local currency acquired by the Government was used, or was to be used, to meet certain Governmental expenses abroad.

[7] For some suggested changes in the investment guaranty program designed to make it more attractive to business, see Maffry, A., *Program for Increasing Private Investment in Foreign Countries, op.cit.*, pp. 25-30.

In general, the U.S. Government approves applications on investments that seem likely to reduce the need of the country in which the investment is made for financial assistance from the U.S. Government.

[8] In addition, certain previous guaranties were increased by $0.2 million; but others were diminished by $2.6 million, including some cancellations and some

covered investments in Turkey, the first to be issued for investments outside Western Europe. Total commitments outstanding at the end of the year amounted to less than $35 million (covering investments in France, Germany, Italy, Turkey, and the United Kingdom), of which only $1.6 million covered guaranties against expropriation—for investments in Berlin and Italy. The Government had not been called upon by the end of 1952 to make any disbursements against these commitments and had collected $647,000 in fees.[9]

b. TAX REFORMS AND CONVENTIONS

The Administration continued during 1952 to seek bilateral tax conventions, designed to eliminate double taxation of income earned in one country by nationals or corporations of another and to prevent fiscal evasion. Usually two conventions were involved, one with respect to income taxes and one with respect to taxes on estates and inheritances, and, in general, these agreements provide for credits against domestic taxes for taxes paid to foreign governments. Negotiations were carried out during the year with Australia, Austria, Finland, and Belgium. No accord had been signed with the first two countries as the year ended but both types of conventions were signed with Finland, and a supplementary protocol was signed to an as yet unratified income tax treaty with Belgium. The Senate gave its advice and consent to ratification of the treaties with Finland and to the estate tax convention signed with Switzerland during the previous year,[1] but the convention and protocol with Belgium were still pending at year's end. The Union of South Africa completed ratification of the two conventions, together with protocols to each, ratified by the U.S. Senate in 1951. These, together with the estate tax convention with Switzerland, thus entered into effect, but those with Finland

reductions in face value as a result of the conversion into dollars of foreign currency earnings effected through regular banking channels.

[9] For more details on the operation of the investment guaranty program, see Export-Import Bank of Washington, *Fourteenth Semiannual Report to Congress, op.cit.*, pp. 28-29, and Appendix J, pp. 77-79, and Export-Import Bank of Washington, *Fifteenth Semiannual Report to Congress, op.cit.*, pp. 22-23, and Appendix J, pp. 79-80.

Details as to the administration and procedures employed in the program may be found in Mutual Security Agency, *Investment Guaranty Manual*, Wash., D.C., June 1952.

[1] See *Exec. Rpt. No. 13*, U. S. Senate, 82d Cong., 2d Sess., June 23, 1952.

(and Greece) still awaited action by the Governments of those countries.[2]

The Economic and Social Council of the United Nations again considered the question of providing tax incentives to international private investment. A draft resolution, introduced by Cuba, calling for a declaration approving the principle that earnings from foreign capital invested abroad should be taxed only in the country in which they were earned was supported by representatives of many of the so-called underdeveloped countries. The United States representatives did not openly oppose the resolution; but they had, apparently, notified the sponsors of the resolution that the U.S. Government did not feel in a position to take a firm stand on the proposal at that time, and in the public debates they argued that it raised a series of complex technical problems needing further study. Representatives from several of the other highly industrialized countries took a similar position, and the resolution, as finally approved, merely took note of double taxation as a deterrent to international investment and of the failure of measures already undertaken to overcome it, and then called upon the Fiscal Commission of the UN Department of Economic Affairs to make further studies of the problem and to report to the Council in 1953.[3]

Congress again failed in 1952 to take action on an Administration-supported bill, long urged by the business community,[4] to postpone the taxation of income earned by branches abroad until it was brought home, as existing law permitted in the case of foreign subsidiaries.

[2] For a calendar of tax conventions in effect at the beginning of 1952, see *Survey—1951*, Appendix Table IX, p. 308.

For a discussion of the then current tax exemptions, partial exemptions, and postponements for income earned abroad, see Gordon, N. N., "U.S. Taxation of Income from Abroad," *Foreign Commerce Weekly*, September 22, 1952, pp. 17-18.

[3] Economic and Social Council Resolution 416 D (XIV). For the debates on this resolution, see Economic and Social Council, *Official Records*, Fourteenth Session, 626th Meeting, July 1, 1952. It may be noted that the UN Department of Economic Affairs had already published a three-volume work on this subject: *International Tax Agreements*, UN Publication Sales Nos.: 1948.XVI.2; 1951.XVI.1; 1951.XVI.5.

[4] For example, see National Foreign Trade Council, *Tax Session-Forum*, Report of Proceedings at the 39th National Foreign Trade Convention, New York, November 19, 1952. See also Maffry, A., *Program for Increasing Private Investment in Foreign Countries, op.cit.*, pp. 30-37, and The President's Materials Policy Commission, *Resources for Freedom, op.cit.*, Vol. I, pp. 69-72 for a number of suggestions for tax incentives designed to encourage private foreign investment.

c. INVESTMENT TREATIES

Spokesmen for the business community continued to urge the Government to negotiate treaties of friendship, commerce, and navigation (commonly called "investment treaties"), and there was nothing to indicate that the Administration had changed its conviction that these treaties, which define how businessmen may operate in each other's country, would contribute to the development of a more congenial climate for private foreign investment. Nonetheless, the only major negotiations on such a treaty during the year were with Japan, and the only new agreement signed was a protocol to the 1934 treaty with Finland, slightly broadening the assurances of national treatment in regard to acquisitions of property.[5] Treaties that had been signed in earlier years with Colombia, Israel, Ethiopia, Denmark, and Greece, and a supplementary agreement to the 1949 treaty with Italy were considered by a subcommittee of the Senate but they were not reported out during the year, so no action was taken by the Senate.[6]

d. REMOVAL OF OBSTACLES TO PRIVATE FOREIGN INVESTMENT BY FOREIGN COUNTRIES

Government officials continued during 1952 to profess their belief that most of the action to encourage greater private capital outflows must come from those countries that wanted to receive foreign investment; the business and financial community held this view even more strongly. The Sawyer Mission, in adding its concurrence, stated that American capital could not be "talked into" other countries, but that given favorable conditions abroad it would flow of its own accord. The record on changes in the so-called investment climate abroad was mixed during 1952. Some countries, notably India and Pakistan, took action designed to entice private capital,[7] but Bolivia nationalized the tin mines,

[5] See *Survey—1951*, p. 87, and the references cited there for information on investment treaties in the years prior to 1952. For a calendar of such treaties in effect at the beginning of 1952, and so at the beginning of 1953, see *ibid.*, Appendix Table X, p. 309.

[6] See "Commercial Treaties," *Hearings*, U.S. Senate, Subcommittee of the Committee on Foreign Relations, 82d Cong., 2d Sess., May 9, 1952.

No reason was given for the failure of the Committee on Foreign Relations to report out the treaties; probably it was due to the pressure of other work rather than opposition to them.

[7] See, for example, Wilson, F. S., "Point IV Conditions the Investment Climate in Asia and Africa," *Foreign Commerce Weekly*, September 22, 1952, pp. 15ff;

including those with large United States investments, Guatemala, in effect, virtually confiscated many of the plantations owned by the United Fruit Company, and no settlement was reached in the Iran–Anglo-Iranian Oil Company dispute.

In the United Nations, spokesmen for the underdeveloped countries continued to show no great enthusiasm for private foreign investment, expressing fears that it would result in "interference" in the economic and political affairs of their countries and in "exploitation" of their national wealth and peoples. However, many of them stated that obtaining foreign capital by one means or another was a matter of great concern to their countries and, as compared with the previous years, they appeared more willing to accept private foreign capital, provided that it would contribute to a "balanced" economic development and would limit itself to "reasonable" returns on original investments. Late in the year, however, an unexpected development occurred, which, to judge from the immediate reaction of financial circles in the United States, seemed likely to make United States private investors even more cautious in making foreign investments. The delegate from Uruguay introduced a resolution in the Second Committee of the General Assembly calling upon the member states to "respect the right of each country to nationalize and freely exploit its natural wealth, as an essential factor of economic independence." The United States delegate argued that the resolution was unnecessary, since the right to nationalize was already well recognized internationally. It appeared, however, that the resolution would be approved, and the United States delegate therefore offered an amendment calling upon members to guarantee "just compensation" to owners of nationalized properties. This amendment was rejected. India had proposed a weaker amendment, recommending that member states in the exercise of their rights to exploit their natural wealth and resources should show regard for "the need for maintaining the flow of capital in conditions of security, mutual confidence, and economic cooperation among nations." The United States representative regarded the Indian amendment as inadequate, but it was adopted by the Com-

"New Trends Condition Investment in India and Pakistan," *Foreign Commerce Weekly*, November 3, 1952, pp. 13ff; and Binney, R. M., "World-Wide Credit Situation and Our Foreign Investments," *Commercial and Financial Chronicle*, February 26, 1953, pp. 12-13.

mittee. Subsequently, with strong support from the delegates of Iran, Bolivia, and several other Latin American countries, the Uruguayan resolution, as amended by the Indian proposal, was adopted by the Committee, with thirty-one votes in favor, the United States alone voting against it, and nineteen countries abstaining. Shortly thereafter the draft resolution was approved by the General Assembly in plenary session.[8]

Private Capital Movements[9]

Despite the continuing efforts by the U.S. Government to expand private United States investment abroad, the estimated *net* outflow during 1952 was about one-sixth smaller than it had been in the previous year and was nearly one-third less than in 1950. The decline, however, was due entirely to a sharp reduction in portfolio and short-term investments, and private direct investments in 1952 exceeded those of the previous two years.

a. LONG-TERM[1]

As Table 11 shows, private long-term portfolio investments during 1952 were only one-third those recorded in the previous year. In 1950 and 1951, United States investors had purchased large amounts of Canadian securities, especially municipal and provincial bonds. These purchases fell off during the first half of

[8] General Assembly Resolution 626 (VII), December 21, 1952. The more important documents relating to this resolution are: UN Doc. A/C.2/L.165; UN Doc. A/C.2/L.188; and General Assembly, *Official Records*, Seventh Session, Second Committee, 231st-238th Meetings, December 6-12, 1952. For a summary discussion of the entire issue, see *United Nations Bulletin*, January 1, 1953, pp. 41-46.

[9] For details on United States foreign investments during 1951 and earlier years, see Department of Commerce, *Balance of Payments of the United States 1949-1951*, Wash., D.C., 1952, pp. 80-113, 152-165. This document provides much detailed statistical information on private capital investment during the period as well as information on the methods used by the Department of Commerce in calculating and collecting such data. For additional data on 1952, see the following issues of Department of Commerce, *Survey of Current Business*, Wash., D.C.: June 1952, p. 11; August 1952, pp. 8ff; September 1952, pp. 7ff; and March 1953, pp. 7-12.

[1] Few data have been published as to the movement of foreign long-term capital into and out of the United States. The Department of Commerce estimated that during 1952 foreigners purchased a *net* of approximately $300 million of long-term U.S. Government bonds—as contrasted with a net liquidation of nearly $300 million in 1951—and invested a *net* of only $115 million in other long-term commitments. Of the latter, Western Europe accounted for one half and Canada for one third.

1952 as Canada relaxed credit restrictions and as the Canadian dollar rose in terms of the United States dollar, making borrowing in the United States by means of United States dollar-denominated bonds (a type increasingly resorted to, beginning in 1951) less attractive to the Canadians, in that the premium on the Canadian dollar, to the extent it was considered temporary, increased the effective rate of interest. During the last half of the year, there was a net inflow of portfolio investment from Canada, generally thought to be due to United States investors "cashing in" on the premium that had developed, as a consequence of the appreciation of the Canadian dollar, on the previously purchased Canadian dollar-denominated bonds. For the year as a whole the net outflow to Canada was estimated at only $8 million, as compared with $220 million in 1951. A small net outflow to Europe ($22 million) was also recorded during the year, arising in large part from the taking by private banks of a portion of the loan to Belgium negotiated by the Export-Import Bank. These small outflows were virtually offset by a net inflow from Latin America and the net rise of $120 million in portfolio investments for the year

TABLE 11

Net Outflow of Private Long-Term United States Capital, 1946-1952

(millions of dollars)

Year	*Total Outflow*	*Direct Investments*[a]	*Portfolio Investments*[b]
1946	59	183	—124
1947	810	724	86
1948	748	684	64
1949	796	786	10
1950	1168	702	466
1951	963	603	360
1952[p]	831	711	120

p) Preliminary.

a) Direct investments consist of (1) the United States equity in foreign incorporated companies in the management of which United States investors have an important voice and (2) the foreign branches of United States companies, including partnerships and sole proprietorships.

b) Portfolio investments consist of investments in stocks, bonds, real estate, etc. in which United States investors do not have an important voice in management. Included are the net purchases of debentures sold and guaranteed by the International Bank for Reconstruction and Development.

Sources: Department of Commerce, *Balance of Payments of the United States 1949-1951*, Wash., D.C., 1952, pp. 91-100, 156, and Department of Commerce, *Survey of Current Business*, Wash., D.C., March 1953, pp. 8-9.

was approximately equal to purchases of International Bank bonds and securities guaranteed by the Bank.

Estimated at $711 million, the *net* outflow of direct investments was the highest of any year since 1949. However, these investments fell off sharply during the last half of the year, when they were at an annual rate of just over $300 million, as compared with the all-time-high annual rate of $1.1 billion during the first six months. The major factor in the decline during the last six months was the completion of many previously initiated facilities in the oil industry in Latin America and the Middle East, together with an increase in the world supply of oil products relative to demand that reduced the need for further expansion. It was also probable, though confirmation was lacking, that the continuing trend toward nationalization of production facilities abroad contributed to the decline. Important shifts were registered in 1952 in the areas receiving direct investments from the United States. Some 53 percent of the net private direct investments in 1952 were in Canada, as compared with 45 percent in 1951. More striking was the fact that during the last half of the year under review over five sixths of the total net direct investments went to that country, and the Department of Commerce reported that "nearly every industry in [Canada] is being expanded by United States capital."[2] Latin America continued to be the second major recipient of direct private investments from the United States, receiving some 27 percent of the total for the year, but during the last half of 1952 this dropped to just over 10 percent. The net outflow of some $83 million to Western Europe and its dependencies in 1951 was replaced by a net inflow of some $54 million in the year under review. Details as to the area distribution of the rest of the direct investments have not been published, but it appears probable that less of it was in the Middle East than in the immediately preceding years and more in Africa and the Far East. Details on the industrial distribution of private direct investments in 1952 were also not available as this document went to press, but the Department of Commerce reported that, as in the preceding year, they were more diversified than in earlier postwar years, with less new

[2] Department of Commerce, *Survey of Current Business*, Wash., D.C., September 1952, p. 7.

A great many of the Canadian projects in which United States capital was participating were still in the early stages of development at the end of the year and it could therefore be anticipated that large additional investments would be made in the future.

investment, both absolutely and proportionately, going into petroleum and more into mining and smelting, manufacturing, distribution, and agriculture.

The value of private direct long-term investments abroad is also affected by the reinvestment of earnings—defined as undistributed profits of foreign incorporated subsidiaries.[3] Data on reinvested earnings during 1952 have not yet been published, but, as Table 12 shows, such reinvestments have been substantial in recent years and in 1951 they exceeded the net new capital outflows. In the period from the end of World War II through 1950 this factor had accounted for over four fifths of the estimated net additions to the value of manufacturing investments, about one half in the case of distribution, two thirds in agriculture, and one third in mining and smelting, and it had exceeded by a substantial amount the net additions to the value of public utility investments. In contrast, during the first five postwar years only about one sixth of the additions to the value of foreign petroleum investments were attributable to such reinvested earnings, and the fact that over half of the increase in value during 1951 was due to this factor represented a striking shift.[4]

b. SHORT-TERM

The recorded net outflow of private short-term capital (claims with maturity of one year or less) declined during 1952 to an estimated $65 million, the smallest amount for any of the postwar years except 1949, when there was a large net inflow. The short-term capital movements were dominated by a huge increase (nearly $200 million) during the first half of the year in unpaid commercial drafts on Latin American importers, mostly in Brazil; there was a small decline in the total amount of these credits outstanding during the last half of the year. Except for Latin

[3] Entirely apart from possible inaccuracies in the data on reinvested earnings, it must be recognized that they may not, for any given time period, give an accurate picture of capital formation in the sense of investment in plant, equipment, and necessary working capital. For example, the undistributed profits of subsidiaries may result from the unwillingness of foreign authorities to permit the transfer of profits, and such funds may then not be reinvested in the usual sense but simply accumulated as idle balances.

[4] Details are not available as to the amount of investment in the petroleum industry (or in any other industry) arising from reinvested earnings of branches, as distinct from subsidiaries, since the reinvestments of branch earnings are included in new capital outflows.

TABLE 12

Factors Affecting Value of United States Private Direct Investments Abroad, 1950 and 1951[a]

(millions of dollars; reduction [—])

	1950			*1951*		
Area and Industry	*Capital Movements*	*Reinvested Earnings*	*Total*	*Capital Movements*	*Reinvested Earnings*	*Total*
Area						
Canada	265	224	489	271	228	499
Latin America	191	76	267	187	252	439
OEEC Countries	75	64	139	77	134	211
OEEC Dependencies	9	—12	—3	5	—2	3
Other	162	78	240	63	124	187
Total	702	430	1132	603	736	1339
Industry						
Manufacturing	119	292	411	140	365	505
Petroleum	364	46	410	184	206	390
Mining and Smelting	68	37[b]	105	96	80[c]	176
Distribution	59	27[d]	86	81	64	145
Agriculture	—4	7	3	37	3	40
Public Utilities	16	14	30	—12	4	—8
Miscellaneous	80	7	87	77	14	91
Total	702	430	1132	603	736	1339

a) These data are provisional and were in the process of revision in 1952 as the result of a new census. The first tabulation of the new data was published in Department of Commerce, *Survey of Current Business*, December 1952, pp. 7ff., and showed the total value of American direct investments abroad as of December 31, 1950 as some $1.7 billion less than was shown in the sources from which the data in the above table were taken. Major factors in this decline were the elimination of enterprises now within Communist territories; more accurate data on the extent of war damage in Germany, Austria, and the Far East; and the reduction in the dollar value of foreign enterprises resulting from currency devaluations. Data have not yet been published as to the effect of these adjustments on the yearly figures cited above.

b) Includes —$2 million of "other factors," chiefly losses on liquidation.

c) Includes $33 million of "other factors," chiefly adjustments of book value, such as write up of assets.

d) Includes —$11 million of "other factors," chiefly losses on liquidation.

Source: Department of Commerce, *Survey of Current Business*, Wash., D.C., September 1952, p. 8. See this source for additional details.

America, and for Western Europe, which recorded a small net outflow, there was a net inflow during the year from all the other major areas of the world, principally the result of foreign official institutions' and foreign banks' repaying loans granted earlier by United States banks.

Note on German and Japanese Debt Settlements

Negotiations to settle Germany's external debts, which were begun in 1951, were continued throughout 1952. At an early point in the negotiations the U.S. Government agreed, on condition that a "reasonable" settlement be made with respect to Germany's prewar external debts, to reduce its claims on payment for postwar aid from $3.2 billion to $1.2 billion (37 cents on the dollar), and the British and French Governments, on the same condition, agreed to reduce their smaller claims on payment for postwar assistance in lesser proportions.[5] Following these decisions, the Tripartite Commission on German Debts (France, the United Kingdom, and the United States) called a London Conference on German External Debts, at which were represented Germany and twenty-two creditor countries, including representatives of both official and private creditors. This Conference negotiated an Intergovernmental Agreement on German External Debts, which dealt with the external claims against Germany arising prior to World War II. Reparations and analogous claims arising out of World War II and debts of the city of Berlin and its public utilities were excluded from the negotiations.

A series of formal agreements covering both the official and the private claims was signed in February 1953; when ratified by Germany and the other countries concerned, it will provide for the payment by Germany of the equivalent of $3.27 billion to creditors in thirty countries. Of this total, $1.75 billion will be paid to the U.S. Government and its nationals, with the U.S. Government receiving approximately $1.3 billion[6] and private creditors receiving $450 million. Payments to the U.S. Government and its nationals were scheduled to begin in April 1953, with total payments of $50 million a year for five years and $90 million a year thereafter until all the obligations were paid.

With respect to the holdings of private creditors, the settlement

[5] See *Survey—1951*, p. 47n.
For a charge by Senator Gillette that the effect of the Government's action was to transfer to the United States taxpayers the load of individual bondholders, and a reply by Assistant Secretary of State McFall, see Department of State *Bulletin*, March 24, 1952, pp. 473-477.

[6] The payments to the U.S. Government include $1 billion for postwar aid, excluding surplus property; $200 million for surplus property provided after the war by the U.S. Government; and $97.5 million in settlement of awards to the U.S. Government by the Mixed Claims Commission.

included the claims of the holders of the Dawes Loan and the Young Loan, as well as other bonds of German public bodies and German corporate bonds. For the most part, principal on these obligations was not reduced, but maturities were extended, and in most cases interest rates were reduced. It was agreed that loan contracts containing gold clauses would be paid as if the currencies of issue had been defined in United States dollars instead of in gold and that bondholders who agreed to accept payment in deutsche marks would receive more rapid amortization.[7]

During the summer the American Foreign Bondholders Protective Council carried on negotiations in New York with Japanese Government officials with the aim of arranging a settlement of $76.2 million of prewar Japanese bonds payable in United States dollars and the $50 million of interest arrearages on them that had accumulated since 1942. Parallel discussions were held at the same time between Japanese officials and representatives of British and French bondholders. The French and Japanese negotiators were unable to reach an agreement, but an accord was arrived at in late September between Japan and the United States and British negotiators that gave exceptionally favorable treatment to the creditors. The Japanese Government assumed responsibility for the bonds issued by various cities and corporate bodies and the services on outstanding issues were resumed at once and at the full contractual rates. The maturity dates for the outstanding bonds were extended for ten years, except for a few non-dollar issues that were extended for fifteen years, but all other contractual obligations were honored. The interest arrearages were to be paid in full in equal installments during the next ten years, and payments on interest arrearages and on principal were scheduled to begin in late 1952.[8]

[7] For the full text of the Intergovernmental Agreement on German External Debts, see Department of State *Bulletin*, August 18, 1952, pp. 252-260. For a schedule of major German issues known to be outstanding in the United States and the German law of August 1952 on validation, designed to separate valid obligations from those looted or otherwise acquired illegally during the war, see Department of State *Bulletin*, October 20, 1952, pp. 608-614. For a discussion of the various agreements signed in February 1953, see Department of State *Bulletin*, March 9, 1953, pp. 373-380.

[8] For details on the Japanese settlement, see *Journal of Finance and Commerce* (Tokyo), August 15, 1952, pp. 15-18, and November 15, 1952, pp. 2ff. Summary statements of the agreement can be found in *New York Times*, September 29, 1952, p. 1, and *Wall Street Journal*, September 29, 1952.

V · INTERNATIONAL FINANCIAL RESOURCES: THE BANK, THE FUND, AND PROPOSED NEW INSTITUTIONS

DESPITE growing opposition from many members, the U.S. Government during 1951 had continued to support the International Monetary Fund in its major policies of carefully husbanding its resources, of assuring itself that the prospects of early repayment were good before approving any withdrawals by members, of insisting that while there were many impediments to an immediate and complete relaxation of exchange restrictions there were many instances where such restrictions could and should be relaxed, of favoring fixed over flexible rates of exchange, and of opposing any change in the United States price of gold or the policy of regarding the primary role of gold to be that of serving as international reserves.

During 1951 the Fund actively searched for new principles that would permit it to expand its lending activities and it abandoned its earlier policy of attempting to specify the conditions under which the gold-producing nations could sell gold at premium prices. Still, some members favored making fundamental changes in its policies and terms of reference. The U.S. Government, however, while recognizing that many exceptions to the Fund's "rules of conduct" might be called for, continued to believe that the Fund's approach and objectives were still the proper ones and that if they were abandoned there was no likelihood in the foreseeable future of obtaining international agreement on principles to replace them.[1]

The U.S. Government in 1951, as in previous years, was also satisfied with the level of operations of the International Bank and with its policy of largely restricting its loans to aiding the so-called

[1] For a summary of the Fund's activities during 1951 and earlier years, see *Survey–1951*, pp. 127-141, and the references cited therein.

underdeveloped areas.[2] United States officials disagreed with those members of the Bank who urged that institution greatly to expand its level of operations, and they strongly, but unsuccessfully, opposed a move in the United Nations to consider the possibility of creating a new International Development Authority that would make grants-in-aid and low-interest, long-term loans to help the underdeveloped countries accelerate their economic development. The United States did, however, agree on the desirability of exploration of the possibility of establishing an International Finance Corporation to make equity investments and to lend to private industries operating in the underdeveloped countries.

A. *INTERNATIONAL MONETARY FUND*[3]

When the Fund began operations in March 1947 it was hoped that by the end of five years the repair of the disruption and dislocation caused by World War II would have been substantially completed, that a balanced system of multilateral world trade and payments would have been attained, and that restrictions and discrimination in trade and payments would no longer

[2] For a summary of the Bank's activities during 1951, see *Survey—1951*, pp. 120-126.

Membership in both the Bank and the Fund was raised to fifty-four during 1952 with the signing of the Articles of Agreement by Burma, Japan, Western Germany, and Jordan. These new members raised the total amount of the Fund's quotas to just over $8.7 billion and the subscribed capital of the Bank to the equivalent of over $9 billion. The Boards of Governors of the two institutions at their seventh annual meeting in September formally approved the applications for membership of Haiti and Indonesia but by the end of the year these two countries had not yet taken formal action ratifying their membership.

[3] The more important official sources for information on the policies and activities of the Fund are the following publications of the International Monetary Fund, all published in Washington, D.C.: *Annual Report, 1952*, June 1952; *Third Annual Report on Exchange Restrictions*, May 1952; *International Financial News Survey* (weekly); *International Financial Statistics* (monthly); the various mimeographed *Documents* prepared for the Seventh Annual Meeting of the Board of Governors of the International Monetary Fund, held at Mexico City in September 1952; and *Summary Proceedings of the Seventh Annual Meeting of the Board of Governors*, 1952. See also the following publications of the National Advisory Council on International Monetary and Financial Problems: *Third Special Report to the President and to the Congress*, Wash., D.C., June 1952 (also available as *House Document No. 522*, 82d Cong., 2d Sess.); *Semiannual Report to the President and to the Congress for the Period October 1, 1951—March 31, 1952*, Wash., D.C., June 1952; and *Semiannual Report to the President and to the Congress for the Period April 1—September 30, 1952*, Wash., D.C., January 1953.

be considered necessary by most, if not all, member governments. That is, 1952 was to witness the end of the transition period.

The Fund acknowledged in its 1952 *Annual Report* that stable international equilibrium had not been attained, that international payments difficulties had been recurrent or continuous, and that most countries had made little or no progress toward the Fund's objectives of general convertibility of currencies and unimpeded multilateral trade or had found it necessary to reverse some of the steps taken in that direction. In other words, the Fund, and so the United States National Advisory Council on International Monetary and Financial Problems, recognized that the world for which the former was designed did not yet exist.

The Fund cited special disturbances that had complicated international trade and payments problems for its various members, but it stated that the frequent recurrence of balance of payments difficulties suggested that an explanation should be sought "in terms of more fundamental and pervasive influences." In the judgment of the Fund's Executive Directors, the most basic reason for the persistence of these problems after the restoration of high levels of production was that many countries had followed fiscal and monetary policies aimed at achieving higher levels of consumption and investment than could be covered out of the resources available.[4] They recognized these policies as efforts to translate into reality the widespread desire of people for economic betterment and security, and they acknowledged that the added burden of increased armament had been undertaken by many of these countries.[5] Nonetheless, it was argued that inflation must result from such policies, though it might temporarily be held in check by price controls and subsidies, and that as a consequence demands for imports would be increased while the availability of goods for export would be reduced. In these circumstances, it stated, the use of import restrictions and exchange controls seemed inevitable to many countries.

While the Fund officials stated that the repeated occurrence of

[4] In its *Annual Report* the Fund noted with approval the increased use of fiscal and credit measures in 1951 and early 1952 to combat inflation.

[5] The Czechoslovak representative in ECOSOC during the year charged that this inflation was almost entirely the result of the "capitalist armaments drive." (UN Economic and Social Council, *Official Records*, Fourteenth Session, 584th Meeting, May 29, 1952.)

difficulties in international payments was to be explained mainly in terms of inflationary pressures, they also believed that restrictionist trade policies by payments-surplus countries contributed importantly to the international imbalance. Agricultural protection and other protective policies of the United States were specifically criticized. The *Annual Report* also cited other complicating factors: the inadequacy of international reserves outside the United States, the disruption of the private international short-term capital market, the decline of East-West trade, and various political influences and tensions.

John W. Snyder, Secretary of the Treasury of the United States and Governor of the Fund for the United States, fully concurred in and approved the Fund's report during the meeting of the Governors of the Fund in Mexico City in September.

Lending Policy and Operations

For at least two years prior to the annual meeting of the Governors of the Fund in 1952, the policies and practices by which the Fund's resources were made available to members had been under review by the Executive Directors and staff with a view toward increasing the use of these resources, while assuring that such use would be only temporary and would tend to further the basic objectives of the institution. One proposal had been advanced in May 1951 but by the end of that year had found no takers.[6] Later that year a new schedule of charges for the use of resources was announced that was intended to encourage short-term use of the Fund's currencies and to discourage longer-term use.[7]

On February 13, 1952 the Executive Board issued another policy statement, which it regarded as a liberalization of the criteria for the use of its resources and one further designed to end the period of its relative inactivity. Two basic principles of the new policy were (a) that currencies purchased from the Fund should not remain outstanding beyond the period "reasonably

[6] For an account of this proposal, its reception, and the failure of the members to make any immediate increase in the use of the Fund's resources, see *Survey—1951*, pp. 128-130.

[7] For the old and new schedules of charges, see International Monetary Fund, *Annual Report, 1952, op.cit.*, Appendix II, p. 91, or any issue of International Monetary Fund, *International Financial Statistics*, from March through December 1952. The lengths of time loans could be outstanding before consultation was required were also reduced.

related" to the payments problem for which the purchases were made[8] and (b) that the granting of access to the Fund's resources would depend in large part on whether the policies the member planned to pursue following the receipt of currency from the Fund would be adequate to overcome the payments problem within the period. It was specified in the general policy statement that access to the Fund's resources would not be denied to a member because that member was in difficulties; that "credit-worthiness" would be taken into account; that there was no intent to limit drawings to any previously determined specific and defined difficulties; that the "overwhelming benefit of any doubt" would be given to drawings within a member's so-called "gold tranche"; and that the Fund would consider extension of the repayment time under certain circumstances. The possibilities were also held out that concurrence might be reached in advance for drawings should certain agreed-upon developments occur and that arrangements might be made for drawings to meet "special short-run situations."[9]

The Fund stated that in implementing the new lending policy it would proceed on a "case-by-case basis," with the hope that a body of practical criteria would be built up so that members would be better able to judge how any request they made would be received. This statement, together with the decision on drawings within the gold tranches, reflected the attempt by the Executive Directors to establish working procedures of some sort to resolve the long-extant differences of view among members as to whether access to the Fund should be "automatic." The U.S. Government had long opposed any automatic access and while it approved the new approach it emphasized that under the existing circumstances, "Each case of a drawing must be considered on its own merits by the Fund. . . ."[1]

[8] It was stated that as a general rule this period should not exceed three to five years, and that it would become shorter as successive tranches of the members' quotas were used. This was the most specific definition the Fund had yet given to its criteria for "temporary use" of its resources.

[9] For the text of the policy statement, see International Monetary Fund, *Annual Report, 1952, op.cit.*, Appendix I, pp. 87-90.

A member wishing to purchase currencies from the Fund was expected under the new policy to include in its request a statement that it would comply with the principles of this policy. The policy enunciated in February was to be effective until December 31, 1953 and was to be reviewed before that date.

[1] National Advisory Council, *Third Special Report, op.cit.*, p. 17.

Notwithstanding this liberalization in the Fund's lending policy, Managing Director Rooth stated in September, "I do not believe that we can be satisfied that we have done all that is necessary to facilitate the use of the Fund's resources for attaining the purposes of the Fund."[2] He stated that in a world where total exports were at the rate of the equivalent of $80 billion annually and where international reserves were low and international short-term credit limited, there were well-founded needs for a wider use of the Fund's resources.[3]

The Governor for the United Kingdom recalled at the September meeting the "disillusionment" that had attended the Fund's earlier operations, and he applauded the statement of the Managing Director as well as the policy declaration of February, which he described as "unfreezing" the Fund's resources. However, he saw this as only the beginning and asserted that, since the world had not developed into the kind of place that had been envisaged by the creators of the Fund, the Fund should go further in considering how it could adapt its policies to make itself into the kind of mechanism that would serve the world that existed. This general sentiment for expanded operations by the Fund was common among many of the Fund's members and was repeatedly voiced both at the annual meeting and in the United Nations. The U.S. Administration, on the other hand, stated that it believed the Fund "has made as much progress as could be expected in view of the postwar economic situation and the policies of the member countries," and that it did not believe any amendments to the Articles of Agreement should be made at that time.[4]

The Fund made six sales of currency during 1952, all of United States dollars, totalling $85.1 million, as shown in Table 13. This was more than twice the amount in the previous year and may be compared with no sales at all in 1950. The Brazilian purchase of $37.5 million and the Iranian purchase of $2.2 million had been

[2] International Monetary Fund, *Summary Proceedings of the Seventh Annual Meeting of the Board of Governors, op.cit.*, p. 19.

[3] Currency sales by the Fund during the entire period from 1947 through 1952 were $897 million, of which $193 million had been repurchased. This amount may be compared with total assets of the Fund of more than $8.5 billion, of which more than $3.5 billion was in gold and United States dollars.

[4] National Advisory Council, *Third Special Report, op.cit.*, p. 18. For an unofficial analysis urging revisions in the Articles of Agreement, see Triffin, R., "Monetary Reconstruction in Europe," *International Conciliation*, June 1952, pp. 268-278.

TABLE 13

International Monetary Fund Exchange Transactions, 1947-1952

(millions of dollar equivalents)

	1951	*1952*	*Total 1947-1952*
Currency Sold	*34.6*	*85.1*[a]	*897.0*[b,c]
U.S. dollars	6.6	85.1	851.6[c]
British pounds	28.0	0	34.0
Belgian francs	0	0	11.4
Currency Bought	*34.6*	*85.1*	*897.0*[b,c]
Australian pounds	0	30.0	50.0
Belgian francs	0	0[a]	33.0
Brazilian cruzeiros	28.0	37.5	103.0
British pounds	0	0	300.0
Chilean pesos	0	0	8.8
Costa Rican colones	0	0	1.3
Czechoslovakian korunas	0	0	6.0
Danish kroner	0	0	10.2
Egyptian pounds	0	0	3.0
Ethiopian dollars	0	0	0.6
Finnish markkas	0	4.5[a]	4.5
French francs	0	0	125.0
Indian rupees	0	0	100.0
Iranian rials	6.6	2.2	8.8
Mexican pesos	0	0	22.5
Netherlands guilders	0	0	75.3
Nicaraguan cordobas	0	0	0.5
Norwegian kroner	0	0	9.6
Paraguayan guaranies	0	0.9	0.9
Turkish liras	0	10.0	15.0
Union of South Africa pounds	0	0	10.0
Yugoslav dinars	0	0	9.0
Currency Repurchased	*46.7*	*113.0*	*192.8*
U.S. dollars and gold	46.7	113.0	192.8
Other currencies	0	0	0
Currency Resold[d]	*46.7*	*113.0*	*192.8*
Belgian francs	0	0	21.6
Brazilian cruzeiros	0	65.5	65.5
Chilean pesos	3.4	3.7	7.1
Costa Rican colones	0	0	2.2
Egyptian pounds	0	0	8.5
Ethiopian dollars	0.3	0	0.6
Lebanese pounds[d]	0.9	0	0.9
Mexican pesos	22.5	0	22.5
Netherlands guilders	0	27.3	27.3
Nicaraguan cordobas	0	0	0.5
Norwegian kroner	9.6	0	9.6
Peruvian soles[d]	0	3.1	3.1
Swedish kronor[d]	0	8.0	8.0
Syrian pounds[d]	0	0.4	0.4
Turkish liras	0	5.0	5.0
Union of South Africa pounds	10.0	0	10.0

(Notes at bottom of next page)

negotiated before the Executive Board's new policy decision was proclaimed but they were within its terms. The purchases of $30 million by Australia and $4.5 million by Finland were hailed by the Fund as fulfilling the intent of the February decision, and the purchases by Turkey and Paraguay came within the terms of the new gold-tranche policy.

A new type of service made available to members during the year, and anticipated in the February decision, was a stand-by commitment for the sale of foreign currencies. Under this arrangement, a member could obtain the right to draw amounts up to an agreed limit at any time within six months, renewable for successive six-month periods up to a total of five years, without any new investigation at the time of drawing. Belgium obtained a stand-by commitment for $50 million in June (see below for details) and renewed it in December. Finland obtained a similar stand-by commitment for $5 million in December. No drawings had been made under either of these commitments at the end of the year.[5]

For the third successive year repurchases from the Fund exceeded new sales, as seven countries bought back the equivalent of $113 million of their own currencies, a total greater than the

a) There were outstanding on December 30, 1952 commitments on stand-by agreements to buy members' currencies totalling the equivalent of $55 million, consisting of a commitment to purchase amounts up to $50 million of Belgian francs and a commitment to purchase amounts up to $5 million of Finnish markkas.
b) There were no currency sales by the International Monetary Fund in 1950.
c) This sum is not consistent with totals appearing in previous editions of the *Survey* because of a change in the Fund's manner of reporting a transaction that occurred in 1948. In that year Norway purchased $6.1 million for gold, in compliance with the Articles of Agreement of the International Monetary Fund, which provide: "Any member desiring to obtain, directly or indirectly, the currency of another member for gold shall, provided that it can do so with equal advantage, acquire it by sale of gold to the Fund." (Article V, Section 6a.) This purchase by Norway is no longer reported as an "Exchange Transaction" in *International Financial Statistics.*
d) Repurchase obligations of members are not restricted solely to cases where purchases have been made by a member from the Fund but may also arise from original payment of less than 25 percent of a member's quota in gold, or from other cases where the Fund acquires amounts of a member's currency in excess of its quota. (Article V, Section 7.)

Sources: Statistical data from International Monetary Fund, *International Financial Statistics*, Wash., D.C., February 1953, p. 6. Notes from various other International Monetary Fund publications.

[5] Finland made a purchase of $2 million in January 1953.

sum of all previous repurchases from the Fund (see Table 13). Still, of the equivalent of $704.2 million purchased from the Fund and un-repurchased at the end of 1952, some $570 million represented purchases made in 1947 and 1948, $300 million of it by the United Kingdom and $125 million by France. That is, a large part of the pre-1952 drawings had in effect become long-term loans.[6]

Another aspect of the Fund's lending policy that again received attention during the year was the role that it should play in connection with problems created by widespread depressions. An international committee of experts in 1951 had recommended, among other things, that the resources of the Fund be increased and that the Fund be prepared greatly to liberalize its lending policies in the event of a major recession.[7] These recommendations received support from the representatives of many countries, but in the United Nations Economic and Social Council debates on them in 1952 the delegate for the United States expressed regret over the failure of the experts to recommend *national* measures to increase international reserves, pointed out that the Fund already had substantial resources that were not being used, suggested that increasing the Fund's resources would be a difficult problem, and, finally, gave assurances that if the time came when the Fund ran short of resources, the United States would "give the matter proper consideration."[8]

Officials of the Fund recognized that it had important responsibilities in these matters and stated that the Fund could assist members with serious balance of payments difficulties in times of depression. But they insisted that the basic problems of depression could not be overcome with short-term credit and that the principal anti-cyclical activities must be national measures to "stimulate effective demand," chiefly within the large industrialized nations. The Fund's Executive Directors stated that they had con-

[6] During the fiscal year ending April 30, 1952 the Fund's total income was $3.3 million, as compared with expenditures of $4.8 million, leaving a deficit of $1.5 million. Comparable figures for the previous year were $2.7 million, $4.6 million, and $1.9 million, respectively. The net excess of expenditures over income from the inauguration of the Fund in 1947 through April 1952 was $7.2 million.

[7] See *Measures for International Economic Stability*, Report by a Group of Experts Appointed by the Secretary-General, UN Publication Sales No.: 1951.II. A.2, pp. 11-13, 32-41. See also the related recommendations in 1949 and the Fund's reaction to them in *Survey—1950*, pp. 161-166.

[8] See UN Economic and Social Council, *Official Records*, Fourteenth Session, 624th Meeting, June 30, 1952.

sidered the proposal for enlarging the resources of the Fund but had concluded that such an increase "is not a question for action at the present time."[9] This conclusion was emphasized when the National Advisory Council told Congress in midyear that it believed "that the Fund's dollar resources are adequate for present needs, or requirements in the near future, so that it does not recommend a change in the United States subscription at this time."[1]

The final resolution passed by the Economic and Social Council expressed confidence that the Fund would act to lessen the impact of depressions on members' balances of payments and urged the Fund to apply its rules flexibly, to give careful consideration to the recommendations made in the UN experts' study, and to be prepared to use its resources promptly and as fully as would be consistent with its Articles of Agreement.[2] Managing Director Rooth stated to the Council that he would "bear in mind" the experts' recommendations.

Foreign Exchange Rate Policy

a. EXCHANGE RESTRICTIONS

The Articles of Agreement of the International Monetary Fund[3] provided a transitional period of five years during which members could maintain restrictions on current-account transactions, engage in discriminatory or multiple-currency practices, and place limits on the conversion of foreign-held balances without violating the obligations of membership. But the Articles of Agreement also required that any member still retaining such restrictions at the end of that time must consult the Fund about their further retention, and that similar consultations must be made annually thereafter until all such restrictions were removed. This transition

[9] International Monetary Fund, *Annual Report, 1952, op.cit.*, p. 46.

[1] National Advisory Council, *Third Special Report, op.cit.*, p. 18.

[2] Economic and Social Council Resolution 427 (XIV), July 10, 1952.

In another resolution, the Economic and Social Council called upon the Secretary-General to appoint a new committee to prepare, in the light of recent experience in various parts of the world and pertinent UN studies already available, a report on national and international measures to reconcile the attainment and maintenance of full employment with avoidance of the harmful effects of inflation. This committee was to report to the Council in 1953.

[3] Particularly Art. XIV, Sect. 2.

period expired in March 1952, at which time only seven[4] of the fifty-four members were not availing themselves of the transitional period privileges and had accepted the obligations of convertibility. The series of compulsory consultations began in the spring of 1952, but they were confidential and no details on substantive issues were provided the public.

Before the discussions began, it was recognized by the Fund, as well as by most member governments, including that of the United States, that the ideal of a more or less complete abandonment of exchange restrictions by early 1952 would not be possible. Nonetheless, the U.S. Government hoped that the consultations might at least serve to bring "a measure of order out of the existing mass of restrictions" and to reduce "their discriminatory impact."[5] Spokesmen for the Fund maintained earlier in the year that some relaxations were feasible and desirable and they repeated during the year previous statements that restrictive practices offered no appropriate or lasting solutions to fundamental economic difficulties, that they were appropriate only when necessary to protect a country's balance of payments and only when accompanied by parallel measures to insure their temporary character. The Fund also stressed that restrictions by some countries tended to impede the efforts of others to abandon them, helped to distort price relationships, and sometimes served to permit a delay in the making of needed fundamental readjustments.

During the September meetings of the Board of Governors in Mexico City, United States Secretary of the Treasury Snyder "noted with satisfaction" the Fund's consultations on exchange restrictions, and he took occasion again to say that the United States had continually stressed the desirability of the members' moving toward nondiscrimination, multilateral trade, and payments free from exchange restrictions. Although the official position of the United States on these matters was unchanged, the press reported that when it came to individual cases United States officials were more sympathetic than in the past with the arguments of those nations that decided to maintain restrictions.[6]

There was no publicly available evidence during the year that

[4] Canada, El Salvador, Guatemala, Honduras, Mexico, Panama, and the United States.

[5] National Advisory Council, *Third Special Report*, *op.cit.*, p. 13.

[6] *New York Times*, September 3, 1952, p. 39.

the Fund consultations had resulted in any appreciable relaxation of exchange restrictions or that, except in the case of Belgium,[7] the Fund had advised any member to do so. For the world as a whole it appeared that exchange restrictions were greater at the end of 1952 than at the beginning.[8]

* * * * *

There were repeated press reports during the year that the British Government and the authorities in the other sterling area countries were actively and seriously seeking for ways to restore the convertibility of sterling and much time was spent in discussing this question at the Commonwealth Economic Conference, held in London in late November and early December. Official statements as to the precise nature of the proposals under discussion were not published and the official communiqué issued at the end of the conference was notable for its platitudes and generalities. This communiqué stated that it was agreed that it was important for both the sterling area and the rest of the world that "sterling should resume its full role as a medium of world trade and exchange" but that "the convertibility of sterling . . . can only be reached by progressive stages." It went on to state that the achievement of convertibility would depend, basically, upon three conditions: (a) the continuing success of the sterling Commonwealth countries in combatting internal inflation, establishing "an adequate and stable external balance," increasing their international reserves, and expanding the production of essential supplies; (b) "the prospect that trading nations [it was clearly implied that the United States had especially large responsibilities here] will adopt trade policies which are conducive to the expansion of world trade"; and (c) "the availability of adequate financial support through the International Monetary Fund or otherwise."[9] The press commonly interpreted the communiqué to mean that no precise plans had yet been agreed upon but that there was going to be a creep rather than a dash toward convertibility and that no move would be made until, among other

[7] See Chapter VI, Section D, below.

[8] For details of the currency restrictions in effect in each country belonging to the Fund as of early 1952, see International Monetary Fund, *Third Annual Report on Exchange Restrictions*, Wash., D.C., May 1952.

[9] For the full text of the communiqué, see Department of State *Bulletin*, March 16, 1953, pp. 397-399.

things, the United States—directly and/or via the Fund—agreed to provide a sizeable "cushion of liquidity." Since the end of World War II the United States Executive Branch had been keenly interested in the return to convertibility of sterling but the outgoing Administration in Washington in the fall of 1952 made no public statements as to its reaction to the discussions in London. As the year ended plans were being made for financial discussions between British and American officials in Washington sometime in the spring of 1953, after the new Republican Administration had taken office.

Fund officials also made no public statements during the year on the specific question of sterling convertibility, but at the annual meeting in September the Managing Director of the Fund took occasion to point out that exchange restrictions in an important country could seriously affect the payments position of other countries, and he stated that if countries occupying key positions in international trade could restore convertibility, others would benefit and a general move to convertibility might be facilitated. On the other hand, the press reported there was some concern and even displeasure from various members of the European Payments Union over the rumored proposals to make sterling convertible. These spokesmen were reported as fearing that the convertibility of sterling might complicate their problems, both by possibly resulting in the tightening of import restrictions by sterling area countries on non-dollar imports and by causing Continental importers to hold back their sterling earnings from the European Payments Union's monthly clearings, thus making Britain such a large creditor of the Union as to "wreck the whole mechanism."[1] It was reported that the European officials expressing these views were urging that no move be made to make sterling convertible except as part of a concerted action to restore convertibility to all major European currencies.[2]

[1] *The Economist*, January 31, 1953, p. 295.

[2] For more details on some of the issues involved in a resumption of sterling convertibility as seen by persons in the United Kingdom, see Robbins, L., "The International Economic Problem," *Lloyd's Bank Review*, January 1953, pp. 1-24; *The Statist*, January 17, 1953, pp. 77-78, and January 24, 1953, pp. 114-115; *The Banker* (London), December 1952, pp. 319-324, January 1953, pp. 7-15, and February 1953, pp. 67-72; *The Bankers Magazine* (London), January 1953, pp. 1-5; *Journal of the Institute of Bankers in Ireland* (Dublin), January 1953, pp. 33-63; Gaitskell, H., "The Commonwealth Conference," *The New Statesman and*

b. PAR VALUES AND EXCHANGE RATES

No Fund members changed the par value of their currencies during the year but Ceylon established an initial par value for its currency that was the same as that in effect since the September 1949 devaluation. No important policy issues were raised by this action. Of the fifty-four members of the Fund at the end of 1952, ten had never established a par value—Austria, Burma, China, Greece, Italy, Thailand, Uruguay, and the three newest members: Germany, Japan, and Jordan—and three—France, Peru, and Canada—had, with various degrees of "acceptance" by the Fund, abandoned earlier agreed par values and established fluctuating rates. The French franc was kept stable vis-à-vis the dollar during the year and the Peruvian sol was permitted to fluctuate within only narrow limits. The Canadian dollar, on the other hand, rose from approximate parity with the United States dollar at the beginning of the year to a premium of around 4 percent at midyear, declining to approximately 3 percent by the end of the year.

Gold Policy

In September 1951 the Fund, on the stated ground that it was not practicable for all members to take uniform measures, abandoned its previous efforts to eliminate premium gold markets and to restrict the flow of gold to private hoards by specifying the conditions under which gold-producing countries could sell their metal abroad for other than monetary purposes.[3] Specifically, the Fund, with United States support, reiterated its belief in the principles that premium sales should be discouraged and that, except for bona fide industrial, professional, or artistic purposes, gold should be directed into official reserves, but it left to individual members the operating decisions involved in enforcement of these policies and the decision of the extent to which each member would implement them.

As anticipated by the Fund, subsequent to this announcement several members that had not previously been doing so began to

Nation, December 20, 1952, pp. 744-746; *Westminster Bank Review* (London), November 1952, pp. 6-10; and *The Economist*, December 20, 1952, pp. 837-838. A series of articles proposing an Atlantic Payments Union appeared in *The Economist*, November 22, 1952, pp. 579-596, and December 6, 1952, pp. 678-679.

[3] See *Survey—1951*, pp. 137-139.

permit sales of newly mined gold in premium markets against United States dollars—Canada, Australia, Southern Rhodesia, and the British Crown Colonies of Fiji, Kenya, Tanganyika, and West Africa. At first, Southern Rhodesia and the Crown Colonies limited sales to 40 percent of new production, but beginning in May 1952 these restrictions were removed. While no quantitative limits were imposed on sales by Canada and Australia, producers in the former country who chose to sell in the premium markets were disqualified from receiving the subsidy paid by the Canadian Government for newly mined gold.[4] South Africa, the largest gold producer and the most vocal critic of the Fund's gold policy, announced after the September 1951 change in policy that it would continue to allow its miners to sell in the premium market and its regulations governing such sales were unchanged. All of the countries engaging in foreign gold sales at premium prices took certain measures designed to reduce the evasions of the gold regulations in the countries of immediate destination but it appeared that these were frequently something less than completely successful. During 1952 gold production, outside the United States and Russia, was estimated at some $790 million, about 3 percent more than in 1951, of which about two fifths went into official monetary reserves. The proportion going into monetary reserves was thus about twice that in 1951; this decline in the amount of gold going into private hoards or otherwise unaccounted for was thought to be due principally to the abatement of inflationary pressures in Europe and the Middle and Far East, together with some reversal in expectations of currency devaluations in certain European nations.[5]

Immediately following the Fund's action in September 1951, the price of gold in premium markets traded directly with U.S. dollars declined on the average by the equivalent of $2 per ounce and moved in a range of $38-39 per ounce for several months. By the end of April 1952 the price was down to about $37 per

[4] Following consultation with, and approval by, the Fund, the Canadian subsidy was extended for two years on January 1, 1952. In November 1952 it was decided by the Canadian Government that beginning in January 1953 the subsidy would be increased as costs of gold production rose and returns fell, the latter reflecting the rise in the U.S. dollar value of the Canadian dollar.

[5] See Kriz, M. A., "Gold," *Engineering and Mining Journal*, February 1953.

ounce and fluctuated around this figure for the remainder of the year.

The official price of gold was again a much-discussed issue at the Fund's annual meeting of its Board of Governors. Mr. Havenga, of the Union of South Africa, led the proponents of an increase in the price of gold,[6] and in 1952 he had a greater measure of public support from representatives of other nations, especially those from the sterling area countries, than in former meetings. He argued that a higher gold price would result in greater international liquidity and would thus facilitate progress toward convertibility. Mr. Havenga stressed the fact that the dollar price of gold had not increased in nearly twenty years while other prices had risen a great deal, and he also cited the fall in the ratios of the value of gold reserves to foreign trade, to national debts, and to money supplies as evidence of the "need" for an increase in the gold price. He commended the Fund's change in policy on premium gold sales but stated that the fact that at least four fifths of the gold mined in 1951 went into private hoards showed "there must be something wrong" with the gold price policies that were followed. In supporting this case the Governor for Australia stated that inflationary dangers often attributed to a rise in the gold price were exaggerated. The United Kingdom representative took no public position on this issue but Foreign Secretary Eden stated in a press conference at the end of the Commonwealth Economic Conference in December that the dollar price of gold was "of great interest to the Commonwealth."[7]

Despite this clamor for a higher official gold price, there was no evidence during the year that either the Executive Directors of the Fund or the U.S. Government had changed their policy of supporting the existing price.[8] Secretary of the Treasury Snyder stated at a press conference during the meeting of the Fund's Governors that the United States policy of a stable price had

[6] More specifically, he requested a uniform change (downward) in the par value of all member countries' currencies.

[7] *The Economist*, December 20, 1952, p. 838.

[8] For an unofficial analysis supporting the existing price of gold, see Kriz, M. A., "The Price of Gold," *Essays in International Finance*, No. 15, International Finance Section, Princeton University, July 1952. See also National City Bank of New York, *Monthly Letter on Economic Conditions and Finance*, January 1953, pp. 3-8, and Collins, E. H., "Raising the Price of Gold," *New York Times*, December 15, 1952, p. 34, and December 22, 1952, p. 32.

promoted stability in the United States and that the existence of a stable link between the United States dollar and gold enabled greater confidence to be put in both throughout the world. Later in the year there was a spate of unofficial speculation in the press that the United States would raise the price of gold in the near future, $52.50 per ounce being a frequently mentioned price. There was, however, no indication from U.S. Government official sources or from any officer of the International Monetary Fund that such a move was contemplated. Nor was there any indication that the new Republican Administration would be receptive to suggestions that the price of gold be raised.

The large flow of gold into the United States that began in the second half of 1951 continued during early 1952 with the United Kingdom, together with Mexico, accounting for most of the sales. As the balance of payments position of the sterling area improved, net sales of gold to the United States declined sharply and the flow was reversed during the third quarter, when the United States sold a net of $1 million. In the last quarter of the year sales by the United States rose rapidly, reaching $268 million, chiefly as the result of the United Kingdom's, the Netherlands', and Mexico's converting part of their rising dollar reserves into gold. As a result of these transactions, plus purchases and sales in the domestic market, the official gold reserves of the United States increased to $23.3 billion, 64 percent of the world's gold reserves (excluding Russia) as compared with about 60 percent at the end of 1945.

As a consequence of the gold purchase and sale services instituted by the International Monetary Fund,[9] together with the settlements under the European Payments Union, the volume of gold transfers among foreign countries was much larger in 1952 than in previous years, but a smaller proportion involved the United States.

The Fund and the European Payments Union

The Fund had been, at best, lukewarm to the establishment of the European Payments Union and through 1951 there had been

[9] In March 1952 the Fund established a regular procedure whereby, for a fee of 1/32 of 1 percent in dollars from each party, it would put members desiring to sell gold in a particular center in touch with others wishing to buy.

TABLE 14

Net Foreign Gold Transactions by the United States, 1952

(net purchases [+]; net sales [—])
(millions of dollars)

Country	*First Half*	*Second Half*	*Year*
Western Europe (other than United Kingdom)	+31	—146	—115
United Kingdom	+520	—80	+440
Union of South Africa	+11	—	+12
Canada	+7	—	+7
Latin America	+98	—40	+57
Asia	—5	—2	—7
Bank for International Settlements	+2	—2	0
Total	+663	—269	+394

Details do not add to totals because of rounding.
Source: Board of Governors of the Federal Reserve System, *Federal Reserve Bulletin*, Wash., D.C., March 1953, p. 211.

virtually no cooperation or consultation between them. In 1952 F. A. Southard, Jr., U.S. Executive Director of the Fund, publicly expressed concern lest the Union have the effect of reducing the incentive of its members to make their currencies convertible into the dollar,[1] and in its *Annual Report* the Fund's Executive Directors took occasion to point out that the various measures that had been taken by the Union "may help temporarily to suppress the payments disequilibrium within Europe, but at the cost of retrogression in the field of liberalization."[2]

Nonetheless, during the year there was established the first concrete, albeit somewhat tenuous, financial relationship between the two organizations and some thought that it might point the way toward further cooperation. As a part of the June 1952 arrangements for settling Belgium's extreme creditor position in the Union,[3] it was proposed that Belgium fund $50 million of her credit in the form of a loan repayable by the Union in five equal installments, beginning in June 1953. Before agreeing to this plan Belgium, with, according to the press, encouragement from the U.S. Government, attempted to borrow an equivalent amount from the Fund, to be repaid out of the yearly installments

[1] For his comments, see "Mutual Security Act Extension," *Hearings on H.R. 7005*, House of Rep., Committee on Foreign Affairs, 82d Cong., 2d Sess., p. 475.
[2] International Monetary Fund, *Annual Report, 1952, op.cit.*, p. 19.
[3] See Chapter VIII.

due from the Union. For several reasons the Fund found it impossible to link its operations so closely with those of the Union[4] but Belgium did succeed in obtaining a special stand-by arrangement with the Fund entitling it to purchase up to $50 million in foreign currencies from the Fund.[5] The Fund did not publicly state that this credit was designed to help finance the European Payments Union, but it did say that in granting Belgium's request for such a credit it recognized that "Belgium's payments position was the key to a significant part of the payments problems of a number of other Fund members in Western Europe."[6]

Shortly after this stand-by credit arrangement was agreed upon, the Managing Board of the European Payments Union stated that it planned to examine the possibility of "establishing closer relationships" with the Fund (and the International Bank), but nothing was published during the year as to the results of this examination and no further financial relationships between the two organizations were recorded.

B. *THE INTERNATIONAL BANK*[7]

Lending Policies and Operations

There was much less criticism in the public press during the year of the International Bank than there was of the International Monetary Fund. This was in part due to the fact that the latter, by its nature, was more concerned than was the former with

[4] For an unofficial report of these reasons, see *The Economist*, June 21, 1952, p. 840, and June 28, 1952, p. 921.

[5] This agreement was for only six months, but it was subject to successive renewals up to a period of not more than five years.

[6] International Monetary Fund, *Annual Report, 1952, op.cit.*, p. 44.

[7] The more important official sources of information on the activities and policies of the Bank during 1952, and the sources of much of the material presented in this section, are: International Bank for Reconstruction and Development, *Seventh Annual Report, 1951-1952*, Wash., D.C., 1952; International Bank for Reconstruction and Development, *Summary Proceedings, Seventh Annual Meeting of the Board of Governors*, Wash., D.C., 1952; International Monetary Fund, *International Financial News Survey* (various issues); International Monetary Fund, *International Financial Statistics* (various issues); and three reports by the National Advisory Council on International Monetary and Financial Problems: *Third Special Report to the President and to the Congress*, Wash., D.C., June 1952; *Semiannual Report to the President and to the Congress for the Period October 1, 1951—March 31, 1952*, Wash., D.C., 1952; and *Semiannual Report to the President and to the Congress for the Period April 1—September 30, 1952*, Wash., D.C., 1952.

matters that members regarded as infringing on their sovereignty. More important, however, it was a reflection of the increasing scale of the Bank's lending, which reached a total of the equivalent of nearly $300 million during the year.

In 1952, as in previous years, the United States Government stated that it was satisfied with the general policies of the Bank, the level of its operations, and the geographic distribution of loans, and believed that it had achieved "substantial progress . . . in adapting [its] policies and procedures to the changing problems of member countries and in directing [its] resources toward the promotion of economic development. . . ."[8] Many of the other members qualified their public statements of approval of the Bank's record by expressing the hope that even greater lending activity could be anticipated for the future.[9]

The Bank itself recognized, as it had before, that the present flow of international investment was "clearly inadequate to the needs," but it was much more optimistic than in immediately preceding years as to the possibility and feasibility of expanding its scale of operations.[1] While repeating earlier statements that massive injections of capital could not alone produce economic development and that the limiting factor on the ability of would-be borrowers to make "effective" use of loans from the Bank was often the shortage of basic facilities, local capital, entrepreneurs, and technicians, the President of the Bank stated at the annual meetings in September that "it seems to me that if the Bank and its members fully grasp the opportunities they have, the coming year will see a significant increase in the Bank's operations."[2]

He went on to report that in the Bank's view there had recently been some encouraging factors in the situation of many of the less-developed countries that augured well for more loans by the Bank: a growing understanding of the processes of economic development; increasing adoption of techniques needed to bring

[8] National Advisory Council, *Semiannual Report to the President and to the Congress for the Period April 1—September 30, 1952, op.cit.*, pp. 40-41.

[9] For an account of the discussion in the Economic and Social Council on the Bank's activities, see UN Economic and Social Council, *Official Records*, Fourteenth Session, 605th and 606th Meetings, June 16, 1952.

[1] See *Survey—1951*, pp. 120-127, and references cited therein for an account of the policies and activities of the Bank during earlier years.

[2] International Bank for Reconstruction and Development, *Summary Proceedings, op.cit.*, p. 9.

about that development; greater efforts to make use of their own physical and financial resources; and better planning. But this was not all. In the two immediately preceding years the Bank had, as a matter of policy, concentrated its loans almost entirely in the so-called underdeveloped areas, but in 1952 officials of the Bank held out the prospect of supplementing Europe's own capital with dollar loans. Moreover, a possible new trend was indicated when the Bank's President stated that, if called upon, the Bank "would be glad to search for feasible ways to assist"[3] the Schuman Plan in particular and European economic integration efforts in general.

During 1952 the Bank granted sixteen new loans to twelve different countries in an amount of $292.5 million, distributed as shown in Table 15.[4] The bulk of these loans continued to be, as in previous years, for specific and individual basic development projects in the so-called underdeveloped countries: electric power development in Southern Rhodesia,[5] Mexico, and Brazil; railway rehabilitation and modernization in Pakistan, Colombia, and Brazil; port development in Peru; and flood control, irrigation, and power development in Turkey. In addition to these more or less well-established types of loans, several of the credits extended in 1952 were notable because they represented departures from the usual practices of the Bank. A $50 million loan to Australia was for a general program of economic development rather than specific individual projects and was intended to help finance the import of capital goods for agriculture, coal mining, iron and steel production, electric power, transportation, the production of

[3] *ibid.*, p. 9. In 1951 the Bank had reported that the nonavailability of capital goods resulting from the rearmament programs of highly industrialized countries might constitute a serious obstacle to a greater volume of loans. In September 1952, President Black reported that post-Korean developments had disturbed the Bank's operations "remarkably little." A special section of the Bank kept itself informed during the year as to the supply situation for capital equipment in various countries and helped borrowers to obtain priorities where needed.

[4] The Bank continued during the year to provide technical assistance to its members. These services were extended through general economic survey teams, which visited members upon request, and through smaller specialized missions, which had been requested to advise on technical, financial, and administrative matters. The Bank reported that its technical services were well received by the members, and the U.S. Government at various times expressed complete satisfaction with this phase of the activities of the Bank.

[5] Southern Rhodesia is not itself a member of the Bank, but as a self-governing colony of the United Kingdom it had access to the Bank's resources through the membership of the latter country, which guaranteed the loan.

TABLE 15

International Bank: Loans Granted and Disbursed, 1947-1952

(millions of dollar equivalents)

	Loans Granted			Loans Disbursed		
Country[a]	*1951*	*1952*	*1947-1952*[b]	*1951*	*1952*	*1947-1952*
Australia	0	50.0	150.0	36.9	43.2	80.1
Belgium—Belgian Congo	70.0	0	86.0	0.7	25.6	38.4
Brazil	0[d]	37.5[c]	142.5	28.7	20.4	95.9
Chile	1.3	0	17.3	1.6	5.1	12.6
Colombia	18.9	25.0	55.0	5.6	12.3	22.7
Denmark	0	0	40.0	0	0	40.0
El Salvador	0	0	12.5	3.4	4.2	7.6
Ethiopia	1.5[c]	0	8.5	2.0	2.6	4.6
Finland	0	23.5	38.1	4.2	7.1	17.7
France	0	0	250.0	0	0	250.0
Iceland	3.5	0.9	4.3	0.7	1.7	2.4
India	0	31.5[c]	90.3	10.2	5.7	50.7
Iraq	0	0	12.8	0.1	4.6	4.7
Italy	10.0	0	10.0	0	5.1	5.1
Luxembourg	0	0	11.8	0	0	11.8
Mexico	0	29.7	80.3	13.8	17.1	47.8
Netherlands	0	7.0	221.9	1.7	5.6	217.0
Nicaragua	5.3	0	5.3	0.1	2.7	2.8
Pakistan	0	30.4[c]	30.4	0	5.7	5.7
Paraguay	5.0	0	5.0	0	0	0
Peru	0	3.8	3.8	0	0.7	0.7
Thailand	0	0	25.4	3.7	9.0	12.7
Turkey	0	25.2	50.6	0.7	3.7	4.4
Union of South Africa	50.0	0	50.0	10.8	22.0	32.8
United Kingdom (Southern Rhodesia)	0	28.0	28.0	0	6.5	6.5
Uruguay	0	0	33.0	4.0	3.4	7.4
Yugoslavia	28.0	0	30.7	0	11.7	14.4
Total	193.5	292.5	1493.5	128.9	225.7	996.5

a) For details of individual loans—principal amounts, dates of agreement, maturities, interest rates—see: for loans made prior to July 1, 1951, International Monetary Fund, *International Financial Statistics*, September 1951, p. xv, and October 1951, p. xv; for loans made after June 30, 1951, *ibid.*, February 1953, p. 9.

b) The total amount of loans granted prior to cancellations was the equivalent of $1524.3 million.

c) As of December 31, 1952, part or all of these loans still required action by the borrower and/or member government before becoming effective.

d) A 1949 loan of $75 million was increased by $15 million in January 1951. The International Bank does not regard this increase as a new loan.

Source: International Monetary Fund, *International Financial Statistics*, Wash., D.C., January 1952, p. XV, and February 1953, p. 9.

metals and minerals, and manufacturing industries.[6] A $31.5 million loan to the India Iron and Steel Company, Limited for the expansion of blast furnace capacity was the first loan made by the Bank directly to a private manufacturer. The loan was, of course, guaranteed by the Government of India, but the Bank also took as security a first mortgage on the Company's fixed properties and a first charge on its other assets. A loan of $7 million to the Royal Dutch Airlines for the replacement of part of its fleet was noteworthy because it was the first time the Bank had made arrangements prior to the conclusion of a loan for a portion of the obligations to be sold to a private commercial bank.[7]

The Bank made no "local currency" loans during the year, as it had to Italy in 1951, nor did it pursue further the policy inaugurated in 1950 of lending to local development banks or consortia of commercial banks to facilitate their relending to small private borrowers.[8] Indeed, the $10 million line of credit opened in 1950 for a consortium of commercial banks in Mexico, intended to be lent by them to small and medium-sized firms, expired on June 30, 1952, after only six loans, totalling less than $0.6 million, had been made. The Bank reported that the reason for the small use of the loan was that subsequent to its extension foreign exchange became more plentiful in Mexico, making resort to the International Bank unnecessary.[9]

Disbursements on loans granted by the Bank amounted to the equivalent of $225.7 million during the year, again the highest figure reached since 1947, bringing total disbursements since the Bank began operations in 1947 to the equivalent of nearly $1 billion. As Table 16 shows, disbursements to borrowers in U.S. dollars were $161.3 million in 1952. At 72 percent of total dis-

[6] A previous loan of this type had been made to Australia in 1950 and others similar to it in scope had been made in 1951 to Italy, Yugoslavia, and the Belgian Congo. The Bank implied that such broad-purpose loans continued to be the exception rather than the rule.

[7] Chase National Bank purchased $3.5 million of these obligations.

Later in the year, the Bank of America National Trust and Savings Association and the Chase National Bank agreed at the time the loan was made to take nearly $0.5 million of the obligations from a loan to Pakistan.

[8] See *Survey—1951*, pp. 123-124.

[9] Following the report of a Bank mission in 1951, the Government of Costa Rica began to make specific plans for certain projects that had been recommended by that mission. The Costa Rican authorities, however, notified the Bank early in 1952 that due to an improvement in the country's financial position it could proceed with its immediate developmental projects without any external aid.

bursements to borrowers, this was, by a small amount, the lowest ratio of dollars to total disbursements in any year since the Bank was established. These figures, however, underestimate the reliance of the Bank on dollars since some of the other currencies

TABLE 16

International Bank: Currencies Disbursed and Currencies Repayable, 1947-1952[a]

(millions of dollar equivalents)

Currency	*Currency Disbursed to Borrower* 1952	*Currency Disbursed to Borrower* Total 1947-1952	*Currency in Which Loans Repayable* 1952	*Currency in Which Loans Repayable* Total 1947-1952
U.S. dollars	161.3	839.2	191.5	930.4
Canadian dollars	13.1	48.2	12.7	30.3
Pounds sterling	29.3	44.5	4.4	7.2
Belgian francs	2.8	28.5	1.3	3.4
Swiss francs	4.3	17.0	6.7	14.8
French francs	7.4	8.3	6.5	7.5
Swedish kronor	0.8	3.3	0.1	0.1
Deutsche marks	2.8	2.8	—	—
Italian lire	2.0	2.1	1.2	1.3
Netherlands guilders	0.5	1.0	0.1	0.1
Danish kroner	0.6	0.8	0.5	0.7
South African pounds	0.6	0.6	0.6	0.6
Norwegian kroner	0.2	0.2	0.1	0.1
Total	225.7	996.5	225.7	996.5

a) Included in this table are loans that had been repaid as of the end of 1952 as well as borrowers' obligations that had been sold by the Bank. As noted in the text, the Bank sometimes uses one currency to buy another, with the latter being disbursed to the borrower. In such cases the borrower is required to repay in the currency that the Bank used, rather than the currency received by the borrower. This practice was a consequence of the Bank's policy of not "tying" loans and by it the Bank was not required to take either a long or a short position on any currency. During 1951 some of the members had objected to this practice but there was no evidence that it was seriously objected to during 1952.

Source: International Monetary Fund, *International Financial Statistics*, Wash., D.C., January 1952, p. XV, and February 1953, p. 9.

distributed to borrowers were purchased by the Bank with dollars. In such cases the borrowers are obligated to repay in dollars even though they may have received other currencies. Of the total value of currencies used by the Bank during the year, and so repayable by the borrower, nearly 85 percent was U.S. dollars. High as this was, it was appreciably lower than in 1951; during the entire period of the Bank's operation, including 1952, over 93 percent of the value of currencies used by the Bank was dollars.

The question of the Bank's role in helping combat depressions was discussed again in 1952. In the United Nations, delegates from several countries spoke in favor of a recommendation by a group of United Nations experts that the Bank should stand ready, in the event of a serious recession, to expand greatly its rate of lending.[1] The Bank continued to oppose a policy of using its resources primarily for anti-cyclical purposes. Its spokesmen stated that there was a shortage of projects suitable for the Bank that could be undertaken promptly enough to be effective for anti-depression purposes, that private projects abandoned during a recession would usually not be suitable for Bank financing, and that the Bank could do nothing about the shortage of local currencies usually associated with depressions. He asserted that the Bank intended to keep lending at a steady rate and that this action would be a stabilizing factor. The delegate from the United States, in supporting the Bank's position, warned that anti-cyclical operations by the Bank might conflict with the long-run goal of a steady supply of credit for economic development.[2] A resolution finally passed by the Economic and Social Council called upon the Bank, in assessing a member's credit-worthiness, "not to be unduly affected by the economic situation of that country in time of temporary recession, but to give full consideration to the country's long-run economic prospects."[3] The resolution also called upon individual governments, independently or in cooperation with the Bank, to prepare programs of additional investment to be undertaken in times of depression.

In contrast with the Fund, whose operating expenses had greatly exceeded its current income, the Bank continued to record large net earnings. Gross income exceeded gross expenses by $24.2 million in 1952, resulting in a general reserve account of $65.7 million and a special reserve account of $32.2 million at year's end.

[1] For the experts' report, see *Measures for International Economic Stability*, *op.cit.*, pp. 27-31.

[2] The American delegate countered a proposal that the Bank should assist in achieving another of the experts' recommendations—financing buffer stocks of important raw materials—with the contention that this was the responsibility of nations participating in such commodity agreements.

[3] UN Economic and Social Council Resolution 427 (XIV), July 10, 1952.

Some of the Bank's members interpreted this high level of operating profits as evidence that the interest rates charged by the Bank should be reduced, but there was no evidence that such a policy was being contemplated by the Bank. On the contrary, during the year the interest charged on some of its loans was increased as the cost of borrowing by the Bank went up. The Bank had distributed no dividends among members and the U.S. National Advisory Council stated that in its opinion this had been a wise policy and that it was preferable for the Bank to continue, for the present at least, to use its net earnings to build up reserves.[4] The Articles of Agreement provide that before a general dividend can be declared a preferred dividend of up to 2 percent of the amount of members' subscriptions used in loans must be paid to those members whose currencies have been so used. Inasmuch as most of the loans made from capital subscriptions have come from the United States subscription, practically the entire amount of any such preferred dividends would go to the U.S. Government.[5]

Marketing Operations and Financial Resources

To meet its needs for loanable funds the Bank floated four issues of its own bonds during the year, sold relatively small amounts of its portfolio, and successfully urged a few members to agree to the use by the Bank of that portion of the Bank's paid-up capital represented by the 18 percent local currency contributions. For the first time, an issue of the Bank's bonds (Canadian $15 million) was sold in Canada. The Bank reported that this had been a successful operation and that a wide distribution of the bonds had been achieved. For the fourth time, an issue (Swiss francs 50 million) of the Bank's bonds was sold in Switzerland,[6] a country not a member of the Bank but whose currency was in demand by certain of the Bank's borrowers. As with U.S. dollars, a portion of the Swiss francs disbursed by the Bank was used to

[4] National Advisory Council, *Third Special Report, op.cit.*, p. 8.

[5] All interest payments and repayments of principal that became due to the Bank in 1952 were received. Repayments on principal amounted to the equivalent of $2.8 million during the year, bringing total repayments since the Bank was established to $10.8 million.

[6] A few months prior to this flotation the Bank redeemed the 17 million Swiss franc issue of 1948, due in 1953-1954. The reasons for this were not made public but it doubtless served to create a more receptive market for the larger, 1952 issue.

purchase other currencies for disbursement to borrowers. Two more issues, totalling $110 million, were floated in the United States capital market during the year, both by direct, negotiated sale to an underwriting syndicate. This operation was regarded as highly satisfactory by the Bank even though the generally tighter money market resulted in the Bank's having to pay somewhat higher interest rates than in the past. Previous flotations in the United States market had been on an agency basis, or through competitive bidding, or by sponsorship agency. The Bank had not been satisfied with any of these earlier methods and, in particular, felt that some of the sponsoring groups had held parts of the issue for appreciation, rather than trying to develop as wide a market —both institutionally and geographically—as the Bank wished. Despite a gradually widening distribution of its bonds, the Bank estimated in the late summer of 1952 that approximately 80 percent of all its securities were held within the United States and were divided approximately equally among mutual savings banks, life insurance companies, pension and trust funds, and commercial banks. The holdings of non-United States residents were composed of the non-dollar obligations of the Bank plus some $65-70 million of dollar obligations. The central banks of twelve countries were known to hold a substantial part of the latter. A breakdown of the Bank's funded debt as of the end of 1952 is given in Table 17.

The Bank also increased its liquid resources by selling during 1952 the equivalent of $32.4 million from its portfolio, of which nearly $14.5 million was without the Bank's guarantee. Such sales, which it had been anticipated when the Bank was created would become an important method of reestablishing the international private capital markets, were some six times as large as in the previous year and brought the total of sales to private investors from the Bank's portfolio to the equivalent of $65.7 million, of which $46.5 million was with the Bank's unconditional guarantee and $19.2 million was without recourse to the Bank.[7]

The Bank also continued to report some success in obtaining permission from various of its members to use all or a part of that portion of the Bank's paid-up capital represented by the 18 per-

[7] In late 1952 the Bank estimated that some $11 million of the obligations with the Bank's unconditional guarantee as to principal and interest were held by non-United States residents.

TABLE 17

Funded Debt of International Bank, December 31, 1952

(millions of dollar equivalents)

Payable in United States Dollars		
3% Twenty-five-Year Bonds of 1947	150	
2% Serial Bonds of 1950	100	
3% Twenty-five-Year Bonds of 1951	50	
3¼% Thirty-Year Bonds of 1951	100	
3⅜% Twenty-five-Year Bonds of 1952	50	
3½% Nineteen-Year Bonds of 1952	60	510.0
Payable in Canadian Dollars		
4% Ten-Year Bonds of 1952 (Can. $15.0 million)		13.6[a]
Payable in Pounds Sterling		
3½% Twenty-Year Stock of 1951 (£5.0 million)		14.0
Payable in Swiss Francs		
2½% Serial Bonds of 1950 (S.F. 28.5 million)	6.6	
3½% Twelve-Year Bonds of 1951 (S.F. 50.0 million)	11.6	
3½% Ten-Year Bonds of 1952 (S.F. 50.0 million)	11.6	29.9
Total		567.5

a) This figure is as reported by the International Bank, though it is less than the U.S.-dollar equivalent at any rate of exchange in effect during the period.

Source: International Bank for Reconstruction and Development, *Press Release No. 317*, February 6, 1953, Exhibit A.

cent local currency contribution by each member. The total of such releases during the year was the equivalent of just over $57 million, of which Canada accounted for $41 million—agreeing that the Bank might convert this into any other currency. France released the equivalent of over $12 million in French francs for the specific purpose of helping to finance purchases in the franc area of goods for a railway loan to Pakistan and a loan to Iceland. Most of the other releases were of very small amounts and were also tied to specific loans by the Bank. As of the end of the year, the equivalent of $668.8 million of 18 percent local currency contributions had been made available to the Bank, of which $571.5 million represented the United States subscription and $58.5 million the Canadian subscription. The total amount of the 18 percent subscriptions as of the end of the year was over $1.6 billion and the Bank, with United States support, continued to urge many of its members to release at least a portion of these funds, which, it was thought, would enable the Bank to expand its operations in nations that found themselves in great difficulties with respect to financing additional dollar debts but that could service external obligations in other currencies.

C. *PROPOSED NEW INTERNATIONAL FINANCIAL INSTITUTIONS*

In addition to trying to make easier their access to the resources of the Fund and the Bank, many of the so-called underdeveloped countries had for several years been urging the creation of various new international financial institutions whose main task would be to provide greater assistance for economic development.[8] The U.S. Government, along with most of the other historically capital-exporting countries, had been either opposed or at best lukewarm to such proposals, but they received important new support in March 1951 when the United States International Development Advisory Board, in the so-called "Rockefeller Report," recommended that the United States "take the initiative in creating an international finance corporation" that would make loans to private enterprises without governmental guarantees, and equity investments in participation with private investors. In the same document this Board proposed that the United States support the creation of an International Development Authority to help finance basic development and public works projects that could not be "financed entirely on a loan basis."[9] A short time later a United Nations committee of experts recommended that the United Nations "establish an International Development Authority" and "explore the possibility of establishing an international finance corporation."[1]

At its thirteenth session (1951) the Economic and Social Council considered these and related proposals and, in a resolution sponsored by the United States, referred the proposal for an international finance corporation to the International Bank, directing

[8] See *Survey—1951*, pp. 90-95, and references cited therein.

[9] See *Partners in Progress*, a report to the President by the International Development Advisory Board, Wash., D.C., March 1951, pp. 72-75, 84-85.

[1] See *Measures for the Economic Development of Under-developed Countries*, Report by a Group of Experts Appointed by the Secretary-General of the United Nations, UN Publications Sales No.: 1951.II.B.2, pp. 82-88, 95.

the latter to present a report on the contributions that such a corporation might be able to make toward hastening economic development. The delegates to the United Nations from the prospective capital-receiving countries were not enthusiastic about establishing such a finance corporation but they vigorously supported the proposal that an International Development Authority be created. The United States, supported by the other highly industrialized nations, was equally vigorous in opposing at that time even a discussion of such an authority. The United States and its supporters were in the minority, however, and the General Assembly in early 1952 passed a resolution asking the Economic and Social Council to submit at the next regular session of the General Assembly a detailed plan for establishing a special fund to make grants and low-interest loans to help the underdeveloped countries accelerate their economic development.[2]

An International Finance Corporation

The International Bank presented its report on the international finance corporation in May 1952, stating that it had been prepared by the Bank's staff but that the Executive Directors of the Bank were expressing no opinion on the merits of the proposal nor any opinions on behalf of the governments they represented.[3] The report first reviewed the need for private international investment and the current obstacles to its resumption at a high level. It discussed the limitations on the ability of the Bank to encourage investments in private, as distinct from public, enterprises abroad, arising from the requirement that the Bank's loans must be guaranteed by member governments and the Bank's lack of authority to engage in equity financing. The report then outlined a possible international finance corporation whose purpose would be to promote economic development through the stimulation of private investment "by bringing together investment opportunities, capital (both domestic and foreign) and experienced management, and by helping to finance private productive undertakings through equity investments and loans without government guarantee." The report recommended that the proposed corporation be affil-

[2] General Assembly Resolution 520 (VI), January 12, 1952.

[3] International Bank for Reconstruction and Development, *Report on the Proposal for an International Finance Corporation*, Wash., D.C., 1952 (also distributed as UN Doc. E/2215, May 1, 1952).

iated with the International Bank, but that its resources be subscribed directly by member governments and not taken from the Bank's funds. A capitalization of $400 million was suggested, with one third initially paid in and the rest subject to call. It was recommended that wide discretion be permitted the management concerning the uses of the corporation's resources, both as to types and degrees of participation by other suppliers of capital, domestic and foreign, and as to types of equity and debt instruments eligible for the corporation's purchase. The corporation, as outlined, would not hold a controlling position in any enterprise nor would it accept responsibility for managing an undertaking in which it had invested. As a matter of policy, the proposed new institution would revolve its funds as fast as possible by selling securities from its portfolio whenever it was possible to do so at a "fair price."

The corporation was presented as an experiment in stimulating private investment and it was recommended that operations should begin on a small scale. The report warned that the corporation could not be expected to provide from its own resources "a large volume of foreign capital, measured by the world's needs for development financing"; and stated that its creation would not obviate the need for other action to increase the international flow of private capital. Nonetheless, the report concluded that the proposed institution would fill a gap in the existing international machinery for private investment, that it would strengthen confidence in international investment and lead to an improved climate for such investment, that its success should be measured not only by the size of its own operations but also by the other additional investment it generated, and that there were "good reasons for concluding that over a period of years the Corporation would be able to give a substantial stimulus to the growth of private enterprises and thus contribute significantly to the further development of the Bank's member countries."

The report elicited a wide variety of opinions when it was discussed in the United Nations Economic and Social Council in mid-1952.[4] In general, the representatives of the underdeveloped countries were apathetic toward the proposal. As in earlier years,

[4] For a full account of the debates, see UN Economic and Social Council, *Official Records*, Fourteenth Session, 606th-610th and 613th-615th Meetings, June 16-23, 1952.

they said that for the present reliance must be put on attracting public rather than private capital since the latter could not be expected to undertake the financing of most of the basic development projects, which were the most immediate and urgent need. In addition to this consideration, some felt the proposal was too modest, some believed the corporation would only become a substitute for existing sources of funds, and some feared that it and the private investors would be motivated chiefly by the quest for profits and would have little regard for the economic development plans and objectives of the recipient countries. The attitude of the richer and more industrialized countries toward the proposal was also not one of enthusiastic support, though generally for different reasons than those mentioned above. Some of the spokesmen for these countries stated that their governments were not in the position to make a financial contribution at that time, one urged caution in establishing a new institution on the ground that its opportunities were not as great as believed, another argued that the corporation should have a voice in the management of any enterprise in which it invested, still another talked of the importance of considering the inflationary effects of a large export of capital equipment from certain of the industrialized countries, and others repeated the warning against thinking of the problem of economic development almost exclusively in terms of its financial aspects. The United States delegate thought that the association of public and private capital in sharing the risks and gains of international investment was a novel and interesting idea but he expressed concern lest the proposed corporation merely replace resources available from existing agencies and thought that the relationship between the finance corporation and existing foreign lending agencies (such as the Export-Import Bank and the International Bank) needed further study. He stressed, as he had in 1951, the importance of an increased flow of domestic savings in underdeveloped countries into productive activities.[5]

[5] Several members of Congress expressed favorable interest in the proposal and an amendment to the Mutual Security Act was proposed that would have authorized the use of up to $100 million of the appropriation under that Act for contributions to the proposed international finance corporation. This amendment was not added on the ground that, whatever its virtues, the proposed corporation would not be ready to receive funds during fiscal year 1953.

The National Foreign Trade Council expressed "strong disapproval" of the proposal in November, arguing that it would foster "uneconomic enterprises and

There was general agreement that the proposal required further study and, under a resolution cosponsored by the United States, Canada, Pakistan, and the Philippines, the Economic and Social Council requested the Bank to continue its study of the corporation, in consultation with member governments and interested business groups, and to report back to the Council in 1953.

An International Development Authority

Following the January 12, 1952 request of the General Assembly that the Economic and Social Council submit a detailed plan for establishing a special fund to make grants or low-interest loans for the purpose of basic economic development in the poorer countries of the world, the Secretary-General of the United Nations, in May 1952, presented to the Economic and Social Council a report to serve as the basis for the Council's discussion.[6] This report, called a working paper, was in the form of alternative approaches to the problem and a listing of some of the considerations that would bear upon the choices among them, rather than of specific recommendations. The report stated that no consideration had been given to the question of whether such a fund was "needed" or whether circumstances permitted its establishment. The Secretary-General did state that he would consider it a "serious mistake" to contemplate creating "still another international organization," but that "every possibility" of merging such a fund with the International Bank or with the United Nations should be examined.

Using this document as a basis for discussion, ECOSOC members considered the adoption of a draft resolution presented by Cuba, Egypt, Iran, and the Philippines, which stated that a preparatory commission[7] should be set up to work out detailed

would serve to deter rather than promote 'mechanisms' for encouraging savings and capital formation."

[6] For the text of the Secretary-General's report, see UN Doc. E/2234, May 27, 1952. See also a memorandum submitted by U. Rao, one of the earlier supporters of the concept of a new international development authority, in UN Doc. E/C.2/333, June 20, 1952.

[7] The preparatory commission was to be composed of nine persons, chosen by the Secretary-General for technical competence and having no governmental affiliation; the latter qualification was inserted by the authors of the resolution because they anticipated that the opposition to the fund by the governments of the industrialized nations would, from the authors' point of view, unfavorably prejudice technical discussion among government officials.

plans for the Authority and report to ECOSOC not later than March 1, 1953.

In the debate on this resolution, representatives of the underdeveloped nations stressed that one of the fundamental objectives of the United Nations was that of increasing the living standards of all peoples, of maintaining full employment, and of fostering economic advancement throughout the world. They warned that the underdeveloped countries could not support fully the collective security programs of the United Nations unless the other purposes of that organization were fulfilled. The Chilean representative emphasized that "world economic stability and even the maintenance of peace depend on economic development."[8] Other delegates asserted that the industrialized countries should make firm commitments to contribute to the fund as a means of improving relations between the developed and underdeveloped countries.

As in the previous year, representatives of the underdeveloped countries maintained, among other things, that their nations were too poor to accumulate sufficient savings internally to meet their "requirements" for economic development; that they were not able to "close the gap between their foreign exchange requirements and earnings from their own sources"; that raw material price fluctuations made earnings from exports of such commodities unsuitable for financing long-term development; that the International Bank imposed "unsuitable conditions" on its lending, thus making it impossible for many countries to borrow from it; and that nothing they could do would entice the needed funds from private sources abroad.[9] They concluded therefore that it was necessary and desirable to establish a special fund to make grants and long-term, low-interest loans to finance such projects as the construction of roads, the building of public utilities, electric power projects, housing, and the irrigation and improvement of agricultural lands.

[8] *United Nations Bulletin*, July 15, 1952, p. 69; for a full report of his statement, see UN Economic and Social Council, *Official Records*, Fourteenth Session, 609th Meeting, June 18, 1952.

[9] See UN Economic and Social Council, *Official Records*, Fourteenth Session, 606th-610th and 613th-615th Meetings, June 16-23, 1952, and *United Nations Bulletin*, July 15, 1952, pp. 68ff. The Czechoslovakian delegate joined in attacking the "discriminatory" lending policies of the International Bank. (See UN Economic and Social Council, *Official Records*, Fourteenth Session, 606th Meeting, June 16, 1952.)

As compared with the discussions in 1951,[1] some of the representatives from poverty-stricken nations were less insistent that the proposed foreign financing be largely on a grant basis, pointing out that grants might be exceedingly difficult to distribute "equitably" among projects and countries and that therefore, perhaps, attention should be focused on extending loans with lenient terms. Most of these officials reiterated their earlier statements that no political interference would be brooked in members' affairs as a condition of receiving funds. The Argentine delegate asserted that any "scheme of financing economic development should be based upon a fair distribution of resources made without regard to profit and without the intervention of private interests."[2]

The representatives from the more industrialized nations reiterated their conviction that economic development demanded domestic policies of reducing the disparity in incomes, of mobilizing internal savings, of land reform, and of providing incentives to private foreign investment. The United States delegate repeated the basic United States position outlined the previous year: that the U.S. Government was sympathetic to the economic development aspirations of the poorer nations of the world but believed that the creation of a new International Development Authority to foster this goal would be premature and was undesirable and unnecessary because (a) existing loan resources were adequate for the immediate future at least, (b) foreign grants, especially from an international agency, were, except for "special" cases, an inappropriate method of financing economic development, and (c) under existing conditions such an Authority would have to rely almost entirely on the United States for its funds, and, with the present rearmament burden, the United States was not prepared to make such contributions. Despite these fundamental objections, the United States delegate said, in a reversal of the position taken in 1951, that his Government would support a resolution calling for continued study of the proposal. Delegates from several of the other historically capital-exporting nations supported the United States position and some specified that,

[1] See *Survey—1951*, pp. 92-95.

[2] UN Economic and Social Council, *Official Records*, Fourteenth Session, 609th Meeting, June 18, 1952, p. 302.

despite their sympathy with the objectives of the proposed fund, their countries could not contribute to it.

In sum, the debate offered no evidence that the differences between the two groups of countries—the underdeveloped and the historically capital-exporting—were significantly less than they had been during the sharp debates of 1951.[8] The opposing positions were compromised by a proposal for further study. The spokesmen from the underdeveloped countries in general took the attitude that, though the case for the establishment of an international development fund was beyond dispute, they would patiently cooperate with the "Great Powers" and agree to another year's postponement. For their part, the delegates from the richer nations took the position that, although the proposals were clearly impractical and ill-timed, they would show their desire to help the underdeveloped countries by agreeing to further study.

The resolution as approved established a nine-man preparatory commission to work out a detailed plan for the proposed Authority. The resolution stated that the study should be guided by the "propositions, principles and alternatives" set forth in the Secretary-General's working paper. Among these principles were (a) recognition that many underdeveloped countries "cannot adequately accelerate" their development from their own savings or from foreign loans; (b) the desirability, nevertheless, of these countries' providing "the bulk" of the effort and the funds for their own development; (c) the need of the poorer countries for aid to meet a general insufficiency in financial resources, rather than to finance particular projects; (d) the need for "integrated" and "harmonious" economic development programs; (e) the desirability of spreading the benefits of development without regard to political, racial, or religious distinctions; (f) the need for recipient countries to demonstrate ability to mobilize their own re-

[8] A third group existed, the Communist countries, which agreed with neither of the other two. Its representatives in the Economic and Social Council attacked the whole notion of development with an International Development Authority as a means of supporting the capitalistic West, which, they stated, required an increasing outflow of capital to prevent it from "collapsing." They also attacked the United States for its program of developing sources of raw materials abroad and for what they called "dictating" the prices of exports from and imports into the underdeveloped countries. They also took this occasion to upbraid the United States for "forcing" unwanted technical assistance on Indonesia, Burma, and Syria. (See UN Economic and Social Council, *Official Records*, Fourteenth Session, 615th Meeting, June 23, 1952.)

sources and to make effective use of the aid received; (g) the desirability of a system of voluntary pledging of contributions to the proposed fund; (h) the necessity that minimum initial contributions, estimated at $200-300 million, be accumulated before the fund was established; and (i) the need for a degree of convertibility of the fund's resources sufficient to permit the fund's beneficiaries "reasonable freedom" in what they buy and where they buy it. Although these "principles" reflected the concern of each of the two groups, the emphasis seems to have been on those aspects of the problem that had been stressed by the United States and other potential large contributors to the fund. The preparatory commission was directed to be convened not later than December 1952 and no reports on its progress were issued during the year.

VI · RECIPROCAL TRADE AGREEMENTS PROGRAM

THE Reciprocal Trade Agreements Program, the core of United States international commercial policy since 1934, suffered several setbacks in 1951. Although important reductions in duties were made during that year at the third round of tariff negotiations under the General Agreements on Tariffs and Trade (GATT), the United States failed to obtain any relaxation (except with respect to Canada) in the British imperial preferences—long a major goal of United States policy. More significantly, the Administration late in 1950 abandoned its efforts to gain approval of the International Trade Organization Charter and in 1951 adopted a defensive attitude toward Congress in asking for an extension of the Trade Agreements Act; but even its modest request for legislation that would merely permit a consolidation of past actions was not fully granted by Congress. That body weakened the foundations of the Program by inserting in the Act an escape clause and restoring a peril-point provision, designed to increase the protection afforded United States producers against foreign competition. Further, Congress not only failed to approve the customs simplification bill and made it plain that it had not endorsed the GATT, but passed *legislation that required new and stringent quotas on imports of* dairy products. As 1951 ended, there were many observers who believed that the United States was in danger of losing the role of leader it had held so long in the program for expanding trade throughout the world and lowering barriers to it.[1]

There was evidence throughout 1952 that a growing number of people in the United States, and abroad, were becoming increasingly skeptical as to the wisdom and feasibility of continuing the huge aid programs that had characterized American foreign economic policy for many years. The prospect of a decline in exports, which would result from a cut in aid, and a growing

[1] For an account of United States activities and policies under the Trade Agreements Program during 1951, see *Survey—1951*, Chapter V.

public awareness of the dependence of the United States on imported raw materials gave new force to the arguments of those who, for other reasons as well, argued that it was in the nation's interest to pursue a more liberal import policy. Symptomatic of this concern was the wide currency and lip service given to the slogan "Trade, not aid," apparently coined in the British Treasury.[2]

Business opinion in the United States in favor of reducing barriers to imports grew noticeably more vocal during the year. Such organizations as the Committee for Economic Development, the United States Council of the International Chamber of Commerce, the National Association of Manufacturers, and the National Foreign Trade Council called attention time and again to the "need" for larger imports and the unwanted consequences of a fall in exports, recommended further tariff reductions, urged renewal of the Trade Agreements Act when it expired in 1953 (frequently asking that, as a minimum, it also be freed of such weakening amendments as the peril-point provision), asked Congress to simplify customs administration and to liberalize or repeal the "Buy American" Act, and recommended that many of the import quotas on agricultural products be removed or liberalized.[3] Great publicity was given to a statement of policy by the Detroit Board of Commerce advocating the eventual elimination of all tariff

[2] Although there was much public discussion of future commercial policy during the year, there was virtually no grappling in public with the question of whether the concepts underlying the Reciprocal Trade Agreements Program were adequate for a world in which, entirely apart from rearmament programs, many nations were firmly committed to policies of full employment, internal economic stability, and direct state control over many economic transactions. (For an essay raising some of these questions, see Diebold, W., Jr., "The End of the I.T.O.," *Essays in International Finance*, No. 16, International Finance Section, Princeton University, October 1952, pp. 30-37.)

An important study, prepared at the New York Federal Reserve Bank and published during the year, indicated that price changes, especially in manufactured goods, have had a greater influence on the volume of imports than many had assumed. (See Adler, J. H., Schlesinger, E. R., and Van Westerborg, E., *The Pattern of United States Import Trade since 1923*, Federal Reserve Bank of New York, 1952.)

[3] See, for example, National Foreign Trade Council, *Final Declaration of the Thirty-Ninth Annual National Foreign Trade Convention*, New York, November 17-19, 1952; Committee for Economic Development, *Britain's Economic Problem and Its Meaning for America*, New York, March 1953; and United States Council of the International Chamber of Commerce, *The Expansion of Trade*, New York, April 1953. For an account of the views of the National Association of Manufacturers, see *New York Times*, November 7, 1952, pp. 24, 33, and December 4, 1952, p. 1. The recommendations of these various organizations were not, of course, identical and there was considerable difference in emphasis.

barriers in the United States and to a subsequent statement by the President of the Ford Motor Company urging, among other things, "the most rapid possible elimination of all tariffs," the immediate repeal of the tariff on automobiles, the dropping of all quotas, and the repeal of the "Buy American" Act.[4]

Three important studies during the year sponsored by the Administration—but in the preparation of which non-official persons participated in varying degrees—did not go as far as the statements of the spokesmen from Detroit in their recommendations, but, with varying stress and emphasis, came to conclusions similar to those in the reports of the other private organizations cited above. One asserted: "There is urgent need for a new United States trade and tariff policy. The trading regulations of this country are governed by a collection of laws, programs, and administrative procedures that do not meet the needs of the present situation and that are frequently in conflict with each other. What is necessary now is a trade policy in the national interest, not one designed merely to protect small groups of domestic producers from competition from abroad."[5]

Some interpreted these various statements as reflecting a basic shift in United States attitudes toward trade and tariff policy. But, there was virtually no evidence during the year of significant changes in the convictions of those persons and groups in the United States who had in the past favored relatively high protection, even though they were much less vocal than those who favored lowering barriers.[6]

Those who argued that there was, as yet at least, no appreciable increase in public sentiment in favor of more liberal trading policies could cite the presidential campaign. The platform of the victorious Republican party stated that "We favor the expansion of mutually advantageous world trade." But it went on to say that to

[4] See *New York Times*, February 18, 1953, p. 1, and February 22, 1953, p. E-8.

[5] Public Advisory Board for Mutual Security, *A Trade and Tariff Policy in the National Interest* (commonly referred to as the Bell Report), Wash., D.C., February 1953, p. 1. The other two reports referred to were: The President's Materials Policy Commission, *Resources for Freedom*, Wash., D.C., June 1952, especially Vol. I (often referred to as the Paley Report), and the report of the so-called Sawyer Mission, reprinted in *Foreign Commerce Weekly*, December 22, 1952, pp. 15-20.

[6] Professor Clair Wilcox asserted at the end of the year, "The fight on trade policy is not over. It has barely begun." (*New York Times*, December 23, 1952, p. E-8.)

further this objective the party would press for elimination of foreign "discrimination" against United States exports and that the Trade Agreements Program would be carried out "on a basis of true reciprocity" and would be administered so as to "safeguard" American enterprisers and workers against "unfair import competition."[7] The platform of the Democratic party stated that that party had always stood and would continue to stand "for expanding trade among free nations," noted that "our own economy requires expanded export markets," and asserted that "we vigorously oppose any restrictive policies which would weaken the highly successful reciprocal trade program. . . ."[8]

During the campaign both candidates spoke of the necessity of finding some "solution" for the apparent failure of the rest of the world, especially Europe, to earn all the dollars they wished to spend. On several occasions Mr. Stevenson talked of the "necessity" of the United States' lowering barriers to imports. The victorious candidate, General Eisenhower, also aligned himself with the economic internationalists, but he rarely talked specifically of trade and tariff policy and then in such qualified terms as these: ". . . while maintaining tariff policies that operate in the interest of our agriculture and industry, we should seek out opportunities to increase imports . . . which will improve our own economy and help make our Allies self-supporting."[9] Judging from the campaign platforms and the statements made by the candidates during the campaign, there did appear to be important differences in the policies the two candidates would pursue if elected; but perhaps the most important fact was that, despite this, the question of United States commercial policy was not an issue in the campaign, reflecting, it may be presumed, a general lack of interest in the problem among most of the electorate.

Whatever the immediate future might bring, and there were many differences of opinion as to the appropriate policies within the Republican party, the trend toward greater protectionism noted in the previous year was not reversed in 1952, as the account of activities in the rest of this chapter shows.

[7] *New York Times*, July 11, 1952, p. 8.
[8] *ibid.*, July 24, 1952, p. 16.
[9] A speech before the *New York Herald Tribune* Forum, October 21, 1952.

VI. TRADE AGREEMENTS PROGRAM

A. *TARIFF NEGOTIATIONS AND TRADE AGREEMENTS*

In asking Congress to extend the Reciprocal Trade Agreements Act in 1951, the Administration stated that, except for the negotiations then in progress under the General Agreement on Tariffs and Trade at Torquay, England, no extensive negotiations or concessions were contemplated for the next three years.[1] These spokesmen, however, did not rule out the possibility of limited bilateral negotiations, and in August 1952, following several months of discussions, a new agreement was signed supplementing and amending the 1939 bilateral undertaking with Venezuela.[2] The most important concessions granted by the United States were on imports of crude petroleum, topped crude petroleum, and residual fuel oil. By the terms of the 1939 agreement, the United States had imposed an excise tax of 10½ cents a barrel on such imports up to 5 percent of the crude petroleum processed in domestic refineries during the preceding calendar year and 21 cents per barrel on imports in excess of this quota. From 1943 to 1950 these rates were superseded by the trade agreement with Mexico, which eliminated the quota provision and applied the 10½-cent-a-barrel tax to all imports. With the termination of the Mexican agreement in 1950, the 1939 rates in the Venezuelan agreement again came into effect.[3]

The Trade Agreements Act, as amended, authorized the Administration to reduce this tax to 5¼ cents per barrel, and the President stated that the "majority" of the representatives of private business who appeared before the Tariff Commission and the Committee for Reciprocity Information while preparations were being made for the negotiations had urged that the maximum possible concession be made. As finally negotiated, however, the tax was set at 5¼ cents per barrel only for such imports as were derived from petroleum having a specific gravity test of under 25 degrees API (American Petroleum Institute rating) and at 10½ cents per barrel for imports testing 25 degrees API or more.

This case was significant not only because crude oil was an im-

[1] See *Survey–1951*, pp. 143, 164-169 for a summary account of the results of the Torquay negotiations.

[2] Turkey and the United States formally terminated their 1939 agreement, which had been superseded by Turkey's accession to the General Agreement on Tariffs and Trade in 1951.

[3] See *Survey–1950*, p. 189.

portant United States import (in accordance with the Trade Agreements Act, tariff concessions apply to imports from all non-Soviet-bloc sources) and because these products have constituted in recent years about 90 percent of the value of all Venezuelan exports to the United States, but also because it involved, for the first time, the peril-point procedure.[4] In 1951 Congress had reinstituted the provision in the Trade Agreements Act, which required the President to notify Congress whenever he proposed to reduce a tariff below the minimum (peril point), as determined by the Tariff Commission (with the advice of other Departments), necessary to prevent serious injury or threat of serious injury to the domestic industry producing the same or similar goods.[5] A majority of the Tariff Commission could not agree on a specific peril point with respect to crude petroleum, and there was consequently some question as to the legal position, but the concessions negotiated went beyond the points found by all of the Commissioners. President Truman therefore made a report to Congress in which he asserted that earlier experience had indicated that imports subject to a tax of 10½ cents a barrel were not likely to hinder domestic oil-drilling or -development programs, and the reduction would stimulate the development of proven oil resources in other countries of the Western Hemisphere; he pointed out that most of the United States crude oil products had a specific gravity rating in excess of 25 degrees API, whereas about one third of the Venezuelan output tested less than this.[6] Further, he said, most of the imported lower-gravity crude oil did not compete in the same markets with similar domestic crude, and since the lower-testing crude was cheaper, a lower specific tax was "appropriate." He also drew attention to the conclusion of the Tariff Commission that the lower tax would not alter the existing trend toward greater use of coal in East Coast manufacturing and power plants. Nevertheless, at the turn of the year there were indications that spokesmen for both the coal industry and the so-called inde-

[4] The Tariff Commission made peril-point determinations in 1948-1949, but the provision was repealed in 1949 and no concessions were actually granted while the peril points were a part of the law.

[5] See *Survey—1951*, pp. 151-154, and *Survey—1949*, p. 155.

[6] The text of the President's letter was reprinted in Department of State *Bulletin*, September 15, 1952, pp. 401-403.

pendent oil companies were planning to urge the new Congress to reimpose restrictions on petroleum imports.[7]

In addition to the concessions on petroleum imports, the United States bound existing duty-free treatment of iron ore imports[8] and granted concessions on a few other minor items. Altogether, United States concessions involved trade in 1950 valued at about $175 million. In return, Venezuela granted new or greater concessions on some 179 tariff items, the imports of which from the United States in 1950 were valued at $104 million.[9]

In compliance with the 1951 amendments to the Reciprocal Trade Agreements Act requiring that the President withdraw any concessions granted under it to Communist-dominated countries,[1] the Treaty of Friendship, Commerce, and Consular Rights with Poland was terminated in June following Poland's refusal to reply to the United States suggestion that only the most-favored-nation clause of the treaty be cancelled.[2] The following month the United States suspended the concessions extended Hungary under the most-favored-nation clause in a similar treaty with that country, thereby completing the cancellation of all concessions that had been contractually granted to the designated Communist countries.[3]

[7] See, for example, *New York Times*, December 28, 1952, p. F-1; January 18, 1953, p. F-1; and February 3, 1953, p. 38. In its report *A Trade and Tariff Policy in the National Interest, op.cit.*, pp. 35-37, the Public Advisory Board for Mutual Security concluded that there was "no good reason" for maintaining even the existing import taxes on crude oil and petroleum products.

[8] Some of the iron ore deposits in Venezuela, and other countries, were being exploited with the assistance of private United States capital.

[9] Venezuela withdrew earlier concessions on imports valued at $12 million in 1950 and imposed higher rates than those set in the 1939 agreement on 1950 imports valued at $6 million.

For an official discussion of the supplementary agreement, see *Foreign Commerce Weekly*, September 8, 1952, p. 3. The text of the agreement may be found in Department of State *Bulletin*, September 29, 1952, pp. 487-489.

The new agreement also included a provision whereby each signatory would impose no quantitative restrictions on imports from the other, except with respect to agricultural products where such restrictions were considered necessary "to secure the effective operation of governmental measures . . . to regulate or control the production, market supply, quality or price of like domestic articles."

[1] See *Survey—1951*, pp. 157-159.

[2] Department of State *Bulletin*, June 16, 1952, pp. 946-947.

[3] See *Survey—1951*, pp. 170-171 for action taken under this provision of the law during that year. In what was regarded as routine compliance with the Act, the President added Tibet to the list of areas and nations in which generalized extension of the most-favored-nation treatment should be withdrawn, even though

B. *ACTION UNDER THE ESCAPE CLAUSE*

A great deal of attention, in the United States and abroad, was focused on the activities under the escape clause that Congress had inserted in the Trade Agreements Act in June 1951. This clause was designed to provide greater protection to domestic producers claiming injury from tariff concessions than had been afforded by the standard escape clause embodied in the General Agreement on Tariffs and Trade and formerly written into United States trade agreements by administrative practice and, later, by Executive Orders.[4] Indicative of the encouragement the new provision gave domestic producers to seek relief from foreign competition was the fact that between June 1951 and the end of 1952 the Tariff Commission received twenty formal applications to carry out investigations with a view toward withdrawing or reducing concessions, as compared with twenty-three filed in the more than three years between April 1948, when the first application was made, and June 1951.[5]

It was also noteworthy that during 1952 the Tariff Commission recommended some increase in the duties on hatters' fur, watches and parts, figs, and garlic; and, in early 1953, on briar pipes. Under the previous procedures they had recommended that the escape clause be invoked in but one case, that of fur felt hats and hat bodies.[6] Less publicity was given to the fact that the Tariff Commission found during 1952 that there was no justification for invoking the clause with respect to motorcycles and parts, spring

---

the United States in 1952 had no trade agreement or direct trade with that country. (Department of State *Bulletin*, June 30, 1952, pp. 1018-1019.)

[4] For a description of the new clause and a summary of action taken under both the old and the new procedures through 1951, see *Survey–1951*, pp. 146-151, 171-172, and references cited therein.

For official accounts of escape-clause action, see U.S. Tariff Commission, *Fourth Report on Operations of the Trade Agreements Program, July 1950–June 1951*, Wash., D.C., 1952, and U.S. Tariff Commission, *Thirty-Sixth Annual Report*, Wash., D.C., January 1953. The Tariff Commission also periodically publishes the full texts of the results of its investigations in a series entitled *Report to the President on the Investigation under Section 7 of the Trade Agreements Act of 1951.*

Applications for investigation of claims of injury and the disposition of these applications are regularly reported in *Foreign Commerce Weekly* as they are made.

[5] Eight applications were filed in the second half of 1951 and twelve in 1952. Four applications (covering hatters' fur, blue-mold cheese, watches and parts, and motorcycles and parts) on which action had not been completed when the Act was amended were treated by the Tariff Commission under the new clause.

[6] See *Survey–1950*, pp. 186-188, and *Survey–1951*, p. 173n.

clothespins, groundfish fillets, *glacé* cherries, tuna and bonito in brine and bonito in oil,[7] wood screws, and bicycles and parts; and, in early 1953, with respect to certain types of china dinnerware.[8] (The Commission stated that it could make no finding on blue-mold cheese while Section 104 [see Section F (a), below] was in effect.) At the turn of the year investigations were under way on handblown glassware, cotton-carding machinery and parts, wood-screws (second investigation), estrogenic substances, whiting, wood-wind musical instruments and parts, screen-printed silk scarves, rosaries and similar articles of religious devotion, metal

[7] No concessions had been granted under the Trade Agreements Act on imports of fresh or frozen tuna and, in an attempt to provide immediate and temporary protection for the domestic fishing industry, which was reported idle because of growing imports of fresh and frozen tuna from Japan and, to a lesser extent, from Peru and other South American countries, the House in late 1951 passed a bill imposing a duty of 3 cents per pound on imports of these products until 1953. This bill also directed the Secretary of the Interior and the Tariff Commission to make studies of the competitive position of the domestic industry to aid Congress in determining what changes, if any, should be made in the duty. The Senate Finance Committee reported the bill out favorably in 1952 but it was subsequently rejected by the Senate. Acting on a later resolution of the Finance Committee, however, the Tariff Commission undertook a study of the industry and was to report its findings to the Finance Committee by March 1953.

The tuna case is interesting not only as an example of a method of providing relief against imports on which no concessions have been made and of efforts by Congress again to legislate tariffs on individual commodities but also because there were sharp differences of opinion within the Administration on the bill. The spokesmen from the Department of the Interior approved the bill, the Department of State shifted its position during the consideration of the bill from one of modified support to one of opposition, the Department of Commerce opposed it, and the Department of Agriculture did not object to the bill. Those opposing the measure did so on the grounds that by restricting Japan's second most important dollar export it would increase the pressures on that country to trade with Communist China and that it might lead to retaliation by the Latin American countries—which had recently been developing their industry with the help of the International Bank and private American investors. The East Coast canners opposed the bill because it would cut off an important part of their tuna supply. (See *Congressional Record*, June 24, 1952, pp. 8031-8048, and "Tuna Imports," *Hearings on H.R. 5693*, U.S. Senate, Committee on Finance, 82d Cong., 2d Sess., February 4-7, 1952.)

[8] Section 336 of the Tariff Act of 1930 permits petitions to the Tariff Commission to investigate, and then to inform the President, as to the duties necessary to equalize domestic and foreign production costs of specific commodities; the President in turn is authorized to proclaim the imposition of such duties. This section thus affords one possible method of escape from injury when an import is not subject to a trade agreement concession. Congress passed a resolution in 1952 (S. Res. 253) directing the Tariff Commission to investigate imports of certain types of Japanese chinaware (on which concessions had not been granted) under this section. The Commission had already denied the industry's application for an investigation. This inquiry, the only one before the Commission in 1952 under Section 336, had not been completed by the year's end.

watch bracelets and parts (other than those of gold or platinum), and hard fiber cord and twine.[9]

President Truman reluctantly approved and put into effect the recommended partial withdrawals of tariff concessions on imports of dried figs and hatters' fur. In implementing the Tariff Commission's recommendation on hatters' fur, the President stated that "While we must be alert to safeguard American industry from actual or threatened serious injury, we must be equally alert to insure that trade agreement concessions are not modified for a period longer than is necessary to prevent or remedy the injury." He warned that if the higher rates were maintained longer than necessary this would encourage retaliation, would unnecessarily raise prices to consumers in the United States, and would, by denying foreigners an opportunity to earn dollars, obstruct other foreign policies of the United States, especially the mutual defense program.[1] Soon thereafter, under terms of Article XIX of the General Agreement on Tariffs and Trade (GATT), Belgian officials consulted with the U.S. Government on the increase in these duties and, failing to arrive at what they regarded as a satisfactory solution, announced their intention to withdraw the concession on industrial wax that had been negotiated by the Benelux countries with the United States at Geneva in 1947.[2]

The President accompanied his proclamation of an increased duty on dried figs with the statement that there was some indication that the necessity for this step was due to abnormal crop and seasonal factors and that the situation was of a temporary nature. He said that the Tariff Commission and the Department of State would keep the domestic and foreign situations under review so that if conditions changed appropriate recommendations might be made before the 1953 marketing season.[3] As noted in Section D, below, this increased duty led to complaints by

[9] See *Journal of Commerce*, New York, June 17, 1952, p. 1, and *Foreign Commerce Weekly*, October 27, 1952, p. 28 for a discussion of some of these cases.

[1] Department of State *Bulletin*, January 21, 1952, pp. 96-97. The President recommended establishing a system of periodic review of all modification of tariff concessions under the escape clause and a few months later formal procedures were set up for such reviews. (The Presidential Order was published in Department of State *Bulletin*, November 3, 1952, pp. 712-713.)

[2] See *New York Times*, April 24, 1952, p. 12. In the 1947 negotiations the Benelux countries had bound their low duty on industrial wax in exchange for the United States duty reduction on hatters' fur.

[3] Department of State *Bulletin*, September 1, 1952, pp. 337-338.

Greece and Turkey at the Seventh Session of the Contracting Parties and, in early 1953, President Eisenhower requested the Tariff Commission to investigate whether the higher duty on figs remained "necessary."

President Truman took a strong position against what he termed the "protectionist overtones" of the escape clause in his rejection of the Tariff Commission's recommendations on garlic and on watches.[4] In the case of garlic, the President found the evidence for reimposing restrictions "tenuous and unpersuasive," and added, "The claim that American producers of garlic have been seriously injured by imports is mere assertion."[5] He noted that production of garlic was a very small element in the United States economy and that it was grown as an incidental part of a much larger vegetable and beet sugar business; he concluded that farmers dissatisfied with their return from garlic could readily turn to other remunerative crops. He asserted that the growth of garlic imports from Italy should be welcomed, not discouraged, if the United States wished to continue its policy of strengthening that economy. He emphasized that the objective of the Trade Agreements Act was to promote and not to contract foreign trade and he stated that the Tariff Commission should carry out its activities "in the light of this general objective, despite protectionist pressures."[6]

In rejecting the Tariff Commission's recommendations that the existing duties on certain classes of watch movements be raised substantially, the President again disagreed with the finding that the present level of imports threatened serious injury to the domestic industry.[7] He said he could not support the "share doc-

[4] President Truman left to his successor the responsibility for dealing with the Tariff Commission's recommendation, in early 1953, that the duties on briar pipes be raised. President Eisenhower made an interim decision not to raise these duties pending the development of the new Administration's trade policies and asked the Tariff Commission for additional data on which he might base the final ruling on the case. (See *New York Times*, January 11, 1953, p. 1; February 19, 1953, p. 1; and March 7, 1953, p. 23; and *Foreign Commerce Weekly*, March 2, 1953, p. 28.

[5] The text of the President's letter to the Chairman of the Senate Committee on Finance and the Chairman of the House Committee on Ways and Means was reprinted in Department of State *Bulletin*, August 25, 1952, pp. 303-305.

[6] It should be remembered, however, that the legislation under which the Tariff Commission operates confines its "findings" to determining specific facts, and in its recommendations the Commission is not permitted to take into account many broad national policy considerations.

[7] The Tariff Commission divided evenly on the issue of whether the industry

trine": that serious injury was indicated by the fact that, even though the total market had increased, the expansion of domestic production had not kept pace with the expansion of imports. He emphasized the "extremely serious" impact of such a tariff increase on Swiss-American relations, noting that watches and watch movements constituted over half of United States imports from Switzerland, that restrictive policies had already curtailed imports of Swiss cheese and almonds, that the United States sold twice as much to Switzerland as it bought from her, and that Switzerland was one of the few countries without quota restrictions on dollar imports.

In his statements on the garlic and watch cases, President Truman also noted the fears engendered abroad by the number of applications for relief under the escape clause. This foreign apprehension had been officially expressed earlier in the year by the Italian Government in a note to the State Department asserting that recent United States import restrictions had damaged Italian trade with the United States and that further restrictions would seriously impair the domestic economy of Italy. The statement expressed fear lest any success in marketing Italian goods in the United States be greeted with demands for further import barriers.[8] A few months later the British Government took a similar position in a memorandum to the State Department, stating that the "most disturbing increase" in the number of appeals for relief under the escape clause was having a discouraging effect upon the willingness of British and other exporters to take risks in developing the American market. Yet, the memorandum asserted, Britain and the other countries must greatly increase their dollar earnings if "deplorable" restrictions on trade were to be avoided and if dependence on United States aid were to be ended.[9]

was then suffering serious injury, but a majority of four found that a threat of serious injury existed. For details on this case, see *Foreign Commerce Weekly*, August 25, 1952, p. 2, and *New York Times*, August 15, 1952, pp. 1, 8. The text of the President's letter on this case can be found in Department of State *Bulletin*, August 25, 1952, pp. 305-307.

[8] The text of the Italian note may be found in Department of State *Bulletin*, April 28, 1952, pp. 661-665. See also *New York Times*, February 14, 1952, p. 1, and April 18, 1952, p. 3 for comment on the Italian note and the United States reply to it. The official State Department reply was reprinted in Department of State *Bulletin*, April 28, 1952, pp. 660-661.

[9] The text of the British memorandum and Secretary Acheson's press statement

In reply, the State Department affirmed its position that "modifications of duty concessions should only be made in cases of genuinely serious injury or threat of injury" and agreed that obligations under the GATT should be "scrupulously observed" and that the escape clause "should not be invoked merely because a concession results in more vigorous competition from imports." The Department reiterated the conviction of the Executive Branch as to the necessity for reducing and minimizing trade barriers. Western European spokesmen welcomed these reaffirmations of Administration policy, but at least one official spokesman took occasion to point out that it was the policy of Congress, not of the Truman Administration, that was causing anxiety abroad.[1]

The 1951 extension of the Trade Agreements Act also required the President, "as soon as practicable," to include the escape clause in all existing trade agreements and to report semiannually to Congress on what had been done.[2] His initial report, in January 1952, stated that all but six agreements contained such clauses. One of these, the bilateral agreement with Turkey, was terminated on August 4, 1952, following the accession of Turkey to the General Agreement. A second, the 1939 bilateral agreement with Venezuela, was supplemented in August by a new agreement containing an escape clause applying to concessions in both the original and the supplemental agreement. At the end of the year discussions were still in progress with Ecuador as to the possible inclusion of an escape clause in that agreement, but the Trade Agreements Committee had determined that it was not then "practicable" to negotiate for inserting the clause in the agree-

regarding it were reprinted in Department of State *Bulletin*, May 12, 1952, pp. 737-738. The formal State Department reply may be found in Department of State *Bulletin*, June 2, 1952, p. 858.

[1] See *New York Times*, April 18, 1952, p. 3 for this statement by an Italian Foreign Ministry spokesman. Other European comments are reported in the *New York Times*, April 19, 1952, p. 1, and April 25, 1952, p. 5.

Unofficial foreign reaction to the "flood" of applications for relief under this clause echoed the anxiety expressed in official quarters. This concern reached its height just before the President's decision on the watch case and was widely reported in the New York press. His rejection of higher duties for watches, following close on the heels of his refusal to restrict garlic imports, received a warm reception from exporters to the United States and from domestic importers. (See, for example, *New York Times*, August 16, 1952, p. 1; August 18, 1952, pp. 25, 26; and August 17, 1952, pp. E-8, F-3.)

[2] See *Survey—1951*, pp. 146-147.

ments with the three remaining countries—El Salvador, Guatemala, and Honduras.[3]

C. *CUSTOMS SIMPLIFICATION*

As a part of its program of liberalizing restrictions on trade, and of discharging obligations assumed under the GATT, the Administration, supported by many private groups, had for several years been urging Congress to pass a customs simplification bill. A specific proposal was introduced into Congress in May 1950 and reintroduced in 1951, and an amended version was adopted by the House of Representatives in October 1951.[4] The Senate Finance Committee held hearings on the bill in April 1952 and the discussion was for the most part a repetition of that during the 1951 House hearings.[5] The Senate committee, however, did not report the measure out before Congress adjourned and announced that action on the measure had been deferred indefinitely.[6]

The failure of Congress to take action was generally attributed to lack of interest in the complex and technical proposal rather than to outright opposition to it. Administration spokesmen, those making officially sponsored studies and reports on future United States international economic policy,[7] and such influential private

[3] The Administration reported that many of the products from these countries on which the United States had granted concessions were on the free list and that most of the others were not likely to be commercially produced in the United States. On the other hand, it was said, a substantial portion of the concessions granted the United States by these countries were on products that competed with their domestic output. It was concluded, therefore, that opening negotiations for an escape clause would probably lead to a renegotiation of the existing agreement on terms less favorable to the United States.

[4] A summary of the major provisions and the debate on them may be found in *Survey—1950*, pp. 190-194, and *Survey—1951*, pp. 160-164.

[5] Administration spokesmen appearing before the Committee in 1952 endorsed the bill as it stood, despite the fact that several proposals sponsored by the Administration in the original measure had been eliminated by the House. The Treasury representative stated that his Department did not propose reinstating the controversial provision that would abolish "American selling price" as a basis for determining the value of certain imports. ("Customs Simplification Act," *Hearings on H.R. 5505*, U.S. Senate, Committee on Finance, 82d Cong., 2d Sess., April 22-29, 1952.)

[6] *Foreign Commerce Weekly*, July 21, 1952, p. 2.

[7] The so-called Sawyer Mission reported that Europeans believed that simplifying United States customs procedures was as important as the lowering of tariff barriers in "promoting healthy international trade." (*Foreign Commerce Weekly*, December 22, 1952, p. 15.)

The Public Advisory Board for Mutual Security, in its *A Trade and Tariff*

organizations as, among others, the Committee for Economic Development, the National Foreign Trade Council, the United States Council of the International Chamber of Commerce, the National Association of Manufacturers, and the National Council of American Importers continued to recommend early passage of the bill. President Eisenhower, in his first State of the Union message, also endorsed customs simplification.[8]

Some progress was made during the year toward the acceptance of simplified customs procedures internationally when the Seventh Session of the Contracting Parties to the GATT, after study by a working party of proposals originating in the International Chamber of Commerce, drafted and referred to governments for further action an International Convention to facilitate the importation of commercial samples and advertising material, and codes of standard practices simplifying documentary requirements and consular formalities.[9]

D. *SEVENTH SESSION OF THE CONTRACTING PARTIES*[1]

The Contracting Parties to the General Agreement on Tariffs and Trade (GATT) meet from time to time in "sessions" to consult, and to discuss and take decisions on broad policy issues as well as specific problems that have arisen under the operation of the Agreement. The seventh such session was held in Geneva

---

Policy in the National Interest, op.cit. (the so-called Bell Report), Chapter VII, concluded that while the proposed measure should be enacted promptly, "nothing less than a basic reform of customs administrative law is required." See this report for an informative account of the inequities, delays, and uncertainties arising from existing customs procedures. Chapter VI of this study provides much specific information on the extreme complexities of the United States tariff schedules. These complexities, related to the problem of customs administration, the study found, provide a great deal of protection over and above that given by the actual duties. This group therefore recommended that an entirely new "Tariff Simplification, Consolidation, and Reduction Act," designed to reduce many of the current rates of duty and to eliminate the existing uncertainties in classification of imports, be enacted by Congress. The group also recommended that the President be given authority to enter into reciprocal trade agreements without time limitations.

[8] See *New York Times*, February 3, 1953, p. 14.

[9] The Convention will become effective after ratification by fifteen nations, and the State Department planned to submit it to Congress for approval in 1953. The Administration also planned to submit the codes to Congress for approval by means of a joint resolution. (For further details, see *New York Times*, December 7, 1952, p. F-1, and *Foreign Commerce Weekly*, December 1, 1952, p. 16, and December 15, 1952, p. 8.

[1] For a brief account of the earlier sessions, see *Survey—1951*, pp. 172-180, and references cited therein.

from October 2 through November 10, 1952 and was attended by representatives of thirty-one of the thirty-four Contracting Parties to the Agreement,[2] and observers from nine non-members and seven international organizations. The agenda included many important items, but the discussions were carried out in an atmosphere of much uncertainty since Britain and some of the Commonwealth countries had previously shown growing doubts as to the advantages they were reaping from participation and future United States policy was to be determined by a new Administration and Congress.[3]

Complaints against the United States

Delegates from eight of the Contracting Parties had complained at the Sixth Session, in 1951, that the restrictions imposed in the United States on importations of dairy products under Section 104 of the Defense Production Act were a "nullification and impairment" of the benefits expected and violated the Agreement. The United States delegates did not deny the charges and recognized that injury had been caused but stated that the Executive Branch was trying to get Congress to repeal the provision. The Contracting Parties therefore agreed to leave the matter on the agenda and counseled the offended members to wait and see if Congress would remove the amendment before applying retaliatory measures. Congress insisted on retaining the provision, with certain ameliorative amendments, however (see Section F, below), and at the Seventh Session several delegates again registered complaints.[4] Some took occasion to point out that these quotas made it difficult for their countries to eliminate their "need" for financial aid from the United States. Others, including some from countries that did not export dairy products, stated that it was this type of legislation that discouraged exporters and

[2] Liberia, Peru, and Nicaragua were not represented.

[3] An official summary of the decisions taken during this session may be found in Department of State *Bulletin*, December 1, 1952, pp. 876-879. More detailed statements, the sources of most of the information given here, were published in European Office of the United Nations, *International Trade News Bulletin*, Geneva, November 1952, pp. 512-523, and in the various press releases issued during the session.

[4] The texts of several of the statements and official summaries of others may be found in European Office of the United Nations, *Press Release GATT/90* and *Press Release GATT/91*, Geneva, October 28, 1952.

their governments from attempting to develop a market in the United States, as they had so often been encouraged to do by the U.S. Government. Many delegates stressed that an important question of principle was involved and others said that such actions by the United States contributed to the severity of the dollar import restrictions maintained in some countries. It was also asserted that while the modifications introduced into Section 104 and the subsequent administration of it during the year had had the desirable effect of permitting larger cheese imports they had also introduced discrimination as among types of cheese and exporting countries.

In reply, the United States delegate pointed out that his country had played a leading role in the liberalizing of trade since the war and that the dairy products case had attracted so much attention precisely because it was a deviation from the nation's general policy. He denied that the 1952 liberalization of the quotas had introduced discrimination as to source but acknowledged that Section 104 was in conflict with the GATT provisions and recognized the right of other Contracting Parties to retaliate by withdrawing concessions. He stated, however, that retaliation was not a remedy and that the Administration's objective was the complete elimination of the quotas.

It was generally agreed that the U.S. Executive Branch had tried to get the amendment repealed and most delegates held that taking compensatory action was not a satisfactory solution to the problem. Therefore, the U.S. Government was again formally asked to continue its efforts to secure the repeal of the offending section. The Netherlands, however, asked for and received authority to compensate for the damage caused it by reducing for the year 1953 the maximum imports of wheat flour from the United States from 72,000 tons to 60,000 tons. Other countries reserved the right to take retaliatory action later and the item was left on the agenda for the next session.[5]

As noted above, during the summer President Truman invoked the "escape clause" under the Reciprocal Trade Agreements Act (and Article XIX of the GATT) in the case of dried figs, and the rate of duty on this commodity was raised from the 2½ cents per

[5] It was agreed that a special session would be called if any other member requested permission to take compensatory action.

pound agreed upon in the Torquay negotiations in 1951 to 4½ cents per pound. At the Seventh Session of the Contracting Parties in October the delegates from Greece and Turkey complained that this action was adversely affecting their exports. The United States delegate "expressed sympathy" with the situation in these countries and, following consultations and pursuant to a resolution by the Contracting Parties, the U.S. Administration agreed to ask the Tariff Commission to review the facts of the case as soon as practicable;[6] the Turkish Government decided to raise duties on certain of its imports from the United States so long as the United States increased duty on figs remained in effect; and the United States and Greece initiated a study of their trade to determine whether the former might make some compensating concessions to Greece.

The United States agricultural subsidies also came in for criticism at the session. Delegates from Greece and Turkey, supported by those from several other countries, stated that the United States practice of subsidizing the production and export of raisins was depriving them of traditional markets in third countries.[7] The spokesman for the United States replied that the issue was part of a much larger problem faced by many countries—how to reconcile domestic agricultural policies and international commercial policies. In this particular case, he said, the purpose of the subsidy was to counteract other countries' import restrictions on raisins from the dollar area and that the effect had been to maintain United States exports at about the prewar level. Nonetheless, he expressed a willingness to consult with the officials from the affected countries and it was agreed that such consultation would take place and the matter would be put on the agenda of the next session.[8]

[6] In March 1953 President Eisenhower asked the Tariff Commission to investigate whether the higher duty was still necessary. (*Foreign Commerce Weekly*, March 23, 1953, p. 31.)

[7] Article XVI of the GATT, commonly regarded as a weak provision, requires each member to notify the Contracting Parties if it grants subsidies, including income or price supports, that have the effect of increasing exports or decreasing imports. If the interest of another Contracting Party is seriously damaged, the member granting the subsidy is requested to discuss the possibility of limiting the subsidization. Many spokesmen at the Seventh Session, but not those from the United States, argued that the provisions in the Agreement against export subsidies should be made more stringent.

[8] Official summaries of the debate are given in European Office of the United Nations, *Press Release GATT/87*, Geneva, October 17, 1952.

Dollar Import Restrictions by Belgium

At the Sixth Session, in 1951, the United States and Canada had complained that the quantitative restrictions imposed by Belgium on certain dollar imports in September of that year had damaged their trade and constituted a violation of the GATT.[9] The Contracting Parties decided not to press for any formal action after the Belgian delegate gave assurances that his country intended to abide by the rules of the GATT, and that the restrictions would be removed as soon as possible. At the Seventh Session the Belgian Government stated that it was planning within two or three months to relax "significantly" its quotas on dollar imports. The spokesmen for the United States and Canada expressed satisfaction with this decision and agreed that the matter need not be pursued further for the time being. Delegates from France, Italy, and the Netherlands, however, expressed concern lest the proposed Belgian measure result in deterioration of the balance of payments positions of other European countries whose exports had benefited from the Belgian quotas on dollar imports. The United States and Canadian delegations replied in strong terms that they could not condone any intra-European arrangements that discouraged a country in Belgium's position from relaxing restrictions on imports in conformity with its international obligations.[1]

Consultations on Quantitative Restrictions

The GATT, in general, bans the use by members of quantitative restrictions on imports and exports but Article XII permits their use in certain circumstances, especially when determined to be necessary to safeguard a member's balance of payments and international reserves, and Article XIV permits the discriminatory application of such restrictions during the so-called postwar transition period. The General Agreement provides, however, that any intensification of restrictions under Article XII requires consultation among the members and, from 1952 onward, members

[9] These restrictions were intended by Belgium to redirect some of her imports to European sources in order to reduce her European Payments Union surplus. (See Chapter VIII, Section A.)

[1] European Office of the United Nations, *Press Release GATT/101*, Geneva, November 11, 1952. See also *New York Times*, November 2, 1952, p. 9.

maintaining discriminatory restrictions are required to hold yearly consultations with the Contracting Parties.

At the time of the Seventh Session twenty-one of the thirty-four Contracting Parties stated that they were maintaining quantitative restrictions on imports to safeguard their balances of payments and were exercising some degree of discrimination among sources of supply. Two others reported that they were maintaining non-discriminatory restrictions.[2] Several members had intensified their import restrictions during 1952 but in many cases these were applied more generally than in earlier years and discrimination against dollar imports therefore became somewhat less marked.[3]

During the Seventh Session consultations were held by the Contracting Parties with several of the members and it was planned to carry out at a later date similar consultations with others. The official statements emphasized that the purpose of these consultations was to "provide for a full and frank exchange of views," and that every effort was made to avoid any feeling that those maintaining restrictions were "defendants" and the other members "plaintiffs." Further, no attempt was made "to seek collective pronouncements on the justification of the discriminatory policies of countries under review." The delegates from the countries whose restrictions were the subject of the consultations stated, however, that they would convey to their governments the views expressed by the other members. In the discussion there was a growing recognition that internal inflation was one of the basic causes of balance of payments difficulties and that the restrictions were, in fact, giving protection to certain domestic industries and were resulting, in some cases, in "uneconomic" production. It was also found that in certain instances discrimination, by a concentrated favoring of imports from certain areas, had driven up prices and so tended to aggravate the balance of pay-

[2] Only Belgium, Canada, Cuba, the Dominican Republic, Haiti, Luxembourg, Nicaragua, Peru, and the United States reported they were not taking advantage of Article XII. Burma and Liberia had not advised the Contracting Parties as to their practices.

[3] For more details on these restrictions, especially on the discriminatory aspects, see Contracting Parties to the General Agreement on Tariffs and Trade, *Third Report on the Discriminatory Application of Import Restrictions*, Geneva, November 1952. This report and European Office of the United Nations, *Press Release GATT/78*, Geneva, October 8, 1952, and *Press Release GATT/96*, November 11, 1952 are the sources of most of the information in this section.

ments difficulties of the countries applying the import restrictions and had also given incidental protection to some supplying countries, thus making probable difficult adjustments when the discriminations were removed. Several countries reported that they were, by various measures, trying to avoid some of these consequences.

Waivers for the Schuman Plan

The European Coal and Steel Community (see Chapter VIII) raised another serious problem for the Contracting Parties. All the members of the proposed Community were also signatories to the GATT but the provisions of the Treaty establishing the Community collided in several respects with the members' obligations under the General Agreement, especially with the most-favored-nation and nondiscriminatory commitments.[4] In applying for a waiver of their obligations under the GATT, the six members of the Community argued that the effect of creating a single regional market for coal and steel products would be to increase the supply of coal and steel products available to outside countries and to widen the market within the Community for the products of the other Contracting Parties.[5] Although most of the other Contracting Parties agreed on the desirability of the Community and were anxious to facilitate its creation, some of the members expressed concern over its effect on their trade and asked that assurances be given by the Community that it would pursue a liberal trade policy with respect to non-members.[6] The delegate of the United

[4] Under the Community all import and export duties on coal and steel products were to be abolished among the members of the coal and steel pool without these benefits being passed on to the other GATT members; quantitative restrictions on coal and steel trade were to be eliminated among the members of the Community but not on trade between the Community and non-members; Holland, Belgium, and Luxembourg planned to withdraw certain concessions already granted under the GATT by imposing tariff quotas for steel imports during a transitional period of the Community, to be followed by an increase in certain of their present tariffs on steel products; and Belgium planned for a period to protect its coal industry by imposing quantitative restrictions on imports.

[5] For official details on the discussion and the action taken, see European Office of the United Nations, *Press Release GATT/77*, Geneva, October 7, 1952, and *Press Release GATT/102*, Geneva, November 10, 1952. See also the account given in *The Economist*, November 22, 1952, p. 524. These documents are the sources of most of the information given here.

[6] The Czech delegate to the GATT session was apparently alone in his insistence that the Community was in conflict with the spirit as well as the letter of the GATT and that the two institutions could not legally be reconciled.

States, whose policy was to support the Community, was cautious in his official public utterances.[7] He stated that the Schuman Plan should be viewed with great sympathy, that the problems between the GATT and the Community were important ones, and that the waivers should not be granted without careful study. In his eyes the critical issues were whether the Community in its operations would be less restrictive on trade than its individual members were and whether it would maintain the "spirit" of GATT. He concluded that the answer was in the affirmative in both cases.

In the event, the Contracting Parties granted the necessary waivers after the members of the Community agreed "to take account of the interests of third countries," "to further the development of international trade," and to insure that "equitable prices" would be charged for its exports, that no "unreasonable barriers" would be placed on exports to third countries, and that the members would "harmonize" the various duties and other trade regulations upon a basis "which shall be lower and less restrictive than the general incidence of the duties and regulations of commerce" then being applied by individual members.[8] The agreement made no provision for sanctions should these generally worded commitments be violated.

Accession of Japan

The Government of Japan notified the Contracting Parties in July that it wished to engage in multilateral tariff negotiations under the GATT with a view to subsequent accession. Discussion of the request was postponed until the Seventh Session, at which time the delegate from Japan emphasized the importance of international trade to his country and stated that "profound changes" had taken place in Japan since the war; in particular, he stressed that real wages had risen and several fair trade practice laws had been passed. The United States delegate spoke in general terms of the importance of Japan's taking her place "as soon as possible" in the international trading community, and he urged that the matter be approached "constructively." Nonetheless, he suggested that, in view of (a) the desire of the other member countries to

[7] The press reported, however, that in the confidential discussions the United States delegate was one of the strongest proponents for granting the waivers.

[8] *Press Release GATT/102, op.cit.*

obtain more concrete information on Japan's commercial policies and practices and (b) the fact that no general tariff-negotiating conference was contemplated in the immediate future,[9] the question be referred for study to an intersessional committee. He did not find it necessary to mention that the fate of the Trade Agreements Act, the legal basis for United States participation, would be in the hands of a new Administration and Congress. Representatives from Turkey, Germany, Sweden, Pakistan, Indonesia, and Ceylon spoke in favor of quick and favorable action on the Japanese request, but the British and French delegates (whose exporters were facing increasingly severe competition from Japanese traders) argued that the question should be thoroughly and closely examined in view of the complicated issues involved.[1] Those favoring a delaying action won the day and the Japanese request was referred to an intersessional committee, which was to make a detailed examination of the application and then to report to the Contracting Parties.[2]

Administration of the GATT

After the United States abandoned the ITO Charter[3] the Administration urged that the Contracting Parties create some permanent administrative machinery for the General Agreement. The British Government, and others, demurred on this at the 1951 session and apparently the question was not raised at the Seventh Session, where it was agreed to reestablish the Ad Hoc Committee for Agenda and Intersessional Business to perform various administrative functions for the GATT until the Eighth Session,

[9] Provision was made in the Sixth Session, however, for special intersessional negotiations under the GATT.

[1] Several delegates pointed out that negotiations with Japan under the GATT would be especially complex because of the size of her overseas trade and the fact that once Japan acceded she would be entitled to the concessions members had previously granted others. The British delegate stated that in the case of past tariff concessions the Parties had given relatively little attention to the cost of extending these concessions *de jure* to possible future acceders and that they would therefore have to consider "very closely" whether they could retain the old concessions in the "new situation" that would exist if Japan joined.

[2] An official summary of the discussions may be found in European Office of the United Nations, *Press Release* GATT/82, Geneva, October 13, 1952.

[3] For an analysis of why the Charter was dropped by the United States, see Diebold, W., Jr., "The End of the I.T.O.," *Essays in International Finance*, No. 16, International Finance Section, Princeton University, October 1952.

scheduled to open in Geneva in September 1953.[4] There was, apparently, no formal continuation of the discussions held at the previous session of the need for calling a constitutional session of the Contracting Parties to make a thoroughgoing reexamination of the GATT.

Other Major Activities

The proposal offered by France in 1951 that the tariffs of all members should be lowered by 30 percent in three yearly stages of 10 percent was studied by a special working party during the year. At the Seventh Session the Contracting Parties "noted the progress" made in resolving some of the problems and instructed the working party to continue its studies, taking into account a new proposal submitted by the French delegation. The Contracting Parties also extended the time limit Brazil, Nicaragua, Korea, and the Philippines had for signing the Torquay Protocols and the one Uruguay had for signing both the Annecy and Torquay Protocols. Austria and Germany carried out certain limited tariff negotiations during the Session providing for concessions in addition to those negotiated at Torquay in 1951.

The Contracting Parties heard a complaint by Norway that West Germany was discriminating against Norwegian sardines, and Germany accepted a recommendation of the Parties that she consider ways of removing this discrimination. The Contracting Parties also recommended that Belgium remove the discrimination arising from a special import tax designed to countervail a system of family allowances in effect in Belgium and discussed possible measures for reconciling some of the Indian-Pakistani trade disputes. Ceylon was given permission, under Article XVIII, to impose some additional protective measures designed to hasten her economic development. Italy was given permission to continue exempting certain imports from Libya from customs duties for three more years. Greece, on the recommendation of the Contracting Parties, agreed to undertake to reduce certain increased customs duty "coefficients." The Contracting Parties found that

[4] The Public Advisory Board for Mutual Security recommended in early 1953 that Congress should take whatever steps were necessary to enable the United States to join in establishing a formal international organization for promoting the objectives of the General Agreement. See their *A Trade and Tariff Policy in the National Interest, op.cit.*, pp. 72-74.

the United Kingdom had modified its domestic purchase tax system so as to remove its discriminatory effects on imports. As noted in Section C, above, the Contracting Parties also made certain recommendations for simplifying customs procedures.

* * * * *

As in earlier years, the discussions of the Seventh Session were not widely publicized, but from the available data it appeared that the declining support of the GATT that had been recorded in 1951 had at least not been accentuated and may have been arrested. Several troublesome trade disputes had been disposed of, at least temporarily, at Geneva with relatively little retaliation. Moreover, the economic correspondent in Europe for the *New York Times* reported, there had been a "tremendous growth in the interest in and support of the General Agreement as an institution by countries that in the past have been either cynical or purely passive about this experiment. . . ."[5] It was perhaps also significant that the communiqué issued at the close of the London meeting of the British Commonwealth Ministers in December 1952 indicated that while these countries might ask for certain amendments to the provisions of the GATT, especially to those that prohibited new preferences, there was no present intention of withdrawing from the Agreement—a possibility that had been suggested by British spokesmen in 1951.[6] On the other hand, the U.S. Congress had shown no greater sympathy for the GATT than it had in 1951 when it had gone out of its way to insist that it was an executive agreement and had not yet been approved by the Legislative Branch.

E. *MISCELLANEOUS ENCOURAGEMENT OF IMPORTS*

One of the few measures taken during 1952 to stimulate imports was the revision of the regulations governing the operations of the foreign trade zones. The 1950 amendments to the Celler Foreign Trade Zones Act permitted limited manufacturing and exhibiting in the zones, and in the year under review the regulations were revised to encourage further such operations by permitting zones or sub-zones to be established in business centers

[5] *New York Times*, November 9, 1952, p. 12.

[6] See *The Economist*, December 20, 1952, pp. 840-841, and *Survey—1951*, p. 179.

physically outside the existing zones but remaining under zone jurisdiction. It was anticipated that this action would permit trade shows at locations convenient to buyers and exhibitors without the expense of customs bonds or other restrictions and without special Congressional action permitting imports for such occasions. The new regulations also simplified the customs rules governing zone operations.[7]

The proposed Second International Trade Fair in Chicago was not held, but several international "shows" and "expositions" were held in various American cities and the President signed a Congressional joint resolution approving the holding of an International Trade Fair, and the establishment of an Inter-American Cultural Center, in New Orleans in 1953 to celebrate the sesquicentennial of the Louisiana Purchase and to foster "improved relations and increased trade with other nations."[8]

F. *CONFLICTS BETWEEN TRADE AND AGRICULTURAL POLICIES*

Major conflicts arose during 1952, as in previous years, between United States domestic agricultural policies and international trade policies, with such conflicts usually being resolved in favor of the former.

Direct Import Controls

a. FATS AND OILS—THE "CHEESE AMENDMENT"

Despite strong objections from the Administration, supported by many importers, exporters, and consumers, Congress in June 1951 substantially extended the scope of previous import controls on fats and oils by adding the so-called "cheese amendment" (Section 104) to the Defense Production Act of 1950. This provision added cheese and other dairy products to the commodities subject to import quotas and provided new and broadened criteria for imposing them.[9] Several friendly countries had protested these

[7] For an official analysis of the revised trade zone rules, see *Foreign Commerce Weekly*, July 28, 1952, p. 3.

[8] P.L. 290, 82d Cong.

[9] For a brief history of import controls on fats and oils in previous years, see *Survey—1951*, pp. 182-184. The import control provisions of the Second War Powers Act, which Section 104 replaced, had authorized quotas when they were essential to the acquisition or distribution of products in short world supply, or

import restrictions on the grounds, among others, that they violated obligations assumed by the United States under the GATT and impaired and nullified the efforts taken by them, in complete accord with the Marshall Plan, to become independent of outside financial assistance. Even more disturbing to many foreign countries was the fact that they discerned in these restrictions and in the growing number of petitions, noted in Section B, above, from United States producers for relief under the escape clause of the Trade Agreements Act, a trend toward heightened protectionism in United States trade policy.[1] At the Torquay session of the GATT in 1951 the Administration persuaded the offended countries to delay taking retaliatory action pending possible Congressional repeal of Section 104. Despite Administration efforts to secure an early repeal, the Senate three times sent back to committee a special bill to terminate the "cheese amendment."[2]

In a message to Congress in early 1952 urging extension of the Defense Production Act, President Truman again asked for a quick end to the "cheese amendment." "Otherwise," he stated, "the friendly countries who are being hurt by this amendment may retaliate—as they have a right to do—against American exports of

---

were essential to the orderly liquidation of temporary surpluses of stock owned or controlled by the Government. It did not specify cheese or dairy products. The Secretary of Agriculture had also imposed quotas under the general authority given the President by Section 101 of the Defense Production Act of 1950 "to allocate materials and facilities in such manner, upon such conditions, and to such extent as he shall deem necessary or appropriate to promote the national defense." (P.L. 774, 81st Cong.) The "cheese amendment" explicitly required that "no imports of any such commodity or product shall be admitted . . . which the Secretary of Agriculture determines would (a) impair or reduce the domestic production of any such commodity or product below present production levels, or below such higher levels as the Secretary of Agriculture may deem necessary in view of domestic and international conditions, or (b) interfere with the orderly domestic storing and marketing of any such commodity or product, or (c) result in any unnecessary burden of expenditures under any Government price support program." (P.L. 96, 82d Cong.)

[1] See *Survey—1951*, pp. 172, 174-175, and *New York Times*, July 6, 1952, p. F-1; July 14, 1952, p. 1; July 15, 1952, pp. 7, 20, 29; and July 20, 1952, p. E-7.

At the Sixth Session nine countries had entered complaints of injury and had claimed nullification of tariff concessions, principally on cheese, by the United States.

[2] For the Senate debate on this bill, S. 2104, during the second session of the 82d Congress, see *Congressional Record*, January 23, 1952, pp. 429-447; January 28, 1952, pp. 526-549, *passim*; January 29, 1952, pp. 573-584, *passim*; and January 30, 1952, pp. 635-647.

apples, tobacco, and other products."[3] In hearings before House and Senate committees, Administration spokesmen asserted that the existing law was inconsistent with United States commitments under the GATT and the Trade Agreements Program, that it conflicted with United States policies designed to liberalize world trade, and that it negated twin Congressional objectives of making Europe self-supporting and preventing the spread of Communism. They also pointed out the adverse effects on United States agricultural exports of reducing European dollar earnings, emphasizing that American farmers rely heavily on foreign markets for sale of their products and that in 1951 the United States had exported $121 million worth of dairy products as compared with only $25 million worth of imports.[4] Finally, they maintained that the "cheese amendment" was not only unwise but also unnecessary because other existing safeguards, such as Section 22 of the Agricultural Adjustment Act and Section 7 (the escape clause) of the Trade Agreements Act,[5] were fully adequate to prevent injury to domestic producers.

These and similar arguments against continuing the "cheese amendment" were also voiced at the Congressional hearings by numerous private organizations representing non-dairy farmers, exporters, importers, and consumers.[6] Congressmen representing the agricultural exporting states and those from urban areas where the consumer interest in cheese was strong were particularly outspoken opponents of the amendment during the floor debates.[7]

[3] *Congressional Record*, February 11, 1952, p. 979.

[4] "Defense Production Act Amendments of 1952," *Hearings on H.R. 6546*, House of Rep., Committee on Banking and Currency, 82d Cong., 2d Sess., April-May 1952, Part 1, p. 252, and Part 2, pp. 1655-1656.

[5] In a letter recommending repeal of Section 104, President Truman pledged his intention to apply promptly these remedial provisions whenever imports threatened farm producers with serious injury. (*Hearings on H.R. 6546, op.cit.*, Part 2, p. 1552.)

Supporters of repeal cited this pledge as further evidence of the sufficiency of existing legislation. Advocates of the "cheese amendment" seemed less sanguine about implementation of the pledge. (See *Congressional Record*, January 30, 1952, p. 640.)

[6] Among the private groups opposing Section 104 were the American Farm Bureau Federation; the National Farmers Union; the National Cotton Council of America; the National Council of American Importers; the Boston, Philadelphia, and New York Chambers of Commerce; the International Section of the New York Board of Trade; Tobacco Associates; the Dried Fruit Export Association; and the Congress of Industrial Organizations. For a complete listing of such groups, see *Hearings on H.R. 6546, op.cit.*, Part 2, pp. 877-878.

[7] For arguments against the law, see *Hearings on H.R. 6546, op.cit.*, Part 1,

A group of foreign cheese producers' organizations placed large advertisements in some of the metropolitan newspapers drawing to the attention of consumers the effect of the amendment on supplies in American stores. Important sectors of the press also editorially opposed the law.[8]

Butter, cheese, and dairy interests and the Congressmen representing the dairy states were the chief proponents of retaining the quotas. Also supporting these import restrictions were the National Renderers' Association, producers of inedible tallow and grease, and representatives of the West Coast tree nut industry. The latter group asked for a broad extension of Section 104 to include such "other commodities . . . as [the President] shall deem necessary or appropriate to promote the national defense, upon investigation and recommendation of the Secretary of Agriculture in the case of agricultural commodities . . . or upon . . . recommendation of the Secretary of Commerce, in the case of nonagricultural commodities. . . ."[9]

Spokesmen for the amendment from the dairy industry held that it was essential for national security because repeal would allow an influx of butter and disastrous competition for domestic cheese producers, thereby accelerating what they testified was already an alarming decline in the dairy cow population. Moreover, they continued, unrestricted imports might jeopardize government price-support programs and unnecessarily burden taxpayers with price-support purchases. They admitted that in recent

pp. 250-272, 573, 648, and Part 2, pp. 872-891, 897-915, 1522, 1655-1656; "Defense Production Act Amendments of 1952," *Hearings on S. 2594 and S. 2645*, U.S. Senate, Committee on Banking and Currency, 82d Cong., 2d Sess., March 1952, Part 1, pp. 302-304, 398-399, 581, 671-685, 806-834, 856, and Part 2, pp. 1573-1574, 1663-1664, 1666; and *Congressional Record*, February 18, 1952, p. A961; April 24, 1952, p. A2620; May 20, 1952, p. 5653; May 23, 1952, p. 5955; May 26, 1952, p. 6060; May 28, 1952, pp. 6183-6184; June 18, 1952, pp. 7677-7678, 7688-7689; and June 19, 1952, pp. 7776-7778.

[8] See, for example, *New York Times*, March 4, 1952, p. 37; April 7, 1952, p. 12; April 18, 1952, p. 24; and April 20, 1952, p. E-10.

[9] Amendment introduced by Congressman Hunter of California (H.R. 7432) and advocated by the Sunkist Growers, California Walnut Growers Association, California Almond Growers Exchange, and Northwest Nut Growers. *Hearings on H.R. 6546, op.cit.*, Part 2, p. 1041.

Senators Mundt and Young also introduced an amendment to reenact Section 104 and to add oats, rye, barley, and feed wheat to the commodities regulated. (*Congressional Record*, June 2, 1952, p. 6376; June 3, 1952, pp. 6531-6536; and June 4, 1952, pp. 6664-6665.)

years dairy exports had exceeded dairy imports but contended that these exports were, to a significant extent, financed by foreign aid grants and "give-away" programs and hence were not indicative of normal trade relationships. These spokesmen and their Congressional supporters argued also that remedial action under Section 22 of the Agricultural Adjustment Act and the escape clause of the Trade Agreements Act had proven too slow and too cumbersome to provide adequate protection to domestic producers and that therefore a mandatory bill with specific and explicit instructions requiring the Administration to act was needed.

In reply to the charge that the law violated United States commitments under the GATT, the proponents of the "cheese amendment" frequently asserted in the hearings and the floor debates that it was consistent with such United States obligations because the wording of the amendment clearly stated its purpose was to protect national security and the GATT allowed measures for this purpose. A few Senators went beyond this position, however, and asserted that the GATT was an illegal executive agreement that had been launched with the idea of "greasing the way for the ITO." Several agreed with the member who stated that repeal of the cheese quotas was part of a State Department scheme to secure "inch-by-inch ratification of various parts of [the GATT] and thus build up an argument that all of it has been approved."[1]

Efforts to repeal outright the controversial amendment were unsuccessful and Section 104 was extended in modified form until June 30, 1953. The modified version of the law continued the previous provision that imports of fats and oils[2] "shall be limited

[1] *Congressional Record*, January 23, 1952, p. 430.

Completing the roster of arguments for retaining the "cheese amendment" were contentions that inasmuch as other countries maintained extensive restrictions against United States imports they should not complain about United States import quotas; that the amendment protected the consumer against uninspected and, it was claimed, frequently unclean foreign cheese; and that the restrictions were necessary to protect American labor.

For arguments favoring the "cheese amendment," see *Hearings on H.R. 6546, op.cit.*, Part 1, pp. 255-261, and Part 2, pp. 807-871, 919-954, 1041-1045, 1411-1412, 1420-1421, 1618-1630; *Hearings on S. 2594 and S. 2645, op.cit.*, Part 1, pp. 249-321, 386-387, 471-472, and Part 2, pp. 1213-1216, 1405-1420, 1434-1436; and *Congressional Record*, June 2, 1952, p. 6376; June 3, 1952, pp. 6531-6536; June 4, 1952, pp. 6668, 6677-6678; June 18, 1952, p. 7677; and June 19, 1952, p. 7777.

[2] "(including oil-bearing materials, fatty acids, and soap and soap powder, but

to such quantities as the Secretary of Agriculture finds would not (a) impair or reduce the domestic production of any such commodity or product below present production levels, or below such higher levels as the Secretary of Agriculture may deem necessary in view of domestic and international conditions, or (b) interfere with the orderly domestic storing and marketing of any such commodity or product, or (c) result in any unnecessary burden of expenditures under any Government price support program." However, the previous legislation was eased in that the new law provided for the imposition of quotas by specific types and varieties of each product listed rather than requiring across-the-board restriction on *all* types and varieties of each commodity, as the Secretary of Agriculture had interpreted the 1951 law to demand. The Conference Committee explicitly amplified this point by stating that "this authority [to impose restrictions] is not to be exercised with respect to types of cheeses, such as Roquefort and Switzerland Swiss, which, because of their United States selling price, are clearly not competitive with domestically produced cheeses."[3] Some flexibility in administering the law was also introduced by allowing the Secretary of Agriculture, after he had determined the amounts of imports to be permitted under the general criteria mentioned above, to permit *additional* imports of each type and variety of the specified commodities to an amount not exceeding 15 percent of the established import limitation. The law authorized the Secretary to permit such additional imports if he deemed it advisable after "taking into consideration the broad effects upon international relationships and trade."[4]

Soon after the passage of the new law, the Secretary ended all quota restrictions on imports of Swiss, Gruyère process, Roquefort, and several Italian sheep's milk varieties of cheese. He also increased the quotas on certain other types of cheeses of historical interest to Denmark, Italy, and the Netherlands.[5]

---

excluding petroleum and petroleum products and coconuts and coconut products), peanuts, butter, cheese and other dairy products, and rice and rice products. . ."

[3] *Congressional Record*, June 28, 1952, pp. 8585-8586.

[4] P.L. 429, 82d Cong., Title I, Section 103.

[5] See *New York Times*, July 6, 1952, p. F-1, and July 16, 1952, p. 33, and *Foreign Commerce Weekly*, July 14, 1952, p. 2.

The Secretary of Agriculture removed from quota restrictions imports of rice meal, rice flour, rice polish, rice bran, rice starch, brewer's rice, and certified rice

This relaxation of import restrictions, however, did not remove the basis for the charge of violations of the GATT leveled against the United States in 1951 by eight signatories to the General Agreement and, as discussed in Section D, above, strong complaints were again registered against the policy at the Seventh Session of the Contracting Parties to the GATT, in October. Early in the fall the Secretary of Agriculture removed quotas on several other relatively minor types of cheese and raised quotas on others, announcing in some instances that the action was taken with a view toward improving international relations and trade with other countries. Any such results were seriously prejudiced, however, by the Secretary's decision in late December to impose drastic restrictions on imports of dried whole milk, dried buttermilk, and dried cream; this action was taken to reduce expenditures under the Government price-support program for butterfat and milk solids.[6] New Zealand, Australia, and Canada quickly sent notes protesting this action and President Truman again condemned the law.[7]

b. RESTRICTIONS ON MEAT AND LIVESTOCK IMPORTS

In September 1952 the United States removed its six-year ban on imports of livestock from Mexico, imposed because of the prevalence of foot and mouth disease in that country,[8] but the previous embargo on meat and livestock imports from parts of Europe, Asia, and South America was continued. An outbreak of the disease in Canada in early 1952 led to the extension of the embargo to meat imports from that country. This action set in motion a widely publicized trade switch in meat worked out between the Governments of Canada, the United Kingdom, and New Zealand. The United Kingdom, which had planned to purchase certain quantities of New Zealand beef, agreed to substitute Canadian beef, and New Zealand in turn shipped to the United

seed for planting, as well as flaxseed screenings, flaxseed scalpings, flaxseed chaff, and flaxseed scourings.

[6] In March 1953, the Government imposed an embargo on dried milk imports. Throughout 1952 imports of butter and peanuts were embargoed.

[7] For an account of the President's statement, see *New York Times*, January 1, 1953, p. 32.

[8] During the period of the embargo the United States had contributed over $88 million to a cooperative effort with the Government of Mexico to control and eradicate the disease.

States the beef that she otherwise would have sold to England. The New Zealand meat was sold at exceedingly low prices by the American distributors,[9] and the press reported that housewives "mobbed" stores where it was being sold. United States cattlemen thereupon complained of the "bad effects" these sales were having on domestic meat prices and a subcommittee of the House Agriculture Committee initiated an investigation. The total imports of New Zealand beef from September 1952 to March 1953 amounted to only some 60-75 million pounds, and on March 1, 1953 the embargo on imports of Canadian beef was lifted, presumably ending the import of low-priced New Zealand meat. Citing the New Zealand incident, however, the subcommittee urged the use of import quotas as one of several measures to bolster the falling cattle prices,[1] and, subsequently, tariff quotas were reestablished on meat imports from Canada.

c. SUGAR QUOTAS

The Sugar Act of 1948, as amended, provides for an import quota system designed to guarantee a market for domestic sugar producers and to maintain what are regarded as "equitable" domestic market prices.[2] As discussed in the following chapter, the U.S. Government also participated in the International Sugar Council and in 1952 supported a request to the Secretary-General of the United Nations that he call a 1953 international conference to negotiate a new International Sugar Agreement.

Under the Sugar Act, the Secretary of Agriculture estimates the total amount of sugar needed to meet the "requirements" of continental United States consumers, this amount being such that it will result in prices to consumers that are "not excessive" and that will "fairly and equitably maintain and protect the welfare" of the domestic sugar producers. Against this total figure, a specific quota is set aside for domestic producers and for imports from Hawaii, Puerto Rico, the Virgin Islands, and the Philippines. The

[9] The press reported, but it was not confirmed, that the Canadian Government agreed to reimburse New Zealand for any financial loss the operation might entail.

[1] See *New York Times*, February 21, 1953, p. 8.

[2] A brief discussion of this Act during earlier years may be found in *Survey—1951*, pp. 186-187, and references cited therein.

For a critical analysis of the U.S. Government sugar policy, see Swerling, B. C., "A Sugar Policy for the United States," *American Economic Review*, June 1952, pp. 347-357.

Department of Agriculture then apportions the difference between these statutory allocations and the total consumption figure to other producing areas, with Cuba obtaining most of such allocations.

Late in 1952 Secretary of Agriculture Brannan set an over-all quota for calendar year 1953 of 7.8 million tons. He stated that this quota was 400,000 tons short of the estimated 1953 consumption but that it could be raised during the course of the year as sugar prices achieved a "fair relationship with prices of other commodities," pointing out that in his judgment the prices during most of 1952 had been "below the levels indicated as desirable" by the Sugar Act.[3] At the public hearings on setting the 1953 allocations domestic sugar producers, as usual, argued for smaller quotas than those finally set, asserting that their prices were "unreasonably" low in comparison with their costs and with the general price level, while industrial users (chiefly candy and soft drink manufacturers) asked for larger quotas on the ground that sugar prices were too high. Following the fixing of the quotas, Dominican Republic officials announced that in view of the small quota allotted to their producers their Government intended to switch a "large part" of their country's dollar purchases from the United States to Britain, which country was paying dollars for its sugar imports.[4]

d. TARIFF AND OTHER QUOTAS

Tariff quotas prescribed in the Tariff Act of 1930, as amended, and within limits provided in the General Agreement, were continued at the 1951 level on whole milk and cream.[5] The tariff

[3] *New York Times*, December 6, 1952, p. 29. The Secretary followed a similar procedure in 1952, twice boosting the originally established quota. The final quota for 1952 was 7.9 million tons.

[4] *New York Times*, December 18, 1952, p. 47. Although many regarded the United States sugar policy as being at least "cartel-like," United States officials actively participated during the year in the *ad hoc* committee established, on United States initiative, in the Economic and Social Council in 1951 (see *Survey—1951*, p. 187n.) to prepare proposals for an international agreement to prevent "harmful" cartel practices. No report was issued by this committee during 1952 but the State Department repeated its earlier statements that it favored safeguards against such restrictive commercial practices. (See, for example, Department of State *Bulletin*, September 22, 1952, p. 458. See also The President's Materials Policy Commission, *Resources for Freedom, op.cit.*, Vol. I, p. 79.)

[5] Information on these quotas may be found in the monthly issues of *American Import and Export Bulletin*, New York. Butter, also subject to a tariff quota, was

quota applying to imports of groundfish was changed during the year to permit an increase in the quantity of imports allowed entry at the lower trade agreement rate. This quantity is equal to 15 percent of average domestic consumption of the fish over the previous three years.[6] The tariff quota on imports of potatoes (other than certified seed) was raised from approximately 40 million bushels to nearly 134 million bushels for the twelve-month period beginning September 15, 1952, in accordance with the provision in the General Agreement that the tariff quota on imports of table stock potatoes for a given quota year shall be increased by the amount by which the estimated domestic crop was less than 350 million bushels.[7] As noted earlier, the quota on petroleum imports was dropped and duties reduced in the late summer under the United States–Venezuelan supplementary trade agreement. The import quotas applied under the provisions of the Philippine Trade Act of 1946 remained unchanged during the year under review. These quotas cover buttons, cigars, coconut oil, cordage, rice, sugar, and tobacco.[8]

The Tariff Commission in 1952 recommended increased import restrictions on almonds and filberts, under the authority provided by Section 22 of the Agricultural Adjustment Act of 1937, as amended.[9] The President proclaimed additional import fees on

---

excluded under Section 104 of the Defense Production Act, described earlier in this chapter.

[6] For details, see *Foreign Commerce Weekly*, February 2, 1953, p. 20. See also the testimony on quotas given by the head of the quota section of the Bureau of Customs in "Tuna Imports," *Hearings on H.R. 5693, op.cit.*, pp. 268-270.

[7] For details, see *Foreign Commerce Weekly*, October 20, 1952, p. 3.

[8] The Philippine Trade Act of 1946 provides for duty-free trade (though some commodities are subject to quotas in each country) between the two countries until early 1955 and for a subsequent twenty-year period of declining customs preferences. Several officials in the Philippines urged during 1952 that the period and extent of duty-free trade on certain commodities be reduced on the grounds that the Islands needed tariffs to protect some of their new industries and as a source of Government revenue. They also urged that duty-free treatment by the United States be accorded indefinitely to certain items, such as sugar, coconuts, and hemp, that bulked large in the Philippine export trade. (See *Foreign Commerce Weekly*, April 21, 1952, p. 17; June 30, 1952, p. 20; and July 21, 1952, p. 26.)

[9] Section 22 provides for imposition of quotas and/or import fees within specified limitations when imports threaten to render ineffective, or materially interfere with, any Department of Agriculture price-support program. Under this section the Tariff Commission also initiated an investigation of a recommendation by the Department of Agriculture that import fees be imposed on wool and wool tops so that the cost of imported wool would be equal to at least 90 percent of the

shelled and prepared almonds for the 1952-1953 marketing year but concluded the imports of filberts did not constitute a sufficiently severe threat to the domestic industry to warrant imposition of new restrictions.[1] Section 22 import quotas on cotton, cotton waste, wheat, and wheat flour continued unchanged during the year and amounted to a virtual embargo.

Export Subsidies

Total expenditures for export subsidies under Section 32 of the Agricultural Adjustment Act, as amended, amounted to approximately $16 million in 1952, as compared with $23 million in the previous year.[2] (These data do not include the cost to the U.S. Government of fulfilling its obligation under the International Wheat Agreement; this is discussed in the following chapter.) Commodities covered in the 1952 program of subsidizing the export of agricultural products declared by the Secretary of Agriculture as surplus to domestic needs under the various price-support programs were fresh and processed oranges, lemons, and grapefruit; dried raisins; dried prunes; and extracted honey. Late in the year the Department of Agriculture renewed its export subsidy programs, with amendments, for raisins and citrus fruits for the 1952-1953 marketing season but the program for prunes was not extended because of the unusually small domestic production. Section 32 subsidy payments are in most cases made only on shipments to traditional export markets and not on those to countries that commercially produce the goods or that border on the United States. Still, as noted earlier, the export subsidy program did give rise to complaints at the Seventh Session of the Contracting Parties

domestic parity price. This recommendation met heavy opposition from domestic wool manufacturers, domestic importers, and foreign wool producers. No report regarding this investigation had been issued by the Tariff Commission at year's end. For further information, see *Foreign Commerce Weekly*, September 15, 1952, p. 2, and December 1, 1952, p. 4. For a criticism of the proposal on the grounds that it would result in still greater penalties—already high because of the tariff—on the consumption and production of woolen goods to the benefit of synthetic fibers, see Public Advisory Board for Mutual Security, *A Trade and Tariff Policy in the National Interest*, *op.cit.*, pp. 25-26.

[1] For a text of the President's statement, see Department of State *Bulletin*, November 10, 1952, p. 743.

[2] For some official details on the Section 32 program of subsidizing export of surplus agricultural commodities, see *Foreign Commerce Weekly*, September 8, 1952, p. 3, and October 6, 1952, p. 28.

that it was depriving certain of the members of their traditional markets in third countries.

The Department of Agriculture made no donations, authorized in the Agricultural Adjustment Act of 1949, during the year of surplus agricultural commodities in danger of spoilage to private United States welfare organizations for the assistance of needy persons abroad. The support-price value of such donations during 1950 and 1951 had totalled just over $81 million.

The economic survey mission headed by Secretary of Commerce Sawyer recommended late in the year that the United States "immediately" terminate subsidies whose value to the American economy was small in relation to the damage they caused to the exports of friendly countries, citing as a case in point the subsidies on dried fig exports.[3] The so-called Bell Report also frowned on export subsidies and recommended that they be used only "to maintain foreign markets for traditional export commodities that could be sold abroad if currency and commodity discriminations were not directed against these products . . . ," and that such subsidies should not be higher than justified by such restrictions.[4]

[3] *Foreign Commerce Weekly*, December 22, 1952, p. 18.

[4] Public Advisory Board for Mutual Security, *A Trade and Tariff Policy in the National Interest*, *op.cit.*, p. 60.

VII · STRATEGIC ASPECTS OF COMMERCIAL POLICY

THE Reciprocal Trade Agreements Program, the cornerstone of United States long-term commercial policy, was not designed to cope with many of the problems that arose when the nation undertook a large-scale rearmament program. As security considerations became dominant in determining the country's international commercial, as well as other, policies, increasing attention was therefore put on such strategic problems as controlling exports, restricting non United States East-West trade, stockpiling strategic and critical materials, and allocating among friendly nations the available supply of materials the demand for which had greatly expanded as the result of the military build-up.

A. *EXPORT CONTROLS*

Export controls—the requiring of a license issued by the Department of Commerce before a given commodity can be exported from the United States—continued during 1952 to be used to prevent "excessive" drains of scarce materials from the United States, to direct exports to friendly foreign countries so as to strengthen their ability to resist aggression, and to prevent exports to potential enemies that might contribute to their military strength.[1]

As production of many items in the United States increased and inflationary pressures subsided, non-security export controls on many goods were relaxed, reversing the trend of the previous year. In general, the relaxations on domestic controls were paral-

[1] See *Survey—1951*, pp. 190-194 for a summary of United States export control policies and activities in earlier years. For official details on the policy of controlling United States exports during 1952, see the quarterly reports of the Secretary of Commerce entitled *Export Control*, Wash., D.C. Many details may also be found in the various issues of Department of Commerce, *Foreign Commerce Weekly*.

The statement on page 190 of the 1951 *Survey* that the Export Control Act had been extended that year until June 30, 1952 was in error, Congress having extended it until June 30, 1953.

leled during the year by a similar easing of export controls. Thus, not only were 117 commodities removed completely from the Department of Commerce's Positive List of Controlled Commodities—except in the case of shipments to Soviet-bloc countries, Hong Kong, or Macao—but many of the quantitative export quotas on goods still subject to license were taken off or enlarged and certain of the licensing requirements were simplified. Controls were reimposed or tightened for supply reasons on a few commodities—notably rice and, for a time during and after the steel strike, steel products. At the end of the year over 1000 commodity classifications[2] were still under control, but most of them for security, rather than short-supply, reasons.

As in previous years, the export controls were also used to allocate scarce commodities among friendly foreign countries, the general aim being that such goods should go to countries where their use would contribute most to the security of the United States.[3] In addition to granting export licenses, the Government continued to assign domestic supply priorities, under the Defense Production Act, to what were regarded as the most essential needs of friendly foreign countries—especially for items directly contributing to rearmament programs and to the production of strategic and critical materials. The demand for such assistance declined greatly as the year progressed, reflecting the increases in production of such goods in the United States and abroad. It was anticipated as the year ended that these domestic priorities would soon be confined to commodities for military use only.

The major purpose of the export controls continued to be preventing the export of strategic goods to the Soviet bloc—either directly or indirectly. Exports of *all* goods to these countries required a license and the controls on direct shipments were so strict during the year as to amount to a virtual embargo. The total value of United States exports and reexports to the Soviet bloc during 1952 was $1.1 million (more than half of which was for tobacco) as compared with $2.8 million during 1951, $130

[2] This figure is not comparable to those given in earlier *Surveys* since major revisions were made during 1952 in the classification procedures that had the effect of increasing the number of classifications.

[3] See *Survey—1951*, pp. 191-192 for a detailed statement of the priorities that had been established for allocating exports among friendly foreign countries. No reports were issued during 1952 on the extent to which each of these priorities had been satisfied.

million during 1950, and $188 million in 1949.[4] Approximately three quarters of these exports during 1952 went to East Germany and to Poland; no exports were recorded for North Korea or mainland China. Much attention was given during the year to preventing indirect shipments to Russia and the satellite countries, that is, reexports or diversions, with major reliance being placed on increasingly stringent requirements that the importer provide, as a condition for the granting of an export license to his United States supplier, evidence from his government that the goods were to be imported into the approved country and, in some cases, evidence subsequent to shipment that such goods had in fact been so imported.[5]

There was little discussion or criticism in Congress or in the press during the year of the administration of the export controls, but it was generally recognized that the effectiveness of the controls imposed for security reasons depended on other countries' following similar policies. Those responsible for administering the United States controls, therefore, cooperated closely with the officials administering the Battle Act, discussed in the following section, and followed the general practice of refusing to grant licenses for goods when the importing country did not adequately control shipments of similar goods to the Soviet bloc.

B. *RESTRICTIONS ON NON UNITED STATES EAST-WEST TRADE*

In the years immediately following World War II the U.S. Administration shared the hopes of the authorities of many of the other non-Communist nations that there would be a revival and expansion of the prewar trade between the Soviet-dominated countries and the rest of the world. By 1948 these hopes had been dimmed, and as the United States began to apply security controls on its own exports the Administration also asked its major allies to apply similar export controls and to cooperate with the

[4] The value of imports from the Soviet bloc declined from $174 million in 1949 and $228 million in 1950 to $110 million in 1951 and $67 million in 1952.

[5] The controls on shipments to Hong Kong were eased somewhat during the year following a "general tightening" of the Crown Colony's controls over shipments to Communist China and North Korea. The general policy of the United States was (a) to permit such exports as would allow essential manufacturing establishments there to operate and (b) to prevent large-scale unemployment and unrest.

United States in restricting the flow of strategic items to potential aggressors. In that same year Congress began, by amendments to various statutes, to develop the doctrine that United States aid should be denied to any country that did not restrict its exports of strategic goods to the Soviet bloc. Sharp disagreements arose after Korea between the Administration and Congress as to the most desirable and effective means of restricting non United States East-West trade, with Congress tending to favor applying more extreme pressure on foreign countries to gain their cooperation, and to interpret more broadly the definition of "strategic" goods.[6]

In October 1951 Congress approved the Battle Act (Mutual Defense Assistance Control Act), which supplanted the earlier legislation and declared that—in order to increase the strength of the United States and its allies; to "impede the ability of nations threatening the security of the United States to conduct military operations"; and to help "nations under the domination of foreign aggressors to reestablish their freedom"—it was United States policy to place an embargo on shipments to any nation threatening United States security of specified categories of goods regarded as of high strategic importance and that no U.S. Government aid should go to any nation that knowingly permitted the export of these goods to the potential aggressors. The President was authorized, however, to waive the termination-of-aid provision with respect to shipments of certain of these goods if he determined such termination would clearly be detrimental to United States security. For working purposes the Administration referred to these embargoed commodities as ones of "primary strategic importance," defined as goods the export of which *in any quantity* would contribute significantly to the Soviet war potential.

The law also directed the Administration to negotiate with each aid recipient with a view to its undertaking an export control program, similar to that applied by the United States, for goods that were not subject to embargo but that, in the judgment of the Administration, should be restricted in order to strengthen the

[6] See *Survey—1951*, pp. 194-206, and the references cited therein for an account of the policies and activities of the United States with respect to East-West trade during 1951 and earlier years.

security of the United States and her allies. The Administration referred to these commodities as ones of "secondary strategic importance," defined as goods the export of which *in large quantities* would contribute significantly to Soviet war potential.

In late 1951 the Administration prepared a list, sending copies to all aid recipients, of the items of "primary strategic importance"—subject to embargo under the Act—and divided this list into two categories: A and B.[7] Category A covered arms and munitions, implements of war, and atomic energy materials; Category B covered petroleum, transportation materials of strategic value, and items of primary strategic significance used in the production of war matériel.[8] The President's authority to waive the termination-of-aid provision in the law applied to shipments of Category B items only.

During the year no case was discovered in which an aid recipient knowingly permitted the shipment of Category A items to the Soviet bloc, but there were six instances—two involving Italy and one each involving France, the United Kingdom, the Netherlands, and Denmark—of shipments of Category B items. Each of these transactions grew out of commitments that had been made prior to the coming into effect of the Battle Act and in each case President Truman made a determination that "cessation of aid would clearly be detrimental to the security of the United States." In justifying these decisions to Congress President Truman stressed that these countries were making major contributions to the defense of Western Europe, and so of the United States, and stated that if aid were terminated these countries would be unable to carry out the military burdens they had assumed, with the result that the whole North Atlantic Treaty Organization defense system would probably "collapse." He also pointed out that for several years these countries had cooperated generously with the United States in the programs for controlling the shipment of

[7] Most of the information in this section on the administration of the Battle Act during 1952 was taken from Mutual Security Agency, *Mutual Defense Assistance Control Act of 1951, First Report to Congress*, Wash., D.C., October 1952; Mutual Security Agency, "Problems of Economic Defense," *Mutual Defense Assistance Control Act of 1951, Second Report to Congress*, Wash., D.C., January 1953; and Department of State, *Export Controls and Free World Security*, Publication 4626, Wash., D.C., July 1952.

[8] During the year these lists were kept under constant review and several items were added to the B list.

strategic items to Russia and her satellites and that if aid were withdrawn they would have to rely more on Eastern Europe for supplies, with the consequence that the flow of strategic goods to the Iron Curtain areas would increase.[9] During the year, at the request of the United States, the question of prior commitments on the part of persons in some European countries to ship goods to Soviet-bloc countries was "reviewed" and approximately one quarter of the value of such projected shipments was cancelled. But as 1952 ended several of the Western European countries still had pre-Battle Act commitments that they felt must be honored.

The Administration reported that "substantial progress" was made during the year in discharging the second major task given it by the Battle Act: negotiating with aid recipients for the curtailment of exports of strategic items not subject to embargo in the law. But it was also recognized that "It would . . . be unrealistic to pretend that everything is as rosy as we would desire it to be."[1] Some of these negotiations were carried out on a bilateral basis but most of them took place in an informal international committee, which had been created in 1950 and held its meetings in Paris, and in which officials from the United States, Canada, most of the Western European countries, and, from mid-1952, Japan participated.[2] In addition, a special informal committee was established in 1952 for the specific task of improving the controls on shipments to North Korea and Communist China.

Controls on these commodities of "secondary strategic importance" were constantly changing since they were designed not to stop all trade but only to prevent such trade as would strengthen the East more than the West. Although resistance to more stringent controls was sometimes encountered by the Administration in friendly nations that relied heavily on the East for imports of such important items as timber, grain, and coal, the United States was successful in getting many of the authorities to tighten their export controls on several items.[3] More difficult

[9] For the text of the President's letters, see *Mutual Defense Assistance Control Act of 1951, First Report to Congress, op.cit.*, pp. 47-57, and *Mutual Defense Assistance Control Act of 1951, Second Report to Congress, op.cit.*, pp. 75-86.

[1] *Mutual Defense Assistance Control Act of 1951, Second Report to Congress, op.cit.*, p. 5.

[2] See *New York Times*, August 3, 1952, pp. 1, F-1, and *The Economist*, August 9, 1952, p. 328.

[3] See, for example, *New York Times*, April 18, 1952, p. 1; April 29, 1952, p. 9;

was the task of enforcing such controls.[4] Since export restrictions normally apply to shipments *originating* in the country, one of the most troublesome problems, apart from outright smuggling, was preventing diversions of shipments to the Soviet bloc while goods were in transit. The United States took the position, in various "intensive discussions," that a country through which controlled goods were passing in transit should assume responsibility for preventing such diversions. Many nations were reluctant to accept this task, however, primarily on the ground that it would slow up and might curtail legitimate commerce that was an important source of income to them. Still, some progress was reported on this score during the year when Japan, Canada, and the United Kingdom, together with the United States, adopted a system whereby a special license was required before goods in transit in these countries could be reshipped. It was hoped these arrangements might be extended to other countries. During the year eleven other nations also joined with the United States in working out the so-called import-certificate–delivery-verification system, whereby the country of origin, before granting an export license, required the importer to obtain an import certificate from his own government. In some cases, after the goods were shipped the country of origin also requested an official certificate verifying the delivery.[5]

The Battle Act also directed the Administration to invite nations not receiving aid from the United States to cooperate in

May 7, 1952, p. 6; July 13, 1952, p. E-7; September 6, 1952, p. 6; December 19, 1952, p. 5; and January 26, 1953, p. 27. There was much less criticism in the European press than during the previous year on the United States policy of restricting East-West trade.

[4] In addition to extending and coordinating export controls, the Administration attempted to restrict shipments of strategic items to the Soviet bloc (and in particular to Communist China and North Korea) by negotiating agreements with various foreign governments whereby those governments agreed to follow the United States practice of prohibiting flag ships' carrying such items to the embargoed ports. Such agreements were negotiated during 1951 with Panama, Costa Rica, and Honduras, and in 1952 with Liberia. In early 1953 similar agreements were reached with Greece. Evidence was not available as to the effectiveness of these prohibitions.

To help prevent evasions, an agreement was made in early 1953 with the French and British Governments whereby they refused to allow ships to touch or to bunker at British or French ports if they were engaged in carrying strategic items to Soviet-bloc countries. (See *New York Times*, March 31, 1953, p. 9.)

[5] For details on this scheme, see the quarterly reports of the Secretary of Commerce entitled *Export Control*, Wash., D.C., 1952.

controlling the export of strategic items, and discussions were held with several of these countries during the year, the most important being those with Sweden, Switzerland, and Ceylon. In the case of the first two countries—which had long followed a policy of neutrality—the discussions centered on proposals by the United States as to measures these countries might take to insure that supplies entering them from the United States and the other cooperating nations were not subsequently transshipped to the East. Details as to the agreements reached, if any, were not published. The United States failed in its efforts to prevent Ceylon from concluding in late 1952 a five-year trade agreement with Communist China under which Ceylon promised to deliver large quantities of crude rubber in return for rice. Prior to signing the agreement, Ceylon sent a Government mission to the United States to discuss the possibility of buying rice from and selling rubber to the United States and of receiving a $50 million five-year economic aid program. The United States offers to buy rubber and sell rice at the world market prices and to negotiate a "Point Four" agreement were unacceptable to the Ceylon officials.

The value of *all* exports of the Western European countries and the Far Eastern countries to the Soviet bloc (data from all countries for the complete year are not available) apparently did not decline during 1952 as compared with 1951,[6] but the Administration concluded that the rate of the Soviet military build-up had been slowed by the operation of the export control systems of the non-Communist countries, and that, on balance, the West had obtained more benefits than the East from the existing East-West trade. Many in Congress, however, were not satisfied that the Battle Act itself was adequate or that it was being properly administered and in May the Senate, by a vote of 40 to 32, approved an amendment to the Mutual Security Act of 1952 that would have supplanted the Battle Act and have had the effect, most observers believed, of forcing countries receiving aid from the U.S. Government to establish an embargo on virtually all exports

[6] For an article concluding that for the period 1948 through 1951 the restrictions of the West "can be considered successful only insofar as [they] prevented the Soviet orbit from obtaining the pre-war levels of import trade . . ." and that they had "not brought about the expected over-all decline from 1948 levels," see Spulber, N., "The Effects of the Embargo on Soviet Trade," *Harvard Business Review,* November-December 1952, pp. 122-128.

to the Soviet bloc. This amendment was removed in the conference between the two Houses on the legislation but the debates in the Senate showed that there was a great deal of support for the proposal.[7]

The Administration insisted in its reports to Congress that even a perfect system of export controls by the non-Communist nations—which it was frankly admitted had not been achieved—could only slow down Russia and her satellites and not prevent them from building a "tremendous" war potential. It was also repeatedly pointed out during the year by the Administration and by various private groups in the United States[8] that the policy of decreasing exports from the countries in the free world to the Soviet-dominated countries meant also a decrease in imports from the latter and that, if the policy were to be successful in increasing the strength of the West relative to the East, alternative markets and sources of supply must be found for Western European and other friendly countries.[9] In particular, the policy was seen by many as making it necessary for the United States to face such issues as: Was it prepared more actively to help expand

[7] For the debate on this amendment, see *Congressional Record*, May 28, 1952, pp. 6276-6280, and June 9, 1952, pp. 6936-6945, 6954-6964.

[8] See, especially, United States Council of the International Chamber of Commerce, *The East-West Trade Controversy*, New York, August 1952.

[9] The Executive Branch insisted during the year that it favored increased trade between the East and the West in non-strategic goods, but it also pointed out that basic Russian policy was one of autarky over the long run and that the rest of the world should not plan on carrying out large trade with the Soviet bloc. (See, for example, *Mutual Defense Assistance Control Act of 1951, Second Report to Congress, op.cit.*, pp. 33-40.)

In August the Economic Commission for Europe cancelled plans for discussions on methods of increasing East-West trade after the Eastern European Governments failed to reply to an invitation to participate, although expanded trade with the West had been the ostensible reason for the holding of the International Economic Conference in Moscow earlier in the year. (See *New York Times*, August 19, 1952, p. 10.) In the United Nations the Russian delegates repeatedly asserted that Russia and the Eastern European countries wished to expand their trade with the West, that they could "meet the majority of the needs" of the Western European countries, and that the "pressure" from the United States to disrupt such trade had resulted, in Western Europe, in a decline in industrial production, an increase in inflation, and a deterioration in the living conditions of the people. (See, for example, UN Economic and Social Council, *Official Records*, Fourteenth Session, 591st Meeting, June 5, 1952, pp. 150-154.)

For a detailed study analyzing the continuing shrinkage of trade between Eastern and Western Europe in 1951 and the first half of 1952, see UN Economic Commission for Europe, *Economic Bulletin for Europe*, Second Quarter, 1952, Geneva, November 1952, pp. 34-78.

sources and markets in the so-called underdeveloped areas?[1] Was it ready, if it became necessary, to reduce its consumption of certain items in order to provide goods no longer obtainable by its allies from the Soviet bloc? Was it willing to reduce its barriers to imports so that friendly exporting nations could earn more dollars to buy goods from non-Soviet sources? And would it, in the meantime, be prepared to provide additional aid to its allies to permit them to buy in other markets the goods presently or formerly obtained from Russia and her satellites?

Note on United Nations Activities

In May 1951 the United Nations General Assembly passed a resolution recommending that its members embargo shipments of certain strategic items to Communist China and North Korea.[2] This resolution was only a recommendation, but by mid-1952 forty-five countries had notified the United Nations that they were applying the embargo or that they did not normally produce or export such items.

The Collective Measures Committee, established pursuant to the United Nations "Uniting for Peace" Resolution in 1950 to consider military and economic measures that might be taken against some future unnamed aggressor, prepared during 1952 an arms embargo list and a list of other strategic items to which selective controls might be applied. It was hoped that the prior preparation of such lists would expedite the application of restrictions on exports in the event such were decided upon.[3] The Committee found that the direct economic burdens that participating countries might have to bear as a result of the imposition of collective measures against those in the future who threaten peace were certain to be spread unevenly and that it was important that the principle be accepted that efforts be made by all members to equalize such burdens. The Committee reported

[1] The so-called Sawyer Mission recommended that greater emphasis should be given under the Point Four Program to developing sources of supply in the free world for some of those foodstuffs and raw materials Western Europe had traditionally obtained from Eastern Europe. (See *Foreign Commerce Weekly*, Wash., D.C., December 22, 1952, p. 19.)

[2] See *Survey—1951*, p. 205.

[3] This Committee also studied the potential roles that the various United Nations organizations and specialized agencies might fulfill in the event of future aggression.

that this might be achieved by, among other things, direct assistance in cash or kind from one member to another, the provision of alternative markets and sources of supply, commodity purchase agreements, and compensatory adjustments of tariffs. But the Committee, on which the United States was represented, concluded that it was impossible to determine in advance of a specific situation what methods and procedures would be most appropriate.[4]

C. STOCKPILING

To reduce a possibly dangerous and costly dependence during wartime upon foreign sources of certain essential raw materials, the U.S. Government has, since the end of World War II, been accumulating a stockpile of strategic and critical materials designed to make up the difference between probable supplies and the estimated needs, both civilian and military, during an all-out war. Certain domestically produced goods are purchased for the stockpile but the great bulk of the expenditures—probably more than three quarters—have been for imported commodities.[5]

In its June 1952 report, The President's Materials Policy Commission (the so-called Paley Commission) found that the legislation under which the nation's stockpiling program was being carried out was in general "sound"—a conspicuous exception being the "Buy American" provision—and that during the latter part of 1951 and early 1952 it had been well administered. The Commission also found, however, that in the past the procurement program had been often characterized by too little procurement when

[4] United Nations, Report of the Collective Measures Committee, General Assembly, *Official Records*, Seventh Session, Supplement No. 17 (A/2215), New York, 1952.

[5] For a summary of the stockpiling policies and activities in earlier years, see *Survey—1951*, pp. 206-216, and the references cited therein. Detailed information on the program during 1952, and the sources of most of the information included here, may be found in Munitions Board, *Stockpile Report to Congress*, Wash., D.C., August 15, 1952 and February 15, 1953; "Independent Offices Appropriations for 1953," *Hearings*, House of Rep., Subcommittee of the Committee on Appropriations, 82d Cong., 2d Sess., Part III, pp. 1420ff.; "Independent Offices Appropriations, 1953," *Hearings on H.R. 7072*, U.S. Senate, Subcommittee of the Committee on Appropriations, 82d Cong., 2d Sess., pp. 772ff.; "Second Annual Report of the Activities of the Joint Committee on Defense Production," *S. Rpt. No. 3*, U.S. Senate, 83d Cong., 1st Sess., pp. 72-80; and The President's Materials Policy Commission, *Resources for Freedom*, Wash., D.C., June 1952, Vol. I, pp. 162-164, and Vol. V, pp. 107-149.

supplies and prices were generally favorable and recommended that purchases be made in a more orderly manner in the future. The report also warned against using stockpile purchases and sales as an economic stabilizing device as had sometimes been the case in the past and recommended that withdrawals from the stockpile should be permitted only when the national security "emphatically" required it. The Commission found that the seventy-four materials then selected for stockpiling were well chosen, but it concluded that in determining the stockpile objectives more weight should be given than in the past to the vulnerability to enemy attack of the production facilities in the United States, Canada, and Latin America.

Program

Each year the stockpile objectives are reviewed, both as to kind, quality, and quantity of materials to be included, in the light of the then currently anticipated military requirements, essential civilian requirements, and the nation's industrial capabilities, including possible expansion in time of war. As the result of such a review during 1952, two goods were added to the list and two others were deleted, while the objectives for ten commodities were increased and those for twelve were decreased. The net effect of these adjustments, together with a decline in the prices of many materials, was to reduce the value of the total objectives from $9.3 billion at the beginning of the year to $7.5 billion, in current prices, as of December 31, 1952. Apparently some two thirds of this decline reflected the fall in prices of raw materials during the year.[6]

The Administration requested Congress to appropriate only $225 million in cash for stockpiling purposes for the year beginning in mid-1952, including $70 million to liquidate previous contract authorizations, as compared with $790 million appropriated for the previous fiscal year and over $3 billion during fiscal year 1951.[7] Administration spokesmen explained that the decline in

[6] For security reasons, data on the stockpile objectives by commodity and by quantity were not made public.

[7] These figures are cash appropriations. Taking account of contract authorizations, both new contract authority granted and cash to liquidate previous contract authority, the *net* new obligational authority provided during fiscal year 1951 was $2.9 billion, and in fiscal year 1952 was $590 million. *Survey—1951*,

the amount requested was due in large part to the fact that there would be an estimated three quarters of a billion dollars of previously appropriated funds still available; during the preceding months some of the materials for which the stockpile authorities had planned to obligate funds had been channeled into the current rearmament program. It was believed that the requested funds, plus the carryover, would permit a slight increase in the then current rate of stockpile accumulation. Members of Congress showed no disposition to curtail the stockpiling activities and evidenced no concern, as they had before Korea, as to the possible threat of a large stockpile to domestic producers of these commodities. The Administration included in its request some $20 million for the building of storage facilities but Congress concluded the Government could and should rent commercial space and so reduced the request accordingly. After making some small reductions in the amount requested for administrative expenses, Congress appropriated $204 million, raising the total appropriations for stockpiling purposes since the beginning of the program in 1946 to $5.2 billion, including some $85 million of outstanding contract authority.

Procurement and Supply Development

The stockpiling goals had been increased greatly during 1950 and 1951 but there had been in those years no comprehensive review of the Government's procurement and supply development policies, although in the last half of 1951, as the stockpiling operations began to impinge on the domestic rearmament program, an extensive reshuffling of the complex administrative structure responsible for building up the official stockpile took place. This had the effect of transferring much of the responsibility for policy determination from the Munitions Board of the Defense Department to a civilian agency, the Defense Production Administration. In early 1952 a thorough review of the nation's stockpiling policies was begun with the aim of determining the appropriate policies for a period of partial, as well as of full, mobiliza-

---

p. 208 erroneously reported the net obligational authority provided by Congress for fiscal year 1952 as $790 million, having failed to take account of the fact that $200 million of the cash appropriation was to be used for liquidating previous contract authority.

tion. This review had not been completed by the end of the year, but the Defense Production Administrator early in the year established the following general priorities for allocating scarce materials: (1) military and atomic energy production to meet United States and allied needs; (2) defense-supporting and "essential" civilian production, including exports; (3) additions to the stockpile; and (4) other civilian production.

a. PROCUREMENT

In spite of the relatively low priority assigned to stockpiling, the problems of acquiring materials for the stockpile became progressively easier during 1952 as production of many items increased, military and industrial demands leveled off, and prices for many of the commodities fell.[8] The bitter disputes with foreign interests as to "price gouging" that had characterized some of the procurement during 1951[9] abated as world prices fell and as the United States effectively removed ceilings on the prices private importers could pay for tin and copper.[1] The earlier charges that the United States was "hogging" the market were generally dropped and foreign countries once again urged the United States to increase its rate of procurement as a means of helping them increase their dollar earnings. Withdrawals from existing stocks for current use by United States industry and diversions to cur-

[8] The international allocations of raw materials discussed in the following section had a bearing on the United States stockpiling activities, as did the United States export controls discussed in the first section of this chapter.

[9] See *Survey—1951*, pp. 211-212.

[1] See the following sections for a brief statement of the various long-term tin contracts entered into by the U.S. Government during the year. The negotiations with Bolivia (see *Survey—1951*, p. 212) were complicated in 1952 following that Government's nationalization of the tin mines, but large quantities were purchased at prices of around $1.17 per pound, as compared with the price of $1.50 a pound that Bolivia had asked in 1951. In late July the U.S. Government authorized private importers to resume importing at any price. (See *New York Times*, January 15, 1952, p. 36; January 23, 1952, p. 35; March 14, 1952, p. 43; April 4, 1952, p. 38; June 27, 1952, p. F-1; July 17, 1952, p. 6; August 1, 1952, p. 21; November 5, 1952, p. 9; and January 17, 1953, p. 23 for unofficial accounts of the negotiations with Bolivia.)

In May the Chilean Government cancelled an earlier agreement by which it had been supplying copper to the United States at 27½ cents a pound—3 cents above the price ceiling established by the Office of Price Stabilization for domestically produced copper but less than the prices other countries were reported to be paying for Chilean copper. Shortly thereafter, the Office of Defense Mobilization authorized United States importers to pay the free market price for copper imports and permitted increases in the domestic price ceiling on copper products.

rent use of supplies under contract for the stockpile also declined sharply as the year progressed and had virtually ceased by December, at which time total withdrawals since 1946 amounted to only $60 million and diversions to $186 million.

Deliveries to the stockpile during the year totalled $918 million at current prices and were the largest in value for any year since the program had begun, raising the total in inventory to some $4 billion. An additional $1.8 billion worth of materials was under contract at the end of the year. That is, in value terms, the stockpile on hand at the end of the year was equal to some 53 percent of the total program and the inventory plus materials under contract for future delivery accounted for 78 percent of the program. The Munitions Board also reported at the end of the year that the stockpile was in better balance than in the past and that for approximately two thirds of the items 80 percent or more of the objective was either on hand or under contract for delivery. As a result of this improvement, it was decided during the latter part of the year to complete the goals for many of the items at a gradually decreasing rate so as to withdraw slowly rather than precipitously from the commodity markets.

The Emergency Procurement Service of the General Services Administration, acting as agent for the Defense Materials Procurement Agency, was responsible for the procurement of materials for the stockpile and the bulk of the acquisitions during the year were by direct purchase from funds specifically appropriated for this purpose. Small amounts were also provided by other methods, however. The Commodity Credit Corporation was authorized in 1949 to barter surplus agricultural products for strategic and critical materials produced abroad. During 1952, approximately $17 million worth of such goods was sold by the Corporation to the General Services Administration, raising the total value of such transactions to $50 million. In previous years the Economic Cooperation Administration had committed some of the European counterpart funds reserved for United States use to the purchase of strategic and critical materials, but during 1952 such commitments, handled by the Defense Materials Procurement Agency, were very small, having been less than the equivalent of $1 million during the first half of the year, raising the total since 1948 to the equivalent of $83 million. Actual deliveries under such purchase contracts through mid-1952 totalled $76 million.[2] Data on commitments and deliveries against counterpart funds during the last half of the year were not available as this document went to press.[3]

b. SUPPLY DEVELOPMENT

The general policy was established during 1952 that, whenever it was judged that there would not be enough of any of the strategic and critical materials to meet the current requirements—or those it was anticipated would arise during a period of full mobilization—for at least the first three priorities mentioned above, the Defense Materials Procurement Agency should prepare and carry out programs for expanding the production of such items. Most such programs applied to domestic sources and are therefore outside the scope of this document.[4]

As to expanding production abroad, two of the more effective devices were placing long-term purchase contracts and making advances against future production out of the appropriations for stockpiling. Further, as noted in Chapter IV, above, an increasing amount of the loans of the Export-Import Bank went to develop new, and extend old, sources of supply of such commodities; in addition to making some $115 million of loan authorizations for strategic material production from the Bank's own funds, the Bank authorized $44 million of loans for especially risky ventures from funds made available under the Defense Production Act of 1950, as amended in 1951. The latter loans, made after receipt of "cer-

[2] P.L. 152, 81st Cong. provided that the various executive agencies could accept strategic and critical materials in lieu of cash payments due under leases or sales of Government surplus property. As of the end of 1952, some 36,450 tons of pig aluminum had been transferred to the stockpile under this law. Arrangements were also made whereby certain seizures by Customs officials may be awarded to the General Services Administration free of charge. Through 1951 diamonds valued at approximately $1 million had been so awarded; these were gem-quality stones and it was planned to trade them for an equivalent value of industrial stones.

[3] For an account of the procedures and practices of the Economic Cooperation Administration-Mutual Security Agency with respect to both purchase and supply development of critical materials, see The President's Materials Policy Commission, *Resources for Freedom*, *op.cit.*, Vol. V, pp. 125-128.

[4] For details on some of these domestic programs during 1952, see *Stockpile Report to Congress*, August 15, 1952, *op.cit.*, pp. 21-34; *Stockpile Report to Congress*, February 15, 1953, *op.cit.*, pp. 5-6, 19-32; and "Second Annual Report of the Activities of the Joint Committee on Defense Production," S. *Rpt. No. 3*, *op.cit.*, pp. 72-80.

tificates of essentiality" issued by agencies of the Government other than the Bank, usually carried with them contracts providing for the sale of at least part of the materials produced to the United States, with the first such sales proceeds being assigned to the Bank to repay the loan.[5] Also, the International Bank, as discussed in Chapter V, granted several loans whose purpose was to increase the production abroad of scarce materials, and some emphasis was given to such activities under the Point Four Program, as surveyed in Chapter II, and in the various programs for encouraging private foreign investment outlined in Chapter IV.[6]

The Mutual Security Administration, through the Defense Materials Procurement Agency, continued the practice of the Economic Cooperation Administration of providing dollars and counterpart funds to expand the output of strategic materials, mostly in the dependent overseas territories of the Western European nations. These funds were made available on a loan basis and were repayable, with interest, in the materials produced; in most instances the United States also retained an option to buy additional quantities. During the first nine months of 1952 (details for the full year are not available) approximately $4 million in dollars and the equivalent of nearly $41 million in counterpart funds reserved for United States use were disbursed for these pur-

[5] The so-called Paley Commission recommended that when these special provisions of the Defense Production Act expired a permanent Government lending agency should be set up to finance foreign materials production in cases where the need for materials by the United States was compelling and the lending risks were greater than could be assumed by the Export-Import Bank under its own Act. It was proposed that such an agency be given authority to make long-term purchase arrangements, including price guarantees, and, if the Government investment exceeded 75 percent of the total, to enter into management contracts or arrangements providing for sharing the profits of such enterprises. The Commission also found that a shortage of equity capital—both local and foreign—constituted one of the greatest deterrents to larger loans by the Export-Import Bank and the International Bank for the development of sources of supply of strategic and critical materials abroad. For details on these findings and recommendations, see The President's Materials Policy Commission, *Resources for Freedom, op.cit.*, Vol. I, pp. 76-77, and Vol. V, pp. 116-124.

[6] The Paley Commission recommended that, in addition to the methods already being used to encourage private investment in foreign projects producing raw materials needed in the United States, certain tax changes favoring such investments should be made; in particular, it suggested permitting the deferment of the reporting of income from overseas *branches* until the income was remitted (already permitted in the case of overseas *subsidiaries*) and permitting the deduction from taxable income of certain outlays for exploration and development activities.

poses, raising the total since 1948 to $19 million in dollars and $64 million in counterpart funds. (Commitments as of the end of 1952 totalled $24 million and $105 million, respectively.) In addition, the Defense Materials Procurement Agency, in a program initiated in 1952, authorized the investment in similar projects of some $9 million in dollars provided under the Defense Production Act and disbursed $4 million.[7]

Assistance for increased investment in the production of such materials abroad was also provided by the granting of export priorities and licenses for needed machinery and equipment, as discussed earlier in this chapter. As in previous years, the Department of Agriculture continued to carry out research and experimentation in several foreign countries with the aim of increasing the production of agricultural-type strategic materials and the Reconstruction Finance Corporation continued to finance certain projects for the development and maintenance of abaca production in Latin America under terms of the Abaca Production Act of 1950.

D. *INTERNATIONAL COMMODITY ARRANGEMENTS*

After a long period of opposition to intergovernmental commodity agreements, the United States during World War II accepted "in principle" that such agreements for primary goods might be desirable in peacetime on condition that both producing and consuming interests were represented, that full publicity was given to any such agreements, that there existed or threatened to develop burdensome surpluses and/or unemployment that was not likely to be corrected in a short time by normal market forces, and that the objective of such agreements was to expand consumption or shift resources out of industries with persistent surpluses. Provisions for such agreements were made in Chapters V and VI of the ill-fated International Trade Organization Charter and they are also permitted in the General Agreement on Tariffs and Trade. In mid-1952 the Paley Commission reported that it was convinced "that the solutions to the problem of materials market instability must be sought through international agree-

[7] The Mutual Security Agency authorized no new releases of counterpart funds reserved for the depositing country's own use in increasing the production of critical and strategic materials.

ments in which the United States will have to take a leading part."[8]

For several years the U.S. Government has participated in six intergovernmental commodity groups (or committees) concerned with wheat, sugar, rubber, tin, cotton, and wool, but, except for the first, these organizations in recent years have had only research and advisory functions. After the outbreak of war in Korea, in the face of a "mad scramble" among the rearming nations for many raw materials, the United States, along with Britain and France, took the initiative in establishing an International Materials Conference.[9]

International Materials Conference

The International Materials Conference, on whose seven commodity committees (pulp and paper, sulphur, cotton–cotton linters, wool, copper-zinc-lead, manganese-nickel-cobalt, and tungsten-molybdenum) twenty-eight nations were represented, accounting for between 80 and 90 percent of the free world's production and consumption of the various commodities, was intended to provide a loose institutional framework for international consultation where the members could review the supply of and demand for the selected commodities, try to develop measures for increasing the production and conservation of them, and attempt to reach agreement on the international allocation of available supplies. The approach of the Conference was one of voluntary cooperation; the organization had no authority to apply sanctions and the member governments were free to accept or reject the recommendations.

Through 1951 the problems of collecting data and recommending allocations had taken up most of the time of the various committees. Specific international allocations had been recommended

[8] The President's Materials Policy Commission, *Resources for Freedom*, *op.cit.*, Vol. I, p. 86. The question of unstable prices for primary products was also extensively discussed in the United Nations during the year in connection with the debates on economic development. Over United States opposition, the General Assembly passed a resolution calling for three studies designed to make recommendations for measures to achieve an "adequate, just, and equitable relationship" between the prices of manufactured goods and those of primary products. (See *United Nations Bulletin*, January 1, 1953, pp. 3-6, 36-40.)

[9] For a survey of United States policies and activities with respect to international commodity agreements during 1951 and earlier years, see *Survey—1951*, pp. 216-227, and the references cited therein.

—and in large part implemented by the members—for sulphur, tungsten, molybdenum, copper, zinc, nickel, cobalt, and newsprint. It had been concluded that there were adequate supplies of lead, manganese, cobalt, and cotton and cotton linters, but the wool group had been unable to agree as to either the dimensions of the shortages or steps to be taken to allocate available supplies. In April 1952 the Conference issued a report on its first year of operations, stating that while it had to date been concerned primarily with short-run and emergency problems and that it was anticipated that allocations would continue to be made for many of the commodities through 1952 at least, it was now turning its attention also to the longer-run problems of "expansion of production, economic utilization of available supplies, substitution of other materials, and end use control measures."[1]

The Administration, and many unofficial observers, believed throughout 1952 that the Conference had done its job well; had contributed, by assuring members of continuing supplies, to reducing the hoarding and panic buying of scarce materials and so helped reverse the upward trend of prices for many of the commodities; had helped to distribute the affected raw materials in a manner calculated to achieve the maximum defense of the members as a group against Communist aggression; and had "proved to be a means of bringing into a world situation, which threatened to be a source of international ill-will, a form of international collaboration which has led to the substantial satisfaction of all countries concerned."[2] Some also cited the Conference as demonstrat-

[1] International Materials Conference, *Report on Operations 1951-1952*, Wash., D.C., April 1952, p. 2. This document gives a detailed statement of the organization, operation, and problems of the International Materials Conference through March 1952. A similar account, through March 1953, giving details on production, exports, and imports of the materials may be found in International Materials Conference, *Report on Operations 1952-1953*, Wash., D.C., April 1953. Other sources that were heavily drawn on in the preparation of this section were the periodic press releases of the International Materials Conference (frequently reprinted in whole or in part in the Department of State *Bulletin*); "Defense Production Act Amendments of 1952," *Hearings on S. 2594 and S. 2645*, U.S. Senate, Committee on Banking and Currency, 82d Cong., 2d Sess., Part 1, pp. 69-73; "Defense Production Act Amendments of 1952," *Hearings on H.R. 6546*, House of Rep., Committee on Banking and Currency, 82d Cong., 2d Sess., Part 2, pp. 1423-1439, 1637-1647; and *Congressional Record*, January 31, 1952, pp. 695ff.; February 4, 1952, pp. 759ff.; February 18, 1952, pp. 1088ff.; March 17, 1952, pp. 2383ff.; June 4, 1952, pp. 6654ff.; June 11, 1952, pp. A3781ff.; June 19, 1952, pp. 7755ff., A4038ff.; June 26, 1952, p. 8252; and June 28, 1952, pp. 8609ff.

[2] Department of State *Bulletin*, February 18, 1952, p. 279.

ing that effective cooperation among nations need not involve grandiose institutions, large secretariats, and elaborate rules and articles of agreement.[3]

But bitter opposition to the institution developed in Congress. It was initiated by Senator Ferguson of Michigan, who considered that the unemployment then being suffered in the automobile industry was the result of a shortage of copper and that this in turn was the result of insufficient allocations of copper to the United States by the International Materials Conference. Other members of Congress quickly joined him, charging that unemployment in their constituencies was also due to shortages of certain materials that could be traced to the operations of the Conference. These spokesmen took issue with the assertions of the Administration that the allocation of materials had "regularly been much larger than our pre-Korean share of the international supply" or that the current difficulties with copper in particular were due primarily to the inability to find foreign sellers at the United States ceiling price.[4] As the debate continued, additional objections were raised to the Conference: it had never been specifically approved by Congress, and even worse, it was the "creation" of the State Department and Secretary Acheson; it was an international cartel, a "supergovernment" and "socialistic"; and it was another "backdoor attempt" to bring the International Trade Organization Charter into being. The Administration, and its supporters in Congress, denied the last two "charges," stressed the voluntary nature of the organization, stated that formal Congressional approval was not necessary inasmuch as the authority for participation came from the President's authority to negotiate with other nations, and reported that the United States participation was in the hands of the Defense Production Administration and not the State Department.[5] Despite the appeals

[3] See, for example, *The Economist*, May 3, 1952, p. 333, and *Strengthening the Free World Economy*, a report by Klaus Knorr of a conference held at Princeton, Center of International Studies, Princeton University, February 1953, p. 44.

[4] Department of State *Bulletin*, February 25, 1952, pp. 297-302. In the early summer, the Office of Price Stabilization amended its ceiling price regulations so as to permit importers to pay any price they chose for imported copper and to pass most of any such increase on to the consumer.

[5] Nonetheless, Congress added a clause to the act appropriating funds to the State Department for fiscal year 1953 specifying that none of the monies could be used to pay any expenses incidental to or in connection with participation in

by the Administration that the Conference had worked to the benefit of the United States defense effort, both the House and the Senate approved amendments to the Defense Production Act that, most observers agreed, would have had the effect of making it impossible for the Conference to continue to function. In the conference between the two Houses to reconcile differences in the proposed legislation, however, there were some second thoughts on the matter and the final law merely stated that the United States could agree to international allocations recommended by the International Materials Conference only if such agreements authorized United States importers to purchase any allocations granted to other nations that were not used by such nations.

In the face of this Congressional hostility, together with the earlier opposition by the producing countries to a draft of a four-year plan to increase tungsten production that had been prepared by the Tungsten-Molybdenum Committee,[6] the International Materials Conference abandoned for all practical purposes its plans to deal with the long-run problems of increasing production, conservation, and substitution, and of improving end-use controls. Further, the number of commodities being allocated was gradually reduced during the year in the face of increases in production and, in some cases, declines in the amounts being demanded. In June, the member governments decided to disband the Cotton–Cotton Linters Committee, which had never found it necessary to recommend any allocation of these goods. An emergency allocation of newsprint was made in the first quarter of 1952, but no allocations of wood pulp had ever been recommended and in September it was decided to disband the Pulp and Paper Committee. The Wool Committee had not been able to reach agreement as to allocations in 1951 and early 1952, and in September, as a result of evidence that wool was no longer "in short supply," this Committee too was dissolved.

The Copper-Zinc-Lead Committee had not found it necessary to recommend allocations for lead, and allocations for zinc were

---

the International Materials Conference. Apparently the Administration thereafter used funds appropriated to other agencies, the Defense Production Administration in particular, for these purposes.

[6] See International Materials Conference, *Report on Operations 1951-1952*, *op.cit.*, p. 52.

suspended during the second quarter of 1952; copper continued to be allocated throughout the year but in the light of improved production this too was discontinued in early 1953. The Committee continued in existence in order to keep the position of these metals "under review." Sulphur was also subjected to allocations through the year 1952, but, since production increased and the amount demanded decreased, allocations were discontinued as of March 1, 1953 and the Sulphur Committee was disbanded as of the end of April.

The Tungsten-Molybdenum Committee recommended international allocations of both these materials throughout 1952 but decided in late December that the steady increase in production of tungsten made it possible to discontinue allocations after the end of the year. Although it was estimated that the production of molybdenum during the first quarter of 1953 would be at a rate 75 percent above that of 1950, the Committee found the amounts being demanded still greatly in excess of the amounts being supplied, and international allocations for this commodity were continued. The Manganese-Nickel-Cobalt Committee had never found it necessary to recommend allocations for manganese and in November 1952 it announced that, since the production of cobalt had increased during the past two years by over 30 percent, allocations of this commodity would be discontinued as of the end of the year. Supplies of nickel, on the other hand, were regarded as falling well below the amount being demanded and it was anticipated that allocations would be necessary for some time. Of the two commodities still under allocations on March 1, 1953, the United States relied almost entirely on imports for one—nickel—but was the world's largest exporter of the other—molybdenum.

Thus, by early 1953 the International Materials Conference appeared well along the way toward self-dissolution. The Director of Defense Mobilization, however, stated on January 1, 1953: "Even after all of the commodity committees can be disbanded . . . the Central Group should continue as a stand-by organization for quickly mobilizing international collaboration in case the raw materials situation again seriously deteriorates."[7]

[7] Director of Defense Mobilization, *Eighth Quarterly Report to the President*, Wash., D.C., January 1953, p. 22.

Commodity Study Groups and Agreements[8]

a. INTERNATIONAL COTTON ADVISORY COMMITTEE

The International Cotton Advisory Committee met in Rome in May and spent most of the session discussing proposals prepared by the United States for an "international cotton contract" that would have established export quotas and buffer stocks. (In earlier years, the United States had opposed the creation of an intergovernmental cotton agreement.) In the discussions, much attention was given to the problems created for such a scheme by the then current practice of charging different prices for comparable cotton according to the currency used for purchase and the difficulties that would arise if the prices determined in various countries under their price-support legislation should—as seemed likely—differ from those that would prevail under an international agreement. This problem, as noted below, had created some problems in the operation of the International Wheat Agreement.

The official communiqués on the meeting were noncommittal but the press reported that several of the major importing countries objected to the United States-sponsored scheme, believing that it was likely to increase the prices they would have to pay for cotton. The proposal was referred to a standing committee, which was asked to undertake further studies and to submit a report to the next meeting, scheduled for September 1953.[9]

Although the delegates to this meeting found that the available supplies of cotton were then in approximate balance with the demand for cotton at current prices, the meeting officially requested other international agencies to support the establishment of regional cooperative research projects designed to increase cotton yields in underdeveloped countries.[1]

[8] See *Survey—1951*, pp. 224-227 for a summary of the work of these organizations in that year. For an official report on these groups, as well as others in which the United States was not represented, see UN Interim Co-ordinating Committee for International Commodity Arrangements, *Review of International Commodity Problems 1952*, UN Publication Sales No.: 1953.II.D.1. This document provides a broad official survey of international commodity problems during the year, including a summary of the discussions in the United Nations on the problem of avoiding large fluctuations in primary commodity prices.

[9] See *The Journal of Commerce*, New York, May 29, 1952, p. 1.

[1] For an official account of the session, see Wall, E. L., "Greater Stability Forecast for World Cotton Trade," Department of State *Bulletin*, August 4, 1952, pp. 185-187.

b. WOOL STUDY GROUP

The Wool Study Group held its fifth meeting in London in November, not having met in the previous year. The delegates "examined" the recent developments in the world wool situation, made public their assessment of the current world wool position, and adjourned without taking any substantive decisions, having agreed that there were no urgent problems to be solved.

c. RUBBER STUDY GROUP

In its meeting at Ottawa in May the Rubber Study Group concluded that production of natural—and possibly synthetic—rubber was currently exceeding consumption and examined various possibilities of increasing consumption, concluding that the best prospects lay in improving and extending highways throughout the world. Representatives from the natural-rubber-producing areas showed much concern over the development of the synthetic industry (it was estimated that the 1952 world production of synthetic rubber would be equal to nearly half the production of natural rubber), the large fluctuations in demand for rubber, and the recent decline in the prices of natural rubber.[2] As in previous meetings, there was a great variety of opinions as to the best methods of solving these problems and the Group, unable to reach any general conclusion, established a special working party, on which the United States was represented, to consider whether it was "necessary and practicable" to take international measures to prevent "burdensome surpluses or serious shortages of rubber," and if so, "to prepare drafts of any agreements required to implement such measures."[3] This working party held inconclusive talks during the summer and adjourned until early 1953. No official reports of their studies were made but the press reported that, since the United States was the world's largest importer of natural rubber and the largest producer of synthetic rubber, the U.S. Government was "apprehensive" of any international control scheme that would be acceptable to other nations.[4] Private manufacturers of rubber products in the United States were strongly

[2] The press reported that some of the delegates charged that prices of synthetic rubber being produced in plants owned by the U.S. Government were below actual cost.

[3] Department of State *Bulletin*, June 9, 1952, p. 913.

[4] *The Economist*, January 10, 1953, p. 110.

opposed to American participation in any international rubber agreement,[5] but the Paley Commission looked with favor on an intergovernmental agreement for rubber combining buffer stocks and quotas on production and exports.[6]

d. TIN STUDY GROUP

The Tin Study Group did not meet in 1952. Sharp disagreements between the United States as a consumer and the various producing countries had characterized the meetings in earlier years and prevented any accord on various schemes that had been presented for the intergovernmental control of tin. The U.S. Government during the year negotiated a series of bilateral agreements to assure itself of adequate supplies of this metal. In January the Reconstruction Finance Corporation entered into a contract to buy from Britain 20,000 tons of Malayan tin during 1952.[7] Shortly afterward a long-term contract was entered into between the Reconstruction Finance Corporation and Indonesian producers whereby the latter agreed to supply from 18,000 to 20,000 tons of tin a year to the United States over a three-year period, and a similar agreement for two years was reached with the Association of Belgian Congo Tin Producers, involving 7,000 to 9,000 tons per year. The prices under all these agreements were approximately the same and clauses were included to the effect that the benefits of a higher price to one producing country would be passed on to the other countries concerned. Negotiations also took place with Bolivia but no long-term contracts had been negotiated at year's end—the problem having been complicated by the nationalization of the tin mines in Bolivia in the autumn. However, "substantial" tonnages of Bolivian tin were purchased by the U.S. Government.

United Nations observers concluded that "in the light of these

[5] See *New York Times*, May 12, 1952, p. 32.

[6] The President's Materials Policy Commission, *Resources for Freedom*, *op.cit.*, Vol. I, p. 88. The Commission favored international buffer stocks without quota provisions for such easily storable materials as copper, lead, and zinc.

[7] See *New York Times*, January 15, 1952, p. 36, and Department of State *Bulletin*, January 28, 1952, pp. 115-116, and February 25, 1952, pp. 297-302. This agreement was part of a larger one in which the U.S. Government agreed to grant licenses for the export of some one million tons of steel to Britain in exchange for the right to buy a large part of the aluminum that was being manufactured in Canada for Britain's account.

agreements at the same or very similar prices, it may be decided to resume negotiations for an international tin agreement."[8] In midyear the Paley Commission recommended that the United States should "consider" participating in an intergovernmental tin agreement involving buffer stocks and quotas on production and exports.[9]

e. INTERNATIONAL SUGAR AGREEMENT

The substantive provisions of the International Sugar Agreement, signed in 1937, have been inoperative, for all practical purposes, since the beginning of World War II and under the terms of the Sugar Act of 1948 the United States has carried out its international sugar transactions within a preferential trading system with a portion of the internal market reserved for domestic producers and most of the balance allocated to Cuba, the Philippines, Hawaii, Puerto Rico, and the Virgin Islands.[1] In 1950 the U.S. Government had supported in principle a proposal presented by Cuba to the International Sugar Council to supplant the existing agreement with a new scheme providing for the international regulation of sugar production and exports and the establishment of minimum and maximum prices. A decision as to whether to request a formal negotiating conference was postponed, however, and a Sugar Council special committee, which had been established in 1948, continued to consider the problem of a new agreement. In October 1952, this committee, on which the United States was represented, informed the Council that in its opinion an international conference should be called to negotiate such an agreement, and in late November the Council took a decision to request the Secretary-General of the United Nations to call such a conference sometime in 1953.[2]

[8] UN Interim Co-ordinating Committee for International Commodity Arrangements, *Review of International Commodity Problems 1952, op. cit.*, p. 9.

[9] The President's Materials Policy Commission, *Resources for Freedom, op.cit.*, Vol. I, p. 88.

[1] See Chapter VI, Section F(c), above. The United Kingdom, together with the Commonwealth countries, also has special arrangements covering trade in sugar.

[2] In June, the United States representative signed a protocol prolonging the life of certain provisions of the 1937 agreement (those having to do with international consultation) for three years from August 1952 or until a new agreement came into force, but the U.S. Senate had not ratified this protocol as the year ended. In July 1952 the Senate approved the protocols, signed in 1950 and 1951, prolonging the agreement until August 1952.

f. INTERNATIONAL WHEAT AGREEMENT

The International Wheat Agreement, which began operations in August 1949, fixes quantities that the exporting countries, including the United States, guarantee to sell when the world price is at or above a predetermined maximum ($1.80 per bushel) and quantities that the importing countries agree to buy when the world price is below a predetermined minimum (originally $1.40 but later progressively reduced to $1.20 a bushel).[3] From the outset, the "free" market price of wheat (and the United States "support" price) had exceeded the maximum price under the agreement by amounts averaging around sixty cents per bushel and this involved the payment of export subsidies by the U.S. Government of over $200 million in calendar year 1951 and over $150 million in 1952.

In the spring of 1952 the International Wheat Council held a series of discussions as to whether the agreement should be extended beyond its expiration date of August 1, 1953. No member country favored abandoning the agreement and the U.S. Government a few months earlier had extolled it,[4] but sharp differences developed on the question of the prices to be set under an extension. The United States representatives, together with those of the other exporting countries, favored a higher maximum and a higher minimum price, while the importers believed that a general fall in commodity prices was imminent and refused to agree to a higher price for wheat. The exporting countries also proposed that consideration be given to adjusting prices in any new agreement at stated intervals to changes in some general price index.[5]

[3] See *Survey—1949* for details on the techniques of this scheme. The agreement was originally intended to cover 456 million bushels, but additional countries joined the plan as importers and other countries had their import quotas increased, with the result that the guaranteed purchases during the crop years 1951-1952 and 1952-1953 were some 581 million bushels—about 30 percent of the production of the four exporting countries (the United States, Canada, Australia, and France) in 1951-1952. The United States quota for the 1951-1952 and 1952-1953 crop years was 253 million bushels. No new countries entered the agreement in 1952 nor were any of the import quotas of existing members increased, although a number of requests that this be done were made. Of the guaranteed sales and purchases, 98.5 percent were consummated in the 1951-1952 crop year. For a summary of the operations under the Wheat Agreement during 1951, see *The Economist*, May 17, 1952, pp. 459-463.

[4] Department of Agriculture, "How Is the Wheat Agreement Working?" *Agricultural Information Bulletin*, No. 74, Wash., D.C., January 1952.

[5] The American Farm Bureau Federation had urged such a proposal earlier in

The press reported that the United States based its request for higher prices on the grounds that the existing price involved a heavy charge on the U.S. Treasury and made the scheme unpalatable to Congress,[6] that the $1.80 maximum price was "unrealistic," and that higher prices would encourage greater production in Canada and Australia.[7] The spring meeting reached an impasse on these price issues and the problem was referred to a special committee, it being planned that the Council would resume formal discussions in early 1953.[8]

E. *TEMPORARY SUSPENSION OF IMPORT DUTIES AND TAXES*

Following the outbreak of war in Korea, many recommended that in view of the existing inflationary pressures and raw material shortages Congress should pass temporary emergency legislation authorizing the Administration unilaterally to reduce or remove tariffs and import taxes on raw materials for which the United States was substantially dependent on foreign sources.[9]

---

the year. (See *New York Times*, April 7, 1952, p. 33.) The Food and Agricultural Organization recommended that the prices in the Agreement be adjusted to changes in the free market prices of wheat and in the price level of world trade as a whole. For other reforms in the Agreement suggested by this organization, see UN Food and Agricultural Organization, *A Reconsideration of the Economics of the International Wheat Agreement*, Rome, September 1952.

[6] It must not be forgotten that a large part—perhaps two thirds—of the subsidized United States exports under the Agreement were sent to various countries as part of official aid programs, thus reducing the direct cost of such aid.

[7] *New York Times*, April 25, 1952, p. 37.

[8] The Wheat Council did agree during the year that the six-cent-a-bushel carrying charge imposed by the exporters in 1951 (see *Survey—1951*, p. 227) could be continued on condition that it not be increased during the life of the current agreement and that it not be regarded as setting a precedent. This question of carrying charges was also being discussed in connection with a renewal of the agreement.

[9] See, for example, *Report to the President on Foreign Economic Policies*, Wash., D.C., November 10, 1950, pp. 78-80, and Council of Economic Advisers, *The Annual Economic Review*, Wash., D.C., January 1951, p. 123. The President's Materials Policy Commission, in its *Resources for Freedom*, *op.cit.*, Vol. I, p. 79, recommended that such legislation be permanent rather than temporary. The Public Advisory Board for Mutual Security, in its *A Trade and Tariff Policy in the National Interest*, Wash., D.C., February 1953, pp. 31-35, recommended that tariffs be permanently reduced and in some cases eliminated on metals and minerals the imports of which were a "major" part of United States supplies and that if, for security reasons, it was deemed desirable to expand domestic production, this be done by special Government purchases and contracts rather than by greater tariff protection.

No such general or broad authority was requested by the Administration but several specific requests to remove such duties and taxes were made in 1951 and 1952. The justification given for these requests was that the domestic production was grossly inadequate to meet urgent current demands; it was argued that since only a temporary suspension was being asked the action would not adversely affect domestic producers or restrain additional investment in local mines. In the cases of each of these commodities the world price was higher than the United States domestic price ceiling by more than the amount of the duty or tax, but it was thought, nonetheless, that suspension of the levies would serve to increase imports, since it was believed that many foreign producers were anxious to create or to preserve American markets and to obtain dollars.[1]

Metal scrap had been scarce in the United States for many years and Congress, by a series of acts, began in 1942 to suspend the duties and import taxes on such commodities. These suspensions had been allowed to lapse in July 1949 but shortly after the outbreak of war in Korea they had been reinstated until mid-1952. In July, Congress approved an extension of this suspension, after excluding lead scrap, until mid-1953.[2] In early February Congress approved measures suspending the duties on imports of unmanufactured lead and zinc until March 31, 1953 (or the termination of the national emergency if this were earlier), the duties to be reinstated if for any one calendar month the average domestic price for either commodity fell below 18 cents per pound.[3] The average domestic price of lead dropped below the 18-cent figure in May and that for zinc in June, and President Truman thereupon reinstated the tariffs on these commodities, effective June 26 and July 24, respectively.

Additional tungsten supplies were also urgently needed for the

[1] See *Survey—1951*, pp. 230-233, and the references cited therein for discussions of the suspension of import taxes during that and earlier years. It should be recorded that the duties and excise taxes on imports of most metals and minerals are low. Many of these have been reduced since 1930 under the various trade agreements and most of them are specific, with the result that their impact has been lessened by the rise in prices.

[2] See S. *Rpt. No. 1830*, 82d Cong., 2d Sess., June 26, 1952, and *H. Rpt. No. 2283*, 82d Cong., 2d Sess., June 23, 1952.

[3] See S. *Rpt. No. 1057*, 82d Cong., 1st Sess., October 20, 1951, and S. *Rpt. No. 1053*, 82d Cong., 1st Sess., October 19, 1951.

rearmament program and late in 1951 the Administration asked Congress to authorize a two-year suspension of the duty on this commodity. The House quickly approved the request, after adding a provision that the President must revoke the suspension if, for any calendar month, the average market price was below the $63 per ton that had been guaranteed for five years for Government purchases under the Defense Production Administration program for expanding internal production. The Senate passed a similar bill without debate just prior to adjourning in July 1952 but, on the subsequent objection by one of the Senators from Nevada, the bill was put back on the calendar, where it remained.

In late 1951 the Administration had also asked Congress to suspend temporarily the duties on aluminum imports but the Legislative Branch took no action on this request in 1952. The question of the import tax on copper, which had been so bitterly discussed in earlier years, was not debated in Congress during 1952, the 1951 law having extended the suspension until June 30, 1953.[4]

[4] Bills were offered, but not approved, in both the Senate and House during 1952 and 1951 to limit by quantitative quotas to 50 percent of the average 1947-1949 level the importation of all products containing raw materials that were subject to United States allocations or priority controls, unless the Secretary of Defense certified that a higher level of imports was "essential" for defense purposes. The proponents of the measure argued that such a law was necessary to protect the future competitive position of American producers whose level of operations was being restricted by Government raw material allocations and that, while consumers might suffer, it was "fair" and the "American way" to distribute the burden of national defense equally among all the people. Opponents of the proposal, including the Administration, argued, among other things, that the existing domestic allocations frequently did not involve a severe reduction in United States production so that the amendments would simply improve the competitive position of the domestic producers at the expense of domestic consumers and foreign producers, that the proposal might lead to retaliation, that it would tend to increase inflationary pressures, and that it would violate commitments under most of the nation's reciprocal trade agreements. (See "Defense Production Act Amendments of 1952," *Hearings on H.R. 6546*, *op.cit.*, Part I, pp. 400-418, and "Defense Production Act Amendments of 1952," *Hearings on S. 2594 and S. 2645*, *op.cit.*, Part II, pp. 1539-1542.)

VIII · EUROPEAN ECONOMIC INTEGRATION

EACH year since 1948 the U.S. Congress, with the approval of the Administration, has expressed in increasingly strong terms its wish that Europe "unify."[1] In the statement of purposes of the law in the Foreign Assistance Act of 1948 (creating the European Recovery Program), it was stated that "it is . . . the policy of the people of the United States to encourage . . . economic cooperation in Europe. . . ." The 1949 legislation added, "It is further declared to be the policy of the people of the United States to encourage the unification of Europe. . . ." In 1950 the word "further" was inserted before "unification of Europe" and in 1951 the Mutual Security Act stated that one of the purposes of the aid program was "to further encourage the economic unification and the political federation of Europe. . . ."

In the public hearings during 1952 on extending the Mutual Security Program there was relatively little discussion of the policy of encouraging European "unification." But this was apparently because almost no one in Congress or among the Administration spokesmen questioned the wisdom of the policy or doubted that most Europeans wanted it.[2] The members of Congress took

[1] The "unification" concept was rarely defined precisely by U.S. Government officials; usually it was spoken of in terms of removing quantitative restrictions and monetary barriers to trade, lowering tariffs within the area, and "pooling" basic resources in the sense of placing them under some sort of supranational authority; establishing a political "federation"; and creating a single European defense force under some degree of supranational direction.

[2] The policy of the United States with respect to the European Defense Community is discussed briefly in Chapter I. Much of the discussion in Congress and in the public press in the United States during the year on "unification" either lumped together economic and political unification or stressed the latter. It is outside the scope of this document to discuss United States policy with respect to encouraging political federation of Europe. It may be noted, however, that the Senate Committee on Foreign Relations took no action during the year (other than to appoint a subcommittee to study the problem) on S. Res. 269, which had been introduced, with the formal approval of President Truman, on January 31 and which declared that the U.S. Government would welcome the calling of the European Constitutional Convention to lay the groundwork of European political federation and

no exception in public to Secretary of State Acheson's statement that the Government's efforts during the preceding years to "speed up" the unification of Europe had been "sound and good and one of the best things that has happened in American foreign policy"[3] or to his conclusion that "If we succeed [in creating a unified Europe] we will have a force which will underpin strength in Europe for generations. If not, we will have an inherent weakness in Europe which will have to be kept propped up—if indeed we can keep it propped up."[4] Even in an election year there was little temptation to criticize such statements, for General Eisenhower was on record as believing that "This [the unification of Europe] is the central goal and the only possible way of creating reasonable security, and insuring at the same time, the improvement in living standards that characterizes Western civilization. Therein lies the real answer to the threat of Communistic inundation." "If these [the European Coal and Steel Community and the European Defense Community] could be supplemented by a Schuman Plan for electric power and for agriculture, along with a system of standardizing money values, the benefits would be

that the U.S. Government would "cooperate" with a European federal government (see Department of State *Bulletin*, February 18, 1952, pp. 275-276).

Senator Connally, Chairman of the Foreign Relations Committee, was the only member of Congress who publicly stated that he did not approve any attempt by the U.S. Government to encourage the political unification of Europe. He said: "I am not in favor of our meddling with the political consolidation of Europe." "That is their business and it is not our business." "We have all we can do to get them to join in and do their part over there [in building up defense forces] without undertaking to force them to unify. I think it would be an impossibility for all of Europe to consolidate into a single state. They would never get their relationships adjusted on earth in any practical way." ("Mutual Security Act of 1952," *Hearings*, U.S. Senate, Committee on Foreign Relations, 82d Cong., 2d Sess., p. 183.) Senator Connally's was a lonely voice, however, and most of the American officials, members of Congress, and general public, so far as could be determined from the public press, were convinced of the desirability of creating a United States of Europe.

In the treaty creating a European Defense Community, as signed in the summer of 1952, a provision was included whereby the proposed European Defense Community Assembly was to prepare proposals for the formation of a European Political Community. At the May 1952 session of the Council of Europe Assembly a proposal was referred to the foreign ministers of the six European Defense Community nations that the Schuman Plan Assembly (including the same nations as the proposed European Defense Community) undertake the preparation of a draft constitution for such a European Political Community. The foreign ministers affected agreed and a subcommittee of the Schuman Plan Assembly was established in September. It was expected that a draft would be prepared by early 1953.

[3] "Mutual Security Act of 1952," *Hearings, op. cit.*, p. 99.

[4] *ibid.*, p. 11.

profound and far-reaching." "Indeed, until this hope ['full political and economic unity'] becomes an accomplished fact, or some miracle brings about a disappearance of the Soviet threat, there will be no confident peace and enlarging prosperity for any part of the free world."[5]

As in previous years, there were several in Congress who favored making United States aid to Europe conditional upon specific programs and concrete steps—"minimum and periodic accomplishments"—toward unification (undefined). Administration spokesmen successfully opposed this, arguing that rapid progress was being made, that effective encouragement could be provided by "persuasion," "assistance," and "advice," and that any formal requirement would probably be considered by the European nations an impairment of their sovereignty and would result in greater resistance.[6]

As finally signed by the President, the Mutual Security Act of 1952 left untouched the statement on unification in the previous year's legislation but added: "The Congress welcomes the recent progress in political federation, military integration, and economic unification in Europe and reaffirms its belief in the necessity of further vigorous efforts toward these ends as a means of building strength, establishing security, and preserving peace in the North Atlantic area. In order to provide further encouragement to such efforts the Congress believes it essential that this Act should be so administered as to support concrete measures for political federation, military integration, and economic unification in Europe." The Administration had also proposed that the law provide that funds appropriated under it might be used to furnish assistance to any "organization, association, or grouping of such [European] nations which, in the opinion of the President, makes a significant contribution toward political federation, military integration, or economic unification of such nations."[7] Congress was sympathetic

[5] Department of State *Bulletin*, April 14, 1952, pp. 576-577.

[6] For evidence of strong Congressional feeling on this matter, however, see *Congressional Record*, May 22, 1952, pp. 5872-5876.

[7] For the Administration's proposals on this matter, see "Mutual Security Act Extension," *Hearings on H.R. 7005*, House of Rep., Committee on Foreign Affairs, 82d Cong., 2d Sess., p. 27. For the text of the final law, see Mutual Security Act of 1951, as amended (P.L. 400, 82d Cong., 2d Sess.). For an account of United States policy and activities regarding European integration in 1951 and earlier years, see *Survey—1951*, pp. 234-269, and the references cited therein.

to the Administration's wishes to stimulate unification by supplying its aid directly to groups or organizations of nations rather than bilaterally to individual nations but did not approve such a general and blanket authority and therefore specified that aid funds could be used to furnish assistance to the North Atlantic Treaty Organization, the European Coal and Steel Community, and "the organization which may evolve from current international discussions concerning a European Defense Community."

The presidential campaign platforms of both major political parties contained planks urging the unification of Europe. The Republican platform stated that "In Western Europe we shall use our friendly influence without meddling or imperialistic attitudes, for ending the political and economic divisions which alone prevent that vital area from being strong on its own right."[8] The Democratic Party statement was: "We encourage the economic and political unity of free Europe and the increasing solidarity of the nations of the North Atlantic community. We hail the Schuman Plan . . . and the European Defense Community. We are proud of America's part in carrying these great projects forward and we pledge our continuing support until they are established."[9] Whether because there was little interest in the question among the voters or because there was no room for partisan debate on the policy, the question was touched upon only briefly and rarely by the candidates during the presidential campaign, but each made it clear that it was planned that his Administration would encourage a greater unification of Western Europe.

A. *EUROPEAN PAYMENTS UNION*

As compared with the previous two years, little attention was given during 1952, in the press and in various official statements, to the European Payments Union, although it and the related trade liberalization measures constituted the main operating instruments of European economic integration. The EPU, in whose creation the U.S. Government had played a major role, began operation in mid-1950 with the immediate objective of creating a multilateral system of payments that would provide for the transferability *within* Europe of the various European currencies.

[8] *New York Times*, July 11, 1952, p. 8.
[9] *New York Times*, July 24, 1952, p. 16.

Those responsible for establishing the Union believed that this would be a major step in creating a single "mass market" in Europe resulting in the intensification of competition and greater international specialization, thus permitting European producers to take advantage of large-scale, low-cost production methods. The results of such competition and production methods, it was anticipated, would be so to increase the production and productivity in Europe as to achieve the other objectives formally set for the Union: those of permitting the area more quickly to dispense with United States aid, facilitating a return to full multilateral trade, and assisting a return to the general convertibility of currencies.

The major issues involved in establishing the Union and its operations, accomplishments, and problems through 1951, together with a description of its mechanisms and those of its predecessors, have been outlined in previous volumes of this *Survey*.[1] The Union is a technically complex institution but its basic operating principles are simple: once a month each country's surpluses or deficits on current account with every other member are set off against one another, leaving each member with a single net surplus or deficit vis-à-vis all the other members as a group, that is, with the Union. This net balance is cumulated monthly and, after certain adjustments, is then applied against the quotas in the Union assigned to each member. Credits (debits) less than a certain portion of the quota are settled by an automatic granting (receiving) of credit to (from) the Union and as the cumulative credit (debit) increases part of it is covered by credits and part by receipt (payment) of gold or dollars from (to) the Union.[2] Thus, the system provides for the complete transferability of currencies among the members within Europe and removes the incentive to discriminate among various European markets.

Through 1951 most observers believed the Union had been an

[1] See *Survey—1951*, pp. 239-259, and references cited therein. For a more detailed and critical account of these regional payments arrangements through 1951, see Diebold, W., Jr., *Trade and Payments in Western Europe*, Council on Foreign Relations, New York, 1952, pp. 15-132. For detailed and brief accounts of operations during 1951 and early 1952, see Bank for International Settlements, *Twenty-Second Annual Report*, Basle, June 9, 1952, pp. 227-249.

[2] These gold and credit percentages are so calculated that once a given country's quota is exhausted a creditor (debtor) has received (paid) 40 percent of the quota in dollars and extended (received) 60 percent in credit.

effective mechanism (at least as compared with what most believed was the actual alternative—a network of bilateral payments and trade agreements) for expanding intra-European trade on a nondiscriminatory basis. Not enough time had elapsed to determine whether the object of a growth in European productivity was being achieved and little, if any, progress had been reported in advancing toward the goals of returning to full multilateral trade and of assisting a return to the general convertibility of currencies. It must be recognized, however, that the impact of the rearmament programs—not foreseen when the Union was established—probably served to make achievement of these goals much more difficult. But there was also evidence by the beginning of 1952 that the Union suffered from some basic defects and was in danger of operating in such a way as to tend to create an increasingly protected soft-currency bloc within Europe.[3]

Operations and Adjustments in Mechanism during 1952

During the latter part of 1951 and the first half of 1952 the major *operating* problems faced by the Union were the excessive creditor positions recorded by several of its members and the related threat to the cash solvency of the Union. These difficulties were the subject of extended discussions and resulted in several adjustments being made before it was agreed in June to continue the Union for another year. During the second half of 1952 the pressures on the Union arising from the extreme positions of several of its members eased considerably, permitting greater attention to be given to the question of whether the Union, as it existed, was the best available means of attaining the objectives that had been set for it.

It is not within the scope of this document to trace the developments, and the reasons for them, in the position of each member of the EPU.[4] The following table, however, gives a picture of the changes in the position of each member of the Union during the

[3] For a discussion of some of these problems as of the beginning of the year, see Fleming, J. M., Hirschman, A. O., and Triffin, R., "Regional Organization of Trade and Payments," *American Economic Review, Papers and Proceedings*, May 1952, pp. 345-368.

[4] For official accounts, see Organization for European Economic Cooperation, *European Payments Union, Second Annual Report of the Managing Board*, Paris, 1952, and Organization for European Economic Cooperation, *Europe—the Way Ahead*, Fourth Annual Report of the OEEC, Paris, December 1952.

TABLE 18

Position of Member Countries with the European Payments Union, 1950-1952
(millions of dollar equivalents)

		Cumulative Net Position:[a] *Surplus (+) or Deficit (−)*			
Member Country	*Quota*	*Dec. 31 1950*	*Dec. 31 1951*	*June 30 1952*	*Dec. 31 1952*
Austria	70[b]	−37.4	−130.6	−142.5	−108.8
Belgium-Luxembourg	360[c]	+21.8	+604.3	+802.2[d]	+761.3[d]
Denmark	195	−38.4	−33.5	−23.9	−27.3
France	520	+212.4	−196.9	−433.6[d]	−625.7[d]
Germany	500	−356.7	+31.4	+299.2	+366.0
Greece	45[b]	−70.8	−186.7	−223.5	−229.0
Iceland	15	−3.3	−8.5	−12.7	−12.5
Italy and Trieste	205	−30.9	+195.2	+166.4	+104.9
Netherlands	355	−107.9	−53.1	+205.2	+266.3
Norway	200	−51.1	−70.1	−59.9	−76.9
Portugal	70	+36.8	+97.4	+88.0	+66.7
Sweden	260	0	+177.2	+225.8	+208.8
Switzerland	250	−12.6	+141.9	+170.6	+185.6
Turkey	50	+5.3	−98.9	−161.0	−218.1
United Kingdom and Ireland	1060	+433.0	−469.0	−900.9[d]	−662.2[d]

a) The "net accounting position" of each member vis-à-vis the Union—the basis for calculating the use of the quota and so the basis for calculating gold payments and/or credit extended to or by the Union—differs from the "cumulative net position" of each member as used in this table. In arriving at the former, account must be taken of "initial positions" (for the first year of the Union's operations certain debtors were allocated "initial credit balances" with the Union to facilitate the settlement of their deficits and certain prospective creditors were assigned "initial debit balances" for which they received an equivalent amount of ECA conditional aid); "existing resources" (bilateral debts—mostly sterling—outstanding on June 30, 1950 for which no specific amortization plans had been agreed bilaterally and that go through the Union mechanism); and "special resources" (dollars provided by the U.S. Government to cover in whole or in part the deficits of Austria, Greece, Iceland, and Turkey). The above cumulative net position figures do include interest paid or received on loans granted to or received from the Union by members. Further, as noted in the text, the cumulative accounting position of Belgium was reduced by $322.9 million in July and that of Portugal by $3 million.

b) By decision of the OEEC Council, the quota for this country is frozen when it is in a debtor position.

c) The effective quota is $331 million when Belgium-Luxembourg is a creditor.

d) For reasons noted in the text, the cumulative net position of Belgium was reduced on July 1, 1952 by $50 million, while the cumulative positions of France and the United Kingdom were increased by $25 million each.

Source: International Monetary Fund, *International Financial Statistics*, Wash., D.C., February 1951, January 1952, July 1952, and February 1953.

year and reflects the fact that the members did not constitute a balanced trading system, despite various efforts of the EPU Managing Board and the OEEC Council to, among other things, increase the imports from and decrease the exports to the other members by the net creditors. During the year only one member (the Netherlands) changed from a cumulative net deficit position to a net creditor position, and there were no changes in the other direction. Of the persistent debtors only Denmark and Austria were able to end the year with a cumulative deficit less than at the beginning, and of the persistent creditors only Italy and Portugal recorded surpluses that were less than they had been as the year began. The other ten members accentuated their deficit or surplus positions and so intensified the strains that were being placed on the Union. The picture is somewhat different if one compares the end of the year with the situation at the end of June. During this six-month period no country changed from a net debtor to a net creditor position but four of the creditors reduced their net surpluses and three debtors reduced their net deficits. Still, at the end of the year, *if one excludes the various special arrangements that were made to take care of extreme positions*, five of the fifteen members were in excess of their quotas, the same number as at the end of 1951.[5]

The agreement setting up the Union set no time limits upon the life of the organization, but the financial commitments of the members expired in mid-1952 and much time was spent during the first half of the year discussing changes in the agreement that would be necessary if it were to operate after June 30. The most pressing problem faced by the Union was that posed by the extreme creditor position of Belgium-Luxembourg and the lesser ones of Portugal and Italy. Efforts in 1951 and early 1952 by Belgium, on the recommendation of the Managing Board of the Union, to increase imports from Europe and decrease those from the dollar area and to decrease exports to European Payments Union countries met with some success during the first part of

[5] After taking account of the various special arrangements, only Belgium-Luxembourg as a creditor and Turkey and France as debtors were in excess of their quotas as of December 31, 1952. On the same basis, three members had exceeded their quotas as creditors as of the end of 1951 (Belgium-Luxembourg, Italy, and Portugal) and one member (Turkey) had exceeded her quota as a debtor.

1952; but Belgium's surplus continued to mount,[6] and by June 30, 1952, Belgium had extended credit to the Union in excess of its quota in an amount of nearly \$223 million. As a condition for remaining in the Union Belgium wished to receive a large part of this in gold. With total dollar and gold assets of just under \$460 million the Union felt unable to meet this request. After lengthy negotiations, in which U.S. Government officials participated, the Union agreed to pay Belgium \$80 million in gold against its credit and Belgium agreed to a supplementary quota of just over \$85 million—this had the effect of putting \$42.6 million of Belgium's earlier credit *within* its quota. Of the remaining \$100 million of Belgian credit, \$50 million was funded in a special credit to be repayable over six years.[7] Before Belgium agreed to this she made arrangements with the International Monetary Fund (and so with the approval of the U.S. Government) whereby she received a stand-by line of credit of \$50 million; this action assured Belgium of being able to obtain the \$50 million in advance if needed.[8] The remaining \$50 million of the Belgian credit was transferred, in equal parts, to the United Kingdom and France, which countries agreed to repay it by delivering defense products of an equivalent value to Belgium within two years.[9] To offset the adverse effects

[6] For a brief account of the reasons why Belgium has had such large surpluses, see New York Federal Reserve Bank, *Monthly Review*, August 1952, p. 115.

Arrangements were made during 1951 and early 1952 to finance any such surplus beyond the quota up to June 30, 1952 by approximately 50 percent in gold payments by the Union to Belgium and 50 percent in credit from Belgium to the Union. In view of her deficit in the dollar area and the inflationary impact of extending credit for a part of her exports, Belgium was reluctant to accept these arrangements, but the Union concluded its gold and dollar reserves were inadequate to pay Belgium 100 percent in gold for any such surplus. The Union also hoped that these 50-50 arrangements would provide additional incentives to Belgium to reduce her European surplus.

[7] The repayment obligation of the Union was not specified to be in dollars; rather, repayment is to be made by adjusting Belgium's position in the Union. The extent to which such adjustments will result in dollar payments to Belgium by the Union will depend upon the cumulative accounting position of Belgium at the time of the adjustment.

[8] For additional details on the settlement with Belgium, see European Payments Union, *Second Annual Report, op.cit.*, pp. 43-45. See also Wolff, S., "EPU Revised," *Swiss Review of World Affairs* (Zurich), August 1952, pp. 9-12.

[9] That is, the United Kingdom and France took over the Union's obligations and had their positions in the Union credited by an equal amount. Since the United Kingdom at that time was paying 100 percent in gold for her deficits with the Union the effect of this was that she received gold payment in advance for the defense items to be delivered. France was not at that time in excess of her quota and so received only a partial payment in gold.

on employment in Belgium of receiving military supplies that country might otherwise have produced for itself, the U.S. Government agreed at the same time to place orders of about $50 million for "offshore" military purchases in Belgium. None of these arrangements was designed to prevent Belgium from continuing to run a surplus, and it was therefore agreed that for the year ending in mid-1953 any Belgian credit surplus beyond her quota up to $250 million would be settled by the Union's paying 50 percent in gold and Belgium's extending 50 percent in credit to the Union.

Portugal had also run up a large surplus beyond her quota in late 1951 and early 1952 and had agreed to finance a limited amount of any excess beyond the quota by an approximately half-gold, half-credit arrangement. Beginning in early 1952, following consultations with EPU officials, Portugal, among other things, eased internal credit conditions, removed certain barriers to imports from the other members, undertook to substitute imports from Europe for those from the dollar area, and agreed to restrict, by direct controls, exports to the EPU countries. By June these measures had taken effect and Portugal's position in excess of its quota had fallen from its earlier level, so that the only adjustment made when the Union was extended for another year was the waiving of the Union's right to recover $3 million in gold already paid by the Union to Portugal. For the year ending in mid-1953 it was agreed that any surplus beyond $55 million that Portugal recorded in excess of her quota would be settled by a half-gold, half-credit arrangement. As the year progressed, however, Portugal's cumulative surplus continued to decline and she reimposed some of the import quotas previously rescinded, giving emphasis to the tendency of EPU members quickly to resort to quantitative restrictions when balance of payments difficulties threatened.

Italy had also exceeded her quota as a creditor in late 1951 and had agreed to finance temporarily any excess on a fifty-fifty basis. But as a result of a more liberal import policy, the maintenance of internal financial stability, and the restrictions placed on imports in late 1951 and early 1952 by the United Kingdom and France, the Italian surplus had been reduced to well within her quota by mid-1952 and in the June arrangements no action was taken on her existing position. It was agreed, however, that any surplus up to $100 million that Italy might record beyond her quota through June 1953 would be settled 50 percent in gold and 50 percent in credit. It appeared for a time that Switzerland would exceed her quota. By mid-1952 she had not done so and therefore no special arrangements were made for settling her current creditor position, but, as a precaution, it was agreed that any surplus beyond her quota up to $125 million that might be recorded during the following year should be settled on the fifty-fifty basis. No decisions with respect to Germany or the Netherlands were taken in June but each of these countries continued during the summer to report large surpluses and, while they had not reached the limits of their quotas at year's end, both were requested by the OEEC in December to relax further their quantitative restrictions on imports from the EPU countries. Germany was also asked to hasten the liberalization of invisible transactions and the Netherlands was also urged to encourage the stockpiling of raw materials, especially those coming from EPU countries, and to make "the greatest possible use . . . of the productive resources of the country."[1]

As noted in Table 18, above, several members of the Union were in extreme debtor positions during the year. Except for the change in the gold/credit scales noted below, no general decisions designed to relieve these positions were taken at the time of the extending of the agreement for another year. As in previous years, the Managing Board of the Union reluctantly gave its blessing to such members' imposing, or reimposing, quantitative restrictions on their imports as their debtor positions reached extreme limits and, in some cases, that of France in particular, recommended that more stringent measures be taken to control the internal inflation.[2]

During the discussions in 1952 on changes in the rules of conduct of the Union the Managing Board considered increasing the quotas of the members but finally decided against it on the

[1] Organization for European Economic Cooperation, *Press Release* A(52)87, Paris, December 9, 1952.

[2] In order to postpone a part of the gold payment France was obliged to make to the Union, the Managing Board in February granted her a special short-term credit of $100 million. This was repaid in June. In November the EPU granted Turkey a special credit of $20.3 million to be repaid by the end of February 1953.

grounds that such an increase would enlarge the potential demands on the Union's convertible assets inasmuch as it would increase the gap between the gold payable by debtors in the early tranches of their quotas and the amounts of gold payable to creditors. The Managing Board had insisted during the discussions on extending the Union that its convertible assets (gold and dollars) needed to be augmented so as to (1) insure that the Union could meet any difference that might arise between the payments of gold by debtors and the payments due creditors, (2) enable the Union to extend, if the need arose, special assistance to members, (3) provide a greater feeling of security to its creditors that their credits to the Union would be paid if and when the Union should be liquidated, and (4) give the general public some tangible evidence of the solvency of the Union. The Organization for European Economic Cooperation was reported to have asked the United States to make an additional contribution of some $200 million to the central fund of the Union, but the U.S. Administration took the view that while an increase in the dollar assets of the fund was desirable on its own merits there were more important and critical needs for any dollars Congress might provide for aid to Europe. They also took the position that the EPU was at that time successfully established and ought in the future to be financed by the Europeans themselves.[3] While it was not so specified in the official statements, it was reported unofficially that in addition to these reasons this decision was a reflection of the feeling among an increasing number of officials in Washington that the Union was "positively bad for Europe," and among others that the Union had already demonstrated that it was not an appropriate mechanism for meeting many of the international financial problems of Europe and that the time had come to look for more fundamental solutions.[4] During the year the United States did supply some $82 million directly to the Union via payments (the so-called "special resources" of the Union) to cover all or part of the deficits incurred by Austria,

[3] "Mutual Security Appropriations for 1953," *Hearings*, House of Rep., Committee on Appropriations, 82d Cong., 2d Sess., pp. 584-585, and "Mutual Security Act Extension," *Hearings on H.R. 7005*, House of Rep., Committee on Foreign Affairs, 82d Cong., 2d Sess., p. 1065.

[4] Hoffman, M. L., "European Payments—An American View," *Lloyds Bank Review*, July 1952, pp. 13-27.

Greece, Iceland, and Turkey, but these fell off sharply as the year progressed, with less than $6 million of the total being supplied during the last six months. In addition, the U.S. Government indirectly supplied dollars for the members to use with the Union by the expanding program of purchasing military supplies in Europe with dollars.[5]

In any case, the cash assets of the Union rose from $217 million on January 1 to $460 million on June 30, primarily because Britain and France reached the upper tranches of their debtor quotas and so paid increasing percentages of their deficits in gold. The EPU officials, however, still regarded their cash reserves as inadequate and in order to relieve possible future strains on these assets it was agreed to change the gold/credit ratios applied to debtors by increasing the percentage of gold payable to the Union in the earlier tranches while compensating for this by decreasing the ratio in the later tranches.[6] It was also hoped that the new schedule would provide additional incentives for debtors to take measures to reduce their deficits. In addition, it was agreed by the members that if the Union's convertible assets would otherwise fall below $100 million members would, according to the size of their quotas, make temporary gold loans to the Union, with the Union's creditors being called upon first and the obligation of all the members as a group limited to $100 million. Following the special arrangements, mentioned above, that were made with Belgium, the Union's cash reserve totalled $351.2 million on July 1 and it rose to $375 million at year's end, so no calls were made to members for such temporary contributions.

[5] During the year the United States also paid approximately $53 million to the United Kingdom (completing such payments and raising the total to some $93 million) pursuant to the 1950 agreement whereby ECA had agreed to reimburse Britain for the loss of gold or dollars to the Union to the extent that such loss was caused by the use of previously accumulated sterling balances by EPU net debtors to cover their deficits in the Union.

[6] The original schedule provided that debtors would pay no gold on the first fifth of their quota, 20 percent on the second fifth, 40 percent on the third, 60 percent on the fourth, and 80 percent on the final tranche. The new schedule provided that no gold would be paid on the first tenth of the quota, 20 percent on the second tenth, 30 percent on the second fifth, 40 percent on the third fifth, 50 percent on the fourth fifth, and 70 percent on the final tranche. Under both the old and new schedules a debtor using all his quota would pay 40 percent in gold and 60 percent in credit but since the first tranches of a quota are called upon before the later ones the theoretical maximum drain on the Union's cash resources was reduced.

Early in 1952 the Managing Board of the Union stated that consideration should be given to enlarging the powers and responsibilities of the Managing Board so as to permit it more effectively to "harmonize" the internal and external policies of the various members. United States officials publicly stated that they "wholeheartedly" approved the proposal but no such reforms were made in the June revisions. The reasons were not made public, but that there was likely to be serious opposition to enhancing the authority of the Board from some of the larger members of the Union was indicated in the spring of 1952 when it appeared that the Managing Board had almost no success in exercising any influence over the actions taken by the British and French Governments as their debt position reached extreme levels. Toward the end of the year the OEEC Council did amend the Managing Board's mandate in certain respects, with the aim of enabling it to propose action to a member whenever the Board believed a "critical situation" was likely to occur, rather than waiting until extreme situations had developed.

Accomplishments and Problems

As 1952 ended the European Payments Union was under less intense pressure and facing less difficult current operating problems than when the year began. But, so far as one could tell from the public record, there was a growing body of opinion holding that the Union at best had continued, and perhaps consolidated, the accomplishments of the previous year but had not—and perhaps could not have—made much progress toward the goal of facilitating a return to multilateral trade and general currency convertibility.[7]

The major accomplishment of the Union during 1952, as in the previous year, was that it did provide what most regarded as a

[7] For some unofficial statements and analyses in varying degrees critical of the potentialities of the Union, see Hoffman, M. L., "European Payments—An American View," *Lloyds Bank Review*, July 1952, pp. 13-27; Bennett, J. F., "Europe's Money Game," *The Journal of Finance*, September 1952, pp. 434-446; Bresciani-Turroni, C., "Monetary Anomalies," *Review of Economic Conditions in Italy* (Rome), July 1952, pp. 271-277; Brown, G. C., "EPU—Has It Been a Success?" *The Bankers Magazine* (London), July 1952, pp. 23-28; and *Strengthening the Free World Economy*, a report by Klaus Knorr on a conference held at Princeton, Center of International Studies, Princeton University, December 1952.

For an analysis more favorable to the Union, see Triffin, R., "Monetary Reconstruction in Europe," *International Conciliation*, June 1952, pp. 282-308.

more satisfactory method than had existed in the years just before it was established for handling international payments among the members and apparently there was during the year no revival of the old maze of bilateral agreements. Thus, the Union permitted almost all transactions within the area to be on a multilateral, nondiscriminatory basis.[8] The multilateral clearing and settlement mechanism continued to work well, with nearly 80 percent of the total monthly bilateral surpluses and deficits being settled by the process of multilateral compensation and the operation of the cumulative principle. The balance was settled by gold payments to (including payments of dollars by the U.S. Government to cover all or a part of the deficits of Greece, Turkey, Austria, and Iceland) or from the Union and credit extended by or to the Union.

Almost everyone who spoke in public on the accomplishments of the Union, and the related trade liberalization measures, continued to stress its great contribution in expanding the amount of intra-European trade.[9] But as the table below shows, the value of such trade fluctuated very closely with the value of Europe's total trade and there were no significant changes, as compared with 1950 and 1951, in the percentage of Europe's total trade that was represented by intra-European trade.

Many of those who in public defended the Union during the

[8] However, for reasons that have not been made public, the monthly bilateral surpluses and deficits cleared through the Union totalled only the equivalent of some $3.4 billion, as compared with nearly $4 billion during 1951; and of the 1952 total, $1.9 billion took place during the first half of the year. This decline was doubtless in part a reflection of the approximately 5 percent decline in the total value of all European exports and imports during 1952, as compared with the preceding year. It may also have been the result of an increase in the amount of bilaterally balancing trade between the various pairs of members, though no supporting statistics are available.

From the beginning of operations to mid-1952 (information for the last half of the year is not available) no member had taken advantage of its right (see *Survey—1950*, p. 245) to use bilateral credit in place of credit granted by the Union. Nor had any member requested to use currencies other than dollars or gold to settle with the Union.

[9] Among the little-publicized accomplishments of the Union was its facilitating the repayment and/or redistribution of the equivalent of $861 million of accumulated intra-European indebtedness that had been outstanding on June 30, 1950. By mid-1952, $587 million of this had been repaid. For details on these operations, see Organization for European Economic Cooperation, *European Payments Union, Second Annual Report of the Managing Board, op.cit.*, pp. 19-20 and Appendix Table III, and Bank For International Settlements, *Twenty-Second Annual Report, op.cit.*, pp. 238-241.

year did so not on the grounds of its positive accomplishments but with the claim that it had prevented chaos. The Managing Board of the Union itself stressed this aspect, arguing that had the Union not existed members "probably" would have been forced to adopt rigidly balancing systems of bilateral settlements with each other, for few of the members could, except through a

TABLE 19

Value of Intra-European Merchandise Trade as Percentage of Members' Total Trade, 1938, 1948-1952[a]

(monthly averages)

Year		*Exports*	*Imports*
1938		50	39
1948		45	32
1949		46	35
1950		49	40
1951	first quarter	50	39
	second quarter	48	37
	third quarter	47	38
	fourth quarter	48	40
1952	first quarter	46	38
	second quarter	47	39
	third quarter	49	42
	fourth quarter	50	45

a) These data refer to trade among the metropolitan countries only. The trade liberalization measures adopted by the member countries were in part extended to their overseas territories but not as completely or as rapidly as had been expected. Imports are on a c.i.f. and exports on an f.o.b. basis.
Source: Calculated from data given in Organization for European Economic Cooperation, *General Statistics*, Paris, March 1953, pp. 64-65.

mechanism such as the Union, have "afforded" to permit the development of any large imbalance in their bilateral trade; any such balancing, it was argued, would "almost certainly" have reduced the volume of intra-European trade and increased discrimination, which, in turn, would "necessarily hamper considerably the defense efforts of Member countries and seriously impede progress towards a general increase in productivity."[1] On the other hand, the Managing Board did not say that the Union had made any significant contribution toward increasing productivity in Europe.

The changes made in June in the operating rules of the Union

[1] Organization for European Economic Cooperation, *European Payments Union, Second Annual Report of the Managing Board, op.cit.*, p. 50.

contributed to progress toward the short-run objective of a more smoothly functioning mechanism for another year[2] but it was generally recognized that they did not provide a solution to what many regarded as basic weaknesses of the Union: the facts that there was no inherent tendency toward an equilibrium of payments among the members and that the Union provided inadequate incentives and lacked sufficient authority to force the debtors to be net earners in other areas; the fact that the Union exercised but little influence on the internal economic and financial policies of members, especially the United Kingdom and France; the assumption that all member currencies were equally valuable at the established rate of exchange; the great temptation inherent in such a regional scheme under the foregoing conditions to keep the system functioning by adopting policies whose object was to create a more nearly balanced trading system *within* Europe and so perpetuating rather than progressively abandoning discrimination against the dollar area; and the fact that the Union, by making prevailing maladjustments easier to bear, served to distract attention from the fundamental task of Europe—establishing a pattern of production and consumption that would bring balance of payments equilibrium within an enlarged volume of trade throughout the world.

The Managing Board of the Union itself was remarkably frank in concluding in mid-1952 that progress toward the general convertibility of currencies could not be achieved "merely by the adaptation and improvement of existing payments mechanisms."[3] Rather, its report stressed that this goal would be achieved only when the members established and maintained a "real equilibrium" in their entire balances of payments and that this required not only that the members achieve and maintain internal financial stability at a high level of economic activity, achieve and maintain increased productivity, and maintain exchange rates that "adequately reflected the purchasing power" of their currencies, but also that the United States adopt a more liberal import policy,

[2] The officials of the Union recognized that the problem of how to treat extreme creditors had been only temporarily and provisionally solved and that the change in the gold/credit ratio might make debtor countries more cautious in removing barriers to imports.

[3] Organization for European Economic Cooperation, *European Payments Union, Second Annual Report of the Managing Board*, *op. cit.*, p. 54.

that the European countries intensify their efforts to increase exports to the dollar area, that the flow of long-term investment funds from the creditor to the debtor countries be enlarged, that means be found to dampen the price fluctuations of the more important raw materials that enter international trade, and that the international reserves of the member countries be increased.

While recognizing that most of these matters were outside the area of responsibility of the Union, the Managing Board reported that it planned to consider what modifications, if any, in the EPU arrangements might assist in solving the basic balance of payments problems of its members. It mentioned as possibilities the extension of the area covered by the Union to include other countries, in particular the Latin American nations, and the establishment of closer relations with the International Monetary Fund and the International Bank. Later in the year the press reported[4] that after studying the effect on the Union of including the Latin American countries it seemed unlikely that these countries would be invited to become full-fledged members and there were no public indications by the end of the year that any new arrangements were being worked out between the Union and the Fund and Bank.

Of more immediate concern to the Union officials as the year ended were the possible effects on the institution when and if sterling were made convertible. As 1953 began there had been no official statements as to precisely what, if anything, was being contemplated by the sterling area authorities in the way of convertibility and the Managing Board had not made public the results of the studies it had undertaken on the impact of sterling convertibility on the Union.[5]

[4] See *The Economist*, October 25, 1952, p. 255.

[5] Many private observers anticipated that if current earnings of sterling were convertible the other members would be tempted to restrict their imports from the sterling area (which might lead to retaliatory import restrictions by Britain and thus do great damage to the trade liberalization program) and to convert the proceeds of their exports to the sterling area outside the Union. In the face of such actions, some thought, Britain might consider it necessary to withdraw from the Union, since otherwise she might be forced to extend large amounts of credit to the Union to cover a portion of the deficits of her EPU debtors and to suffer a large and persistent drain on her gold reserves. (For a discussion of some problems for the Union arising out of sterling convertibility, see *The Banker*, March 1953, pp. 130-133; *The Economist*, July 26, 1952, pp. 205-208; and letters written by Robert Triffin, who played an important role in the early stages of the European Payments Union, in the *New York Times*, October 5, 1952, p. 8-E, and March 1, 1953, p. 8-E.)

The U.S. Government had been instrumental in creating the EPU and many officials had been enthusiastic as to its potentialities for achieving all of the objectives mentioned above. Official statements during 1952 were, on the whole, much more restrained than during previous years as to what might be expected of this organization. Most of those who talked in public about it emphasized the contribution the Union had made in removing discrimination and promoting the liberalization of trade among the members, including trade needed for the rearmament programs in Europe, and in promoting a greater degree of cooperation among the European economic authorities, but at the same time most of these persons recognized that the Union was only a first and modest step on the road toward economic integration of Europe and that in fact the Union had made little, if any, contribution to solving the so-called dollar problem of Europe. In a report released early in 1953, the National Advisory Council stated that during the period of the defense build-up the United States Government should continue to support "effective measures to provide for a satisfactory functioning of the EPU" but that in its existing form the Union was "to be considered as transitional to a system of nondiscriminatory multilateral trade with convertible currencies, and leading to full integration, and possibly political federation, of certain members." The report went on to specify, however, that the operations of the Union should not conflict with the obligations of its members to the International Monetary Fund or with the policies embodied in the GATT, that the United States policy vis-à-vis the Union should be reviewed annually, that the United States should continue to oppose action by the Union designed to improve the balances of payments of certain European countries that resulted in discrimination against the United States,[6] and that the United States should continue to support policies that strengthened the weak EPU currencies and should discourage policies that placed pressures on stronger currencies.[7]

[6] At the Seventh Session of the Contracting Parties to the General Agreement on Tariffs and Trade in November, the United States delegation insisted that Belgium should relax her restrictions against dollar imports even though the French, Dutch, and Italian delegates said that such action might result in a deterioration in the balance of payments positions of other European countries.

[7] National Advisory Council, *Semiannual Report to the President and to the Congress, April 1–September 30, 1952*, Wash., D.C., January 1953, p. 22.

B. *TRADE LIBERALIZATION MEASURES*

Intimately associated with the United States-encouraged efforts to economically "unify" Europe by removing monetary barriers to trade were measures to remove or relax trade barriers, it having been recognized from the beginning that there were both financial and trade aspects to convertibility—or transferability. For various reasons[8] it was decided that the Organization for European Economic Cooperation and its agencies should concentrate on the relaxation of quantitative restrictions. The general approach agreed upon was that each member would remove quotas on *private account* imports from the other OEEC members as a group[9] to an agreed-upon percentage[1] of its imports from them in a base year—1948, except for Germany, where it was 1949—but a series of escape clauses were inserted for countries suffering adverse balances of payments.[2] These percentages applied—up to 60 percent—separately to each of three major categories of imports: foodstuffs, raw materials, manufactured goods. Under the original rules each member was free to choose the particular commodities that made up its lists and inasmuch as it was unlikely that any one commodity would be on everyone's list and so be able to compete throughout the entire European market, the above arrangements were supplemented in 1951 by the drawing up of a list of commodities—the so-called "common list"—that each member who reached a liberalization figure of 75 percent was asked to include in the category of goods not subject to import quotas.

It had been the announced objective of the OEEC to have all members reach a minimum of 75 percent by February 1951 but by the beginning of 1952 only seven of the members had achieved this objective. By the end of 1952 ten of the member countries

[8] See *Survey—1951*, pp. 254-255.

[9] The trade liberalization measures adopted by the member countries were in some instances extended to their overseas territories but not as completely or as rapidly as had been expected.

[1] Any given percentage (for example, 50 percent) means that quantitative restrictions had been removed from imports that accounted for 50 percent of the given member's total intra-European imports in 1948.

[2] For a brief summary of these, see *Survey—1950*, pp. 257-259. For details on these decisions, see Organization for European Economic Cooperation, *Code of Liberalisation*, Paris, July 1951.

had reached or passed the 75 percent standard[3] and the OEEC calculated that the average for all of Europe was nearly 70 percent. Yet, on balance it appeared that this trade liberalization program had suffered a setback during the year since the modest increases recorded during that period by Belgium, Denmark, Germany, Norway, Sweden, and Switzerland had apparently been more than offset by the actions of France, which had a liberalization figure of 70 percent on January 1 but, faced with the payments difficulties in the European Payments Union noted above, reimposed import quotas on all those imports from which they had earlier been removed; the United Kingdom, which for similar reasons had reduced her percentage from 60 at the beginning of the year to 46 at the end; and Portugal, which had dropped from 100 percent to 85 percent. To the credit of the OEEC and the member governments it must be recorded that while the members frequently "scurried back to the protection of their quotas" when their balance of payments positions became serious, there was virtually no direct retaliatory curtailment of liberalization during the year.[4]

Following the deliberalization actions by the United Kingdom and France in early 1952, the OEEC created a Steering Board for Trade, on which a representative of the U.S. Government sat as a nonvoting member, and charged it with following up on the execution of decisions taken by the OEEC on trade policy and with proposing new measures for liberalizing trade.[5] The Board was instructed to examine to what extent the economic position of the members enabled them to apply the rules of trade in a "satisfactory" manner and to avoid having recourse to the escape clauses. This Board issued no public reports during the year and the Council of the OEEC did not, as had been planned earlier,

[3] Belgium-Luxembourg, 90 percent; Denmark, 75 percent; Germany, 81 percent; Ireland, 75 percent; Italy, 99 percent; the Netherlands, 75 percent; Norway, 75 percent; Portugal, 85 percent; Sweden, 91 percent; Switzerland, 92 percent. Not all of these countries, however, had removed quota restrictions from all of the items on the "common list."

[4] Following the outbreak of the war in Korea and the resulting shortages of raw materials, quantitative restrictions on exports were greatly expanded and served to restrict trade. The Organization for European Economic Cooperation attempted, without success, to curb this tendency. This problem became much less acute, however, during the latter part of 1952.

[5] OEEC *Press Release* A(52)27, Paris, May 6, 1952. This new Board took over the tasks previously given to the Special Restrictive Committees.

add to the number of commodities on the "common list." In December the Council, presumably on the basis of the recommendations of the new Board, did issue a series of recommendations designed "to maintain, and . . . to extend, the liberalization of trade."[6] The details were not published but it was recommended that the major EPU creditors—Belgium, Germany, the Netherlands, and Portugal—should increase still further their liberalization percentages. It was also recommended that the United Kingdom consider how its import regulations could be adapted to mitigate the damages the earlier deliberalization was causing to exporting interests in France and Italy, and France was, in turn, asked to do the same thing with respect to Italian interests. These recommendations had not been implemented as the year ended.

In its *Fourth Annual Report*, dated December 1952, and in the preparation of which United States (and Canadian) officials "played parts entirely similar to those of the Member countries," the Organization for European Economic Cooperation repeatedly stressed the need for increasing the competitive power of European industries and reiterated its conviction that removing barriers to intra-European trade and payments would stimulate such competition and would result in important economies of large-scale production. The *Report* signified disappointment with the degree of intra-European trade and payments liberalization achieved, and concluded that "New methods must now be devised in order to facilitate a more rapid advance towards this objective than has so far seemed possible." It added, "Up to the present, however, no such methods have been applied or even defined."[7] The report went on to express the hope that those countries that had totally or partially suspended liberalization would soon be able to restore and extend it and that it would be possible to introduce arrangements that would assure that any liberalization undertaken would be of a more permanent nature than it had been in the past.

Apart from the recognized major defects of this percentage approach to trade liberalization,[8] the percentage standard itself

[6] OEEC *Press Release* A(52)88, Paris, December 9, 1952.

[7] Organization for European Economic Cooperation, *Europe—The Way Ahead*, *op.cit.*, p. 166.

[8] There was general agreement that the method suffered at least three serious

was an exceedingly slippery one and any given percentage recorded implied a much greater measure of relaxation or removal of quantitative restrictions than was actually the case. In the first place, the quota applied only to imports on private account, with the definition of such imports being left more or less to the discretion of the individual governments. Details on these decisions are not available but in some cases at least they were highly restrictive and excluded not only such imports as those included in official bulk purchase agreements or those by various government monopolies but also imports that were merely subject to some kind of internal marketing regulations. Secondly, the use of the 1948 base period resulted in some of the "most wonderful pieces of window-dressing of all." The current prices of imports during any subsequent period frequently varied widely from those obtaining in the base period and this fact permitted the "liberalization mathematicians" in each country to pick and choose items for quota removal in such a way that, as a result, the current value of liberalized imports was much less than the theoretical quota values. No detailed account of these practices has been made public but one study published in early 1953 concluded that only some 30 percent of the then current intra-European trade was taking place under the liberalized quotas.[9]

C. *EUROPEAN COAL AND STEEL COMMUNITY*

The proposals by the then French Foreign Minister, Schuman, that the coal and steel industries of France, Germany, and other interested Western European nations be pooled in a single market in the sense of removing all barriers to trade of coal and steel products among the members, prohibiting private cartel arrange-

defects: (1) Each country began with the easy commodities, that is, those not previously subject to quotas or not pressing on them, or that were noncompetitive internally, or that were being kept out by other barriers, especially tariffs; (2) there was little incentive for members to remove quotas on those goods whose importation in the base year had been kept at very low levels by barriers of one kind or another but whose selection for liberalization might be most desirable from the point of view of achieving the most economical use of resources in Europe; and (3) each country was in practice free to select its own particular commodities, with the result that only in rare cases were imports of any one commodity permitted to compete with domestic production in the entire European market. The "common list" was intended to remove this last-mentioned defect.

[9] See Richebacher, K., "Hinter den Kulissen der Liberalisierung," *Der Volkswirt* (Frankfurt), January 24, 1953, pp. 9-10.

ments and excessive concentrations of economic power, and placing the industries under the control, but not under the ownership, of a supranational authority—these proposals were enthusiastically received in most private and official circles in the United States. Only a few in the United States questioned, in public at least, the propositions that such an arrangement would for all practical purposes remove the danger of war between Germany and the other members of the pool, that it was a prerequisite to the incorporation of German forces and productive capacity into the mutual defense effort of the North Atlantic countries, and that it would permit the free play of competition, which in turn would result in increased production and productivity, thus improving European living standards and making the area less dependent on aid from the United States.[1] Following extensive discussions, in which the U.S. Government from time to time intervened, a Treaty constituting the European Coal and Steel Community was signed by representatives of Germany, France, Italy, the Netherlands, Belgium, and Luxembourg in April 1951. A summary of the more important provisions of the Treaty and the responsibilities of the various institutions to be created was given in the volume of this *Survey* for 1951 and will not be repeated here.[2]

Ratification of the treaty by the parliaments of the six member countries was completed in June 1952,[3] and the Community was

[1] For an adversely critical assessment of the economic aspects of the Plan by a senior official of an American steel company, see Randall, C. B., "European Steel: Monopoly in the Making," *The Atlantic Monthly*, October 1951, pp. 34-38. For an account by an American that concludes that the economic benefits of the Community are "remote" and the immediate political gains "negligible," see Parker, W. N., "The Schuman Plan—A Preliminary Prediction," *International Organization*, August 1952, pp. 381-395. For critical but more sympathetic accounts, see Shenstone, M., "The Schuman Plan—'A Leap into the Unknown,'" *International Journal*, Spring, 1952, pp. 116-126; Reynolds, P. A., "The European Coal and Steel Community," *The Political Quarterly*, July-September 1952, pp. 282-292; and UN Economic Commission for Europe, *Economic Survey of Europe Since The War*, Geneva, 1953, pp. 227-231.

For an analysis of the nature of the transfer of sovereignty involved in the Community, see Vernon, R., "The Schuman Plan," *The American Journal of International Law*, April 1953, pp. 183-202.

[2] See *Survey—1951*, pp. 259-265, and references cited therein.

[3] *The Economist*, June 21, 1952, p. 804 stated that the ratification came none too soon, for the delay between signature and ratification had been used by both the French and German officials to attempt to get approval from the OEEC Steel Committee for grandiose plans for the expansion of their national steel industries,

officially brought into being on July 25, with the High Authority formally beginning to function on August 10. The Treaty provided for two transitional periods. The first, the "preparatory period," extended until February 10, 1953 and was used to establish the five institutions of the Community (the High Authority, Common Assembly, Council of Ministers, Court of Justice, and Consultative Committee), to negotiate with nonmembers on relations between them and the Community, and to make preliminary plans for the single market. The second transitional period was to last for five years from February 10, 1953, during which time all the basic substantive provisions of the Treaty were to come into effect, it having been concluded that an abrupt shift from the existing situation to a completely competitive market would result in what most members would regard as intolerable disruptions of established patterns of wages, trade, production, and investment.

By the end of the "preparatory period" all of the institutions had been created and were functioning, and the High Authority had recruited a staff of over 200 persons and established several technical commissions. During 1952 several steps had also been taken to establish relations with outside nations. Formal delegations from the United Kingdom, Sweden, and the United States had been accredited to the Community.[4] The importance the United States attached to the Community was indicated by the fact

---

although one of the main responsibilities of the Community's High Authority was to plan and, within limits, approve or prohibit such investment. See also *The Economist*, July 26, 1952, p. 215 for an account of "Franco-German Steel Rivals."

[4] Britain had refused—to the disappointment of many American officials, especially members of Congress—to join the Community but she had insisted that it was her policy to cooperate with it, and, of the three non-member delegations, the one from the United Kingdom was commonly regarded the most important so far as the day-to-day operations of the Community were concerned. Indeed, a special Joint Committee was formed by the British Delegation and the High Authority in October. The press reported that the strongly manned British Delegation's first responsibility would be safeguarding Britain's continental markets for coal and steel products and assuring Britain of continuing supplies at reasonable prices of those raw materials that were controlled by members of the Community. The Delegation was not willing at the outset to agree on any "general principles" of association between the United Kingdom and the Community and expressed the intention of developing rules and arrangements on the basis of experience in handling specific problems as they arose.

For an analysis of the advantages and disadvantages to Britain of remaining outside the Community, see Krzysztof, Z., "Britain and the Schuman Plan," *Kyklos*, Vol. V, Fasc. 3, pp. 237-250.

that, while the American officials were present formally as "observers," the Delegation head was David K. Bruce, former Ambassador to France and Under Secretary of State.[5] The Community had also established formal relations with the Council of Europe and the Organization for European Economic Cooperation. More important, in the fall the Community succeeded in obtaining from the Contracting Parties of the GATT a formal waiver of several of the obligations that the six members of the Community had assumed when acceding to the GATT but that were inconsistent with their plans to remove barriers to steel and coal trade among themselves but not to such trade with nonmembers. (See Chapter VI, Section D.)

In preparing for the common market the High Authority, whose task was not one of directing the production of coal and steel but one of establishing and maintaining "conditions under which production will develop to the best advantage of the common interest,"[6] as a matter of policy proceeded cautiously and planned to intervene in the markets less than the Treaty permitted.[7] This policy was facilitated by the fact that at the time there were no great shortages or surpluses of coal and steel products at existing prices in Europe. The High Authority in late 1952 did specify, however, that within three months after February 10, 1953 the practice of members' charging discriminatory rates for transportation of coal or steel was to be eliminated. This was regarded as a major step in creating a common market even though it did not call for immediate abolition of the practice of not allowing rates to "taper off" beyond national frontiers. By the end of 1952 the High Authority had reached few firm conclusions on other ques-

[5] The United States stated that henceforth it would deal with the Community rather than individual members on questions of coal and steel and that the final form of association between the Community and the United States would be determined on the basis of the experience in dealing with questions of common interest.

[6] European Coal and Steel Community, *Speeches Delivered by Monsieur Jean Monnet, President of the High Authority*, Luxembourg, 1952, p. 12.

[7] The High Authority decided that for the time being it would not apply the procedures permitted in the Treaty for distributing coal among its members but would participate in discussions and abide by the allocations recommended by the OEEC and the Economic Commission for Europe, which organizations, together with the dissolved Ruhr Authority, had been allocating the coal output of the member nations for several years. (OEEC *Press Release* A(52)60, Paris, August 21, 1952.)

tions of price policy[8] and in its studies had been primarily concerned with the effect on prices of monopolistic practices and government policies as to taxes, social security benefits, and subsidies.

With respect to what many regarded as the most difficult problem immediately facing the Community—eliminating cartels and preventing "excessive concentrations" of economic power—the High Authority, in consultation with the Council of Ministers, had decided to go slow "in view of the delicate and novel nature of the question."[9] Indeed, the Central German Coal Sales Agency, regarded by many as a particularly obnoxious cartel, was reported in the press as one of the most powerful and active bodies at the Community's headquarters despite the fact that the Ruhr Authority had ordered it dissolved forthwith in June, that the German Government had agreed to dissolve it, and that its liquidation was one of the conditions demanded by France during the negotiations on the Schuman Plan. As to investment, the High Authority had concluded that, while in the beginning, at least, the initiative in new investment should come from individual firms, its approval (where required) for new investment would be more easily obtained if emphasis in the steel industry were placed on modernizing existing facilities rather than on building new ones; with respect to coal, it concluded that while some new coal mines might need to be worked the major attention should be on increasing the output per miner.[1] It was estimated by the High Authority that over the next several years annual gross new

[8] The problems here seemed likely to be less difficult in the early stages of the Community's life than had been anticipated since the price differences for coal and steel among the six members were much less during the latter part of 1952 than they had been for several years.

[9] European Coal and Steel Community, the High Authority, *Report on the Situation of the Community*, Luxembourg, January 10, 1953, p. 62. This *Report*—accounts of which were presented in *The Economist*, January 24, 1953, pp. 217-218, and in *The Statist*, January 17, 1953, p. 74, and January 24, 1953, pp. 108-109—is the source of much of the information in this section. See also Wolff, S., "Coal and Steel Pool in Operation," *Swiss Review of World Affairs*, February 1953, pp. 3-10. For a brief account of the position and problems of Germany vis-à-vis the Community, see "The Economic Position of Germany," *The I.I.F. Bulletin*, No. 178, Institute of International Finance, New York University, October 7, 1952, pp. 15-19.

[1] The High Authority gave as its opinion that a basic condition for increasing productivity was an improvement in working conditions and living standards of the workers, especially more and better housing.

investments should be the equivalent of some $400-500 million in the steel industry, of some $400-450 million in the coal industry, and of at least $250 million in workers' housing.

The High Authority had agreed by year's end that the levy authorized in the Treaty should be fixed by July 1953[2] at 0.9 percent of the taxable value (determined by the High Authority) of the coal and steel output of the members. This first "European tax" was to be levied directly on the individual enterprises without the participation of the national governments.[3] The High Authority estimated that this tax would yield the equivalent of $50-60 million annually. In addition to providing funds to meet the expenses of the Community's organizations and to assist in the readjustment, including retraining of workers, of firms that proved unable to meet the competition in the single market being created, it was planned that these monies would serve to build up the credit of the High Authority and thus permit it to contribute to new investment in the coal and steel industry (1) by granting direct loans from borrowed funds and (2) by giving its guarantee to borrowings by individual coal and steel firms.

The High Authority stressed the competitive handicap the high interest rates in Europe created for the Community and, while the official report spoke only of obtaining capital in Europe "and elsewhere," it was assumed by many that a large part of any external capital assistance needed would be sought in the United States. The U.S. Government gave no financial assistance to the Community during 1952 but, as noted above, the Mutual Security Act was amended early in the year so as to authorize the granting of aid to the Community, and the President of the International Bank, in a statement that it may safely be assumed had the approval of the Executive Branch of the U.S. Government, had held out the prospect of assistance from the International Bank.

As the year ended there were no indications that the new

[2] It was set at 0.3 percent in January and was to be progressively increased to 0.9 percent by July.

[3] The Treaty also provided that the High Authority could levy an equalization—pre-equation—tax of up to 1½ percent (to be gradually reduced, and then eliminated after five years) on the selling price of coal in those countries where the average production costs were below the weighted median of the Community as a whole and use these funds to reduce the selling price of Belgian coal, provided the Belgian Government made an equal financial contribution. This levy had not been set at year's end because the Belgian Government had not decided what its contribution was to be.

Administration in Washington would disagree with Secretary Acheson's August statement that "It is the intention of the United States to give the Coal and Steel Community the strong support that its importance to the political and economic unification of Europe warrants."[4]

D. *OTHER INTEGRATION PROPOSALS*

The U.S. Government offered no concrete new integration proposals to the European countries during 1952 and apparently did not resume its earlier efforts to encourage the formation of customs unions within Europe.[5] Administration officials did tell Congress that there would have to be a greater degree of economic unification than existed if Europe were to "stand on her own feet" and several expressed the hope that the Schuman Plan would lead the way to the establishment of other, similar "pools" in Europe.[6] In April, as noted above, General Eisenhower spoke in favor of extending the "pool" concept to agriculture and electric power. United States officials did take occasion during the year to speak out in favor of various proposals that had been initiated in Europe for creating a single market for selected agricultural products—somewhat along the lines of the Coal and Steel Community—but the U.S. Government offered no specific plans for accomplishing this nor did it imply that it was willing to make a financial contribution to such a scheme.[7] This "green pool" notion was discussed by European officials throughout the year, but no concrete

[4] Department of State *Bulletin*, August 25, 1952, p. 285.

[5] The Benelux countries moved no closer to economic union during the year, the major difficulties continuing to arise from the relatively high costs of agricultural production in Belgium, which in turn resulted not so much from differences in efficiency as from disparate government policies toward agriculture in Belgium and in the Netherlands. The year 1952 also witnessed sharp objections from Belgian industries to imports of Dutch manufactured goods and, in some cases, cartel-like agreements were reached by the private organizations concerned. (See *Neue Zurcher Zeitung*, Zurich, September 27 and October 5, 1952 for an account of the pressures being exerted in Belgian industrial circles for securing protection against duty-free imports from the Netherlands.)

[6] See, for example, "Mutual Security Act of 1952," *Hearings on H.R. 7005, op.cit.*, pp. 345, 814.

[7] A special committee of the International Chamber of Commerce concluded in late 1952 that, in the opinion of "representative business men," the pool approach to European integration was "unsound" and would end in the further economic division of Europe. (See International Chamber of Commerce, *World Trade*, January 1953, pp. 3-4.)

agreements had been reached as the year ended and strong opposition to the removal of barriers to agricultural products was being registered on the part of nations whose farmers were thought to be at a competitive disadvantage.[8]

The U.S. Government did welcome the decision in March by the OEEC Council at the Ministerial level to continue to pursue its policies of promoting "economic cooperation" among the members even though the European Recovery Program was being terminated. United States officials actively participated in these various activities by virtue of the informal membership in the OEEC that the United States (and Canada) assumed in 1950. Apart from the trade liberalization program and the European Payments Union, discussed above, and its work in allocating coal output among the European countries and developing a common list of end-use prohibitions for certain scarce strategic and critical materials, the Council's work was essentially the making of studies and recommendations and the providing of a method for consultation among the member states. During the year the OEEC Council concentrated its activities on studying, and subsequently making recommendations to member governments as to, various ways in which total European production could be increased by 25 percent by 1956, and various ways of achieving internal financial stability. With respect to the latter, particular attention was given to recommending policies that would "harmonize" the internal financial and fiscal policies of each member with those of the other members.[9]

In a study published early in 1953 the UN Economic Commission

[8] For accounts of these negotiations and some of the difficulties encountered during 1952, see Papi, G. U., "Myths and Realities of the European Green Pool," *Quarterly Review*, Banca Nazionale del Lavoro, Rome, October-December 1952, pp. 201-214; Fanfani, A., "Italy and the Green Pool," *Review of Economic Conditions in Italy* (Rome), January 1953, pp. 5-8; and Mansholt, S. L., "Toward European Integration: Beginnings in Agriculture," *Foreign Affairs*, October 1952, pp. 106-113. See also UN Economic Commission for Europe, *Economic Survey of Europe since the War, op.cit.*, pp. 233-234.

[9] For a detailed statement of the various "economic cooperation" activities of the OEEC, see that organization's *Europe—The Road Ahead, op.cit.*, and its *European Economic Cooperation, a Third Survey Prepared for the Council of Europe*, Paris, May 1952.

For a review of the effects of internal policies on external financial relations based on a study of the United States, the United Kingdom, France, and Belgium, see Organization for European Economic Cooperation, *The Internal Financial Situation in Members and Associated Countries*, Paris, August 1952.

for Europe concluded that but little progress had been made in economically "re-integrating" Western Europe. This study found that "next to nothing" had been achieved in promoting intra-European mobility of labor and capital, and that "the historical trend towards national autarky has not been clearly reversed." This group also asked "whether the emphasis currently given to economic integration in western Europe does not run the risk of diverting attention from the great readjustments needed in the broader pattern of world production and trade, if western Europe is ever to find its place again in a more freely functioning system of international trade and payments."[1]

E. *EUROPEAN VERSUS NORTH ATLANTIC INTEGRATION*

Some responsible officials in Western Europe, especially in the discussions in the Council of Europe and the Consultative Assembly, continued during the year to urge that European integration efforts be widened to include the United States and Canada. There were, however, no indications that either the U.S. Congress or the U.S. Administration was prepared seriously to consider creating an Atlantic Community in the sense that economic integration was being encouraged in Western Europe. Even such active supporters of intra-European unification as the Director for Mutual Security stated that "it would not seem practical for us" to join such institutions as the European Army and the coal and steel pool.[2] It is perhaps also significant that the tendency during the year in the North Atlantic Treaty Organization was to regard economic problems as "suitable for national action only, or as coming within the province of other international agencies."[3] As noted in Chapter I, the communiqué issued after the December 1952 meeting of the Ministers of the North Atlantic Treaty Organization countries had virtually nothing to say about developing further the economic aspects of an Atlantic Community, which had been discussed in such glowing, be they general, terms at the meeting in Ottawa in 1951.

In the autumn, the press gave much publicity to a so-called

[1] UN Economic Commission for Europe, *Economic Survey of Europe since the War, op.cit.*, pp. 234-235.

[2] See *Hearings on H.R. 7005, op.cit.*, p. 79.

[3] Spofford, C. M., "NATO's Growing Pains," *Foreign Affairs*, October 1952, p. 100.

"Green Book" prepared in the Mutual Security Agency and proposing that the United States take the initiative in creating an Atlantic Reserve System, which apparently would pool the reserves of the members and attempt to coordinate their monetary policies; an Atlantic Economic Board, which would coordinate the various trade policies of the members; and an Atlantic Commodity Board, charged with stabilizing the production and prices of raw materials. The gist of this document, which took as a desideratum close administrative cooperation between the United States and other "like-minded" North Atlantic countries (and so called for important cessions of sovereignty), was "leaked" to the press but the text was not made available to the general public. It quickly was made clear that the document was only a working paper that had not obtained the support of other interested branches of the Administration, especially the U.S. Treasury Department.[4] Although most of the American press supported European economic integration efforts, virtually none of them gave editorial support to the "Green Book" proposals, and there were no indications that the new Administration would embrace them.

The United States did, however, continue to work closely with the authorities of the various European countries in a variety of economic problems, as has been discussed throughout this *Survey*. Some regarded the willingness of the U.S. Government to subject its rearmament program to periodic "review" by the North Atlantic Treaty Organization officials and its willingness to participate in the Organization for European Economic Cooperation's annual "review" of economic and financial conditions and prospects of the European countries and the United States and Canada, made with the object of "harmonizing" their policies, as major steps in the direction of more intimate economic cooperation at the administrative level with Western Europe. It was not possible to tell from the public record, however, whether these reviews resulted in important changes in American defense, economic, and financial policies.

[4] For a brief account of the "Green Book" proposals, see *New York Times*, October 29, 1952, p. 1. Some of the basic issues involved in setting up such an institution are discussed in *Strengthening the Free World Economy*, *op.cit.*, pp. 31-55.

IX · UNITED STATES BALANCE OF INTERNATIONAL PAYMENTS, 1952

THE balance of payments of the United States remained in severe disequilibrium during 1952, but there were some indications during the latter part of the year that a trend might be developing toward greater balance.[1]

The value and volume of both exports and imports of goods and services increased in 1952 over 1951, but the current account export surplus totalled nearly $5 billion in 1952, only some 4 percent less than in the previous year. This huge export surplus, however, hides the important fact that, as compared with 1951, an increasing proportion of U.S. Government grants took the form of military- rather than civilian-type goods. Moreover, the annual rate of the excess of exports over imports declined by one third during the second half of the year as compared with the first six months, despite the fact that the exports of military supplies under the aid programs during the second half of the year were over one-half billion dollars greater than during the first half.

The rest of the world continued to lose gold and dollars to the United States during the first quarter of 1952, but thereafter United States exports of other than military goods and services fell off and imports increased, with the result that, for the year as a whole, the rest of the world accumulated some $1.2 billion in gold and dollar assets in its transactions with the United States.

Statistical details on the developments by major categories of transactions are given in Table 20.

[1] Official publications of the U.S. Government provide accessible and excellent accounts of the balance of payments of the United States and therefore only a brief summary of the major developments is attempted here. Those needing more information are referred to the following issues of Department of Commerce, *Survey of Current Business*, Wash., D.C.: June 1952, pp. 8-12; August 1952, pp.8ff.; September 1952, pp. 5ff.; December 1952, pp. 4ff.; and March 1953, pp. 7-12. Also heavily relied upon in the preparation of this section were the following issues of *Foreign Commerce Weekly*: March 2, 1953, pp. 15ff.; March 16, 1953, pp. 16ff.; and April 13, 1953, pp. 14ff. In addition to statistical data, Department of Commerce, *Balance of Payments of the United States 1949-1951*, Wash., D.C., 1952 provides detailed information on the concepts used and the methods of deriving the United States balance of payments. For detailed changes in foreign gold and dollar assets, see *Federal Reserve Bulletin*, March 1953, pp. 209-216.

TABLE 20

International Transactions of the United States, 1950-1952

(millions of dollars)

Type of Transaction	*1950*	*1951*[r]	1952[p] and by Quarters				
			Total	*I*	*II*	*III*	*IV*
Exports of Goods and Services							
Merchandise, adjusted[a]	10658	15485	15859	4177	4088	3436	4158
Income on investments	1743	1992	1911	422	454	461	574
Transportation	926	1487	1373	392	375	289	317
Travel	377	420	512	102	141	160	109
Miscellaneous services	721	834	1046	254	264	258	270
Total Exports	14425	20218	20701	5347	5322	4604	5428
Imports of Goods and Services							
Merchandise, adjusted[a]	1343	3817	11519	2962	2844	2689	3024
Income on investments	437	398	421	89	109	99	124
Transportation	798	933	1051	245	276	276	254
Travel	727	722	823	132	203	343	145
Miscellaneous services	851	1333	1914[b]	439	435	504	536
Total Imports	12128	15054	15728	3867	3867	3911	4083
Surplus of Exports of Goods and Services							
Merchandise, adjusted[a]	1343	3817	4340	1215	1244	747	1134
Income on investments	1306	1594	1490	333	345	362	450
Transportation	128	554	322	147	99	13	63
Travel	–350	–302	–311	–30	–62	–183	–36
Miscellaneous services	–130	–499	–868	–185	–171	–246	–266
Total Export Surplus	2297	5164	4973	1480	1455	693	1345

Type of Transaction	1950	1951[r]	*1952[p] and by Quarters*				
			Total	*I*	*II*	*III*	*IV*
Net Means of Financing Surplus							
Liquidation of gold and dollar assets[c]	–3629	–442	–1182	382	–404	–765	–395
U.S. Government sources:							
Grants and unilateral transfers	4120	4501	4628[b]	857	1239	1185	1347
Long- and short-term loans	164	163	454	140	210	199	–95
U.S. private sources:							
Remittances	481	412	415	96	94	103	122
Long- and short-term capital[d]	1317	1066	896	235	519	–7	149
Total Net Financing	2453	5700	5211	1710	1658	715	1128
Errors and Omissions	–156	–536	–238	–230	–203	–22	217

p) Preliminary.
r) Revised.
a) Includes goods sold to or bought from other countries that have not been shipped from or into the United States customs area (e.g., with respect to imports, purchases abroad by U.S. Government agencies for transfer to third countries under various foreign aid programs and purchases abroad for the use of American military establishments overseas; with respect to exports, commodities furnished by the U.S. Government from overseas stocks—such as surplus property—and goods sold from overseas purchases, particularly under the various foreign aid programs). The United States customs area includes continental United States, Alaska, Hawaii, Puerto Rico, the Virgin Islands, the Panama Canal Zone, American Samoa, and certain minor American islands in the Pacific.
b) Infrastructure expenditures under the military assistance program are included in this balance of payments statement as miscellaneous services. In the tables in Chapters I and III of this document these expenditures were classified as grants.
c) Includes net dollar disbursements by the International Monetary Fund and the *difference* between the dollar disbursements by the International Bank and the net purchases in the United States of debentures sold or guaranteed by the International Bank.
d) Includes net purchases of debentures sold or guaranteed by the International Bank.
Sources: Department of Commerce, *Balance of Payments of the United States 1949-1951*, Wash., D.C., 1952, p. 120, and Department of Commerce, *Survey of Current Business*, Wash., D.C., March, 1953, p. 8.

IX. BALANCE OF PAYMENTS

A. CURRENT ACCOUNT

Merchandise Trade

a. EXPORTS

Merchandise exports of the United States totalled over $15.8 billion in 1952. This was over a third of a billion dollars greater than in the previous year, but if one excludes from both years shipments of military end-items provided on a grant basis by the U.S. Government it is found that commodity exports declined by approximately three quarters of a billion dollars in 1952 as compared with 1951. This decline in nonmilitary exports was virtually all in volume since prices, on the average, were approximately the same in the two years.

Geographically, most of the decline in nonmilitary goods took place in shipments to Western Europe. Latin America imported about a quarter of a billion dollars less in goods from the United States than in the previous year (the United States still supplied about half of that area's imports, as she had in 1951) and shipments to the Far East declined slightly, but these decreases were almost exactly offset by the increase in United States exports to Canada, which expansion reflected the absence of exchange restrictions in Canada and the exceptionally high rate of production and investment in that country.

There were also important shifts in the commodity pattern of exports during the year under review, with the general trend being a fall in consumers' goods and some increase in certain types of investment goods. The largest absolute declines were in raw cotton and textile manufactures, automobiles, and chemicals. Shipments of coal were also appreciably less in 1952, as were exports of vegetable oils and tobacco. A decline in the exports of wheat was offset by an increase in the exports of other grains, notably rice. On the other hand, larger foreign markets were enjoyed in all of the major geographic areas of the world by the producers of machinery and iron and steel products.

Several factors contributed to the fall in nonmilitary exports. Some of these reflected possible trends toward a sustainable pattern of international trade: the increase in the production abroad of many goods previously purchased in the United States; the more intense competition being faced by some United States exporters in third markets, primarily from European and Japanese producers; and the tightening abroad—especially in Europe—of monetary and fiscal policies. The decline in exports was also due in part to reduced amounts of United States foreign economic aid and to the imposition of more stringent exchange and import controls, particularly in the sterling area and Brazil. Of temporary importance were the declines in imports by the rest of the world from the United States for inventory accumulation purposes; in some instances, there appears to have been a using up of inventories previously accumulated from imports to meet current demands abroad.

b. IMPORTS

The moderate decline in the value of merchandise imports in 1952 from the all-time high in 1951 stemmed entirely from an estimated decline of five percent, on the average, in prices; the volume of goods coming into the United States in the year under review was slightly greater than during the previous twelve months. Slight increases were recorded in the value of imports from Western Europe, Canada, and Latin America; those from the Middle East and Africa were virtually unchanged; but there was a drop of one sixth in the value of goods purchased in the Far East and the Pacific, reflecting the sharp fall in prices of certain raw materials, especially crude rubber and raw wool.

Important changes were recorded in the composition of imports. Most striking was the nearly 60 percent increase in expenditures on nonferrous metals, to meet the needs of expanded rearmament in the United States and of the sustained high level of investment and civilian goods production, despite the fact that the prices of many of these commodities were less than in the previous year. Marked increases were also recorded in payments for (and volume of) imports of petroleum, grains and feedstuffs, industrial machinery, and automobiles. The volume of burlap imports advanced nearly one half but this was offset by a fall in price. The quantity of raw rubber and raw wool imports also increased by small amounts but as a result of the fall in prices total expenditures on these items were some one-half billion dollars less than in 1951. Sharp percentage decreases, in both value and volume, were registered in imports of cattle and meat (largely the consequence of the embargo on meat imports from Canada in effect for most of the year), hides, skins and furs, copra, and industrial chemicals. Sugar imports rose slightly but expenditures on coffee, the nation's biggest single import, were almost identical with those in 1951.

Invisibles

a. INCOME ON INVESTMENTS[2]

After rising steadily since the end of World War II, United States income on foreign investments fell off by about $80 million during 1952 despite an increase in the net value of United States investments abroad during the preceding year of nearly $2 billion. Yet, balance of payments receipts on this account in 1952 totalled over $1.9 billion and they were offset by payments to foreigners on their investments in the United States in an amount of only $421 million, slightly more than during the previous year.

The decline in income in 1952 was concentrated in private long-term investments in Latin America and, to a lesser extent, in Canada. The receipts from private investments in Western Europe and its dependencies were estimated to be the same as in 1951 and slight increases were recorded for the other major areas. It is probable that the fall was the consequence of rising costs, including taxes, combined with stable or declining prices for many of the goods being produced in industries containing United States capital. Details on the sources of investment income during 1952 were not available when this document went to press but estimates for 1951 showed that in that year over $1.6 billion of the total receipts arose from private direct investments abroad, $168 million from private portfolio and short-term investments, and $192 million from foreign loans extended by the U.S. Government. The receipts from private direct investments were heavily concentrated, as were the investments, in the Western Hemisphere and in the petroleum industry, as the following table shows.

In addition to such income, foreign subsidiaries of United States

[2] Income is defined in the official statistics as the sum of interest and dividends from portfolio investments, and dividends, interest, and branch profits from direct investments. Income from direct-investment companies excludes undistributed profits of subsidiaries, which are, however, included in "earnings," and all income as officially reported for balance of payments purposes is taken after the payment of any foreign taxes thereon.

TABLE 21

Direct Investment Income Receipts, by Area and Industry, 1951p

(millions of dollars)

Industry	*Latin America*	*Canada*	*OEEC Countries*	*OEEC Dependencies*	*Other*	*Total*
Petroleum	335	13	15	75	303	741
Manufacturing	84	169	65	2	24	344
Mining and Smelting	87	35	*	14	10	146
Distribution	56	20	31	4	15	126
Public Utilities	23	16	*	*	5	44
Agriculture and Miscellaneous	146	39	12	6	28	231
Total	731	292	123	101	385	1632

* Less than one-half million dollars.
p) Preliminary.
Source: Department of Commerce, *Survey of Current Business*, Wash., D.C., August 1952, p. 9. See this issue of the *Survey of Current Business*, pp. 8ff. for details on "Income on International Investments in 1951." It is the source of most of the information given in this section.

companies had "earnings" that were not distributed and are not included in the above calculations of "income." Information on such undistributed earnings for 1952 is not available, but they totalled just over $700 million in 1951.[8] Thus, total earnings on United States foreign investments during 1951 were estimated at $2.7 billion and the Department of Commerce pointed out that, in interpreting the significance of this huge amount for the balance of payments problems of the rest of the world vis-à-vis the United States, it was important to keep in mind (a) that only some $350 million of it represented fixed interest charges, (b) that direct investment enterprises had made a practice in recent years of reinvesting about half of their earnings abroad; and (c) that the earnings of direct investment companies abroad tend to rise when United States imports go up, in large part because they export directly to the United States, a flexibility that lessens the problem of transferring net earnings. In addition, as has frequently been pointed out, some of these companies produce goods that might otherwise be imported from the United States.

[8] The undistributed earnings of foreign direct investment subsidiaries in the United States amounted to $40 million in 1951.

b. TRANSPORTATION

Balance of payments receipts from the provision of transportation services declined a bit during 1952 from the 1951 level as a result of the reduced tonnage of United States exports,[4] lower freight rates, and more intense competition from the enlarged foreign fleets. On the other hand, *payments* on this account advanced to the highest level since the war and net receipts on transportation account were, with the exception of 1950, the lowest of any year since 1945.

Excluding shipments of Defense Department-controlled, and in-transit cargo, the proportion of the total tonnage of United States water-borne exports carried in American-flag ships declined from 37 percent in the period comprising the first three quarters of 1951 to 31 percent in the same period of 1952, with the decline extending to shipments to every major geographical area but being greatest in exports to Northern Europe, Africa, and the Far East, and least in those to Canada and Southern Europe. The percentage of water-borne imports carried in United States bottoms declined during the same period from 43 percent of the total tonnage to 40 percent, with the fall being distributed fairly evenly among shipments from all areas except Canada, the proportion of imports from that country carried in United States ships having risen.[5]

c. TRAVEL

American tourists spent an estimated $823 million abroad in 1952, over $100 million more than during the previous year. The increase was spread over many areas, but over half of it went to Western Europe. An important factor in the increased travel to Europe was reported to be the rapid growth of the so-called tourist flights by the airlines systems, under which the number of

[4] Earnings by American vessels in foreign trade are greater than the balance of payments statistics show since carriage payments for United States imports transported in American bottoms are not counted as international transactions. The transportation account of the balance of payments is dominated by ocean transportation but it also includes rail and air activities.

In 1951, the last year for which detailed data are available, nearly one quarter of the receipts and one fifth of the payments on transportation accounts represented expenses of foreign carriers in the United States and expenses of American carriers abroad, respectively.

[5] For further details, see *Foreign Commerce Weekly*, April 27, 1953, pp. 17-18.

passengers carried per plane was increased, the incidental services provided reduced, and fares cut. Canada continued to be the largest recipient of tourist dollars from the United States but was followed closely by Europe and Latin America. These three areas accounted for over 90 percent of the total.

The rise in expenditures abroad by United States tourists was almost matched by increased expenditures in the United States of foreign travelers, leaving the United States with an import surplus on this account of slightly more than $300 million. Canadians supplied three fifths of the travel receipts of the United States and accounted for most of the growth during 1952 over 1951. One fourth of the tourist expenditures in the United States during the year under review were made by residents of Latin America and less than one tenth by Europeans.

d. MISCELLANEOUS SERVICES

Expenditures by the United States abroad for miscellaneous services soared to over $1.9 billion in 1952, increasing nearly 50 percent over the previous year. All of the increase and nearly 87 percent of the total expenditures during the year were on Government account and reflecting the growing expenditures abroad of United States troops and the increasing costs of constructing and operating various facilities required in foreign countries by the U.S. Armed Forces.[6] Government purchases of miscellaneous services rose in all areas during 1952, as compared with the preceding year, but the bulk of the increase, and of the total expenditures, was in Western Europe and the Far East. Most of the private payments on this account went to Western Europe and were for reinsurance and communication services.

Receipts for miscellaneous services were also at a postwar high and totalled over $1 billion. Private receipts in 1952 accounted for 60 percent of the total and were estimated to have been the same as in the previous year. Details on the sources of the 1952 receipts were not available, but in 1951 one fifth of the receipts were for film rentals and approximately one fourth each were for reinsurance, management fees and royalties, and foreign repre-

[6] This account, of course, includes only a small part of the total cost of United States military operations abroad since it does not include goods and services used for these operations originating in the United States or that portion of troop pay that was remitted to the United States.

sentational expenses in the United States. Most of the remainder were in payment for communications and services of engineers and contractors. Exports of miscellaneous services on Government account in 1952 totalled $423 million and were double those of the previous year, reflecting the growth in services, including costs of administration, supplied foreigners under the Point Four and the military assistance programs.

Export Surplus

The net result of the various transactions summarized above was that the current account export surplus of the United States during 1952 totalled nearly $5 billion, some 4 percent below the previous year. However, as Table 22 shows, if one deducts aid in the form of military supplies and equipment, the export surplus in 1952 was less than $2.4 billion, as compared with $3.7 billion in the previous year. The decline thus calculated reflected primarily the fall in nonmilitary merchandise exports, for the reasons noted above, and the sharp increase in payments for miscellaneous services on Government account.[7]

Moreover, the export surplus, excluding military aid shipments, declined for all major geographical areas during the last half of the year (the United States had an import surplus, as in the preceding two years, with Eastern Europe and the Western European dependencies) and was at an annual rate during this period of less than $1 billion. Although this sharp fall in the surplus during the last six months of the year was in part the result of seasonal factors and of the steel strike during the summer, it may be that a better balance in the international accounts between the United States and the rest of the world was being established. Geographically, the most striking aspect of the change in the current account export surplus during 1952 as compared with the previous year, after deducting military aid, was the nearly two-thirds reduction in the surplus to Western Europe and the more than two-fifths reduction in that to Latin America.

[7] The latter were, of course, associated with the expanding foreign military activities of the United States and so perhaps should be considered temporary phenomena.

TABLE 22

United States Current Account Export Surplus, by Area, 1950-1952

(millions of dollars)

			1952[p]				
	1950	*1951*[r]	*Total*	*First Quarter*	*Second Quarter*	*Third Quarter*	*Fourth Quarter*
Canada	293	698	875	191	331	157	196
Excluding military aid[a]	(293)	(698)	(875)	(191)	(331)	(157)	(196)
Latin America	357	1033	587	255	248	39	45
Excluding military aid[a]	(357)	(970)	(534)	(223)	(230)	(38)	(43)
Western Europe[b]	1734	3168	2919	907	697	344	971
Excluding military aid[a]	(1221)	(2057)	(773)	(549)	(199)	(−131)	(156)
Western European[b] Dependencies	−312	−475	−489	−165	−136	−74	−114
Excluding military aid[a]	(−312)	(−475)	(−489)	(−165)	(−136)	(−74)	(−114)
Eastern Europe	−44	−64	−27	−7	−8	−5	−7
Excluding military aid[a]	(−35)	(−51)	(−27)	(−7)	(−8)	(−5)	(−7)
All Other Countries	219	798	1087	285	316	239	247
Excluding military aid[a]	(149)	(497)	(692)	(235)	(243)	(99)	(115)
International Institutions	50	6	21	14	7	−7	7
Excluding military aid[a]	(50)	(6)	(21)	(14)	(7)	(−7)	(7)
Total	2297	5164	4973	1480	1455	693	1345
Excluding military aid[a]	(1723)	(3702)	(2379)	(1040)	(866)	(77)	(396)

p) Preliminary. r) Revised.

a) The data on military aid used here were taken from different sources than those used in Chapter I and differ by small amounts from the data on "military end-items" as given in Chapter I. Most of the differences are accounted for by the fact that the contributions to the infrastructure program in Europe are excluded from the data in this table and included in the other tables. It has not been possible to reconcile the other differences but they probably arise because of different treatment given administrative expenses under the military aid programs, and perhaps some difference in the date of recording actual expenditures.

b) Includes OEEC countries, Finland, Spain, and Yugoslavia, except in 1950, when it includes only the OEEC countries.

Source: Department of Commerce, *Survey of Current Business*, Wash., D.C., March 1953, pp. 8-9, and Department of Commerce, *Balance of Payments of the United States 1949-1951*, Wash., D.C., 1952, p. 120.

B. CAPITAL ACCOUNT

Foreign Gold and Dollar Assets[8]

The rest of the world in its transactions with the United States had built up its gold and dollar assets (both long- and short-term) by over $3.6 billion in 1950. In the first half of 1951 these accumulations continued at an annual rate of approximately $2.1 billion. During the last six months of that year, however, net liquidations of such assets were at an annual rate of some $1.2 billion and this trend continued during the first quarter of 1952. The trend was reversed, however, in the second quarter of the year as the value of United States exports other than military supplies provided on a grant basis declined and the value of imports of services of all kinds increased, and for the year as a whole the rest of the world, through its transactions with the United States, was able to build up its gold and dollar assets by approximately $1.2 billion.[9]

Net purchases by foreign persons of long-term dollar assets, customarily not included in calculating a nation's gold and dollar reserve position, apparently were approximately matched by new gold production abroad that went into official channels with the result that, excluding the International Bank and Fund, the rest of the world also increased its gold and *liquid* dollar reserves by approximately $1.2 billion. This raised the total of such known holdings to $20.4 billion,[1] almost the same as the all-time peak reached at the end of 1945 and well above the postwar low of $14.7 billion in September 1948, when the Marshall Plan got under way. In 1945, however, prices and the value of world trade were much lower than in 1952.

Taking into account transfers among foreign countries, as well as their transactions with the United States, and including newly mined gold but excluding changes in long-term dollar

[8] Most of the information in this section was taken from "International Flow of Gold and Dollars, 1952," in Board of Governors of the Federal Reserve System, *Federal Reserve Bulletin*, March 1953, pp. 209-216.

[9] More specifically, in their transactions with the United States the rest of the world made net sales of between $380 million and $400 million of gold (official figures vary on this item) but accumulated a net of nearly $420 million in long-term dollar assets—mostly U.S. Government bonds—and about $1150 million of short-term dollar accounts—mostly short-term U.S. Government securities and, to a lesser extent, bank deposits.

[1] Of this, $11.3 billion was in gold and $9.1 billion in dollar holdings; about half of the latter was owned by private individuals.

holdings, it is seen that the increase in the international reserves of the rest of the world varied widely among areas. Continental Western Europe and its dependencies increased their holdings, as shown in Table 23, by over $1.2 billion, of which approximately half grew out of transactions with the United States and another $275 million represented gold and dollar payments made to them via the European Payments Union by the sterling area. Almost every Western European nation shared in this increase in reserves

TABLE 23

Estimated Changes in Foreign Gold and Dollar Holdings, 1952[a]

(millions of dollars)

Area or Country	*First Half*	*Second Half*[p]	*Total*[p]	*Holdings as of Dec. 31, 1952*[p]
Sterling Area[b]	−639	+145	−494	3242
Western Europe[c]	+536	+719	+1255	8369
Other Europe[d]	−13	+9	−4	350
Canada	+239	+66	+305	2462
Latin America	−60	+56	−4	3356
Asia	+181	+6	+187	2353
Other	+1	−44	−43	285
Total, Foreign Countries	+245	+957	+1202	20417
International[e]	−21	+137	+116	3287
Grand Total	+224	+1094	+1318	23704

p) Preliminary. The differences between total estimated holdings as of the end of 1951 (as given in *Survey—1951*, p. 283) plus changes during 1952 and estimated holdings as of December 31, 1952 result from revisions in the end-of-1951 data.

a) Dollar holdings represent both official and private holdings as reported by United States banks and include deposits, short-term U.S. Government securities (those maturing in twenty months or less after date of purchase), and certain other short-term liabilities. These data do not include long-term dollar assets, gold in private hoards, or private holdings of United States currency, as distinguished from deposits.

b) Excludes Eire and Iceland, which are included in Western Europe.

c) Includes holdings of Western European dependencies, the Bank for International Settlements (including European Payments Union), gold to be distributed by Tripartite Commission for Monetary Gold, and estimates of certain unpublished gold reserves of Western European countries.

d) Excludes gold reserves of, but includes dollar balances held by, Russia.

e) Includes International Bank, International Monetary Fund, and other international organizations except the Bank for International Settlements, which is included in Western Europe.

Source: Board of Governors of the Federal Reserve System, *Federal Reserve Bulletin*, Wash., D.C., March 1953, p. 212.

but the largest amounts were recorded by the Netherlands and Germany, each accounting for over one fifth of the increase, followed by Belgium and Switzerland. The sterling area, on the other hand, suffered a great loss in reserves during the year—nearly one-half billion dollars. Less than two fifths of this arose out of transactions with the United States and most of the rest of it represented payments to continental European countries via the European Payments Union. Virtually all of the decline in the sterling area reserves occurred during the first three months of the year, and during the last six months that area's reserves increased as the previously instituted tighter import restrictions and more stringent monetary policies began to take effect. Unrecorded capital movements may also have been a factor in the growth of sterling area reserves during the last half of the year. Canada continued to accumulate gold and U.S. dollar reserves, but at a much reduced rate during the last half of the year. The loss of reserves during the first six months by Latin America was virtually all recouped during the remainder of the year as several countries in that area imposed more stringent import restrictions, but sizable net losses were suffered by Argentina, Cuba, and Brazil, while Venezuela recorded a large gain. Japan, which benefited from large expenditures by United States troops and purchases of supplies to support the United Nations forces in Korea, augmented her reserves by $200 million after having paid $67.5 million in subscriptions to the International Bank and Fund. Indonesia, on the other hand, suffered a loss of nearly $121 million in reserves as the prices of many of her exports fell. International institutions, primarily the International Bank and Fund, made small net disbursements to foreign countries during the year over and beyond repayments of past loans plus new borrowing by the International Bank and sales from its portfolio, but their gold and dollar assets increased by some $116 million as a consequence of the subscriptions paid during the year by Germany and Japan.

As 1952 ended, balance of payments difficulties appeared to be decreasing for most countries in the free world despite growing defense expenditures. Nonetheless, the strains were still so great, in spite of greater production abroad and the curtailment of inflationary pressures in most areas, that most nations continued to maintain, and some intensified, their vast and intricate network of import and payments restrictions. At the British Commonwealth Conference held late in the year officials of those countries talked in general terms of moving toward freer trade and currency practices but said that this would be feasible only if, among other things, provisions could be made by the International Monetary Fund or "otherwise" for larger international reserves. The U.S. Government, however, gave no indication during the year that it was contemplating making any grants or loans for this purpose.

Other Items

The various means by which the United States financed its export surplus (and a portion of the increase in the reserves of the rest of the world)—official grants and loans, private loans and remittances, and dollar disbursements by the International Bank and Fund—were discussed in some detail in Chapters I through V and need not be summarized here.

C. *ERRORS AND OMISSIONS*

The difference between known dollar payments and receipts—errors and omissions—during 1952 was $238 million, considerably less than during the previous year. This item was notable, however, in that it declined from a net receipt of $433 million in the first half of the year to a payment of $195 million during the last half. This was an extraordinarily large shift, and the Department of Commerce concluded that most of it represented a change in the movement of unrecorded capital flows between the United States and the sterling area and that it contributed to the building up of the sterling area's reserves during the last half of the year, as noted above.

SUMMARY

SECURITY considerations dominated virtually all aspects of United States international economic and financial policies during 1952. In its major outlines the record of the problems faced and the policies and activities pursued followed closely those of the previous year. The Presidential campaign, and the knowledge that 1953 would bring with it a new Administration and a new Congress, resulted in something of a paralysis in policy during the last half of 1952, but there was evidence of a growing dissatisfaction, both in the United States and abroad, with many of the policies being followed and the view was frequently stated that a thorough reassessment of most of them was needed.

The major economic weapon used by the United States to strengthen the defenses of the rest of the free world against possible further aggression by the Soviet bloc continued to be the granting of huge amounts of military assistance to friendly countries. There was widespread agreement that the prior practice of concentrating such aid in Western Europe was still the proper one, it being generally believed that those nations were prepared and able to make the most effective use of such assistance and that the loss of Europe would so strengthen the military potential of Russia as to force the United States to assume a more costly, full mobilization posture. Nonetheless, the existence of warfare in other areas and the constant threat of further hostilities, strengthened by the realization that the areas of possible Russian aggression could not be confidently forecast, were found to justify the sending of larger amounts of military aid to non-European countries than in 1951. It was, moreover, believed by most of those having responsibility for policy formulation that aid designed to raise the standard of living in many of the non-European nations was an effective and feasible method of deterring Communism and so should complement, or in some instances take the place of, military assistance. With respect to Europe, however, the U.S. Government assumed no responsibilities for providing on a grant basis goods and services to further the "recovery" of those economies or to raise levels of civilian consumption or investment.

Many members of Congress had for years viewed with alarm the cost of the official foreign aid programs and had appropriated less funds than asked by the Administration, but the question of the ability of the United States to "bear these burdens" received more attention than usual during 1952 in Congress and in the public press. Those raising the issue rarely attempted to define the capacity of the United States economy to make such transfers, but the conclusion that it was in danger of being exceeded was nonetheless firmly held. Spokesmen for the Administration argued that the national security of the United States was at stake and that the requested funds were carefully calculated to provide more national security than an equivalent expenditure on the Armed Forces of the United States. Congress did not seriously question this argument, but in weighing the threat of Communism against the threat of what many chose to call "national bankruptcy," it cut the Administration's request for funds for the Mutual Security Program for fiscal year 1952-1953 from $7.9 billion to $6.0 billion.[1] The legislators also justified this pruning on the grounds that there were large unspent balances from previous appropriations for military aid, that the rearmament efforts of the European nations were "disappointing" and did not justify the requested aid, and that, in the views of many members of Congress, some of the requested funds were scheduled for purposes not closely related to the security of the United States.

The military assistance provided nations other than those that were members of the North Atlantic Treaty Organization (the major non-European recipients were Formosa and Indochina) was mostly in the form of military end-items and services produced in the United States, and the amount of such aid actually

[1] Virtually all of the nearly $4.8 billion of financial assistance actually provided by the U.S. Government on a grant basis during the calendar year was under the Mutual Security Program, the only important exception being the $154 million of civilian supplies provided by the Defense Department to Korea and the Ryukyus. In addition, a *net* of approximately $400 million of official loans was extended, the most important being those by the Export-Import Bank (both on its own account and for the Mutual Security Agency) and the wheat supplied India on a loan basis under the India Emergency Assistance Act of 1951. Some loan assistance was also provided indirectly by the U.S. Government through the International Bank and the International Monetary Fund.

utilized increased throughout the year, exceeding $450 million and reaching an annual rate of nearly $550 million during the last quarter.[2] In Europe, the military assistance also took two other forms—so-called defense-support aid and offshore procurement. Although defense-support aid was in the form of commodities similar or identical to those provided under the European Recovery Program, its purpose was not to rebuild the civilian economies and to raise standards of living and internal investment; rather, it was to finance the purchase of raw materials and machines to be used directly in the production of armaments in Europe and to finance the import of some goods consumed by civilians so as to facilitate the European nations' diverting more of their own resources into armaments production and away from the production of goods for civilian consumption, domestic investment, and export. The amount of such defense-support (or economic) aid totalled approximately $1.7 billion during 1952, as compared with some $2.5 billion during the preceding year,[3] but European Recovery Program aid in the pipeline accounted for some of the shipments during the year and the annual rate of defense-support assistance during the last quarter of 1952 had fallen to just over $0.8 billion.

The policy decision to spend some one quarter of the funds provided for military end-item assistance to Europe for the fiscal year beginning in mid-1952 on offshore procurement—purchasing in Europe with dollars military end-items in turn to be given to Europe—represented the most important financial innovation in the military assistance program in 1952 and received almost universal approval. This "untying" of American aid was designed to relieve the demands on certain sectors of the American economy already under strain, to make use of certain idle productive capacity in Europe, to expand the production and maintenance of supplies closer to the place of use, and to provide European countries with a source of dollar earnings to help fill the gap left by the termination of the European Recovery Program and aggravated

[2] In addition, nearly $140 million worth of civilian-type goods and services were provided various Asian countries by the Mutual Security Agency. This aid was designed primarily to alleviate the impact on their economies of the expanded mobilization programs but it also had objectives similar to those of the Point Four Program, discussed below.

[3] Including such aid provided on a credit basis.

by the diversion in some countries of production from export goods to rearmament.

From the publicly available data it is impossible to assess with any precision the progress achieved in 1952 in building the "balanced collective forces" of the North Atlantic Treaty Organization countries. The value of United States aid in the form of military end-items and services actually delivered was double that of 1951 and totalled some $2.3 billion, of which only about $80 million represented offshore procurement. The flow of military supplies was increasing as the year ended but shipments were far below the hopes and expectations of the European nations, and just before leaving the White House in early 1953 President Truman stated that "we need to find methods to expedite delivery of end-item military equipment and to achieve the optimum volume of offshore procurement."[4]

The European countries as a group did increase their production of military equipment and supplies and the number of their men under arms, but the specific goals set by the Council of the North Atlantic Treaty Organization early in the year were not fully met. Moreover, during the latter part of the year there were indications that the authorities in these countries had concluded that the threat of Soviet aggression was less imminent than United States officials believed it to be and that, unless United States contributions were increased, the previously planned mobilization goals for 1953 exceeded what the European officials regarded as the economic-political capabilities of their nations. European spokesmen also frequently insisted that it was virtually impossible for them to make or to carry out the long-range mobilization plans urged on them by the United States when the latter's contributions were on a yearly basis and when Congress tended to regard each year's appropriations as emergency measures that carried no commitments for subsequent years. Although it had not yet resulted, so far as the public could determine, in serious frictions, it was more and more apparent as the year went by that there was a fundamental conceptual difference between the United States and the European nations as to the nature of the military assistance program. Most people in the United States, including the

[4] Mutual Security Agency, *Third Report to Congress on the Mutual Security Program,* Wash., D.C., December 31, 1952, p. XII.

majority of Congress, saw the relationship between the two areas as that of a donor and recipient and regarded the flow of goods and services financed by the U.S. Government as "aid" or "grants," whereas in Europe most persons spoke of the relationship as one of equal partners and regarded the transfer of commodities and services as nothing more than the United States share of a joint undertaking.[5]

In the view of the U.S. Government, and of a great many private citizens, the most discouraging aspect of Europe's rearmament endeavors during 1952 was the failure to reach an accord on the incorporation of German forces and productive capacity in the mutual defense effort. For some time the U.S. Government had taken the position that adequate defense of the North Atlantic area demanded the participation of Germany and to facilitate this had, after some hesitation, repeatedly urged that most of the armed forces of Germany, France, Italy, the Netherlands, Belgium, and Luxembourg be incorporated into a single European Army under some form of supranational control along the lines proposed in 1950 by the French Government. To encourage the formation of such a common defense force, Congress in 1952 amended the Mutual Security Act so as to authorize the transfer of funds directly to such an organization if and when it were created. Further, the coming into effect of the contractual agreement, signed in midyear, replacing the occupation statute in Germany, and restoring to German authorities control over most of their internal and external affairs, was made conditional on the creation of a European Army. A treaty constituting a European Defense Community was signed in May by the executive authorities of the six European nations concerned but opposition to it in the signatory countries was strong and no Parliament had ratified the treaty as the year ended.

As a matter of major policy Congress and the Administration, with the support of most of the vocal public in the United States, continued during 1952 to urge that Europe "unify" its economies and "federate" its political structures. Work was started at the

[5] In his final report to Congress on the Mutual Security Program, President Truman stated that "foreign aid" was an "obsolete, unsound and unworthy . . . conceptual basis for the great ventures in international partnership upon which we are engaged."

ministerial level on a draft constitution for the political federation of six Continental nations but agreement had not been reached by the drafters as the year ended. The U.S. Government hailed the formal birth during the summer of the European Coal and Steel Community and the Administration promised, without being specific, to give this organization "strong support." No direct financial aid was provided in the year under review but the International Bank held out the prospect of such aid and the United States did assume a leading role in getting the Contracting Parties to the General Agreement on Tariffs and Trade to grant the necessary waivers so that the members of the Schuman Plan would not be acting in violation of their obligations under the General Agreement. The several institutions of the coal and steel pool were established during the latter part of 1952 and a few substantive decisions were taken by the High Authority. The actual creation of a single market for coal and steel among the members was scheduled to start in early 1953 and it was still to be demonstrated whether the hopes were justified that the Community would make war between Germany and her Western European neighbors impossible and would bring about increased competition, production, and productivity, thus strengthening the defense potential of Western Europe and enhancing that area's ability to provide politically and socially acceptable standards of living to its peoples without help from the United States.

U.S. Government officials repeatedly exhorted Europe to find and adopt new economic integration techniques but put forward no specific proposals, and the European discussions on establishing a single market for certain agricultural products—the so-called green pool—failed to result in any agreement. The European Payments Union and the related trade liberalization measures continued to receive the blessings of the U.S. Government, but the Administration rejected an appeal for additional dollar grants to the Union's central fund and there was some evidence of a growing skepticism in the United States as to the ability of the Union and the trade liberalization measures to make further contributions to the creation of a single, "mass market" in Europe. The Union continued to provide an effective device for facilitating nondiscriminatory multilateral trade *within* Europe, but most observers recognized that it had accomplished virtually nothing toward achieving its other original major objective—assisting members to return to worldwide nondiscriminatory multilateral trade and a general convertibility of currencies. Indeed, the Union's Managing Board reported that this task transcended the inherent possibilities of the mechanism.

The intra-European trade liberalization measures suffered a setback during the year as France and the United Kingdom attempted to correct serious balance of payments deficits by imposing previously removed import restrictions. The resort to, or maintenance of, such controls by nations facing balance of payments difficulties was not limited to the Western European nations. During the year the Contracting Parties to the General Agreement on Tariffs and Trade and the International Monetary Fund carried out consultations with their members (European and non-European) on the retention of the various controls over trade and payments that had been authorized for the "transitional period," scheduled to end in 1952. United States officials, as well as those of most other nations, recognized that the world in 1952 was not the one that had been anticipated when the rules of the Fund and the General Agreement had been agreed upon and, with one or two exceptions, no country was formally urged in the consultations to remove its controls. For the world as a whole, probably more trade was carried out under exchange and direct import and export restrictions in 1952 than in the previous year.

Although the bulk of official U.S. Government aid was designed directly to expand the military potential of other friendly nations and was concentrated in Europe and a few Far Eastern nations, the U.S. Government continued to hold that the Soviet design for conquest in many parts of the world, especially in the so-called underdeveloped areas, relied on subversion as well as military aggression and that it was therefore in the interest of United States security to help reduce poverty and misery in these areas. Most of the discussion on this policy centered around the Point Four Program and the major issue in the Congressional consideration during 1952 was the extent to which this aid should be in the form of commodities as distinct from services. In its request to Congress for funds, the Administration included relatively large amounts for commodities for certain countries, especially India and Pakistan, arguing that these were needed to complement the technical services to be provided, and, more importantly, that they reflected the necessity for accelerating the processes of economic development if the newly established governments of those nations were to survive as independent entities in the face of the rapidly rising expectations of their peoples and the intense pressures being exerted on them by Russia. Many in Congress, however, concluded that a basic change in concept was involved and that the Program was in the process of becoming a big new "give-away" project. In keeping with the prevailing mood that the U.S. Government must reduce, not increase, its foreign "economic" commitments, Congress drastically cut the Administration's request, emphasizing that the Program should concentrate on providing technical assistance and that only those commodities necessary to make the technical assistance effective should be supplied as grants, the rule of thumb being that amounts spent for goods should be no more than three to four times the amounts spent for services.[6]

For the first time, there was some questioning by members of Congress of the basic hypothesis that helping people to raise their standards of living and accelerate the processes of economic development, which inevitably resulted in the disruption of many existing social and economic institutions, was an effective means of reducing the appeal of Communism. The Administration acknowledged that this fundamental assumption had not yet been proven valid but argued that, given the desire of the people of

[6] Apart from the regular Point Four Program, the U.S. Government (through the Technical Cooperation Administration) supplied on a grant basis during the year some $80 million worth of commodities and services to Israel in a program designed to help resettle the post-1948 immigrants in that nation; the U.S. Government also transferred $22 million to the United Nations to help resettle the Arab refugees from the Palestinian war, then located in the surrounding Arab countries. Most of the aid under both of these programs was used to provide goods for current consumption and but little progress was recorded in making either of these groups self-supporting.

As noted earlier, the U.S. Government, through the Mutual Security Agency, also furnished nearly $140 million of economic and technical assistance to various Asian nations—most of it going to Formosa, Indochina, and the Philippines. While this aid was intended in part to accomplish the same things as the Point Four Program, its major purpose was to permit the recipients to make more effective use of the military goods being provided them. Most of this economic aid took the form of commodities rather than services and the operating principles in administering the aid were patterned after those of the European Recovery Program.

these areas to maintain their independence, United States aid would help eliminate the conditions under which totalitarianism tended to flourish. This thesis was accepted by most persons who publicly expressed their views. The extension of aid to the underdeveloped areas was also frequently justified on the ground that it would serve to increase the production of strategic and critical materials needed in the current rearmament program of the North Atlantic nations and for the civilian requirements of an expanding United States economy. In the event, most of the dollar aid to foster the production abroad of raw materials—and the amount was appreciably greater than in the preceding year—was provided on a loan basis by the Export-Import Bank, the International Bank, and by private United States investors; encouragement was also given to expanded production abroad of such goods by the placing of long-term contracts for materials destined for the official United States stockpile.

Although the aspects of anti-Communism and of expansion of production of strategic and critical materials were emphasized before Congress, the Administration repeatedly took occasion throughout the year to emphasize that, even if there were no Communist threat, the Point Four Program was justified on the humanitarian grounds that the United States could and should help others help themselves in building decent conditions of life in which they could find social and political security and that it was in the economic self-interest of the United States to help create conditions in the poorer nations that would be conducive to an expansion of world trade.

The Point Four Program was accelerated during the year but actual expenditures, including contributions to the United Nations Technical Assistance Program, totalled only some $75 million.[7] There were many specific instances where this aid had increased local production and productivity, especially in agriculture, and had improved health conditions, but most of the individual projects were just getting under way as the year ended and it was still too early to determine whether the Program was serving to reduce the appeal of Communism to these peoples and to strengthen the political ties of the aided countries with the

[7] Not included is some $80 million of aid to Israel that was legally but not conceptually a part of the Point Four Program.

United States. The fact that most of the funds were spent to expand agricultural production and to improve health and sanitation facilities led some in Congress to question publicly, for the first time, whether the result of all this might not be merely to increase the number of people living in misery and result in still greater demands for American help to alleviate the suffering of an increased population for which the United States would be at least partially responsible. This important issue was not publicly explored in detail by United States officials and it was too early to determine what effect, if any, the Program was actually having on population growth and on the volume and content of international trade. The most difficult *operating* problem faced in implementing the Program was that of recruiting technicians who were not only competent but who could, or would, adapt themselves to the social and cultural patterns of the countries to which they were sent and who were prepared to resist the temptation merely to transplant the most modern (and expensive) techniques developed in their own countries in favor of applying their knowledge and adapting their techniques to the particular constellation of resources and demands existing in the aided nations.

Experience during the year gave support to the earlier conclusion of many that if technical assistance were to be effective in raising standards of living it must be accompanied by a much larger amount of capital goods than was provided under the Technical Assistance Program. United States officials continued to insist that most of the required investment in capital goods be financed by the underdeveloped countries themselves and again received the reply from the spokesmen for the poorer countries that their national incomes were so low as to preclude adequate internal savings. Spokesmen for the U.S. Government acknowledged that a greater flow of long-term capital from the richer to the poorer areas was desirable but maintained that the bulk of this should come from private sources, supplemented, for certain noncommercial types of basic development, by loans from existing government and international lending institutions.

In furtherance of this policy the Administration continued its efforts, mainly by issuing investment guaranties and attempting to negotiate bilateral tax conventions and investment treaties, to encourage a larger outflow of private United States capital but achieved only moderate success. Spokesmen for most of the poorer countries showed little interest in encouraging private foreign investment but, except for a few glaring exceptions, there seemed to be less open hostility to private capital inflows than in the immediately preceding year. In any event, total net private long-term United States investment declined from the previous year but there was a small increase in net direct private investment; however, over half the $711 million of these net direct private capital outflows went to Canada[8] and most of those in the areas generally regarded as underdeveloped were in petroleum and extractive industries and so did not coincide with the development plans of the officials of the recipient nations.

Several loans for such basic development projects as transportation, power, and irrigation were authorized for borrowers in the so-called underdeveloped countries by the Export-Import Bank and the International Bank, but spokesmen in the United Nations from the underdeveloped countries again insisted that the existing international institutions were inadequate to meet their capital requirements and urged the creation of a new International Development Authority that would extend grants and low-interest rate loans for basic investment projects. The United States, supported by the other historically capital-exporting nations, continued to oppose the creation of such an institution and succeeded in getting a resolution approved calling only for further study of the proposal. Pursuant to a 1951 resolution of the United Nations Economic and Social Council, the staff of the International Bank prepared a report on a proposal to create an International Finance Corporation designed to make, and to encourage private investors to make, equity investments in enterprises located in the underdeveloped nations. Official representatives from neither the potentially capital-exporting nor the potentially capital-receiving nations were enthusiastic over this proposal and it too was remanded for further study.

In these discussions and elsewhere, officials of many foreign governments continued to press the International Monetary Fund to ease the access to its resources. These pleas were given new urgency by the anticipation that the amount of foreign aid pro-

[8] Virtually all of the net long-term portfolio investments during the year were in securities issued or guarantied by the International Bank.

vided by the U.S. Government for other than strictly military purposes was likely to decline in the future. The U.S. Government insisted that the Fund continue to operate according to the principles embodied in the Articles of Agreement and stated that it was not prepared to make additional contributions to the Fund; it did, however, support certain new procedures worked out by the Fund designed to increase its loans and to insure that they would not become long-term. The Fund sold more currencies to its members than it had in either of the two preceding years and repurchases were in excess of all previous years combined. Nonetheless, many were those outside the U.S. Government who asserted that the Fund had taken only a first step in making itself into an institution that would be a significant service to the world as it existed.

The overriding objective of strengthening the defenses of the free world found expression in many economic policies other than those involving the financing by the U.S. Government, in one form or another, of the transfers of goods and services to friendly nations. Expenditures to accumulate an official stockpile of strategic and critical materials continued at approximately the same rate as in the previous year and provided foreign countries with large amounts of dollars, as did the growing payments by the U.S. Government for the construction and maintenance of military facilities and installations abroad and the spending by American forces stationed overseas. Stockpiling procurement problems were eased as demands throughout the world for many of the goods leveled off, supplies increased, and prices fell from their post-Korean peaks. These same factors resulted in a progressive curtailment in the allocation activities of the International Materials Conference and this institution, which had been subjected to severe criticism earlier in the year by some members of Congress but which most observers believed had achieved an international allocation of several critical raw materials that was more equitable and more consistent with the defense needs of the non-Communist countries than would have resulted from the operations of a free market—this institution appeared to be in the process of self-dissolution as the year ended.

The U.S. Government maintained such stringent controls on exports from the United States to Soviet-bloc countries as to result in a virtual embargo. There was no serious questioning of the wisdom, or criticism of the administration, of these export restrictions—the United States historically had engaged in only minor amounts of trade with these countries. But the corollary policy of asking—and applying as a sanction the threat of terminating official aid—other friendly nations to prohibit all exports of primary strategic items to the Soviet bloc and to reduce drastically the export of goods of secondary strategic importance was a source of some friction between the United States and her allies and between the Administration and Congress. In addition to such immediate difficulties as transshipments, diversions, classification of commodities as to their strategic importance, and prior commitments by Western European exporters to ship goods to Eastern Europe, the policy brought to the fore the more basic problem of providing alternative markets and sources of supply for those friendly countries that historically had relied heavily on trade with the East.[9]

The East-West trade question; the growing concern as to the adequacy of domestic supplies of many raw materials; the continuance of an export surplus on current account of nearly $5 billion; the conviction in the United States and abroad that it was neither feasible nor desirable to continue unilateral Government transfers of the dimensions that had been recorded for many years; and the recognition that a decline in foreign aid would injure United States export industries—all these gave a sense of urgency, brought some new recruits, and provided powerful arguments and a new slogan ("Trade, not aid") to those who had earlier, and for other reasons as well, concluded that the United States trade and tariff policy should be thoroughly revised in the direction of reducing import barriers. Authority to make substantial changes in the nation's import policies was in the hands of Congress and that body did not undertake any thorough investigation of this problem during the year; but such piecemeal action as it did take, or did not take, together with developments under the changes made in the Trade Agreements Act of 1951, served to strengthen the fears of many that the policies were veering in

[9] There were many who believed that, apart from the United States insistence that East-West trade be curtailed, the long-term policy of the Soviet bloc was one of autarky and that therefore the free world must, in any event, face the problem of a redirection in its trade patterns.

the direction of providing greater protection to domestic producers and of intensifying the conflicts between trade policy and the other international economic policies of the nation.

The most publicized and most controversial action during 1952 in the field of commercial policy was the continuation by Congress, with a few ameliorative amendments, of the law authorizing stringent import quotas on dairy products. Congress again failed to approve the customs simplification bill despite the fact that few questioned that current United States customs procedures were frequently unfair, uncertain, and time-consuming, and constituted almost as serious a barrier to imports as existing tariff rates. The great increase in applications for relief under the escape clause that had been written into the 1951 Trade Agreements Act resulted in the withdrawal of previously granted concessions in only a few cases and on relatively minor items; nonetheless, these were seen by many as evidence of a trend toward greater protection and as introducing such uncertainty concerning the continuance of any given tariff concession as to constitute a major deterrent to efforts by foreign exporters to develop markets in the United States.

The United States was again found to be acting in violation of some of its commitments under the General Agreement on Tariffs and Trade, but the Seventh Session of the Contracting Parties held in Geneva in the autumn was more noteworthy in that these, as well as several disputes between other participants, were settled, or discussed and action postponed, with but little retaliation. The United States appeared to have suffered no further decline in its leadership in this institution and there was some evidence that others, especially the United Kingdom and some of the other members of the British Commonwealth, were more willing than they had been in 1951 to support the principles of the General Agreement. It was generally recognized, however, that the future of the General Agreement would be determined in large measure by the new Administration and the new Congress in Washington, which, in response to demands from many quarters, had promised a thorough reevaluation and reformulation of all the nation's international economic and financial policies.

INDEX

Abaca, 105tn, 221
Acheson, D. (Secretary of State): on North Atlantic Treaty Organization strength, 44n; on European Defense Community, 49n; on technical assistance, 58n, 59, 66n; on escape clause, 178n; on International Materials Conference, 224; on European economic integration, 236; on European Coal and Steel Community, 263; see also State Department
Act for International Development of 1950, 60, 71; see also Point Four Program
Adler, J. H., 168n
Afghanistan, 58tn, 62, 102tn, 116tn
Africa: see Near East and Africa and individual countries
Agricultural Adjustment Act, 194, 196, 201-203
Agricultural products: import controls on, 167, 192-202; export subsidies on, 202-203; donations of surplus of, 203; bartered for strategic materials, 218; and International Materials Conference, 222-232 *passim*; and European green pool, 263-264, 287; see also individual products
Agriculture, Department of, 102tn; foot and mouth disease operations of, 99; and surplus commodities, 99-100; and tuna fish tariff, 175; and wool tariff, 201n; and export subsidies, 202-203; and strategic materials, 221; see also Agricultural products and Brannan, C. F.
Agriculture, foreign, United States investment in, 273t
Alaska, 269tn
Albania, 102tn
Alien Property Custodian, 103
Allied High Commission, Germany, 88-90
Almonds, 178
Aluminum, 219n, 229n, 234
American and Foreign Power Company, 108n
American Farm Bureau Federation, 194n, 231n
American Foreign Bondholders Protective Council, 129
American Petroleum Institute, 171
American Red Cross, 102tn
"American selling price," 180n
Andrews, S., 71n
Anglo-Iranian Oil Company, 122
ANZUS Council, 52-53
Appropriations: Mutual Security Program, 9, 13-15, 283; transfers between military and economic aid, 11, 33n, 37n; military aid to Europe, 21; Spain, 22; Asia and the Pacific, 24; Latin America military end-items, 26; defense support to Europe, 27; one-year approach, 44; technical and economic aid, 67; Organization of American States technical assistance, 74; United Nations technical assistance program, 74-75; Israel-Palestine refugee programs, 79-84 *passim*; occupied areas, 87-90; Korean aid, 91-92; children's relief, 93-95; migration and escapees, 95-99; stockpiling, 215-216
Arab States: and military assistance, 50n; and Middle East Command, 51; technical assistance to, 63; and Israel, 79, 84n; and Palestine refugees, 79-87; and petroleum, 82; see also individual countries
Argentina: Export-Import Bank credit to, 109n; and International Development Authority, 164; gold reserves of, 280
Asia and the Pacific, 34t, 58t, 101t, 107t, 115t, 127tn, 147t, 279t; Mutual Security Program appropriations for, 9, 15t, 67; technical assistance to, 14-15, 63-64, 68-69; military assistance to, 16, 24-25, 51-53, 283-284; security treaties with, 52; defense-support aid to, 56; contributions to Point Four, 60; economic relief aid to, 65, 94, 284n; United States investment in, 125; gold hoarding in, 144; meat embargo on, 198; United States exports

to, 270; U.S. Armed Forces expenditures in, 275; see also individual countries
Atlantic Commodity Board, 266
Atlantic Community, 44n, 46n, 265-266
Atlantic Economic Board, 266
Atlantic Payments Union, 143n
Atlantic Reserve System, 266
Atomic Energy Commission, 107
Australia, 102tn, 116tn, 136t, 151t; security treaty with, 52; and migrants, 97, 98; Export-Import Bank loan to, 106; tax convention with, 119; and International Monetary Fund, 137; and gold price, 144, 145; International Bank loan to, 150; and United States dried milk embargo, 198; and International Wheat Agreement, 231n, 232
Austria, 38t, 127tn, 143; economic aid to, 27, 88-90; and European Defense Community, 47; and migration, 96, 98; Export-Import Bank loan to, 109; tax convention with, 119; and General Agreement on Tariffs and Trade, 190; and European Payments Union, 241, 246, 249

Baldwin, H. W., 43n
Balkan pact, 37n
Bank for International Settlements, 147t, 279tn
Bank of America National Trust and Savings Association, 152n
Battle Act, 206-213
Belgian Congo, 151t, 152n
Belgian Congo Tin Producers, Association of, 229
Belgium and Belgium-Luxembourg, 38t, 111t, 136t, 151t, 153t, 242t; military assistance to, 27; offshore procurement in, 36n; and European Payments Union, 36n, 147-148, 241-247 *passim*, 256; and European Defense Community, 47, 286; and migration, 98n; Export-Import Bank loan to, 109, 110, 124; tax convention with, 119; and International Monetary Fund, 137, 141, 148; and import restrictions, 176, 185, 186n, 190, 253n, 255, 256; and European Coal and Steel Community, 258, 262n; and Benelux, 263n; increase in reserves of, 280
Bell Report, 169; on customs simplification, 180-181n; on General Agreement on Tariffs and Trade, 190n; on wool tariff, 202n; on export subsidies, 203; on import taxes on metals, 232n
Benelux, 176, 263n
Bennett, J. F., 248n
Bennett, W. T., 67n
Benton Amendment, 31n, 41, 42, 116-117n
Berlin, 47, 119, 128
Bingham, J. R., 68n, 71n
Binney, R. M., 122n
Black, E. R. (President, International Bank for Reconstruction and Development), 149, 150n
Bolivia: and migration, 98n; Export-Import Bank loans to, 108; nationalization by, 121-123, 217n, 229; tin agreement with, 217n, 229
Bolles, B., 43n
Bowles, C. B., 65n
Bradley, General O. N., 8, 18
Brannan, C. F. (Secretary of Agriculture): and "cheese amendment," 195, 197; and sugar, 199-200; see also Agriculture Department
Brazil, 136t, 151t; military assistance agreement with, 53n; and migration, 98; Export-Import Bank loans to, 107, 108, 112; and private short-term capital, 126; and International Monetary Fund, 135; International Bank loans to, 150; and General Agreement on Tariffs and Trade, 190; import controls of, 271; gold reserves of, 280
Bresciani-Turroni, C., 248n
Briar pipes, 174, 177n
British Commonwealth Economic Conference, 141-142, 281
British East Africa, 112
British Ministry of Supply, 107
British West Africa, 144
Brown, G. C., 248n
Bruce, D. K. (Under Secretary of State), 19n, 260
Burma, 58tn, 63, 72, 102tn, 116tn, 131n, 143, 165n, 186n
"Buy American" Act, 168-169, 214

California Almond Growers Exchange, 195n
California Walnut Growers Association, 195n
Canada, 107t, 115t, 127t, 147t, 153t, 277t, 279t; offshore purchases in, 37; and North Atlantic Treaty Organiza-

tion infrastructure, 45n; and migration, 97, 98; strategic materials loans to, 108, 113; investments in United States, 124; United States investment in, 125, 272, 292; and exchange controls, 140n; exchange rate of, 143; and Fund gold policy, 144; and International Bank, 155; and international finance corporation, 162; and Belgian dollar import restrictions, 185; import restrictions by, 186n; and United States dried milk and meat embargoes, 198-199, 272; and East-West trade, 209, 210; and United States stockpiling, 215; and aluminum agreement, 229n; and International Wheat Agreement, 231n, 232; and European Payments Union, 256; and European integration, 265, 266; United States exports to, 270; and tourism with United States, 274-275; gold and dollar reserves of, 280

Capital assistance, 104-129, 148-166, 291-293; United Nations debates on, 73, 76-78; and Export-Import Bank, 106-112; and United States encouragement of private foreign investment, 114-123; and International Bank, 148-158; and European Coal and Steel Community, 262; see also Loans and investments

Capital movements, see Loans and investments

Carnegie Foundation, 117n

Caroline Islands, 102tn

Cartels: and Benton Amendment, 31n; United Nations study of, 200n; and International Materials Conference, 224; and European Coal and Steel Community, 261; and Benelux, 263n

Central German Coal Sales Agency, 261

"Certificates of essentiality," 112, 219-220

Ceylon, 58tn, 102tn; United States aid to, 62, 211; exchange rate of, 143; and General Agreement on Tariffs and Trade, 189, 190; and East-West trade, 211

Chase National Bank, 152n

"Cheese amendment," 178, 182-183, 192-198

Chile, 136t, 151t; military assistance to, 53n, 54; and migration, 98; and economic development, 163; and copper agreement, 217n

China, 101tn, 116tn, 143; and United States export controls, 175n, 205-214 *passim*; see also Formosa

China Aid Act of 1950, 34tn, 101tn

Chinaware, 175

Chinese students, 100

Clapp Mission, 81n

Coal, 270; see also European Coal and Steel Community

Cobalt, 108, 112, 222-223

Collective Measures Committee, United Nations, 213

Collins, E. H., 145n

Colombia, 53n, 54, 108, 121, 150, 151t

Colombo Plan, 68-69n, 76

Commerce, Department of, 111tn; on United States foreign investment, 123n, 125; on "cheese amendment," 195; and export licenses, 204; see also Export controls and Sawyer Mission

Commercial Policy, United States: see East-West trade, Export controls, Export subsidies, Foreign trade zones, General Agreement on Tariffs and Trade, Import controls, Import taxes, International commodity arrangements, International trade fairs, Stockpiling, and Trade agreements program

Committee for Economic Development, 168, 181

Committee for Reciprocity Information, 171

Commodity Credit Corporation, 218

"Common list," 254, 256

Congress of Industrial Organizations, 194n

Connally, Senator T., 12; on defense support, 28; on European economic integration, 236n

Copper: Export-Import Bank loans for, 112; agreement with Chile on, 217n; under International Materials Conference, 222, 224, 225; Paley Commission on, 229n; import tax suspension on, 234

Costa Rica, 136t, 152n, 210n

Cotton: Export-Import Bank loans for export of, 108-109; import quotas on, 202; under International Materials Conference, 222, 223, 225, 227; fall in exports of, 270

Council of Europe, 236n, 260, 265

Counterpart funds, 34tn, 38tn, 101tn; in Mutual Security Act, 31; under Mutual Security Program, 40-42; for strategic materials, 39n, 112, 218,

220, 221; and housing in Germany, 42n; and technical assistance, 68n, 72n; and occupied areas program, 89n; and United States reverse grants, 100, 102; and U.S. Government capital movements, 114; and Benton Amendment, 116-117n
Cowen, M. M., 7n
Cuba, 53n, 54, 120, 186n, 200, 230, 280
Customs, Bureau of, 201n
Customs simplification, 167, 168, 180-181, 192, 295
Czechoslovakia, 23, 102tn, 116tn, 132n, 136t, 187n

Dairy products, import restrictions on, 167, 178, 182-183, 192-198
Dawes Loan, 129
Defense, Department of, 34tn; and military stockpiles and North Atlantic Treaty Organization priorities, 18, 32; civil aid to Korea and Ryukyus by, 32n, 87n, 90-93, 283n; and offshore procurement, 33-36, 109; and aid to Spain, 36n; and North Atlantic Treaty Organization costs, 46n; and "certificates of essentiality," 234n; see also Military assistance
Defense Materials Procurement Agency, 38tn, 115t; use of counterpart funds by, 112-113; and stockpiling, 214-221 *passim*
Defense Production Act: and Export-Import Bank loans, 111-112, 219; Section 104 of, 182-183, 192-198, 201n; and export priorities, 205; and International Materials Conference, 225; see also Defense Materials Procurement Agency
Defense Production Administration: and Export-Import Bank loans, 111-112, 115t; and International Materials Conference, 224; and tungsten production, 233-234; see also Defense Production Act
Defense-support aid, 23, 26-31, 36-42, 284
Democratic Party, platform of: on trade policy, 170; on European integration, 238
Denmark, 38t, 98n, 111t, 121, 136t, 151t, 153t, 197, 208, 241, 242t, 255
Detroit Board of Commerce, 168
Diebold, W., Jr., 168n, 189n, 239n
Director for Mutual Security, see Harriman, W. A.
Director of Defense Mobilization, 226
Discrimination: see East-West trade, European Coal and Steel Community, European Payments Union, Export controls, General Agreement on Tariffs and Trade, and International Monetary Fund
Displaced Persons Act of 1948, 98; see also Migration
Displaced Persons Commission, 98n
Dominican Republic, 53n, 186n, 200
Douglas, Senator P. A., 13n
Draper, W. H., Jr., 19n, 31n
Dried Fruit Exporters Association, 194n

East Germany, 206
East-West trade: restrictions on non United States, 3, 206-214, 294; United Nations activities on, 213-214; see also Export controls
ECOSOC (UN Economic and Social Council): and population problem, 65; and technical assistance program, 73-74; and tax conventions, 120; and International Monetary Fund policies, 138-139; and new international financial institutions for economic development, 158-166
Economic Commission for Europe: on East-West trade, 212n; and European Coal and Steel Community, 260n; on integration, 264-265
Economic Cooperation Act, 31n, 101tn, 242tn
Economic Cooperation Administration, 30n, 34n, 91-92, 218, 220; see also European Recovery Program
Ecuador, 53n, 54, 179
Eden, A. (British Foreign Secretary), 145
Egypt, 50n, 58tn, 102tn, 116tn, 136t
Eisenhower, D. D. (General and President): on cuts in foreign aid, 12; on North Atlantic Treaty Organization goals, 43, 44; on trade policy 170; on escape clause, 177n; on customs simplification, 181; on fig tariff, 184n; on European unification, 236-237; on agricultural and electric power pools in Europe, 236, 263
El Salvador, 140n, 151t, 180
Escape clause, Trade Agreements Act, 167, 174-180, 193, 194, 196, 295
Escapees, 20n, 95-99

Ethiopia, 50n, 58tn, 102tn, 116tn, 121, 136t, 151t
Europe, 15t, 34t, 101t, 107t, 115t, 127t, 147t, 277t, 279t; military assistance to, 1, 2, 5, 9, 16-24, 31-33, 282-286; defense support in, 26-31, 36-42; offshore procurement in, 34-36; industrial and agricultural production of, 39n; pace of rearmament in, 42-46, 285; migration from and refugees in, 84n, 95-99; United States investment in, 123n, 124, 125, 127, 272; gold hoarding in, 144; and currency convertibility, 147; dollar gap of, 170; and meat embargo, 198; and East-West trade, 206-214, 294; dependent overseas territories strategic materials, 220; United States exports to, 270, 271, 276; United States ocean freight to and from, 274; United States travel to, 274; U.S. Armed Forces expenditures in, 276; reserves of, 279-280; see also European Coal and Steel Community, European Defense Community, European economic integration, Mutual Security Program, North Atlantic Treaty Organization, OEEC countries, and individual countries
European Army, see European Defense Community
European Coal and Steel Community, 3, 22, 47, 90n, 236, 238, 257-263, 287; and International Bank, 150; General Agreement on Tariffs and Trade waiver for, 187-188, 260, 287
European Constitutional Convention, 235n
European Defense Community, 3, 14, 21-22, 43, 46-50, 90n, 235n, 236, 238, 286
European Payments Union, 3, 36n, 38t, 102tn, 185n, 238-253, 264, 279tn; and sterling convertibility, 142, 279-280; and International Monetary Fund, 146-148; gold payments in, 146, 279; and International Bank, 148; operations and adjustments in mechanism during 1952, 240-248; accomplishments and problems of, 248-253
European political federation, 235, 237
European Recovery Program, 2, 5, 23, 27, 38tn, 39, 284; and counterpart funds, 31; defense support by, 36n; type of goods provided by, 39; technical assistance by, 55n; and Occupied Areas Program, 88; and investment guaranties, 117; and European economic integration, 235, 264; see also Economic Cooperation Administration.
"Excess" military equipment as aid, 13n, 32n, 54
Exchange rates, and International Monetary Fund, 139-143
Exchange restrictions, 271; and International Monetary Fund policy on, 132-133, 139-142; and General Agreement on Tariffs and Trade, 254
Export controls, by United States, 204-206, 217n; see also East-West trade
Export-Import Bank, 11, 105tn, 115t; and strategic materials production, 4, 107-108, 219, 220, 290; loans by, 35, 106-112, 124; and economic development, 61, 78, 104, 108, 161, 292
Export priorities, by United States, 205n
Export subsidies, 184, 202-203
Export surplus, United States, 276-277
Exports, by United States, 270-271

Fanfani, A., 264n
Far East: and Colombo Plan, 68-69n; and Israel immigrants, 84n; Occupied Areas Program in, 88; see also Asia and the Pacific and individual countries
Fats and oils, import controls on, 192-198
Ferguson, Senator H., 224
Figs, and escape clause, 174, 176, 183-184
Fiji, 144
Finland, 102tn, 107tn, 116tn, 119, 121, 136t, 137, 151t, 277tn
Fleming, J. M., 240n
Food and Agriculture Organization, UN, and International Wheat Agreement, 232n
Foot and mouth disease, 99, 102tn, 198
Ford Foundation: and Point Four, 69-70; and refugee aid, 96n
Ford, H., II, 169
Foreign Assistance Act of 1948, 235
Foreign trade zones, 191-192
Formosa, 58tn, 73t; military assistance to, 24, 51, 283; economic assistance to, 63, 72, 289n; see also China and Asia and the Pacific
Forrest, J. G., 9n
France, 38t, 111t, 136t, 151t, 153t, 242t; import restrictions by, 3, 244,

255, 256, 288; and North Atlantic Treaty Organization, 19, 35n, 44, 46n; and Indochina, 19, 25, 46, 52; defense-support aid to, 27, 28, 37; offshore procurement in, 35; Export-Import Bank loans to, 35, 108; aid to Yugoslavia by, 37n; and European Defense Community, 47-49, 286; and Middle East Command, 51; and migration, 98n, lend-lease returns by, 100; and investment guaranties, 119; and German debt settlement, 128; and Japanese debt settlement, 129; and International Monetary Fund, 138; exchange rate of, 143; and International Bank, 157; and Belgian import restrictions, 185, 253n; and Seventh Session of General Agreement on Tariffs and Trade, 189-190; and East-West trade, 210n; and International Materials Conference, 222; and International Wheat Agreement, 231n; and European Payments Union, 241n, 243, 244-246, 248, 251, 255; and European Coal and Steel Community, 257, 258; and coal cartel, 261
Frankel, S. H., 68n
French Morocco, 113

Gaitskell, H., 142n
Garlic, and escape clause, 174, 177, 178, 179n
General Agreement on Tariffs and Trade: and imperial preferences, 167; Torquay negotiations under, 171; and United States escape clause, 174, 176, 183; Seventh Session of Contracting Parties to, 181-191; and customs simplification, 181; complaints against United States in, 182-184, 193-194, 196; and export subsidies, 184; and dollar import restrictions by Belgium, 185, 253n; consultations on quantitative restrictions in, 185-187; and European Coal and Steel Community, 187-188, 260, 287; accession of Japan to, 188-189; administration of, 189-190; and tariff quotas, 200-201; and international commodity arrangements, 221-222; and European Payments Union, 253; and trade and payments restrictions, 288; United States role in, 295
General Services Administration, 115t, 218
Germany, 38t, 111t, 127tn, 153t, 242t; United States aid to, 21, 88-90; and North Atlantic Treaty Organization, 43; counterpart funds for luxury housing in, 42n; and European Defense Community, 46-50, 286-287; and migration, 96, 98; Export-Import Bank loan to, 108; investment guaranties in, 119; debt settlement by, 128-129; and International Monetary Fund, 131n; and International Bank, 131n, 280; exchange rate of, 143; and General Agreement on Tariffs and Trade, 189, 190; and European Payments Union, 245, 256; trade liberalization measures in, 254-256 *passim*; and European Coal and Steel Community, 257-263, 287; gold reserves of, 280; see also Berlin and East Germany
Giarlino, J. G. del, 97n
Gifts, private, 103, 268t
Gillette, Senator G. M., 128n
Gold: International Monetary Fund and United States policy on, 143-146; transactions by United States in, 146; foreign assets in, 267, 278-281
Gordon, N. N., 120n
Government and Relief in Occupied Areas, see Occupied Areas Program
Greece, 34tn, 38t, 101t, 107tn, 116tn, 242t; military assistance to, 5, 23-24, 50; defense-support aid to, 27, 37n, 51; and Balkan pact, 37n; and North Atlantic Treaty Organization, 43; and migration, 96, 98; lend-lease returns by, 100; tax convention with, 120; investment treaty with, 121; exchange rate of, 143; and United States escape clause, 177, 184; and United States export subsidy, 184; and General Agreement on Tariffs and Trade, 190; and East-West trade, 210n; and European Payments Union, 247, 249
Greek-Turkish Assistance Act of 1948, 34tn, 101tn
"Green Book," 266
"Green pool," Europe, 263-264, 287
Groundfish, tariff quota on, 200-201
Gruenther, General A. M., 10, 19n
Guatemala, 122, 140n, 180

Haiti, 112, 131n, 186n
Hanson, S. G., 68n
Harriman, W. A. (Director for Mutual Security), 13, 17, 19, 31n, 37n, 57-58, 59n, 110, 116n, 118, 265
Hatters' fur, and escape clause, 174, 176

Havenga, N. C., on gold price, 145
Hawaii, 199, 230, 269tn
Hirschman, A. O., 240n
Hoffman, M. L., 246n, 248n
Honduras, 140n, 180, 210n
Hong Kong, export controls by, 205, 206n
Hoselitz, B. F., 68n
Howard, H. N., 68n
Hungary, 102tn, 116tn, 173
Hunter, Congressman A. O., 195n

Iceland, 38t, 111t, 151t, 157, 242t, 247, 249, 279tn
Imperial preferences, 167, 191
Import controls, direct: and International Monetary Fund, 132-133, 139-141; by United States, 167, 172-173, 182-184, 192-202, 234n; and General Agreement on Tariffs and Trade, 182-187; liberalization of by OEEC members, 244, 245, 254-257; and United States exports, 270-271
Import policy of United States, 4, 167-203, 191-192, 294-295; see also Commercial policy, United States
Import price controls, by United States, 217n
Import taxes, suspension of, 232-234
Imports, intra-European, 249-250, 254-257
Imports, United States, 267, 268t, 271-276; see also Commercial policy, United States
Income on private United States foreign investment, 268t, 272-273
India, 58tn, 102tn, 116tn, 136t, 151t; technical assistance to, 62-70 *passim*; Export-Import Bank—Mutual Security Agency loan to, 110-111, 112n; and investment climate, 121-123; International Bank loan to, 152; trade dispute with Pakistan, 190; Export-Import Bank loan to, 283n; economic assistance to, 288-289
India Emergency Assistance Act, 110, 283n
Indochina, 58tn, 102tn; and French North Atlantic Treaty Organization commitments, 19; military assistance to, 24, 25, 51, 52; North Atlantic Treaty Organization support of, 46; economic aid to, 63, 289n; technical assistance to, 72
Indonesia, 51, 58tn, 63, 72, 102tn, 116tn, 131n, 165n, 189
Infrastructure, 17n, 32n, 36n, 45, 269tn, 277tn
Initial credit and debit balances, European Payments Union, 239, 242t
Institute of Inter-American Affairs, 101tn
Integration, European economic: 3, 235-266, 286-287; and Mutual Security Act, 21-22; and defense-support aid, 28; and Germany, 90; and International Bank, 150; and European Payments Union, 238-253; and trade liberalization measures, 254-257; and European Coal and Steel Community, 257-263; miscellaneous proposals for, 263-265; versus North Atlantic Community, 265-266
Inter-American Cultural Center, New Orleans, 192
Intergovernmental Agreement on German External Debts, 128, 129n
Intergovernmental Committee for European Migration, 99; see also Provisional Intergovernmental Committee for the Movement of Migrants from Europe
Interior, U.S. Department of, 175n
International Authority for the Ruhr, 260n, 261
International Bank for Reconstruction and Development, 11, 105tn, 148-158, 269tn, 278, 279tn; loans for strategic materials production by, 4, 220, 290; technical assistance by, 4, 220; loans for economic development by, 61, 78, 292; and colonization projects, 99; and competition with Export-Import Bank, 108n; portfolio sales by, 124, 280, 292n; lending policies and operations of, 148-155, 163; and European Payments Union, 148, 252; and international commodity arrangements, 154n; marketing operations and financial resources of, 155-158; and international finance corporation, 159-161; and tuna industry in Latin America, 175n; and European Coal and Steel Community, 262, 287; gold holdings of, 280
International Chamber of Commerce, 168, 181, 212n, 263n
International Children's Emergency Fund, 15t, 93-95, 101t
International commodity arrangements, 3, 221-232; and International Bank policy, 154n; and United States stock-

piling, 217n; on cotton, 227; on wool, 228; on rubber, 228-229; on tin, 229-230; on sugar, 230; on wheat, 231-232; see also International Materials Conference and President's Materials Policy Commission
International Cotton Advisory Committee, 227
International Development Advisory Board: on purposes of technical assistance, 58n; on purposes of Point Four, 59n; on contributions by recipients, 60; on type of projects, 64n; on new financial institutions, 158
International Development Authority, 56, 78, 131, 158-159, 162-166, 292
International Economic Conference, Moscow, 212n
International finance corporation, 78, 131, 158-162, 292
International Materials Conference, 3, 222-226, 293
International Monetary Fund, 105tn, 130-148, 269tn, 270tn; lending policy and operations of, 133-139, 292-293; and foreign exchange rate policy, 139-143; and exchange restrictions, 139-142; and sterling convertibility, 141-142; and gold policy, 143-146; and European Payments Union, 146-148, 252, 253; credit to Belgium, 243; gold holdings of, 280; reserves of, 278, 281
International Refugee Organization, 95, 101t; see also Migration
International Sugar Agreement, 199, 230
International Sugar Council, 230
International trade fairs, 191-192
International Trade Organization Charter, 167, 221, 224
International Wheat Agreement, 202, 227, 231-232
International Wheat Council, 231, 232
Intra-European merchandise trade, 249-250; see also Trade liberalization measures
Investment, foreign in United States, 124
Investment guaranties, 116-119, 291
Investment treaties, 121, 173, 291
Investment, United States foreign, 273t; encouragement of private, 61, 71, 104, 114-123, 160-161, 163; in petroleum, 104, 125, 126n; in mining, 104, 173; volume of, 104-114, 123-127, 291-292; see also Loans and investments, United States
Iran, 58tn, 116tn, 136t; military assistance to, 22, 23, 50; technical assistance to, 69; investment climate in, 122, 123; and International Monetary Fund, 135
Iraq, 50n, 58tn, 102tn, 151t
Ireland, 38t, 111tn, 255n, 279tn
Israel, 50n, 58tn, 102tn, 116tn; economic assistance to, 15t, 63, 79-87, 95n, 289n, 290n; and Middle East Command, 51; and migration, 98; investment treaty with, 121
Italy, 38t, 111t, 151t, 153t, 242t; offshore procurement in, 35; defense-support aid to, 37; and European Defense Community, 47, 286; and migration, 96, 98; Export-Import Bank loan to, 109n; and investment guaranties, 119; tax convention with, 121; exchange rate of, 143; International Bank loan to, 152; and United States import restrictions, 177-178, 197; and trade liberalization, 185, 253-255; and General Agreement on Tariffs and Trade, 190; and East-West trade, 208; and European Payments Union, 241, 244; and European Coal and Steel Community, 258

Jamaica, 113
Japan, 102tn, 116tn, security treaty with, 52-53; investment treaty with, 121; debt settlement by, 128-129; and International Monetary Fund, 131n; and International Bank, 131n, 280; exchange rate of, 143; and tuna fish, 175n; and chinaware, 175n; accession to General Agreement on Tariffs and Trade by, 188-189; and East-West trade, 209-210; and United States exports, 271; reserves of, 280
Javits, Congressman J. K., 117n
Johnston, Eric, 58n, 117n
Jordan, 50n, 58t, 102tn, 131n, 143; see also Palestine refugees

Keenleyside, H. L., 75n
Kenya, 144
Kerber, E. S., 32n
Kersten, Congressman C. J., 20n
Knorr, K., 224n, 248n, 266n
Korea, 101tn, 116tn; military assistance to, 24; technical assistance to, 72; reconstruction program for, 32n, 90-93, 95n; students, 100; and General

Agreement on Tariffs and Trade, 190; see also North Korea
Kriz, M., 144n, 145n
Krzysztof, Z., 259n

Land reform, 59n, 75n
Latin America, 15t, 34t, 58t, 101t, 105tn, 107t, 115t, 127t, 147t, 279t; military assistance to, 5, 9, 16, 25-26, 53-54; technical assistance to, 60, 62, 63, 68, 69; and International Children's Emergency Fund, 94; and migrants, 97, 98; and strategic materials, 113, 221; and nationalization, 123; investment in United States by, 124; United States investment in, 125, 126, 175n, 272; United States meat embargo on, 198; and stockpiling, 215; and European Payments Union, 252; United States exports to, 270, 276; United States travel in, 275; gold reserves of, 280; see also individual countries
Lead, 222, 229n, 233
Lebanon, 50n, 58tn, 102tn, 116tn, 136t
Lend-lease credits, 101t, 102, 113, 115t
Lenroot, K. F., 94n
Liberia, 50n, 58tn, 102tn, 113, 116tn, 182n 186n, 210n
Libya, 50n, 58tn, 75n, 102tn, 190
Lisbon, Meeting of North Atlantic Council: North Atlantic Treaty Organization goals set at, 10, 14, 17-20, 26, 35n, 42-46; see also North Atlantic Treaty Organization
Loans and investments, United States, 104-129; U.S. Government, 105-114; private, 114-129; income on, 272-273; see also Investment, United States foreign
London Conference on German External Debts, 128
Lovett, R. A. (Secretary of Defense), 8n, 14, 18n, 19
Luxembourg, 151t, 186n, 258, 286; see also Belgium and Belgium-Luxembourg

Macao, 205
Maffry, A., 108n, 114n, 118n, 120n
Malaya, 229
Malenbaum, W., 69n
Manganese, 107, 112, 222, 223, 226
Mansholt, S. L., 264n
Mariana Islands, 102tn
Maritime Administration, 114, 115t
Marshall Islands, 102tn
McFall, J. K. (Assistant Secretary of State), 128n
Mediterranean Command, 46
Metal scrap, import tax suspension on, 233
Mexico, 102tn, 136t, 151t; military assistance agreement with, 53n; technical assistance to, 70; foot and mouth disease in, 99, 198; Export-Import Bank loans to, 108, 112; International Monetary Fund meeting in, 131n, 133, 140; and exchange restrictions, 140n; gold sales to United States by, 146; and International Bank loans, 150, 152; United States trade agreement with, 171
Middle East, see individual countries and Near East and Africa
Middle East Command, 23, 51
Middleton, D., 43n
Migration and escapee assistance, 15t, 20n, 38tn, 95-99, 101t, 102tn; see also Displaced Persons Act of 1948, Palestine refugees, and Israel
Military assistance, see Table of Contents, Chapter I
Mining and smelting, private foreign investment in, 104, 273t; see also individual commodities
Mixed Claims Commission, 128n
Molybdenum, 222, 223, 225
Monnet, J., 260n
Monroe Doctrine, 52n
Moody Amendment, 41-42, 116n
Most-favored-nation clause, 172, 173, 187
Mundt, Senator K. E., 195n
Munitions Board, 214-221 *passim*
Murphy, C. J. V., 43n
Mutual Defense Assistance Act of 1948, as amended, 5, 16n, 101tn
Mutual Defense Assistance Control Act of 1951; 207; see also Battle Act and East-West trade
Mutual Security Act of 1951: and responsibilities of Director for Mutual Security, 31n; on counterpart funds, 31, 41; on reimbursable military aid, 32n; on transfer funds to defense support, 33n; and shipping clause, 39n; and military aid to Latin America, 53; and assistance to Israel, 79-80n; on encouraging private investment, 116n; on European integration, 235
Mutual Security Act of 1952: appropriations authorized by, 15t, 101tn; pos-

sible aid to ineligible recipients, 22-23; and defense-support aid, 30; on encouraging private enterprise in Europe, 31n, 41-42; on loans versus grants, 110; on encouraging private investment, 117; and international finance corporation, 161n; proposed East-West trade amendment, 211-212; and European integration, 237; and European Coal and Steel Community, 262; and European Defense Community, 286
Mutual Security Agency, see Mutual Security Program
Mutual Security Program: and military assistance, 5-54; and aid to underdeveloped areas, 55-78; and miscellaneous activities, 79-102; and Export-Import Bank loans under, 110-111, 111t, 115t, 283n; and strategic materials, 113, 220, 221n; and investment guaranties, 117-119; and European economic integration, 235ff.; see also East-West trade, Export controls, and International Materials Conference

National Advisory Council: on loans to Europe, 11, 110; and International Monetary Fund objectives, 132; on United States subscription to International Monetary Fund, 139; on International Bank reserve policy, 155; on European Payments Union, 253
National Association of Manufacturers, 168, 181
National Cotton Council, 194n
National Council of American Importers, 181, 194n
National Farmers Union, 194n
National Foreign Trade Council, 161n, 168, 181
National Planning Association, 117n
National Renderers Association, 195
National Security Council, 13n
Near East and Africa, 15t, 34t, 58t, 101t, 107t, 115t; military assistance to, 5, 9, 16, 23-24, 50-51; technical assistance to, 62, 63, 68, 69, 70; and Israel-Palestine refugee programs, 79-87; and children's relief, 94; United States investment in, 125; gold hoarding in, 144; see also individual countries
Near East Foundation, 70
Nepal, 58tn, 62, 102tn
Netherlands, 38t, 136t, 151t, 153t, 242t; and migration, 98; gold purchases from United States by, 146; International Bank loan to, 152; and United States "cheese amendment," 183, 197; and trade liberalization, 185, 253n, 255n, 256; and East-West trade, 208; and European Payments Union, 241, 245, 256; and European Coal and Steel Community, 258; and Benelux, 263n; gold reserves of, 280; and European Defense Community, 286
Netherlands-Indonesia, 111t; see also Indonesia
Newsprint, 223, 225
New York Board of Trade, 194n
New Zealand, 102tn, 116tn; security treaty with, 52; and migration, 98; and United States dairy products embargo, 198; and beef exports to United States, 198-199
Nicaragua, 136t, 151t, 182n, 186n, 190
Nickel, 108, 222, 223, 226
North Atlantic Community, see Atlantic Community
North Atlantic Council, 35n, 45n; see also Lisbon and North Atlantic Treaty Organization
North Atlantic Treaty Organization, 6-23, 26-51; and Lisbon goals, 10-11, 17-20, 42-46, 285; and United States aid, 13, 22, 283-284; and defense-support aid, 26-27, 36-37n; and West European exports, 27-28; and supply priorities, 32; and European Defense Community forces, 47; and Pacific pact, 52-53; and escapees, 99; and Battle Act, 208; and European integration, 238, 265-266; and balanced collective forces, 285-286; see also Lisbon and Mutual Security Program
Northern Rhodesia, 112
North Korea, and export embargo, 206-214 *passim*
Northwest Nut Growers, 195n
Norway, 38t, 111t, 136t, 153t, 242t; and migration, 98n; strategic materials loan, 113; and General Agreement on Tariffs and Trade, 190; and trade liberalization, 255

Occupied Areas Program, 87-90, 101t
Ocean freight, United States, 15t, 32n, 274
Office of Defense Mobilization, 217n

Office of Price Stabilization, 217n, 224n
Offshore procurement: in Europe, 23, 34-36, 284; and defense support, 30; *and loan to France, 109*
Okinawa, 88
Organization for European Economic Cooperation (OEEC): and European Payments Union, 238-253; and trade liberalization measures, 254-257; and European Coal and Steel Community, 258n, 260; and East-West trade, 264; other activities of, 264-265
OEEC Council, 241, 242tn, 248, 264-265; see also Organization for European Economic Cooperation
OEEC countries, 102tn, 107tn, 116tn, 127t, 277tn; see also individual countries
Organization of American States, 56, 57, 58tn, 74, 76

Pakistan, 58tn, 102tn, 116tn, 151t; technical assistance to, 62-63; wheat loan to, 112; investment climate in, 121; International Bank loan to, 150, 152n, 157; and international finance corporation, 162; and General Agreement on Tariffs and Trade, 189, 190; trade dispute with India, 190; economic assistance to, 288-289
Palestine refugees, 15t, 58tn, 63, 289n; aid to, 79-87
Paley Commission, see President's *Materials Policy Commission*
Panama, 140n, 210n
Panama Canal Zone, 269tn
Paper, see Pulp and Paper Committee
Papi, G. U., 264n
Paraguay, 98n, 136t, 137, 151t
Parker, W. N., 258n
Peril-points clause, 167, 168, 171-172
Peru, 53n, 54, 136t, 143, 150, 151t, 175n, 182n, 186n
Petroleum: offshore purchases of, 37; United States investment in, 104, 125, 126n, 273t, 292; and trade agreement with Venezuela, 171-173; tariff quotas on, 201
Philippine Rehabilitation Act of 1946, 100
Philippines, 58tn, 101t, 116tn; military assistance to, 24-25, 51, 52; security treaty with, 52-53; economic and technical assistance to, 63, 72, 100, 289n; Export-Import Bank loans to, 108; refunding loan to, 114, 115t; and international finance corporation, 162; and General Agreement on Tariffs and Trade, 190; and proposed *changes in Trade Act of 1946, 201;* and United States sugar quota, 230
Philippine Trade Act of 1946, 201
Pleven, Premier R., 46
Point Four Program, 55-72, 288-291; purposes of, 57-61; methods of financing, 61-62; form and amount of aid for, 62-67; and implementation problems, 67-72; exploration projects, 71n; and United Nations, 72-77; and capital assistance, 77-78; and private investment, 114-123; and civilian aid by military, 284n; see also Export-Import Bank, International Bank for Reconstruction and Development, Technical Cooperation Administration, and Underdeveloped areas
Poland, 23, 102tn, 107tn, 116tn, 173, 206
Population, and United States aid, 65, 97, 291
Portfolio investments, 124, 292
Portugal, 38t, 111t, 241, 242t, 255n, 256
Portuguese Africa, 108
"Positive list," 205; see also Export controls
Potatoes, 201
President's Materials Policy Commission: on Technical Cooperation Administration programs, 71n; on private foreign investment, 114n; on new trade policy, 169n; on stockpiling, 214-215; on strategic materials loans, 220n; on tax conventions, 220n; on international commodity arrangements, 221-222; on international buffer stocks, 229; on tin agreement, 230; on import taxes on metals, 232n
Primary products, prices of, 78n, 222
"Productivity drives," of Mutual Security Program, 40
Provisional Intergovernmental Committee for the Movement of Migrants from Europe, 38tn, 96-99, 102tn; see also Migration
Public Advisory Board for Mutual Security, Report on Trade and Tariff Policy, see Bell Report
Puerto Rico, 199, 230, 269tn
Pulp and Paper Committee, 222, 223, 225

Raisins, export subsidies on, 184, 202
Randall, C. B., 258n
Rao, U., 162n
Rayburn, Speaker S., 13
Reciprocal Trade Agreements Act, see Trade Agreements Act
Reconstruction Finance Corporation, 105tn, 114, 115t, 221, 229
Reimbursable military aid, 26, 32n, 54
Remittances, private, 103, 269t
Republican Party, platform of: on trade policy, 169-170; on European integration, 238
Reynolds, P. A., 258n
Richards, Congressman J. P., 12
Richebacher, K., 257n
Ridgway, General M. B., 43
Robbins, L., 142n
Rockefeller Foundation, 70
Rockefeller report, 158
Rooth, I. (Managing Director, International Monetary Fund), 135, 139; see also International Monetary Fund
Royal Dutch Airlines, 152
Rubber, 211, 228-229
Rubber Study Group, 228-229
Russia, 102tn, 116tn, 144, 146, 206
Ryukyus, 87-88, 102tn, 283n

Samoa, 269tn
Saudi Arabia, 50n, 58tn, 102tn, 116tn
Sawyer Mission: on Benton-Moody Amendments, 42; on East-West trade, 71n, 213n; on investment guaranties, 118; on investment climate, 121; on new trade policy, 169n; on customs simplification, 180n; on export subsidies, 203
Schlesinger, E. R., 168n
Schuman, R. (French Foreign Minister), 257
Schuman Plan, see European Coal and Steel Community
Seager, C. H., 67n
Second War Powers Act, 192n
Sharp, W. R., 75n
Shenstone, M., 258n
Shepler, C. E., 32n
Shipping, Mutual Security Act restrictive clause on, 39n; see also Ocean freight, United States
Sisal, 112
Smith-Mundt Act, 101tn
Snyder, J. W. (Secretary of the Treasury): on exchange restrictions, 140; on gold price, 145; see also Treasury Department
Southard, F. A., Jr., 147
Southern Rhodesia, 113, 144, 150, 151t
Spain, 15t, 38t, 107tn, 116tn, 277tn; military assistance to, 21-22; and defense-support aid, 36n; Export-Import Bank loans to, 109, 110
Special Restrictive Committees, Organization for European Economic Cooperation, 255n
Spofford, C. M., 45n, 265n
Spulber, N., 211n
State, Department of, 115t; on aid to Spain, 36n; on appropriations for Germany and Austria, 89n; on Philippine rehabilitation, 100; on tuna fish bill, 175n; on escape clause, 176, 178-179; and General Agreement on Tariffs and Trade, 196; on cartels, 200n; on International Materials Conference, 224; see also Acheson, D., Bruce, D. K., McFall, J. K., and Thorp, W. L.
Steel, 108, 229n; see also European Coal and Steel Community
Steering Board for Trade, Organization for European Economic Integration, 255
Sterling, convertibility of, 141-142, 252n
Sterling area, 141-142, 271, 279, 279t; see also individual countries
Stevenson, A. E., 170
Stockpiling, 3, 214-221; counterpart funds for, 42; program of, 215-216; procurement and supply development for, 216-221, 290, 293; see also International commodity arrangements and Strategic and critical materials
Strategic and critical materials, 3, 4, 204-234, 290, 293; and Latin America, 25-26, 54; and restrictive shipping clause, 39n; counterpart funds for, 42; technical assistance for, 60-61, 71; and Export-Import Bank, 106-108; Defense Production Administration—Export-Import Bank loans for, 111-112; and Defense Materials Procurement Agency, 112-114; and East-West trade, 204-214; and export priorities, 205; and foreign surplus property, 219n; and International Bank loans, 219-220; see also International commodity arrangements and Stockpiling
Sudan, 82
Suez Canal, 82

Sugar, import quotas on, 199-200
Sugar Act of 1948, 199, 230
Sulphur, 108, 222, 223, 226
Sulphur Committee, 222, 226
Sunkist Growers, 195n
Surplus property, 89n, 113, 115t, 219n
Sweden, 38t, 98n, 111t, 136t, 153t, 189, 211, 242t, 255, 259
Swerling, B. C., 199n
Switzerland, 242t; and migration, 98n; tax convention with, 119; and International Bank, 155-156; and tariff on watches, 174, 177-178; and East-West trade, 211; European Payments Union position of, 245; and trade liberalization, 255; gold reserves of, 280
Syria, 50n, 58tn, 102tn, 136t, 165n

Tanganyika, 144
Tariff Act of 1930, 175n, 200; see also Trade Agreements Program
Tariff Commission: on petroleum tax, 171; and peril-point clause, 172; and escape clause, 174-180; and restrictions on nuts, 201-202; see also Trade Agreements Program
Tariff quotas, United States, 171, 200-202
Taxes, on infrastructure construction, 17n
Tax reforms and conventions, 116, 119-120, 220n, 291
Technical assistance: see Point Four Program and 55-57, 72-77, 150n, 290-291
Technical Cooperation Administration: operating principles of, 56; and goods versus services, 66-67; and Israel-Palestine refugee programs, 79-87, 289n; and loans to Pakistan, 112, 115t; see also Point Four Program
Temporary Council Committee, North Atlantic Treaty Organization, 42
Thailand, 24, 51, 52, 58tn, 63, 72, 102tn, 116tn, 143, 151t
Thorp, W. L. (Assistant Secretary of State), 65n
Tibet, 173n
Tin, 121-122, 217n, 229-230
Tin Study Group, 229-230
Tobacco Associates, 194n
Trade Agreements Act, 167, 168, 171, 294; see also Trade Agreements Program
Trade Agreements Committee, 179
Trade Agreements Program, 167-203, 293-295; tariff negotiations and agreements, 171-173; action under escape clause, 174-180; customs simplification, 180-181; Seventh Session of General Agreement on Tariffs and Trade, 181-191; miscellaneous encouragement of imports, 191-192; conflicts with agricultural policies, 192-203
Trade liberalization measures, Organization for European Economic Integration, 3, 190, 253-257, 264, 287-288
"Trade, not aid," 168, 294
Transportation, 268t, 274; see also Ocean freight
Travel, 268t, 274-275
Treasury Department, 102tn, 115t; and Export-Import Bank dividend payment, 109n; and United Kingdom loan, 113; on customs simplification, 180n; and Atlantic Community, 266; see also National Advisory Council and Snyder, J. W.
Treaties of friendship, commerce, and navigation, 121-122, 173, 291
Trieste, 38t, 98, 242t
Triffin, R., 135n, 240n, 248n, 252n
Tripartite Commission for Monetary Gold, 279tn
Tripartite Commission on German Debts, 128
Truman, H. S. (President): on cut in aid, 14-15; reimbursable aid, 16n, 32n; military matériel priorities, 32, 33; military fund transfer to defense support, 33n, 37n; on one-year appropriations, 44n; on European Defense Community, 49; and military assistance to Latin America, 53; and technical assistance, 58n; on Point Four, 71, 72; on Israel aid, 85; on occupied areas program, 87; on Korean aid, 91; and children's welfare, 94; on aid to migrants, 97, 99; on strategic materials loans, 112; on peril-point clause, 172; and withdrawal of concessions to Communist areas, 173; on escape clause, 176-179, 183; on "cheese amendment," 193, 194n, 198; on almond tariff, 202; on Battle Act, 207-208; on import tax suspension, 233; on European integration, 237; on offshore procurement, 285; and foreign aid concept, 286n
Tuna fish, 175n

Tungsten, 108, 222, 223, 225, 226, 233-234
Tungsten-Molybdenum Committee, 222, 225, 226
Turkey, 34tn, 38t, 101t, 107tn, 111t, 116tn, 136t, 151t, 242t; military assistance to, 5, 23-24, 50; defense-support aid to, 27, 37n, 51; and Balkan pact, 37n; and Mutual Security Program construction project, 40; in North Atlantic Treaty Organization, 43; investment guaranties in, 119; and International Monetary Fund, 137; International Bank loan to, 150; in General Agreement on Tariffs and Trade, 171n; trade agreement with, 171n, 179; and United States escape clause, 177, 184; and export subsidies, 184; and Japanese accession to General Agreement on Tariffs and Trade, 189; and European Payments Union, 241n, 245n, 247, 249

Underdeveloped areas, aid to, 55-78; some general issues in United States aid to, 6-15; and United States bilateral programs, 57-62; and purposes of United States programs, 57-61; and methods of financing, 61-62; and form and amount of aid, 62-67; and Technical Cooperation Administration programs, 67-71; and Mutual Security Agency programs, 72; United Nations Expanded Program, 72-78; and new international financial institutions, 158-166; see also International Bank for Reconstruction and Development, Loans and investments, and individual countries
Union of South Africa, 102tn, 106, 116tn, 119, 136t, 144-145, 147t, 151t, 153t
United Fruit Company, 122
United Kingdom, 38t, 111t, 115t, 136t, 147t, 151t, 153t, 242t; defense-support aid to, 27, 28, 37; offshore procurement in, 35; aid to Yugoslavia by, 37n; and North Atlantic Treaty Organization goals, 44; and European Defense Community, 48-50; and lend-lease returns, 100; United States Treasury loan to, 113; investment guaranties in, 119; and German debt settlement, 128-129; and Japanese debt settlement, 129; and International Monetary Fund, 135, 138; and sterling convertibility, 141-142, 252n; and gold price, 145; gold sales to United States by, 146; International Bank loan to, 150n; and "Trade, not aid," 168; and escape clause, 178; and General Agreement on Tariffs and Trade, 182, 295; and accession of Japan to General Agreement on Tariffs and Trade, 188-189; and imperial preferences, 191; and import restrictions, 191, 244, 255, 256, 288; and Canadian beef, 198-199; and sugar, 200, 230n; and East-West trade, 208, 210; and International Materials Conference, 229; and steel-aluminum agreement, 229n; and European Payments Union, 243, 244, 247n, 248, 251, 252n, 255; and European Coal and Steel Community, 259
United Nations, 58tn, 102tn; technical assistance program of, 55-58, 72-77, 290; and prices of primary products, 78n, 222; and refugees, 81-82, 95-96; and Korean rehabilitation, 91-93; Civil Assistance Command, 93; building loan to, 113, 115t; nationalization resolution in, 122-123; and International Monetary Fund policies, 138-139; and full employment study, 139n; and International Bank policy, 154; and international commodity arrangements, 154n; and study on economic stability, 154; on new international financial institutions, 158-166; and East-West trade, 213-214; on international tin agreement, 229-230; see also ECOSOC, Economic Commission for Europe, International Children's Emergency Fund, and Palestine refugees
United Nations forces, in Korea, 24, 32n, 34tn
United Nations High Commissioner's Office for Refugees, 95; see also Migration
United Nations Korean Reconstruction Agency, 90-93
United Nations Relief and Rehabilitation Administration, 93, 95n, 101t
United Nations Relief and Works Agency for Palestine Refugees in the Near East, 79-87, 95n
United Nations Technical Assistance Board, 76, 77
United States High Commissioner in Germany, 90

"Uniting for Peace" Resolution, United Nations, 213
Uranium, 106
Uruguay, 53n, 122-123, 143, 151t, 190

Van Westerborg, E., 168n
Venezuela: and migration, 98; United States trade agreement with, 171-173, 179; gold reserves of, 280
Vernon, R., 258n
Virgin Islands, 199, 230, 269tn

Wall, E. L., 227n
Walton, C. C., 47n
Warren, G. L., 96n
Watches, and escape clause, 174, 177, 178, 179n
Wheat, 202, 270; see also International Wheat Agreement
Wilcox, C., 169n
Wilcox, F. O., 43n
Williams, J. H., 40n
Wilmot, C., 43n
Wilson, F. S., 121n
Wolff, S., 243n, 261n
Wool, 201n, 222, 223, 225, 228
Wool Study Group, 228

Yemen, 50n, 58tn
Young, Senator M. R., 195n
Young Loan, 129
Yugoslavia, 38t, 101tn, 107tn, 116tn, 136t, 151t, 277tn; military assistance to, 21-22; defense-support aid to, 36n, 37n; and lend-lease returns, 100; International Bank loan to, 152n

Zinc, 112, 222, 223, 225, 229n, 233-234

GPSR Authorized Representative: Easy Access System Europe - Mustamäe tee 50, 10621 Tallinn, Estonia, gpsr.requests@easproject.com

www.ingramcontent.com/pod-product-compliance
Ingram Content Group UK Ltd.
Pitfield, Milton Keynes, MK11 3LW, UK
UKHW010159180926
475586UK00003B/87

* 9 7 8 0 6 9 1 6 2 8 4 0 0 *